Baedeker's
HUNGARY

Imprint

197 illustrations, 16 ground plans, 5 special plans, 8 general maps, 7 drawings, 1 large map at end of book

Original German text: Janos Nemes; Verlag Ikon, Budapest.

Additional material by Dr Bernhard Abend, Dr Peter Jordan, Rudolph Knoll, Ellen Krause, Helmut Linde, Dr Christina Melk-Haen, Dr Lerke von Saalfeld, Hans-Joachim Schmidt, Andrea Wurth

Editorial work (German edition): Baedeker, Redaktion (Andrea Wurth)
(English edition): Crispin Warren

Cartography: Franz Kaiser, Sindelfingen; Gert Oberländer, Munich; Mairs Geographischer Verlag, GmbH & Co., Ostfildern-Kemnat (large map)

General direction (German edition): Dr Peter Baumgarten
General direction (English edition): Alec Court

Source of Illustrations: Archiv für Kunst und Geschichte (1); Baedeker-Archiv (2); Bela Birkeneder (30); Siegfried Bohnacker (1); Peter van Bürck (2); Klaus Görgen (4); Helene Hartl (12); Historia-Photo (3); IFA Bilderteam (2); Institut für Auslandsbeziehungen (3); Bildagentur Jürgens (4); Klaus Kallabis (19); Marton Radkai (5); Bildagentur Schuster (1); Hans-Horst Skupy (33); Staatsgut Tokaj-hegyalja (2); Manfred Strobel (8); Ullstein Bilderdienst (5); Andrea Wurth (18); ZEFA (1)

English translation: David Cocking, Alec Court, Julie Waller, Crispin Warren

Following the tradition established by Karl Baedeker in 1844, sights of particular interest and hotels and restaurants of particular quality are distinguished by either one or two stars.

To make it easier to locate the various sights listed in the "A to Z" section of the Guide, their co-ordinates on the large city map are shown at the head of each entry.

Only a selection of hotels, restaurants and shops can be given: no reflection is implied, therefore, on establishments not included.

In a time of rapid change it is difficult to ensure that all the information given is entirely accurate and up to date, and the possibility of error can never be entirely eliminated. Although the publishers can accept no responsibility for inaccuracies and omissions, they are always grateful for corrections and suggestions for improvement.

1st English edition 1994

© Baedeker Stuttgart
Original German edition

© 1994 Jarrold and Sons Limited
English language edition worldwide

© 1994 The Automobile Association
United Kingdom and Ireland

Prentice Hall General Reference
US and Canadian edition

PRENTICE HALL and colophon are registered trademarks of Simon & Schuster, Inc.

Distributed in the United Kingdom by the Publishing Division of the Automobile Association, Fanum House, Basingstoke, Hampshire RG21 2EA

Licensed user:
Mairs Geographischer Verlag GmbH & Co., Ostfildern-Kemnat bei Stuttgart

The name *Baedeker* is a registered trade mark
A CIP catalogue record of this book is available from the British Library

Printed in Italy by G. Canale & C.S.p.A – Borgaro T.se –Turin

ISBN US and Canada 0–671–89690–3

UK 0–7495–0866–3

Contents

The Principal Places of Tourist Interest at a Glance

Note: The places listed above are merely a selection of the principal places of tourist interest in Hungary, either for themselves or for attractions in the surrounding area. There are, of course, innumerable other sights to which attention is drawn by one or more stars in the text.

Preface

This guide to Hungary is one of the new generation of Baedeker guides.

These guides, illustrated throughout in colour, are designed to meet the needs of the modern traveller. They are quick and easy to consult, with the principal places of interest described in alphabetical order, and the information is presented in a format that is both attractive and easy to follow.

The guide is in three parts. The first part gives a general account of the country, its political and geographical divisions, its landscape, climate, flora and fauna, population, educational systems, government and administration, economy, history, famous people, art and culture. A brief selection of quotations and a number of suggested itineraries provide a transition to the second part, in which the country's places and features of tourist interest – towns, provinces, regions, rivers – are described. The third part contains a variety of practical information. Both the sights and the practical information are listed in alphabetical order.

The new Baedeker guides are noted for their concentration on essentials and their convenience of use. They contain numerous specially drawn plans and colour illustrations; and at the end of the book is a large map making it easy to locate the various places described in the "A to Z" section of the guide with the help of the co-ordinates given at the head of each entry.

Facts and Figures

Even before it once again became accessible to the west, Hungary was always the most popular place to visit in Eastern Europe. Lake Balaton, the "Hungarian Sea", and the capital city Budapest have traditionally been the country's main attractions. In addition, the historic towns situated within the Danube Bend, the celebrated wine town of Tokaj and the Hortobágy Puszta will almost certainly find inclusion in any tour of Hungary. However, even further afield, in the Hungarian countryside, there are many natural sights and cultural monuments awaiting the visitor – low undulating mountain ranges, peaceful river landscapes, historic towns such as Székesfehérvár, Pécs, Győr and Eger, numerous ruined castles and Baroque ancestral houses, which in many cases have been converted into comfortable hotels. Substantial areas of the country, notably in the east, have up until now remained largely untouched by tourism. In these out-of-the-way places there is still many an undiscovered treasure to be found and, even more importantly, the visitor can experience the special charms of rural Hungary.

General

Hungary (the Republic of Hungary; in Hungarian Magyar Köztársaság) is situated in the eastern half of Central Europe and, with an area of 93,031sq.km/-35,919sq.miles, makes up less than 1% of the total surface area of Europe. The country lies between latitudes 45° 45' and 48° 35' (in other words, it is equidistant from both the North Pole and the equator) and longitudes 16° 05' and 22° 55' (1300–1700km/800–1050 miles from the Atlantic Ocean). It thus extends approximately 320km/200 miles from north to south and 520km/325 miles from east to west. To

Hungary
© Baedeker

Situation

the north Hungary is bordered by Slovakia, in the north-east by the Ukraine, in the east by Romania, in the south by Serbia, Croatia and Slovenia and in the west by Austria.

The capital of Hungary is Budapest, which was formed in 1872 from three historic towns, Buda (= furnace), Óbuda (= old furnace) and Pest, and now comprises 22 districts.

Capital city

Topography

Hungary is a typical lowland basin region (it forms part of the Carpathian Basin), with 84% of its area below 200m/650ft and only 2% above 400m/1300ft. The gentle relief of the country reaches its highest point in the north-east (Mátra Mountains, Kékes-tető, 1015m/3330ft). This predominantly low-lying situation has a pronounced influence on the climatic and hydrographic conditions of the country.

◄ Budapest and the Danube

Geological Profile

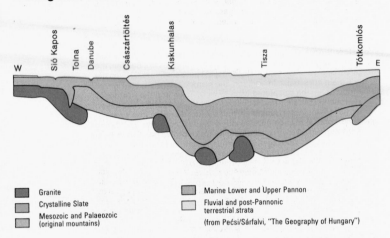

Granite	Marine Lower and Upper Pannon
Crystalline Slate	Fluvial and post-Pannonic terrestrial strata
Mesozoic and Palaeozoic (original mountains)	(from Pećsi/Sárfalvi, "The Geography of Hungary")

Geology

Hungary lies almost wholly within the Pannonic Basin, which is also sometimes referred to as the "Carpathian Basin" or the "Central Danube Basin". This tectonic depression zone is flanked on the west by the Eastern Alps and their foothills. On the north and east the basin is surrounded by the arch of the Carpathians, to the south-east it is bordered by the Transylvanian Alps, to the south-west by the Dinaric Alps. The Pannonic Basin is located within the Alpidic mountain system and is filled with sedimentary beds of varied provenance. Marine deposits, terrestrial sediments, windblown deposits and various residues from rivers can all be distinguished. In the depression the remains have been detected of a Palaeozoic mountain range known as the Tisza Massif. This consists primarily of granite, but also of crystalline slates. It had almost certainly been extensively worn away by the end of the Palaeozoic period.

In the Mesozoic period this mountain range was washed around by the Tethys Sea and would have been flooded in many places. The Alpidic mountain formation which occurred at a later date resulted in the present-day layout of the Alps, Carpathian and Dinaric mountain ranges. The Tisza Massif finally broke up and subsided into several beds of soil of varying sizes. Most of the basin was then flooded by the Miocene Sea. Powerful volcanic activity then occurred along the cleft lines at the edges of the basin. The effects of these upheavals, which vented themselves in the area of Budapest and Lake Balaton, are to be found in the high incidence of thermal springs. Structural movements in the geological plates in due course caused the basin to be lifted up, along with its surrounding mountain ranges, while individual areas actually sank back lower and lower (as much as 3000m/9850ft below sea level!) and at the same time the sea receded. The massive layers of marine sediment were later covered over by river and windblown deposits. The Pannonic Basin did not receive its present appearance until the quaternary period when the Danube and its tributaries washed down considerable quantities of debris and gravel from the surrounding mountain areas. During and after the Ice Age large amounts of fine loess were blown around and drifted and piled up to form dunes.

Mineral resources

In the course of geological history the formation has occurred of various deposits of raw materials which are now able to be exploited on an economic basis. Besides hard coal and brown coal (lignite), these consist principally of bauxite, uranium, copper, iron and manganese, as well as smaller quantities of oil and natural gas. In this connection the frequent occurrence of thermal and mineral waters should also be mentioned.

Geographical Areas

The country can be divided into six main areas: the Great Plain (Alföld), the Little Plain (Kisalföld), the West Hungarian Alpine foothills (Alpokalja), the Transdanubian Highlands (Dunántúli-domb-vidék), the Transdanubian Hills (Dunántúli-középhegység) and the North Hungarian Hills (Északiközéphegység). The present-day national boundaries of Hungary do not follow any natural geographical line; in other words the geographical areas at the edges of the country are the continuation of those in neighbouring states.

The Alföld or Great Plain is the most typical Hungarian landscape, occupying as it does practically half the total surface area of the country. This plain, which was formed by soil deposits, is situated to the east of the Danube and is in geological terms the newest area of Hungary. The area is divided into two by the River Tisza: the area between the Danube and the Tisza to the west (Duna-Tisza köze) and to the east of the Tisza the Tiszántúl (literally: beyond the Tisza). Both parts consist of similar landscape types: the rivers are lined by alluvial flood areas, between which there are higher-lying loess ridges (e.g. Hajdúhát, Békés Ridge). With their deposits of black earth these offer the best conditions for agriculture, together with the Pleistocene alluvial peaks of the Danube and Tisza (e.g. Kiskunság, Nyírség), which display a more varied relief with their drifting sand dunes, which even today are still susceptible to movement. The areas of the plain known as the puszta are famous worldwide. This today mainly treeless landscape is now

Great Plain

Puszta

Landscape in the Great Plain

Topography

a conservation area with parts of it within the bounds of two national parks (Kiskunság and Hortobágy Parks). These national parks, which alternate wide expanses of pastureland with fascinating sand-dunes and shallow salt lakes, have been made easily accessible to tourists, with the exception of some strictly protected biosphere reserves. The puszta, which today is so arid (puszta = barren land), can not be considered a natural landscape, despite its appearance, for it replaced the old wetter wooded steppes, which disappeared as a result of thoughtless forest clearances during the period of Turkish rule in the 16th and 17th c. as well as the large-scale river regulation schemes of the last century.

Little Plain

The landscape of north-west Hungary, through which flow the Danube and its tributaries, shows genetically and morphologically similar features to the Great Plain. The most important area of the Little Plain is the Győr Basin, where the Danube is joined by three tributaries, the Rába, Rábca and Marcal. Particularly attractive from a scenic point of view is the alluvial island of Szigetköz, a large stretch of land (450sq.km/174sq.miles) between the arms of the Danube above Győr, mainly covered with wooded meadowland. The southern shores of Fertö-tó (Neusiedler See) and certain basalt hilltops 3–4 million years old (Somló near Devecser, Sághegy near Celidömölk), which are like islands on the southern edge of the plain, are also of interest.

West Hungarian Border Region

The commonly used Hungarian name for this landscape, Alpokalja (foot of the Alps), is only correct in that the eastern foothills of the Eastern Alps lie along the western border of Hungary. These wooded mountains under 1000m/3300ft high, the Kőszegi-hegység and Soproni-hegység, only show geological similarities with the Alps. The highest point of the Kőszegi-hegység (Irottkő, 883m/2897ft), which for many years was only accessible from Austria, is also the highest point in the whole of Transdanubia. The rest of the West Hungarian border region consists of hilly country (e.g. the Zala Hills) and is heavily intersected by rivers which flow down from the Eastern Alps. Its position on the edge of the country, its many divisions of relief, and the wet, often marshy valleys contribute to the retention of ancient traditions both in popular architecture and folk customs (the ethnographic landscapes of Göcsej and Őrség) which have recently been discovered by the tourist industry. Hungary's petroleum industry started up in this region in the interwar years and although the oil fields are already largely depleted, the deep bore-holes today provide spas with thermal water (e.g. Bükfürdő, Zalakaros).

Transdanubian Hills

The hills of Southern Transdanubia are mainly composed of tertiary marine sediments, in many places covered with a layer of quaternary loess. The area is bounded to the north by Lake Balaton, to the east by the Danube and in the south – along the Croatian-Hungarian border – by the Drau (Dráva). This hilly country displays a relief of considerable diversity. Some parts, such as the 300–350m/985–1150ft high Somogy and Tolna Highlands, have been heavily intersected by valleys. (The Tolna Highlands are also known as "Swabian Turkey" after the "Danube Swabians" ("Donauschwaben") who settled in the area in the 17th and 18th c. after the many years of Turkish rule.) Other parts of the region, on the other hand, such as the loess covered mezőföld (= meadowland) in the east, are rather flat and monotonous. The mezőföld descends steeply down a bank as much as 50–60m/165–200ft high to the Danube and so down to the Great Plain (Alföld). Archaeological finds show that frequent landslides (the last in the area of Dunaújváros and Dunaföldvár in the 1960s and 1970s) have moved this bank about 60–100m/200–330ft to the west since Roman times.

Mecsek Villány

In the south-eastern part of this upland area, to the north and south of Pécs, two Mesozoic ranges, the Mecsek Mountains and those around Villány, tower above the surrounding hills. The larger and higher of the two ranges, Mecsek (682m/2238ft) consists mainly of Trias and Jura limestone com-

Landscape near Villány

plexes with the only significant layers of hard coal in the whole country. Alongside this there are Permian red sands containing some deposits of uranium ore. In the wooded uplands there are also karst formations, including the dripstone cave of Abaliget, the moist air of which is very healthy. The lower mountains of Villány only reach a height of 442m/1450ft. This Mesozoic limestone range has hardly any woods, its bare slopes dotted with the scars left by quarrying. The southern slopes of both mountain ranges are much favoured as wine-growing areas.

From the north-west corner of Lake Balaton to the north-east corner of the country there stretches a line of mountain ranges running in a south-west–north-east direction. The section to the west of where the Danube breaches this chain of uplands is known as the Transdanubian Mountains, the section to the east of the Danube valley is called the North Hungarian Mountains.

Transdanubian Central Mountains

The Transdanubian Mountains are 200km/125 miles long and 40km/25 miles wide and are bordered on the north-west by the Little Plain, and to the south-east by the Transdanubian Hills. These mountains are predominantly composed of Mesozoic sediments (limestone, sandstone and dolomite) and are divided up into several sections by rifts running across from north-west to south-east.

The westernmost section of the Transdanubian Mountains, the Bakony (once known as Bakony Forest because of its extensive woodlands) consists of several parallel ridges divided up by rifts. The higher, more northerly of the mountains are made of limestone (Kőris-hegy, 704m/2310ft) and have a number of small tectonic basins in which nestle small villages. This part of the range is rich in lignite, bauxite and manganese deposits. The mining of them, however, does bring significant environmental problems in its train, as it causes the lowering of the karst water-level. The world-famous Lake Hévíz, which is fed by thermal springs, has a surface area of

Bakony

Landscapes, Lakes and Rivers, Mountains

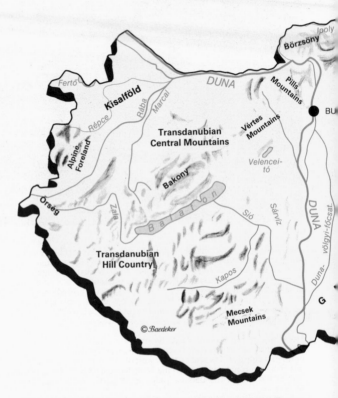

almost 5sq.km/2sq.miles and is thus the largest lake of its kind in Europe. Some time ago this natural monument, which is situated near the town of Keszthely, was saved only after long discussions, when it was agreed to close a bauxite mine.

Balaton Uplands

The more southerly, less hilly section of the Bakony is often called the Balaton Uplands. On the southern edge of the vineyards, in a shallow rift valley parallel to the Bakony, lies Lake Balaton, the largest lake in Central Europe (598sq.km/231sq.miles). Scenically the most beautiful parts of the Balaton Uplands are the Tihany Peninsula, composed of basalt outpourings two to three million years old (including the remains of former geyser peaks), and the Tapolca Basin, which is of similar origins. In the latter, island-like basalt mountains have formed after the clearing away of softer material (e.g. Badacsony, 438m/1437ft). These basalt peaks are often crowned with castle ruins, while on their lower slopes there are vineyards which grow the highest quality grapes.

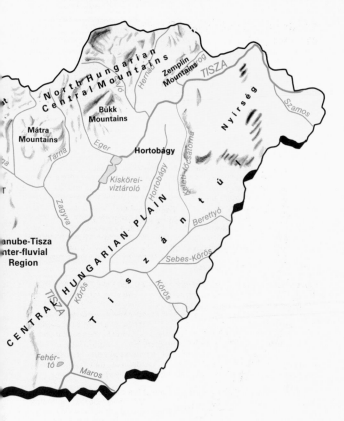

East of the Balaton Uplands are the low limestone and dolomite uplands (now turned to karst) of Vértes (482m/1581ft), in the basin of which bauxite deposits are to be found. In an already partly disused open-cast bauxite mine at Gánt an open-air geological museum has been set up. Near the village of Vértesszőlős, in the proximity of hot springs, finds of cavemen 500,000 years old have been unearthed.

Vértes

To the south of Vértes are the 351m/1152ft high Velencei Hills, which in Hungary are worthy of note because of the way they were formed. The weathered shapes (with names such as "mountain fortress", "sacks of wool") of the Variszic granite outcrops are under environmental protection. On the southern edge of the mountains lies the tiny Lake Velencei with an area of 26sq.km/10sq.miles.

Velencei
Mountains

The north-eastern sections of the Transdanubian Mountains (Pilis, Gerecse and Buda Uplands) are referred to collectively as the Danube Corner Mountains (Dunazug-hegység). The Pilis Uplands, which are made of Triassic

Danube Corner
Mountains

sediments, are, with a height of 757m/2484ft, the highest part of the whole of the Transdanubian Mountains. The surface of the lower Gerecse Mountains (634m/2080ft) consists, on the other hand, of younger Eocene rocks. Lignite mining in the mountain basins (e.g. at Tatabánya) has also led here to a potentially disastrous lowering of the karst water-level. Nor have the thermal springs to be found along the Danube at the edge of the Buda Uplands been spared this process. These springs, even as long ago as Roman times, used to supply baths on the site of present-day Budapest. The horsts of the Buda Uplands, e.g. János-hegy (529m/1736ft), protrude to varying heights. – Budapest itself has certain natural beauties to offer: rising thermal waters have formed interesting caves and some of them e.g. those at Szemlöhogy and Pálvögy, have been lit and made accessible to tourists.

Visegrád Mountains

The Visegrád Mountains (700m/2297ft) are the linking range which connects up with the North Hungarian Mountains. Consisting of volcanic andesites, they form the beginning of a chain of volcanos which appeared along the border between the North Hungarian Mountains and the Great Plain 16–11 million years ago. The Danube Bend (Dunakanyar) is where the Danube forces its way through the mountains and indeed it is the only place in Hungary where the river flows through a narrow valley. This valley was carved into the volcanic rocks of the Visegrád Mountains. Until just recently this landscape, interesting both from a geographical and historical point of view, was threatened with plans for a hydroelectric power station, which would have formed part of the Gabčikovo-Nagymaros reservoir scheme (see Rivers and Lakes).

North Hungarian Mountains

The mountains to the north and east of the Danube Valley form part of the North Hungarian Mountains. Whereas the volcanic formations in the Transdanubian Mountains are no more than elements of pigmentation, here they are of crucial importance to the landscape. The Börzsöny, Mátra and Zempléni Mountains are sections of the range which are all of volcanic origin, and volcanic formations are also to be found in the Cserhát and in the southern part of the Bükk. But the parts of the range which are composed of sedimentary rocks are also rich in natural beauties (e.g. the caves in the Bükk and in the karst at Aggtelek). Incidentally, this mountain landscape has the highest average altitude in the whole country.

Börzsöny

The Börzsöny is the most westerly section of the 200km/124 mile long and 40–50km/25–30 mile wide North Hungarian Mountains. During the Middle Ages Germans and others searched for gold and silver in the valleys at the edge of this densely wooded Andesite range. Today the beauties of the Börzsöny can be enjoyed exclusively by walkers and skiers.
In the higher parts of the range, around the summit of Csóványos (939m/3081ft) it is still possible to uncover morphological vestiges of the former centre of volcanic activity.

Cserhát

The Cserhát is noticeably lower (652m/2139ft) lower than its neighbours. The range contains both Mesozoic sediments (e.g. the cement marl quarries at Naszály above Vác) and also andesite lava flows and coverings (e.g. in the eastern Cserhát). In the north of the range – near the village of Ipolytarnóc – a palaeontological excavation site has been opened up, which has often, if rather exaggeratedly, been dubbed the "Hungarian Pompeii". Under the layer of ashes left by a volcanic explosion occurring some 20 million years ago there are visible traces of the indigenous plant and animal life of that period (e.g. rhinoceroses, different types of birds, palms, cedars and magnolias). Some of the finds can be seen in the well set out open-air museum. In the north-east of the Cserhát, around Salgótarján, basalt peaks 1–2 million years old tower up, often crowned with the ruins of castles (e.g. Salgó, 625m/2051ft).

Mátra

To the east of the Cserhát and separated by the valley of the River Zagyva are the Mátra Mountains which contain the highest peak in Hungary

North Hungarian Central Mountains

(Kékes-tetö, 1015m/3330ft). This former volcanic massif has been compared by some scientists with Mount Etna, but the only signs today of its
immense power are such post-volcanic manifestations as mineral springs,
the waters of which supply a bottling plant in Parádsasvár. The steep
north-facing slopes are used in winter for ski-ing, while the gentler southern slopes constitute a famous vine-growing area, extending to the historic
town of Eger at the south-western end of the Bükk Mountains.

The Bükk Mountains are of a completely different geological composition   Bükk
from those sections of the North Hungarian Mountains so far described.
Large areas of the range have been turned into a national park, while as a
whole it has the highest average height of any Hungarian mountain range.
It is mainly composed of Triassic limestone which has undergone extensive karst development. The high plateau of the Bükk, which is bounded by
steep limestone peaks, known as "stones" (Istállós-kő, 959m/3146ft), is
devoid of water-courses. The karst plateau is 700–800m/2300–2625ft high,
20km/12 miles long and 6–7km/3½–4½ miles wide (a toll road runs across it)
and is dotted with swallow-holes and dolines. The karst water comes to the
surface in plentiful springs at the foot of the high plateau. Large quantities
of lime have collected in many places, for instance in the limestone sinter
terraces of the Szalajka Valley. There are also many caves in this area. In
some of them, e.g. in the caves at Szeleta, traces have been found of Ice Age
hunters and gatherers. The István dripstone cave at Lillafüred is also of
interest.

The longest and also the most beautiful dripstone cave in Hungary is to be   Aggtelek
found in what is known as the Little Karst of Aggtelek (604m/1982ft), the
most recent of Hungary's national parks, which extends from north of the
Bükk to the Hungarian-Slovak border. A length of some 7km/4½ miles of
the Baradla cave (the total length of the cave system – part of which lies the
other side of the border – is about 22km/13½ miles!) has been fitted out and

17

illuminated (conducted tours of different lengths available). The largest hall of the caves is even used in summer for concerts. To the east of the Karst of Aggtelek are the relatively low hills of Cserehát (322m/1056ft), an area surrounded by the valleys of the Rivers Sajó, Bódva and Hernád and with little, if any, touristic development.

Zempléni
Mountains

To the east of Hernád is the final section of the North Hungarian Mountains, the Zempléni Mountains (899m/2949ft), which are another volcanic range. The peaks, which are composed of andesite and rhyolite, are divided up by smaller valleys and basins. On some of the volcanic peaks there are ruined castles (e.g. Boldogkő, situated on a narrow and precipitous tuff ridge). The south-eastern slope of the range, which falls away to the Great Plain, is called Hegyalja (= mountain foot) and includes the volcanic peak of Kopasz-hegy (= bald mountain) near Tokaj, which has shifted as far as the River Tisza. Tokaj is the centre of a wine-producing area located on volcanic rock which is probably the most famous in Hungary.

Rivers and Lakes

"We always have a drought, never any water – and if we do get any water, it is always too much". So says the Hungarian peasant and there is some truth in what he says, as land that is often starved of water can also be susceptible to terrible floods. In terms of hydrography Hungary's location in a basin is of crucial importance: the country receives about 90% of its surface water from its neighbours. The most disturbing thing in the last few decades has been the increasing pollution evident in this water.

Danube

The country's main river is the Danube (Duna) with 417km/259 miles of its length occurring within Hungarian territory, of which some 140km/87 miles form the border with Slovakia. For the whole of this length the river is navigable, but the water flow is unequal. In the Budapest area it is on average 2330cu.m per sec./82,284cu.ft per sec. By comparison the Danube at Ingolstadt has a rate of flow of 308cu.m per sec./10,877cu.ft per sec. and at Vienna 1940cu.m per sec./68,511cu.ft per sec.

As with other rivers in Hungary, there are two high water periods within each yearly cycle. The first major one, known as the "ice flood", occurs at the beginning of spring. It was one of these which caused the high water disaster at Pest in 1838. A second larger flood wave can occur in early summer, known as the "green flood". Many of the places in Hungary which are popular with visitors, such as Győr, Esztergom, Visegrád, Szentendre, Budapest and Mohács, lie directly on the Danube. The most attractive areas of the river's banks and its islands are visited by countless holidaymakers during the summer season. There are facilities for a large number of water sports available here.

Danube Dam
System
Gabčíkovo-
Nagymaros

The large-scale plans, already partially realised, designed to build a gigan-tic system of dams along the course of the Danube between the Slovak town of Gabčíkovo (about 30km/19 miles downstream from Bratislava) and the Hungarian town of Nagymaros (situated in the Danube Bend, opposite Visegrád) have been, and continue to be, surrounded by controversy. The initial idea for such a scheme was set down on paper back in the 1950s. In the mid-1970s it was intended to create a 20km/12 mile-long reservoir just downstream from Bratislava, from which a 25km/16 mile-long artificial power-station canal would branch off with a dam at Gabčíkovo (and a storage station with a capacity of 720 megawatts of electricity). The dam at Nagymaros was intended to even out the tidal effect of the storage power-station at Gabčíkovo and in addition produce 171 megawatts of electricity. The plans, which on the Hungarian side were to a large extent dependent on Austrian finance, aroused a large number of objections from sections of the population concerned about ecological issues, but these protests were

The Danube

hushed up by the one-party dictatorship in power at the time. The opponents of the project feared above all that supplies of drinking water in the vicinity of the dams would be endangered, that the meadowland vegetation would dry out, and that the natural symbiotic balance both along the Danube and in the Danube Bend would be destroyed.

A demonstration calling for a halt to the construction of the dam was held in September 1988, with 35,000 people attending. It turned into a political declaration of strength by the democratic and ecological movements in Hungary. In early 1989 the Németh government ordered building work in Nagymaros to be halted and then in 1992 the agreement relating to the project to build the dam was cancelled. If all goes well, the environmental conditions which once existed in the Danube Bend should be restored by 1994.
Slovakia, now independent, remains committed to the project, however, despite the Hungarian withdrawal, and fully intends to carry it through. In the late autumn of 1992 the two neighbouring states of Hungary and Slovakia became embroiled in a serious legal and diplomatic dispute over the matter. The Danube was diverted on the Slovak side just below Bratislava. On the Hungarian side this led to an immediately noticeable lowering of the water table. The Slovaks' engineering was, however, not able to cope with an early winter high water, so for the moment they have had to draw back, with a consequent relaxation in the political tension. Hungary hopes to gain a solution in the near future by involving the European Community.

The Tisza meanders for 598km/372 miles through Hungarian territory. This river has frequently been dubbed the "blond river" on account of the yellowish shimmering quality created by the vast masses of alluvial material which it carries. The Tisza is characterised by the many channels which have been artificially blocked off from the main river. In regulating the river's flow in the 19th c., the actual length of the river was reduced by a

Tisza

third from what it had originally been. The extremes of the water-flow of the Tisza are also remarkable: the ratio between low and high water can occasionally be as much as 1:80. The Tisza's worst high water disaster occurred in 1879, when the city of Szeged was almost completely flooded. Certain sections of the Tisza's banks, as well as some of the old blocked-off channels, have been turned into recreational areas during the last few years. The largest project of this type is the reservoir at Kisköre, which is being developed into an important holiday region.

Rába

The Rába, the 383km/238 mile-long right-hand tributary of the Danube, rises in the Eastern Alps in Austria (the Wechselgebirge) and flows into the Mosoni-Danube at Győr. The Rába's catchment area is 14,000sq.km/-5400sq.miles in total, of which 5564sq.km/2148sq.miles are within Hungary. The Gyöngyös and the Marcal are important tributaries of the Rába.

Lake Balaton

None of Hungary's lakes is particularly deep. As a result they warm up very quickly in summer but in winter can freeze over in a very short space of time. The largest stretch of water, and without doubt the most popular tourist attraction, is Lake Balaton, not far from Budapest. The lake has an area of 598sq.km/231sq.miles, is 78km/48 miles long and has a maximum width of 15km/9 miles. It was formed about 20,000 years ago along a tectonic depression zone. Just south of the Tihany peninsula, where the lake is only 1.5km/1 mile wide, is its deepest point: 12.4m/41ft. On average, however, the lake is only 3–4m/10–13ft deep. Thus Lake Geneva, which in terms of surface area is roughly the same size, contains 50 times more water than its Hungarian counterpart. The shallowest water in Lake Balaton, mainly to be found along its southern shores, can heat up to as much as 26–28°C/79–82°F in summer!

Lake Balaton is fed mainly by the tiny River Zala and a few small streams. The excess water is diverted along the canalised Sió on the southern shore to the Danube.

Kis Balaton

Near where the Zala flows into the lake is the marshy area known as Kis Balaton (Little Balaton), which is strictly protected as a nature conservation area because of its importance as a resting-place for migratory birds. Some years ago an attempt was made to drain this area but the misguided nature of the plan was realised in time and it was rescinded. As a result the water quality in Lake Balaton began to improve, with floating matter from the River Zala once again being deposited in the basin of Kis Balaton.

Lake Velencei

The 10km/6 mile-long and 2–3.5km/1½–2 mile-wide Lake Velencei (Velencei-tó; 26sq.km/10sq. miles) is also situated in a tectonic depression. The unobstructed surface area is only 16sq.km/6sq.miles. The lake, which has an average depth of only 1m/3ft, is predominantly overgrown with reeds (bird reserve). The proximity of Budapest has enabled Lake Velencei to become a popular recreational area in recent years. Along the southern shore in particular the villages combine to form one continuous holiday area.

Lake Fertő
(Neusiedler See)

Lake Fertő (Fertő-tó; normally known in English by its German name, Neusiedler See, as most of the lake is in Austria) has about a quarter of its surface area (82sq.km/32sq.miles) in Hungarian territory. This lake, on average less than 1m/3ft deep, is heavily overgrown with reeds. As a result of temporary falls in the water level, large areas of the lake dry up from time to time. Sketches survive from the second half of the 19th c. which show that the lake was for a time completely dried up. Until just a few years ago the Hungarian part of the lake formed part of the Iron Curtain but it is now to undergo extensive touristic development.

Lake Héviz

The thermal Lake Héviz (see Topography, Transdanubian Mountains), situated some 6km/4 miles from the north-west shore of Lake Balaton, has a special place among Hungary's tourist attractions. Its slightly radioactive healing water is mainly composed of calcium salts, sulphur and hydrogen carbonates. The lake, which is partly overgrown with waterlilies, has a maximum depth of 35m/115ft and an average temperature of 33°C/91°F.

Hungary is one of the richest countries in Europe for mineral and healing waters. Thermal springs mainly come to the surface along the rifts, both lengthways and crosswise, of the central mountain ranges, but there are also some in the Great Plain. In the Budapest area alone there are 123 thermal springs with temperatures between 24 and 78°C/75 and 172°F, occurring along the so-called Buda Thermal Line. Many hot baths in Hungary have a long tradition; some of these curative springs were known to the Romans. The most important spas in Hungary are Balf, Bükfürdo, Harkány, Héviz and Zalakaros in Transdanubia, Gyula and Hajdúszoboszló in the Great Plain and Eger, Mezőkövesd and Miskolc-Tapolca in the North Hungarian Mountains.

Thermal springs

Climate

Hungary is dominated by temperate-continental climate conditions, resulting mainly from the country's situation in a basin relatively far from the sea and surrounded by mountains. From time to time, however, Atlantic and Mediterranean influences are also felt. The country is small in surface area and has no very pronounced divisions of relief, and there are naturally, therefore, no sharply defined climatic contrasts or distinctive climatic areas. Certain differences are, however, striking. The climate of Hungary is essentially a transitional one between two more extreme types, with the continental qualities becoming far more apparent as one goes east and oceanic influences receding. Even more crucial than this east-west variation is the effect of the basin situation, so that the area of Hungary with the most continental climate (i.e. with the largest temperature variations and the lowest rainfall) is not in the east at all, but in the Great Plain around the town of Szolnok. These differences of location have a bearing on all aspects of the climate.

The average number of hours of sunshine is "only" 1700–1800 hours per year near the western border and in the North Hungarian Mountains, while around Szeged on the Tisza it reaches 2100 hours per year. The hours of sunshine are naturally highest in the summer months.

Sunshine

The annual mean temperature in the west is 8°C/46°F, in the south of the Great Plain 11°C/52°F. The changes in temperature are better reflected by the mean temperatures of the coldest and warmest months, viz. January and July. The mean temperature in January is −1°C/30°F in the Somogy uplands, in the Zempléni Mountains −4°C/25°F; in July it is under 19°C/66°F along the western border, but in the southern part of Tiszántúl, on the other hand, it reaches more than 22°C/72°F. The mean annual variation in temperature along the western border is under 20°C/68°F but in the heart of the Great Plain it exceeds 26°C/79°F. The most extreme temperatures recorded so far in Hungary's history were −35°C/−31°F (in 1940 at Miskolc) and +41°C/106°F (in 1950 at Pécs). Very often there can be an Indian summer with temperature increases being recorded in October. This "grape cooker", as it is frequently called, can have a very beneficial effect on the grape harvest.

Temperature

The rainfall distribution also varies considerably between different parts of the country. The national annual average of 580 to 730mm/23 to 29in. conceals figures of more than 800mm/31in. per year in the Zala Uplands (with extreme measurements of 1400mm/55in. per year) and figures of less than 500mm/20in. per year in the centre of the Great Plain, where some extremely dry years produce only 300–350mm/12–14in. The highest quantities of precipitation are recorded in the west of the country when Atlantic

Precipitation

Climate

Year from
J (= January) to
D (= December)

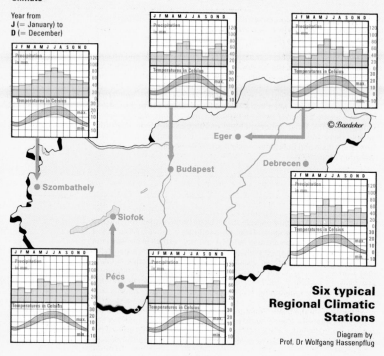

Six typical Regional Climatic Stations

Diagram by
Prof. Dr Wolfgang Hassenpflug

© Baedeker

and Mediterranean air masses meet one another. The mountainous regions with an altitude greater than 700m/2300ft in general receive some 200mm/8in. more precipitation than the surrounding areas. As regards the seasonal distribution of precipitation, there is a maximum, caused by Atlantic cyclones, in the months May–July (60–110mm/2–4in. per month). The most pronounced minimum precipitation figures occur in January and February (30–50mm/1–2in. per month). In the south-west of Hungary there is a second period of high rainfall in the late autumn, which is ascribable to Mediterranean influences.

Snow

In the country taken as a whole, about 10–15% of the annual precipitation falls on average as snow, while in the mountain areas it is some 20–25%. However the snow only remains on the ground for any length of time at altitudes above 800–900m/2600–3000ft, something which severely restricts opportunities for winter sports.

Extreme weather conditions

As Hungary is situated in a transitional zone between quite distinct air masses which are alternately deflected and reinforced by the Carpathian Mountains, deviations from the average statistical figures are not uncommon. They are likely to occur both during changeable weather conditions, when there are heavy thunderstorms, as well as in extreme conditions of longer duration, such as droughts and cold spells.

Föhn influences

Föhn influences are not uncommon along south-eastern facing mountain slopes. These currents of air which descend from the mountains warm up very rapidly and are extremely dry. They are very conducive to viniculture and the growing of fruit.

Plants and Animals

Hungary's position far from the sea, the resulting continental climate, and the occurrence over wide areas of highly fertile brown and black soils have all contributed to a biosphere which, while having certain individual characteristics, can basically be classed as that of a Central European subregion. The vegetation which exists in Hungary today traces its development back to the end of the Ice Age, which did not actually cause any freezing-over in the Carpathian Basin, but instead led to a chilly tundra climate. Rare remains of this glacial and post-glacial plant world (e.g. silver birch moorland) can still be found in the area around Bátorliget in north-eastern Hungary (near Nyírbátor).

Originally, large areas of the country were sparsely covered with deciduous woodland (especially oak). In higher-lying areas, oaks, beeches, limes, maples and chestnuts predominated. In addition there were expanses of steppe composed of woodland and grassland. This natural vegetation has today become limited, and then in a heavily modified form, to just some 10–15% of the country's surface area. As regards its animal kingdom, Hungary lies in an intermediate zone, with representatives of Central European and Pontic fauna occurring.

Biosphere

Flora

Hungary belongs to the Central European flora area, and within that area to the Pannonic (or Hungarian) flora province. Despite its small area, there is a proliferation of species (over 2000), as, in consequence of the very varied climatic influences already mentioned, Hungary is very much a transitional zone between East Alpine, Mediterranean and continental regions.

Deciduous forests are the norm in both the Transdanubian and North Hungarian Mountains. Even the highest summits remain below the zone of coniferous forests (pines and yews occur naturally only in pockets), but in recent times these have been deliberately planted in many places – and unfortunately in some places where they are quite alien to the surrounding environment. In higher-lying areas and on north-facing slopes there are beech forests, while lower down, and on south-facing slopes, oak and ash are found. In the uplands of Transdanubia and in the Mecsek and Villány ranges, Mediterranean tree types occur (e.g. sweet chestnut). Beeches occur in low-lying situations in areas of western Hungary which have a high rainfall. The green alders and different types of fern which are to be found on the uplands of the Kőszegi-hegység and the Soproni-hegység point to Atlantic influences. In the Bakony there are isolated oak forests, while in the karst-developed limestone and dolomite areas there are hornbeam, ash and thickets of wild rose, whitethorn and blackthorn.

Natural vegetation of the central mountains

At the time of the Hungarian conquest (around 900) the vegetation of the Hungarian plains consisted of woodland steppes with sparse forests, moorland, pastureland and meadows along the rivers. The treeless puszta landscape, with its pale-green covering of short grass and the mirages which form over its wide overheated expanses, is for the most part an artificial steppeland created by man's intervention. The last climatically determined steppe period in the Carpathian Basin was at the time of the Boreal phase, about 9000–7500 years before our own time. The areas with sandy or saline soils have their own special vegetation. The sandy soils support a few poplars, oaks, ash and elms. In quite a few places – such as at Bugac in the Kiskunság National Park – junipers are also to be found. The acacia, or robinia, which was introduced from America in the 17th c., is also widespread and in many places helps to bind the drifting sand.

The natural plant world is still best preserved on the soda-rich soils, which are distinguished by panicles, camomile and, not least, wormwood. Loess soils, which are now intensively used for agriculture, yield only the most rudimentary traces of the original natural vegetation.

Natural vegetation of the Hungarian Plains

Plants and Animals

Deciduous forest in the Bükk Mountains   *Silver birches*

Fauna

Experts have counted some 32,000 different animal species in Hungary, of which the majority can be classed as insects. Mammals have now become reduced to just 85 species. In particular, big game has disappeared from the country at a steadily increasing rate over the past few centuries. As early as the 13th c. aurochs had become extinct. The last elks and bisons were seen in the 18th c.

Predators

Wolves, bears and lynxes have retreated into the forests of the Carpathians. These animals only now appear during especially hard winters in the eastern border areas. Foxes, wild cats and martens can still be seen relatively frequently, especially in the North Hungarian Mountains, while martens are even capable of venturing into closely built-up areas. With the disappearance of undisturbed river meadowland becoming more and more evident, it is only a matter of time before the otter becomes extinct in Hungary.

Other wild animals

Large numbers of deer still live in Hungary's forests and pasturelands. The number of red deer alone is estimated to be 30,000. The north of the country is home to a considerable number of wild boars. Fallow deer and moufflons live mainly in the Mátra and Bükk Mountains. Both large and small rodents are to be found over the whole country, while in the last few decades the beaver has been successfully reintroduced. All over Hungary there are plentiful supplies of food to support field hares, rabbits, squirrels, hamsters and field mice.

Birds

Owing to the regulation of river flow and drainage of large expanses of land, the biosphere for birds has become severely restricted. The last few silver herons nest in the reed thickets of Kis Balaton and Fertő-tó (Neusiedler See). Cormorants, waders and razorbills are more often to be seen in the plains. There are also large populations of wild ducks, geese, cranes,

24

A stork   *Hungarian sheepdog*

bitterns, pheasants and Turkish doves. During the spring and autumn months many migratory birds, such as white-fronted geese, visit the area around Hortobágy and Fehér-tó (White Lake; near Szeged). Storks' nests are clearly visible across the whole country, but bustards which were once extremely numerous, have now retreated to the meadowland along the River Tisza. Falcons, owls and eagles are threatened with extinction.

Originally there were a large number of different types of fish but this diversity has been noticeably reduced in recent years through the increasing level of water pollution. Carp, pike-perch, whitefish, eels and catfish are much sought after by anglers. Pike also abound in Hungary's rivers and lakes.

Fish

Since time immemorial animal husbandry has been an inseparable part of the Hungarian way of life. In the past Hungarian pasturage was typified by White Hungarian cattle, but this breed has more recently been replaced by others which are more robust and productive (e.g. Hungarian red-flecked cattle). The situation is very similar in pig-breeding, with the older famous Hungarian fat pig having been ousted by West European meat-producing strains. On the bare pasturelands of the north-east and between the Danube and the Tisza there are extremely large numbers of sheep, including horned zackel sheep, small Hungarian merino sheep and reddish brown Ratzka sheep. Hungarian horse-breeding has also traditionally been of great importance, particularly for thoroughbreds.

Poultry farming should not be overlooked either: chickens, geese, turkeys and ducks form an integral part of the Hungarian farming landscape. The most typical breeds of dog to be encountered are the puli and the Hungarian sheepdog.

Working animals

Environmental Problems

The environmental problems which for some time now have been surfacing in Hungary can probably be directly traced back to measures taken by both the communist party and government which right up to the late 1980s would have followed the guidelines laid down by the communist countries' much vaunted Council for Mutual Economic Aid (Comecon). The alignment of social policies to prevailing communist and socialist principles over several decades has led to misguided developments and initiatives which resulted recently in the Gabčíkovo problem (see Rivers and Lakes, Danube) coming under worldwide scrutiny. A powerful confrontation threatened to develop between the two former socialist nations and neighbours across the Danube, Hungary and Slovakia, because the latter was trying to sweep to one side the misgivings of the former over the ecological implications of the Danube dam project.

Until very recently environmental damage has mainly resulted from such situations as power stations using inferior low-grade fuels, large-scale industrial complexes being established without proper filtration and purification plants, and scant attention being paid to the problem of waste disposal. In agriculture the disproportionate use of pesticides, herbicides, insecticides and artificial fertilisers has given rise to additional problems, which have manifested themselves in contaminated drinking water, general air and water pollution and accumulations in the food chain.

Waterways

The prime carrier of Hungary's pollution burden is the Danube, the flow of which is "regulated" by all manner of water installations and industrial plants. The situation is similar with the Tisza, the second largest river in the country. Various kinds of human intervention have resulted in a drastic lowering of the water table in certain areas. More recently, though, the intention has been expressed of restoring Hungary's waterways to their natural state and it is planned to build large purification plants, particularly near the major towns and cities.

Soil

The short-sighted cultivation of large expanses of land, which had been the norm over the past few decades, is being totally reappraised at the present time. There are now quite a few large agricultural concerns which are calling into question the excessive use of chemicals and instead are going over to more natural farming methods. Areas of land which have either become barren or severely eroded are gradually being reafforested or are being put to new uses.

Destruction of forests

Predictably, Hungarian forests have also been damaged to an alarming degree, principally through acid rain which is produced by the combustion of coal, oil and gas. Domestic users, trade and industry, power stations and individual travellers are the main culprits. Forests on the windward side of the Hungarian mountain ranges are particularly affected, as well as woodland in close proximity to the exhaust fumes of large Hungarian and foreign industrial sites and centres of population.

Emergency measures

The urgently needed improvement in the environmental situation represents a major challenge, which can probably only be met by a concerted effort on the part of Hungary and its neighbours. In particular, the know-how and financial support of western countries are required.

That Hungarians have started to develop an environmental awareness was shown not least in the conflict over the Gabčíkovo project. Far-sighted forces in the world of business and administration have already set about the reconstruction of industrial enterprises to take into account environmental considerations and these same concerns have been paramount in recent legislation which has been passed.

Gemence Forest, a protected area

Nature and Environmental Protection

Nature and environmental protection has been an integral component of Hungarian national planning at least since the middle of the 1970s. The Tihany peninsula on Lake Balaton was made a nature conservancy area as long ago as the 1950s. There are now four large national parks: Hortobágy (52,000ha/200sq.miles including the puszta region around Debrecen), Kiskunság (36,000ha/140sq.miles including the puszta region around Kecskemét, made a biospheric reserve by UNESCO in 1979), Bükk and Aggtelek. In addition there are over 500 more biotopes and landscape areas, some of them very restricted in size, which have been given protected status. Certain key areas of these are out of bounds or may only be entered with special permission.

Unfortunately, during the last few years a thriving tourist trade has developed in certain places closely associated with the romanticism of the puszta (Apaj Puszta, Bugac, Nine Arch Bridge in Hortobágy). This tends to make a mockery of the efforts of the conservationists.

Considerable progress has been made in the last ten years regarding protection of the country's waterways and regulation of access to shorelines and wetlands. For some time now the use of motorboats has been banned on Lake Balaton, the only exception being the Tihany ferry.

The desirability of further regulation of boat traffic and shoreline access is being evaluated. There are equally severe restrictions in force in the area around Lake Velencei, which, like Lake Balaton, is an important recreational area close to Budapest.

Naturally the protection of birds is accorded special attention. River-banks and the shores of shallow lakes and ponds are important staging-posts for large flocks of migratory birds.

[Margin notes:]
Nature conservation areas

Waterside areas

Bird protection

27

Countryside code of conduct

Danger of fire
in woodland and
open country

Prolonged periods of dry weather in Hungary can create a situation where there is a real risk of fires breaking out in either woodland or open country. Lighting open fires is particularly to be avoided during the summer months. When leaving a picnic place where there are special places for lighting a fire, the visitor must be sure to check that any such fire is completely extinguished!

Protection
of plants

It is of the utmost importance not to uproot or dig up plants if these belong to a type that is protected or which are growing in a nature conservancy area.

Hunting, fishing

Hunting wild animals and fishing is permitted only in specially assigned areas and only at certain times.

Nature
conservancy
regulations

Hungarian nature conservancy regulations are continually being updated. It is always advisable to check in advance to ascertain whether any regulations are in force.

Population

Statistics

In 1991 the population of Hungary was 10,354,000; this corresponds to an average density of population of 111 inhabitants per sq.km/287 per sq.mile. In the south and east of Hungary, particularly in the Great Plain, the density, at 60–90 inhabitants per sq.km/155–233 per sq.mile, falls noticeably short of this figure. This regional difference in the population distribution is the result of large-scale immigration after the Second World War and massive industrialisation during the 50s and 60s. Thousands of people left the predominantly agricultural areas of southern Transdanubia and the Great Plain and migrated to the major industrial centres, in particular the capital Budapest and the industrial areas of the central uplands (Tatabánya and Miskolc, etc). Today 61% of the population lives in the northern half of the country, including 20% in Budapest alone. This disparity between the industrial heartland and the other relatively underdeveloped regions has until now been an unresolved problem for Hungary – only the nature of the migration has altered, with about 15% of the working population havng to commute between their home and their place of work.

Population
changes

Any consideration of population changes within Hungary is complicated by the fact that the national boundaries of the country have altered and contracted several times during the last few centuries, and older studies have generally referred to the whole area of the Carpathian Basin. It is estimated that the number of Magyars who migrated into the Carpathian Basin in 900 was around 250,000. The Slav population living there at that time would have been somewhat larger. The high population of 5 million in the 15th c. was reduced to about 2.5 million by the year 1700 as a result of the Turkish Wars. By 1787 the population had recovered to reach 8 million (within the present-day boundaries it would have measured 2.7 million) and in 1840 a population census produced a figure of 11.3 million. In 1920 Hungary had a population of some 20 million, but after the Second World War it fell once again as a consequence not only of war losses and deportations, but also of resettlements and the expulsion of ethnic Germans at the end of the 1940s. In the 1960s and 1970s the population rose sharply again, partly as a result of the rigorous prohibition of abortion in the early 1950s, and reached a temporary high point of 10.7 million in 1980; since 1982, however, population growth has slowed down slightly.

Language

The official language of Hungary is Hungarian, which is spoken by 96% of the population as their mother tongue. Within Central Europe Hungarian occupies a unique position, belonging as it does to the Finno-Ugrian group of languages and being related to Finnish and Estonian. Hungarian has the oldest linguistic monuments (12th c.) of any of the Finno-Ugrian languages. A vast number of words in Hungarian have, however, been borrowed from Latin, Slavic, German and Turkish.

The Constitution of 1949 effectively separated church and state in Hungary. Since then censuses have no longer concerned themselves with an individual's religious denomination and therefore any statistics have to be based on estimates and on figures supplied by the religious organisations, and these often show considerable divergence. With about 6 million members (approximately 60% of the total population), the Roman Catholic Church is the largest denomination. In Hungary there are three archbishoprics (Eger, Esztergom and Kalocsa) and eleven bishoprics; the Archbishop of Esztergom is at the same time Primate of All Hungary. About 19% of the population are Calvinist, while the Evangelical and Greek Catholic churches each claim adherents amounting to 5% of the population. Around 2% of Hungarian citizens are members of the Greek Orthodox Church. The Jewish community in Hungary, notwithstanding the extermination and expulsion of hundreds of thousands during the Second World War, is still, with 80–100,000 members (about 1% of the population), the largest in Central Europe. The Rabbinic Institute, the only Jewish university in Eastern Europe, was set up in Budapest, where most of the Hungarian Jews live.

Religion

Following the religious persecution of the 1950s and early 1960s, involving the proscription of almost all monastic orders, the closure of denominational schools and institutions and the arrest of priests, there has been a gradual decrease in repression since the 1970s. Since the political changes of 1989 the position of the churches has been strengthened again. In most schools optional religious instruction is now available and the establishment of religious orders has once again been permitted. Even the highly vexed question of the return of expropriated church possessions has already been partially addressed.

Role of the churches

Ethnic groups and minorities

Since the Second World War there has not been any significant non-Hungarian element in the population; 90% of the country's citizens classify themselves as Hungarian. However the former multi-ethnic Hungarian state was a land with many minorities: Germans, Romanians, Slovaks, Serbs, Croats and Greeks; in addition there are Jews, Sinti and Roma, not officially recognised as ethnic minorities. Moreover, since the First World War, Hungarians have formed minorities in certain neighbouring states: some 600,000 Hungarians live in Slovakia, 150,000 in the Ukraine, 2 million in Romania, 500,000 in Serbia, Croatia and Slovenia and 10,000 in Austria.

The largest minority in terms of numbers are Germans (about 200–250,000), mainly descendants of original migrants to the east, who settled in the countryside and made their homes in the area around Budapest (traditional German settlements include Budaörs and Budakeszi), near the western border and in the region between Pécs and Baja, known as Swabian Turkey. Before the First World War there were still as many as 500,000 ethnic Germans in Hungary; their numbers contracted as a result of enforced resettlement after the Second World War, with a total of 170–190,000 people leaving the country. Since the 1970s pressure on ethnic Germans within Hungary has considerably lessened. Tangible signs of the more relaxed situation are the numerous institutions set up to protect the German cultural heritage (national associations, German-language schools, cultural societies, German libraries and local history museums, etc.). Even the bilingual village signs to be seen in places such as Villány, are an expression of a renewed sense of national identity.

Hungarian ethnic Germans

Two fine examples . . .   *. . . of the Hungarian arcaded house*

Slovaks,
Southern Slavs,
Romanians

The second largest minority group are the Slovaks (about 110,000), who, apart from the northern boundary of Hungary, mainly inhabit the south-east of Tiszántúl. The Slovak share of the population was considerably reduced by the exchange of citizens which took place between 1945 and 1948 between Hungary and the then Czechoslovakia. Approximately 80–100,000 Southern Slavs (Croats, Serbs and Slovenes) live mainly along the River Drava in southern Transdanubia and in the southern part of the area between the Danube and the Tisza. In the former Serbian town of Szentendre to the north of Budapest the number of Serb families has decreased dramatically. The area of settlement of some 30,000 Romanians in Hungary is to be found along the Romanian-Hungarian border in the south-east of the country.

Gipsies

Between 350,000 and 800,000 gipsies (Sinti and Roma) live in Hungary; they are not recognised as a minority and their integration poses enormous social and political problems. With the exception of the families of certain rich musicians and businessmen, gipsies occupy the very lowest position on the social ladder. In particular their lack of formal education tends to condemn them to unemployment. These social tensions lead to an increased level of criminality and this unfortunately in turn reinforces existing prejudices.

Types of settlement

By the end of the 1980s 59% of the Hungarian population lived in the country's 166 towns, with more than 25% in the Budapest conurbation. The dominant position of this metropolis of 2 million people within Hungary's settlement structure is determined by historical factors. The counter-balancing influence exerted by the former urban centres of the imperial era, such as Bratislava, Košice, Cluj, Zagreb and Timişoara, which since the

First World War have lain outside the boundaries of the Hungarian state, has only partially been replaced by the present-day provincial centres of Debrecen (pop. 215,000), Miskolc (pop. 192,000), Szeged (pop. 177,000), Pécs (pop. 170,000), Győr (pop. 130,000), Nyíregyháza (pop. 115,000), Székesfehérvár (pop. 110,000) and Kecskemét (pop. 105,000).

Various types of urban settlement can be distinguished, according to the way they have been formed. In many cases a fortress was the impetus for the formation of a settlement and provided protection for the latter by virtue of its elevated position (e.g. Esztergom, Buda or Veszprém), or its location in swampy ground (e.g. Csongrád, Gyula, Komárom and Szigetvár). Baja, Mohács, Győr and Pest lie on fords; Eger, Gyöngyös, Hatvan and Miskolc are situated at crossing-points between the plain and the mountains. A typically Hungarian type of settlement is provided by the agricultural towns of the Great Plain. They grew up during the unsettled period of Turkish rule, when large swathes of the plain were laid waste and the population was forced to take refuge in the larger townships, which often enjoyed the protection of the sultan (known as Khas towns). Whereas in the 19th c. at least 50% of those in employment in these towns still worked on the land, today the figure is just 20%. So far these settlements, which are surrounded by fertile agricultural land, have only really acquired the attributes of a town right in their centres, where church, administrative buildings and school are to be found, the outskirts of the town consisting of a broad belt of rural "suburbs" (e.g. Kecskemét).

Towns

Agricultural towns

The geography of the country has produced various forms of village. The smaller villages in the hilly and mountainous areas are situated along roads through valleys or lie scattered, clinging to slopes which are protected from the wind. In the flatter areas villages are larger, but even more scattered. The traditional Hungarian farmhouse is a long, single-storey building with a characteristic leafy walkway, often covered with vines, along one of its longer sides.

Villages

The individual farmhouse, or "tanya", to be found in the Great Plain, can be traced back to the period of Turkish rule. After the withdrawal of the Turks, farmers moved back on to the land from the protection of the towns and there built solitary buildings to serve as temporary working quarters. These later became permanent dwelling-places. During the second half of the 19th c. these single buildings also became a feature of the areas along the River Tisza which were able to be drained through regulation of the flow of the river, and also of the sandy areas between the Danube and the Tisza. Today between 3 and 4% of the Hungarian population still lives on these solitary farmsteads; many of the inhabitants of the rural areas have migrated to the industrial towns, because the deficient infrastructure (lack of electricity and water supplies, etc.) made life in a tanya so arduous and full of hardship. Latterly there has been a trend to improve the rural infrastructure so that the tanyas can be used as second homes and holiday houses.

State and Society

From the year 1000 to the end of the Second World War Hungary was a monarchy. Between the First and Second World Wars, because of a vacancy on the throne, it was ruled by an imperial administrator as head of state. During the communist era the country was a people's republic. Since October 23rd 1989 Hungary has been a republic.

Type of state

The national flag of Hungary is red, white and green. These colours are supposed to have first featured in the country's history when they appeared on a proclamation issued by the Árpád King Andreas II. When the country became a republic in 1989 the historic coat of arms was reintroduced. The left half of the arms has red and silver stipes; the right-hand

Flag and arms

Republic of Hungary
Magyar Köztársaság

Administrative Divisions

National Flag

Regional Administrative
Headquarters

Regional Boundaries

H

International
Vehicle Nationality Sign

National
Coat of Arms

side has the famous double cross, dating back to the 14th c., resting on three green hills. Since the end of the 16th c. the shield has also borne the crown of Stephen.

Constitution

The most recent change to the Hungarian constitution turned the country from a socialist people's republic into a republic based on a parliamentary democracy. The highest powers of the state reside in the National Assembly, a single-chamber parliament with 386 elected representatives, chosen for a four-year term. In March/April 1990 the first free parliamentary elections took place, the method being a mixture of direct mandate (for particular candidates) and election from a party list. The head of state, the state president, is chosen by parliament for a six-year term and is invested with powers which are similar to those of the German president. The first president of the new non-communist Hungary, who took office in May 1990, is Árpád Göncz, president of the writers' association and founder member of the "Alliance of Free Democrats". The Prime Minister is chosen by parliament, but on the suggestion of the state president, in accordance with the parliamentary cycle for a term of four years, and it is he who chooses the members of the government. Since May 23rd 1990 the cabinet of Jószef Antall (Hungarian Democratic Forum) has been in office. Along with the constitutional changes, a new audit division and constitutional court were introduced, the latter comprising fifteen constitutional judges who are chosen by parliament for a period of nine years.

Parties

The political upheavals recently experienced in Hungary have meant the end of the one-party system. Of the political parties now active, most have been newly formed and six of them succeeded in gaining parliamentary representation in the 1990 elections. The largest number of votes was secured by the Hungarian Democratic Forum (President Jószef Antall), which had emerged from the opposition movements of the 1980s and united a broad base of public support behind it. It was able to form a coalition government with the Party of Small Farmers and the Christian Democratic People's Party. At present the opposition parties include the Hungarian Socialist Party, which has inherited the mantle of the former ruling Hungarian Socialist Workers' Party, the Alliance of Young Democrats, which owes its representation in parliament mainly to votes from the

Administrative divisions of Hungary

Divisions/Headquarters	Area (km²)	Pop. (1000)	Pop. density (P/km²)
Budapest	525	2018	3843
Bács-Kiskun/Kecskemét	8362	543	65
Baranya/Pécs	4488	418	93
Békés/Békéscsaba	5631	409	73
Borsod-Abaúj-Zemplén/Miskolc	7247	757	104
Csongrád/Szeged	4263	438	103
Fejér/Székesfehérvár	4373	422	97
Győr-Moson-Sopron/Győr	4012	424	10
Hajdú-Bihar/Debrecen	6211	549	88
Heves/Eger	3637	333	92
Jász-Nagykun-Szolnok/Szolnok	5607	424	76
Komárom-Esztergom/Tatabánya	2251	314	139
Nógrád/Salgótarján	2544	226	89
Pest/Budapest	6394	951	149
Somogy/Kaposvár	6037	343	57
Szabolcs-Szatmár-Bereg/Nyíregyháza	5937	569	96
Tolna/Szekszárd	3703	253	68
Vas/Szombathely	3336	272	83
Veszprém/Veszprém	4689	382	81
Zala/Zalaegerszeg	3784	305	81
Total	93,031	10,354	111

student population, and the Alliance of Free Democrats, the second strongest party in Hungary, which grew out of the radical-intellectual citizen's rights movement.

For purposes of administration the country is divided into 19 regions (Hungarian megyék) and one capital district, Budapest. The large cities of Miskolc, Debrecen, Pécs, Győr, Szeged and Nagykanizsa are on an equal footing with the regions.

Administration

Since the 1970s there has existed in Hungary, alongside the "official", i.e. party-directed, and, albeit not in a strict sense, censored media a kind of "secondary" public domain in which people's opinions and beliefs have been shaped using (illegal) self-produced books, tracts and periodicals ("samisdat"). The political upheavals of 1989 also restored to Hungary the freedom of the press, although a liberalisation of the media had already made itself felt in the previous year. A large number of new publications were set up (in 1988 alone some 30 daily papers appeared), partly using resources provided by foreign investment, though of these many have not survived in the long term. The most important daily newspapers are (1992 circulation levels in brackets): Népszabadság (about 1 million), Népszava (about 500,000), Kurír (about 350,000), Esti Hirlap (about 200,000) and Magyar Nemzet (about 250,000).

Mass media

Education and Science

After the Second World War an elementary school system with eight classes was introduced, which all Hungarian children had to pass through. Apart from a few private schools, which charge quite substantial fees, all

School system

education is provided free of charge. About 50% of Hungarian children, after completing their eight years of elementary education, then follow an apprenticeship which leads to a proficiency examination in their chosen skill. The other half of the school population either attends grammar school (about 23%) or a technical high school (about 27%). Both educational routes lead to a leaver's certificate and entitle the successful student to a place in higher education.

The changes in the education system have also had an effect on teaching methods, with those promoting creativity and the abilities of the individual again coming to the fore. At the same time, and parallel with the state system, new types of school are being tried out, on a private basis, mainly by means of endowments. The Hungarian school system has had a long tradition of specialist educational institutions and initiatives, such as the method of musical instruction developed in the post-war years by the renowned composer Zoltán Kodály (see Famous People), which found and continues to enjoy recognition and influence not only in Hungary itself, but all over the world. Its aims are not, as in the educational institutions of the former Soviet Union, the fostering of talents of highly gifted children from a very early age, but rather the raising of the general level of musical awareness and understanding. The foundation of this method of musical instruction is the wealth of national folk songs.

Universities

The ratio of further education students to the overall population is at 12% quite low compared with other European countries. There are about 100,000 students at Hungary's 58 seats of higher education, of whom 43,000 attend the country's 19 universities. The most important university towns are Budapest, Pécs, Debrecen and Szeged. Education at a centre of higher education normally lasts four years, while university courses last five. Whereas between 1950 and 1970 the number of graduates in higher education rose substantially, in the 1980s the pressure on university places eased off considerably. It may be assumed that the cause of this is the relatively low levels of pay and loss of prestige suffered by the intellectual professions.

Research

The Hungarian Academy of Science (MTA) was founded in 1825 by Count István Széchenyi. After the Second World War various academic institutes, based on Soviet models, were set up alongside the university institutes with the aim of conducting scientific research. The history of Hungarian science can boast many inventions and important contributions to research developments, although many scientists have chosen, especially during the immediate post-war years, to pursue their work outside their homeland, either elsewhere in Europe or in America. Among the most well-known Hungarian or Hungarian-born research scientists, mention should be made of the engineer Kálmán Kandó (inventer of the electric locomotive), the mathematician János (John von) Neumann (see Famous People), Tivadar Puskás (inventor of the telephone exchange), the surgeon Ignác Semmelweis (see Famous People), the electrical engineer Dénes Gábor (inventor of the holograph, see Famous People), the biochemist Albert Szent-Györgyi (Nobel Prize 1937 for the discovery of Vitamin C), the atomic physicist Ede Teller (who took part in the production of American hydrogen bombs between 1949 and 1952) and the Nobel Prize winner of 1963, the physicist Jenö Wigner.

Economy

At the present time it is difficult to write with any degree of precision about the Hungarian economy. Comments which may safely be made about the situation today are likely to be overtaken by tomorrow's events. The economic life of the country is in a state of transition. The Hungarians have to find new ways of regulating possessions and ownership, of coming to terms with previously unknown concepts (at least officially) such as unemployment, of building up new foreign trading contacts. These tasks, and the many others which face them, are by no means straightforward, although the ideological fetters which acted as a strait-jacket on the economy did start to be relaxed as long ago as 1968 (the introduction of the so-called New Economic Direction) and in many cases have even been dismantled. Hungary was the first country in the former Eastern bloc where the application of western capital, joint ventures, etc. was permitted. The high national debt of the 1970s and 1980s created an economic boom in Eastern Europe, previously never experienced and to a large extent illusory, while at the same time making possible an increase in living standards. Today however the country is heavily burdened by the effects of this false boom, any positive results from all this economic activity having at present receded. Foreign capital, on which people were prepared to take risks, flowed into the country, in particular from Austria, Switzerland, certain EC countries (especially Germany and Italy), as well as the United States.

Agriculture and forestry, fishing

Over 70% of usable land in Hungary is given over to agriculture and forestry. More than a sixth of the working population was working on the land at the end of the 1980s. During the same period, however, Hungarian agriculture contributed just under 10% to the gross national product. Just before the lifting of the Iron Curtain 70% of available agricultural lands were worked by agricultural co-operatives, 15% were designated state properties, and only 14% were in the hands of private farmers. Since 1989/1990 privatisation (in many cases re-privatisation) of agricultural land has been in progress. The value of these measures is debatable. Will it gradually lead to a fragmentation of land ownership? Will the more fertile lands fall to poorly equipped and technologically backward small farmers or will a proper farming economy emerge? Can the old collectives, which were partly set up by compulsion, make the transformation into modern "capitalistic" Danish-style co-operatives?

The land in Hungary available for agricultural use (in many cases black earth) is predominantly classified as good to very good and fertile. Potentially negative climatic influences (e.g. droughts) can be combated by the application of advanced agricultural technology (e.g. irrigation measures). Over half the agricultural land is given over to cereal production. In terms of the ratio between surface area devoted to wheat and maize production and population, Hungary is only surpassed by Denmark. Wheat, maize, barley and sunflowers are grown throughout the whole country, the main wheat-growing areas being the Tiszántúl and the Mezőföld. Rye and potatoes are chiefly cultivated in the north-east of the country. In certain climatically favoured places rice can be grown with the help of irrigation.

Farming

Paprika, which is also well-known and much coveted outside Hungary, mainly comes from the area of Kalocsa. The region around Szeged is famous for its sweet paprika. Large amounts of onions and garlic are produced in the south-east of the country. After the Second World War the cultivation of fruit, which had previously really only been carried out on a domestic basis, was dramatically increased. Fruit farms were established on a large scale, chiefly in the north-east of the country around Nyírség and in the area between the Danube and the Tisza. The main fruits grown include apples, pears, plums, apricots, cherries and peaches. Around Lake Balaton almonds and figs are also cultivated commercially.

Vegetable and fruit growing

The high level of sunshine makes vine-growing possible on a large scale, and indeed the vine has been cultivated in Hungary since Roman times. At present 200,000ha/770sq.miles of the total agricultural land area in Hungary is given over to viniculture. One of the largest areas is the series of

Viniculture

35

Harvesting peppers

sandy ridges between the Danube and the Tisza. Good quality vines are cultivated on the slopes of the hilly areas and from the Sopron/Neusiedler See area. The most famous historic wine-producing areas are around Tokaj, Sopron, Eger, Pécs and by Lake Balaton and the Balaton Uplands. In Hungary between 4 and 6 million hectolitres of wine are pressed every year.

Cattle rearing

Cattle rearing has traditionally always been important and initially beef cattle predominated. Cross-breeding of Hungarian white cattle with Simmental cattle produced a bright red-coloured breed which produced good beef and milk yields. A parallel development occurred in the case of pig-breeding: after the Second World War, in response to the tastes of the time, breeding was switched from the traditional Hungarian fatting pig to Western Europeans strains of meat-producing pigs. Sheep rearing (in particular merino and ratzka sheep) is practised on barren sandy and sodaic soils, especially on the Hortobágy puszta, in Transdanubia and in the sandy areas between the Danube and the Tisza. Poultry farming is now of considerable importance, yielding as it does profits no less great than the larger-scale activity of cattle rearing. It is now estimated that there are more than 30 million hens in Hungary, as well as several million geese, ducks and turkeys. The role that beekeeping plays in Hungarian agriculture should not be underestimated; nor should it cause any surprise, given the vast expanse of acacia groves. Besides honey, it provides raw materials for the natural healing industry (e.g. propolis).

Horse rearing has become much reduced in scale since the Second World War because of a lack of demand and the large stud farms have resorted to breeding the kind of thoroughbreds much prized in the West and Arab countries (e.g. Lipizzaners).

Forestry

The timber industry plays a fairly subordinate role in the Hungarian economy. A maximum of 4 million cubic metres/140,000,000cu.ft of oak, beech,

Vines are an important crop . . .   *. . . as is maize*

acacia and poplar wood are felled each year. Since the Second World War a vast programme of afforestation has been pursued. An interesting development in the forestry industry has been the recent growth in shooting as a tourist activity. The possibilities of this market had already been put to the test in communist times when visiting dignitaries were given shotguns and game was frightened into their paths. Today rich trophy hunters from all over the world are attracted here.

Fishing has also been an important activity over many years. A large proportion of the fish (especially carp) come from ponds. In the rivers and lakes (especially Lake Balaton) people fish for catfish, pike and pike-perch, while in the small streams, for instance in the Bükk Mountains, trout are farmed.

Fisheries

Industry

The first area in Hungary to become industrialised was around the lignite coalfields in the Transdanubian and North Hungarian Mountains, where small deposits of iron were also to be found. The first iron works was started at the end of the 18th c. by Hendrik Fazola, an Italian by birth who migrated to Hungary from Würzburg in Germany. His estate near Lillafüred in the Bükk Mountains is now preserved as an interesting industrial monument. The closeness of Austrian markets played a key role in the early industrialisation of the Little Plain (particularly the textile industry). Buda and Pest had already become influential trading centres on the River Danube in the previous century and later grew to be important industrial towns. Because of the excellent availability of raw materials, both branches of the food industry – staple goods and semi-luxury items – were able to play a leading part in Hungarian industrialisation from a very early stage. Capital was provided by big landowners and the organs of high finance,

Historical development

which had become established during the imperial and royal period. After the Second World War socialist and communist governments attempted to counter this traditional dependence of Hungarian industry by a one-sided policy of seeking to force heavy industry into a strong position, thereby disregarding the economic realities of the country.

Mining and energy

Hungary is relatively poor in mineral resources and energy supplies. Nevertheless, there are reasonably large reserves of hard coal in Mecsek which have begun to be exploited; oil occurs naturally at several points in the southern part of the Great Plain and significant fields of natural gas exist in the Tiszántúl area. However it is no surprise that Hungary has to import large quanties of petroleum and is also heavily committed to creating more energy production capacity (hydro-electric power stations on the Danube and Tisza, thermoelectric power stations based on coal and lignite). Along the main mountain axis of Hungary, which runs from southwest to north-east, there are deposits of lignite and brown coal as well as extensive hard coal stocks, although the former are not especially profitable. The most important mineral product is bauxite, which is mined in large quantities in the Bakony and Vértes area. These rich reserves are the basis of the flourishing aluminium industry, which was even able to be developed during the communist period, thanks to COMECON and Russo-Hungarian co-operation in the energy sector. The comparatively rich manganese ore deposits in the Bakony area are assuming greater and greater importance, the manganese being in great demand by industrial enterprises in the European Community.

Heavy industry

As has already been stated, the Bükk Mountains with their iron ore reserves are the focal point of the Hungarian iron and steel industry. With the opening up of certain coal deposits there is a possibility of further development of this branch of Hungarian industry. Even before the Second World War Budapest was able to develop into an important centre for the steel industry. With the help of the most modern technology of the time (including Siemens-Martin procedures), steel was successfully produced from scrap iron. After the Second World War the development of heavy industry was given a high priority. The iron and steel combines on the Csepel island to the south of Budapest, in Miskolc and in Ödz were provided with cheap raw materials from the Soviet Union, as was the steel works of Dunaújváros, which was built on the banks of the Danube in the 1950s. The iron foundry at Győr also received its raw materials from Russia.

Aluminium

Aluminium production using the rich bauxite reserves in the Bakony got underway during the mid 1930s. The mineral was much sought after for the manufacture of aeroplanes and many other uses and there was a ready export market, particularly in Germany. After the Second World War the industry was developed much more extensively. Soviet mineral transporters used to return to the Soviet Union with Hungarian aluminium oxide which they took to the great aluminium foundries which used the hydro-electric potential of the River Volga. The raw aluminium produced on the Volga was then taken back to the great rolling-mills of Budapest and Székesfehérvár for further processing.

Mechanical engineering

Hungarian mechanical engineering has a long tradition which began initially with the need to equip and fit out the early factories and railways (including rolling-stock). The interwar years also saw the establishment of plants for machine and electrical appliance manufacture and the early telecommunications industry. Until a few years ago over three quarters of the jobs in mechanical engineering were concentrated in the Budapest and Győr districts.

Chemical industry

The chemical works situated around Budapest and Debrecen are amongst the world's most important suppliers of pharmaceutical products such as antibiotics, penicillin and morphine. The production of nitrogen fertilisers from coal also has a well-established tradition in Hungary. In addition the manufacture of artificial fibres and rubber (centred around Budapest, Győr and Szeged) has also seen a substantial increase in volume. Products using refined petroleum and natural gas are also fabricated at various places along the Danube (in particular on the island of Csepel in the Danube at Budapest), near the Romanian border and in Transdanubia. Important centres of the paper and cellulose industry are Budapest, Balatonfűfző, Szolnok and Dunaújváros.

There are many places throughout the country where building materials (e.g. cement, finished parts, concrete and bricks), glass, porcelain and ceramics are produced. World-famous examples of the latter do not only come from Herend, known as the "Hungarian Meissen", but also from Pécs and Budapest.

Building materials, glass, ceramics

The Hungarian textiles industry has traditionally always been very strong, based as it is on the rich and varied range of raw materials supplied by Hungarian agriculture. Local linen, viscose, wool, leather and pigs leather are manufactured all over the country in both large and small-scale centres of production. Even the silk industry has gained a foothold in Hungary, silkworms being successfully bred in southern Transdanubia. Imported Egyptian cotton and Australian wool are combed and spun in Hungary and Chinese and Indian silks are also processed in large quantities. During the last twenty years foreign firms with prestigious names have commissioned the production of high-quality textiles and accessories in Hungary.

Textiles, leather goods

Even in the last century the milling industry was important in Hungary and today it continues to be one of the world's major centres. There are factories processing locally grown sugar-beet scattered across the whole country. The same is true of the fruit and vegetable canning industry, which can also rely on home-grown produce. The Hungarian processed meat

Food production

Porcelain production in Herend

39

industry (e.g. salami, szegediner), with its major factories in Budapest, Debrecen and Pécs, is also world-famous. Besides basic foodstuffs, there is an increased range of semi-luxury goods (wine, beer, spirits and tobacco) being produced for the export market. Imported goods also come from the Balkan states and the Middle East for processing.

New trends in
industrial
production

The availability of cheap raw materials, such as iron ore, from the Soviet Union meant that up to a few years ago industrial production in Hungary was often very wasteful in terms of energy. In addition, for many years it had been possible to find ready markets in the Eastern bloc for industrial products, without the need to make any technological innovations. As a result the quality of many Hungarian goods (e.g. railway rolling-stock, buses) was significantly below the standard which obtained elsewhere in the world. Today it is precisely those areas of industrial production which in the past had bothered little about technological improvements (e.g. iron and steel works in the north-east) which are now the most severely affected by crises and unemployment. Even the long-established IKARUS company, which makes buses, vehicle parts, etc., is experiencing hard times since the loss of its previously secure markets in the Soviet Union and East Germany.

On the other hand the firms which have fared best are those which have always had to take account of the realities of world markets, such as the pharmaceutical industry based around Budapest and the meat-processing industry in Debrecen. The potential which exists, however, in industries such as machine and vehicle building, with their well-trained skilled workforce, should soon make it possible for an automobile industry to become established once again in Hungary. The American firm of General Motors has begun production of the "Opel" range at Szentgotthárd on the Austrian-Hungarian border and the Japanese firm of Suzuki has established an assembly plant at Esztergom. A very positive benefit of all this is that the capital city Budapest appears to have lost its earlier domination of the industrial sector. In the 1960s over half of the jobs available in industry were concentrated in Budapest, whereas today the figure is only 20%.

Service sector

After the decades under socialism, when industrial production occupied very much a foreground place, it is now realised that there is a big need to make up lost ground in the area of service industries, especially in providing a suitable infrastructure. A major effort is now being made to modernise and extend the telecommunications systems and a similar drive is in progress to establish a modern transport system.

Of the 4.7 million Hungarians who were in employment in 1992, almost half worked in the tertiary sector (in 1970 it was only a quarter). In 1992 the service sector contributed more than 40% of the gross national product, whereas three years before that the figure stood at 37%. It is therefore to be expected that in the foreseeable future the figure will be comparable to the percentages for neighbouring Austria or Germany.

Recent surveys show that at present 560,000 Hungarians are employed in commerce in some form or another. Almost half a million Hungarians are involved in transport and postal services and telecommunications. The other half of the service sector is employed in a large range of activities such as tourism, banking and insurance and certain advisory services, for instance the law, taxes, engineering consultancy. There have been dynamic developments in commerce (e.g. the establishment of a large number of firms and agencies from former "enemy" countries) and finance (increase in banking and insurance activities). The continuing trend towards privatisation means that many small businesses and family concerns are starting up, often on a relatively informal basis. Joint-stock companies and limited liability companies, based on German and Austrian models, enjoy great popularity.

Within the service sector this so-called "white industry" occupies a key role. In 1992 alone, well over 30 million foreigners travelled to Hungary, of whom more than three quarters spent longer than a single day in the country. In the same year the Hungarians themselves made more than 14 million visits abroad, with over 7 million people crossing the Austrian-Hungarian border. At the same time four fifths of Hungarian accommodation capacity is in private ownership.

The area which comprises present-day Hungary does not have a very long-established touristic tradition. Before the First World War foreign visitors were of virtually no importance, and even between the wars their impact was very small. In the late 1930s Budapest became quite an important destination for visiting Czechs, Austrians and Germans. In addition the various spas scattered throughout the whole country attracted a small number of foreign tourists. Lake Balaton, on the other hand, was visited almost exclusively by Hungarians. After the communist takeover in 1947 the flow of western tourists into Hungary – as with all the countries of the Eastern bloc – came to an almost complete standstill. Tourist facilities were at first geared only to local workers, but from the early 1970s onwards Hungary opened its doors in a much more comprehensive way to tourists from the "socialist brotherlands". By the end of the 1970s, and even before that, Hungary also decided to attract western hard currency into the country. The contacts between Hungary and Austria were particularly welcome, with the compulsory visa and currency exchange requirements being lifted quite early on. Wide-ranging improvements in tourist facilities, in particular the rapid increase in tourist accommodation and the licensing of small single-owner shops and restaurants in private hands, made Hungary very attractive to western visitors. In the 1980s there was an enormous increase in the number of visitors from Austria, Germany, Italy and the Netherlands. The pricing structure developed its own dynamic, so that fewer and fewer tourists from other Eastern bloc countries were able to afford a holiday in Hungary. Nevertheless tourism continued to occupy a position of key economic importance, thereby attracting more and more interest from the authorities. By 1989 Lake Balaton had become a highly popular and easily accessible meeting-place for families and friends from West and East Germany. Since the dismantling of the Berlin Wall and the fall of the Iron Curtain the growth of tourism in Hungary has considerably slowed down. Receipts from foreign tourists at present amount to about 5% of the income derived from exported goods. Quality tourism, a rich source of revenue, is today centred, as it was up to a few decades ago, on Budapest, so often called the "Paris of the East", a city which is held in high regard by visitors connected with the worlds of culture and business. Alongside it, Lake Balaton has been able to hold on to its position as a favoured centre for summer beach-style holidays, and the great spas are also enjoying increased popularity, which may well be attributable not least to the excellent value of the services which they offer. Large tracts of the country, in particular the Great Plain, have hitherto had only a negligible share of the tourist trade, so that it can truthfully be said that tourism contributes only in very small measure to evening out the economic imbalance between the individual regions. Only the once relatively impoverished border area in the west of the country is experiencing an economic upturn because of excursion traffic from neighbouring Austria.

Tourism

Tourist development

Transport

The Hungarian transport infrastructure (motorways and roads, railways, international airport, waterways) is to a large degree based around the capital, Budapest.

Hungary has a well developed road network, the total length of which is roughly 30,000km/18,500 miles. About 90% of roads are asphalted, and

Roads

The Danube, the main shipping artery

some 80% are served by public buses. At the present time there is in excess of 300 kilometres/185 miles of motorways. One problem is that all the main roads radiate outwards from Budapest, with the result that the capital city is heavily congested with through-traffic. To the south of Budapest there are only two bridges across the Danube (at Dunaföldvár and Baja), which makes east-west communications within the country extremely difficult.

Air travel

Ferihegy Airport at Budapest is the busiest in eastern central Europe. Its existing capacities enable clearance of 4 million passengers per year to be carried out and 20,000 metric tons/19,700 tons of airfreight to be transferred. Extension plans for the airport are waiting to be implemented. The national airline MALÉV is significantly increasing its participation in international air transport. For some time now there have once again been domestic flights (especially for business travellers) to all the important commercial and administative centres of Hungary.

Railways

The Hungarian railway network, which was laid down during the last century, was also completely centred around Budapest. To the south of the capital city there is only one railway bridge across the Danube (at Baja), which also has to be used by slow stopping trains. The first stretch of railway line in Hungary was opened in 1846 between Pest and Vác. The present-day network covers 8025km/4988 miles of track, of which some 30% is electrified. As well as the Hungarian State Railway (MÁV) there is the Austro-Hungarian private railway GySEV (in Austria ROEE), which has operated in the west of Hungary for the last 100 years. This 115km/71 mile stretch of railway was even in service during the Cold War.
With the growth in tourism the charms of the old narrow-gauge railways in the Mátra and Bükk mountains are being rediscovered.

Shipping

Hungary has 1622km/1008 miles of navigable waterways which can be used by ships with a capacity up to 1100 tonnes. The main shipping route is the River Danube, which can be rightly considered the backbone of the eastern countries of Central Europe. The principal transshipment port is Budapest with its large free harbour area on the island of Csepel. The Hungarian capital is the most important stopping-place for all river cruisers on the Danube. There are also hydrofoil services from Budapest to Bratislava and Vienna. Many tourists avail themselves of the excursion boats which follow the Danube Bend from Budapest. There are also small steamers which operate on Lake Balaton.

History

From pre-historic times to the Magyar conquest

500,000 B.C.	One of the oldest human finds in Europe is found in Hungary: traces of hunters who settled in Vértesszőlős near Tata, near hot springs, about 500,000 years ago.
150,000–50,000 B.C.	Stone Age finds in the Bükk and Mecsek Mountains suggest the presence of hunters and gatherers who lived chiefly from reindeer hunting.
5th millennium B.C.	People migrating into the Carpathian Basin from the Balkans bring skills in agriculture (wheat, barley, wine) and cattle rearing (goats, sheep, later also cows and pigs). These immigrants settle mainly in the south-east of the Great Plain.
3000–2000 B.C.	During the Copper and early Bronze Ages Indo-European tribes conquer the area around present-day Budapest. The tribal leaders live with their families in earthworks, on the site of which many later stone buildings are to be built. The main feature of this early civilisation is the continued development in agricultural skills and the working of bronze to produce tools, weapons and jewellery.
c. 1000 B.C.	Members of the "urnfield" civilisation, so called because they burn their dead and bury the ashes, are living in western Hungary.
800–400 B.C.	Arrival of Scythians and Celts.
c. 10 B.C.–2nd c. A.D.	Transdanubia is subjugated by the Romans and incorporated into the Roman Empire as the province of Pannonia. Initially the capital of this province is Savaria (Szombathely). After the division of the province into Upper and Lower Pannonia Carnuntum becomes the capital of Upper Pannonia and Aquincum (Óbuda) the administrative centre of Lower Pannonia. From A.D. 105 the Great Plain forms part of the province of Dacia.
2nd–5th c.	In the course of migrations Vandals, Gepids and western Goths invade the Hungarian region.
454–568	The Romans withdraw from Pannonia. The Huns, advancing from Asia, are the first people to unite under their rule the three great areas of Hungary: Transdanubia, the Great Plain and Transylvania.
568–c. 800	Invasion by the Turkish Avars, who rule the Carpathian Basin for more than two centuries. About the year 670, Bulgaro-Turkish tribes arrive, considered by many researchers to be the first Magyars. Between 791 and 803 the Avar empire is destroyed by Charlemagne, the majority of the Avar population abandoning their settlements and fleeing eastwards.
9th c.	The Carpathian Basin is inhabited by a large number of different tribes. Since Charlemagne's occupation Pannonia has been a border province of the Frankish empire, the Little Plain belongs to the kingdom of Greater Moravia and the Great Plain and Transylvania are in thrall to the Bulgars.
894–900 Conquest	Hungarian tribes, whose language belongs to the Finno-Ugrian family (their oldest known homeland is the area of Western Siberia between the Volga and the Urals), invade the Carpathian Basin in several thrusts and bring it under their rule. National tradition has made Prince Árpád, the founder of the first royal dynasty, the single architect of this conquest, but he probably shared the role of the "gyula", highest military leader, with

two other heroes ("Kende" and "Harka"). These tribes, called by their neighbours "Hungarians" (derived from "on ogur" = 10 arrows), styled themselves "Magyars", which more or less means "talkers" (as opposed to the "mutes", members of other tribes whose speech was unintelligible).

The Kingdom of Hungary until the defeat at Mohács

Feared because of their swift horsemanship and superior military tactics, the Hungarians advance westwards and southwards in numerous raids, penetrating far into the realms of their neighbours. Only their crushing defeat at the hands of Otto I at Lechfeld near Augsburg in 955 restrains them from further incursions. The increasing influence of Christianity and the political restraints on the power of tribal princes imposed under Grand Prince Géza smooth the way for a Christian monarchy based on those of West European countries.

10th c.

Hungary ruled by the Árpád dynasty.

972/1000–1301

Stephan I (Saint Stephen), the son of Grand Prince Géza, brought up as a Christian, is the first to be crowned king of the Hungarian realms in 1000. The main residence of the ruler is Székesfehérvár. The tightly controlled administration of the kingdom is safeguarded by the establishment of 40 Komitaten (districts). With the foundation of new bishoprics and monasteries (Pannonhalma), the organisation of the church and the Christianisation of the people make great strides. After Stephan's death (his only son and appointed successor, Prince Imre, predeceases him in 1031) the integrity of the newly-formed state is endangered by almost 40 years of disputes over the succession to the throne.

1000–38

Dalmatia and Croatia become part of the Hungarian kingdom.

1105

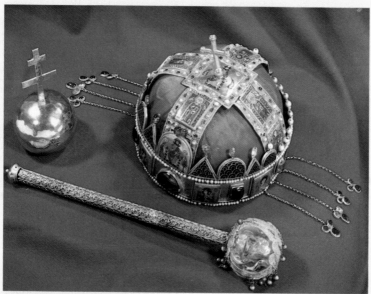

St Stephan's crown, symbol of the Hungarian monarchy

History

1222	The Golden Bull of King Andreas II safeguards the privileges of the feudal lords, including the right to armed resistance against the king.
1241	At the Battle of Muhi in 1241 the Hungarians suffer a decisive defeat at the hands of the invading Mongols. More than half the unfortified settlements in the Great Plain are laid waste by the Mongols, thousands of people are murdered, abducted or killed off by hunger and epidemics.
1308–1445	Hungary under the Angevins and Luxembourgeois. In 1325 Karl I (Robert of Anjou) introduces the minting of the first Hungarian coins (forints). The royal residence moves to Visegrád and Temesvár (Timişoara). Royal power is strengthened by reforms and new sources of income (trade duties, taxes, monopoly of precious metals). The trading agreement reached in 1335 with the kings of Bohemia and Poland in Visegrád regulates trade between east and west. Karl I leaves his son and successor Ludwig I (Nagy Lajos) a well-established state with a flourishing economy. Ludwig I reconquers the provinces of Croatia and Dalmatia which were lost under his predecessors; the latter finally falls to Venice in 1420. Ludwig promotes culture and founds the first Hungarian university in Pécs. King Sigismund from the House of Luxembourg (married to Ludwig's daughter) is in 1433 crowned Emperor of the Holy Roman Empire of the German nation.
1445–90	The head of state János Hunyadi (father of the later King Matthias) defeats the Turkish army at Belgrade in 1456, thereby warding off further invasion by the Turks for many years.
1458–90 King Matthias I	King Matthias (Mátyás), chosen by the regional nobles and the barons, once again centralises the power of the state. A new tax system makes it possible to build up the crown's administrative machinery and maintain a mercenary army subject to the king (known as the "Black Army"). His rule, however, is also marked by foreign policy successes, notably expansions to the north and west (in 1485 Vienna is captured). Most of all, however, King Matthias I takes his place in the history of Hungary as an unprecedented patron of science and the arts (during his reign the royal palace at Visegrád is altered and extended). His reign sees the ideas of the Renaissance arrive in Hungary, with influential scholars preparing the ground for the dissemination of humanism (founding of the Bibliotheca Corviniana).
1490–1526	Matthias I dies without leaving an heir to the throne. The regency of the weak Bohemian kings, Wladislaw and Ludwig, of the Jagiellonan line, is exploited by the Hungarian barons to curtail the power of the crown and to extend their sphere of influence once again (from 1507 the king is kept in check by a royal council).
1514	The Franciscans call for a crusade against the Turks and arm the peasants, who thereupon revolt against the large landowners. The rebellion, led by the officer György Dózsa, is brutally put down and the peasants' subordination "to the eternal chains of the soil" remains a reality for many years to come.
August 29th 1526 Battle of Mohács	The Hungarian army, under King Ludwig II, suffers a crushing defeat at Mohács, about 40km/25 miles south-east of Pécs, at the hands of superior Turkish forces. The king drowns in the Csele brook not far from the battlefield, while fleeing from the enemy. Mohács marks the beginning of the Turkish occupation and the division of Hungary, which disappears from the map of Europe as a separate entity for the next four centuries.

From the beginning of Turkish rule to the reunification of Hungary within the Habsburg Empire.

1526	The struggle for the succession to the throne of Ludwig II is waged between the Austrian Archduke Ferdinand, the brother of Emperor Karl V and King

of Bohemia, and Johann Szapolyai, the claimant supported by the Hungarian nobility. After Szapolyai's death in 1540, the Sultan, on being asked to intercede, enters the fray and in 1541 seizes Buda.

The country is then torn into three parts: the nucleus of the old Hungarian kingdom between Pécs and Szeged in the south and Esztergom in the north is occupied by the Turks. The areas to the east of the River Tisza become the principality of Transylvania, an independent region but recognising the ultimate authority of the sultan. The resulting kingdom of Hungary, which is under a Habsburg regency, now consists of just a narrow strip of land in the north and west of the country, as well as Croatia. 1541

Re-establishment of an eastern kingdom under Johann Sigismund, son of Johann Szapolyai. 1556

The struggle between the Habsburgs and the Szapolyai to determine the border along the River Tisza is finally ended by the peace treaty arranged by the powerful Hungarian magnate István Báthori, in which Johann Sigismund renounces the Hungarian crown and as Prince of Transylvania retains the area east of the Tisza. 1570
Pozsony (Bratislava; today in Slovakia) becomes capital of the Hungarian kingdom.

Calvinism takes root in Hungary, particularly in the eastern areas of the country where many people switch to the new faith and Debrecen becomes a Calvinist stronghold. 16th c.

In 1604 the disputes between the Habsburg realms and Transylvania, which is fast becoming a centre of protestantism and nationalism, erupt into a full-scale anti-Habsburg rebellion, led by the Transylvanian magnate István Bocskai. Aided by the Haiducs he brings the Habsburg territories of Upper Hungary under his control and in 1606 extracts the concession of religious freedom and self-government for the region. Under Gábor Bethlen, Prince of Transylvania, the fight for independence is continued (1619–29). Transylvania, until 1660 a sovereign state, experiences a unique period of cultural and economic prosperity. 17th c.

The kingdom of Hungary remains subject to continual attacks by the Turks. The Habsburgs avoid any direct confrontation with the Turks and use the Hungarian realms as a buffer for their borders. One of the first people to see through this strategy is the military leader and poet Miklós Zrinyi, who rouses the Hungarian nobles to independent action. As a result of the ignominious Peace of Vasvár of 1664, by which the Habsburgs make major concessions despite their victory over the Turks, there is a conspiracy between the Catholic high nobility of Transdanubia and Upper Hungary against the Viennese court (the Wesselényi Revolt). Lacking popular support, the revolt is suppressed and is followed by brutal repression and recatholicisation by the Habsburgs. Thousands of Hungarians flee to the Transylvanian border. 2nd half of the 17th c.

The Hungarians who have fled from the Habsburgs, known as the Kuruzzen, rise up against their imperial rulers under the leadership of Imre Count Thököly, who relies on the support of the Ottoman Empire. 1678–85

With the help of the Holy Alliance against the Turks (Habsburg, Poland, Venice) the Habsburgs succeed in liberating Buda and in 1688 seize Belgrade. The Turks are in retreat. Transylvania recognises Habsburg rule, the Pozsony (Bratislava) parliament and the right of succession of the male line of the House of Habsburg. 1686–87

Peace treaty of Karlóca (Karlowitz): Hungary is freed from 150 years of Turkish domination. 1699

The Turkish Battle, a favourite subject in 17th and 18th c. painting

Hungary under the Habsburgs

1703–11	The final revolt against Habsburg rule is led by the Catholic-raised descendant of the Princes of Transylvania, Ferenc Rákóczi II and begins as a peasants' uprising which soon turns into a national independence movement. The lack of support from the European great powers, the economic weakness of a country still ravaged by years of war, and the superiority of the imperial troops all combine to ensure that the struggle for freedom collapses. At the Peace of Szatmár the Hungarians are granted religious freedom and the constitution of estates is abolished.
Mid-18th c.	The depopulated areas of Hungary in the south are settled by Serbs and Croats, in the east by Romanians, in the north by Slovaks and in Transdanubia by (Catholic) Germans. They turn the puszta into fertile arable land and make Hungary the "granary" of Austria (tobacco, maize, cereals, cattle rearing). The population, which has shrunk to 3.5 million during the 17th c., has risen by the end of the 18th c. to more than 9 million, with the Hungarians forming a minority of only 40%.
1740–80	Maria Theresia encourages the integration of Hungary into the Habsburg monarchy. Jesuits propagate the Counter-Reformation in Hungary.
1780–90	Emperor Joseph II, brought up with the philosophy of enlightened absolutism, rules Hungary according to the motto "Everything for the people, nothing by the people". He abolishes peasants' serfdom, limits the power of the clergy (dissolution of the monasteries, withdrawal of censorship) and of the nobility (abolition of patrimonial jurisdiction, centralisation of the administration, etc.). In the Tolerance Edict of 1781 he restores freedom of worship for Protestants and those of the Greek Orthodox Church. His imposition of German as the official language makes him unpopular with the Hungarian people and causes the first seeds of nationalism to be sown.

The Hungarian Rulers

Joseph II's brother and successor, King Leopold II, is able to appease the Hungarian nobility by recognising Hungary as a sovereign kingdom. Re-introduction of the old regional constitution. — 1790–92

Under the conservative King Franz II (1792–1835), from 1804 Emperor of Austria, the progressive trends in Hungarian life are all reversed and Hungary is once again ruled with absolutist power. The leaders of the Hungarian Jacobins are executed on the "bloody meadow" at Buda. The Habsburgs are forced to recognise, however, that the government of Hungary can no longer be conducted without the regional deputies, to which end the parliament is convoked once more for the first time after a gap of thirteen years. — 1792–1825

The decisions of the parliament of 1825 mark the beginning of a period of reform for Hungary. A steamer service starts between Pest and Vienna; the first railway line is built between Pest and Vác and the first fixed bridge constructed across the Danube between Pest and Buda (the Chain Bridge); the country's first steam mill is built and the flow of the River Tisza is regulated. The outstanding politicians of the reform period are István — 1825–48

The Chain Bridge, the first fixed bridge across the Danube

Count Széchenyi, who is largely instrumental in securing economic reforms, and the jurist and parliamentarian Lajos Kossuth, who fights for wide-ranging social changes, such as the abolition of tax exemptions enjoyed by the nobility, decision-making rights guaranteed to citizens and peasants, civil freedoms, the right to vote given to commoners, etc. In 1847 the liberal opposition joins together to form one party under the leadership of Kossuth, Ferenc Deák and Lajos Count Batthyány. From 1844 Hungarian is the official language.

1848/49

Outbreak of revolution in March 1848. Bloodless revolution on the 15th of the month in Pest; the March Youth led by the poet Sándor Petőfi put forward their demands in twelve points. Vienna accepts Lajos Batthyány as the first Prime Minister of Hungary. Draft laws for the remodelling of the country along democratic lines are passed. In the autumn of 1848 the Habsburgs begin to suppress the revolution. The parliament flees to Debrecen and Lajos Kossuth there proclaims the removal of the Habsburgs; he himself is chosen to be imperial administrator. With the help of the Russians, Austria is able to defeat the revolutionary troops decisively. Kossuth is forced into exile, while Széchenyi dies in 1860 in a psychiatric hospital. The overthrow of the revolution is followed by the most bloody and brutal oppression (execution of thirteen Hungarian generals in Arad in Romania and of Lajos Count Batthyány in Pest).

1867

In the wake of the frustrated revolution Hungary reverts to the status of an Austrian province. The anti-Austrian feelings prevalent in Hungary come to the surface in the form of passive resistance. The failure of Emperor Franz Josephs's brand of neo-absolutism leads to the settlement of 1867, drawn up by Ferenc Deák, which turns the Austrian Empire into an Austro-Hungarian monarchy. The coronation of Franz Joseph takes place in Buda. The prime minister of Hungary is Count Gyula Andrássy.

The country is conceded its own parliament, as well as its own government and armed forces. The politics of magyarisation neglect the many other nationalities, which, when taken together, amount to a majority of the population, outnumbering the Magyars.

Buda, Pest and Óbuda are brought together to form Budapest.
1872

Hungarian nationalism and the Magyars' search for identity finds expression in the many festivities marking the thousandth anniversary of the national conquest (millennium celebrations).
1896

The murder of the successor to the Austrian throne Franz Ferdinand and his wife on July 28th in Sarajevo triggers off the First World War. Austria and Hungary wage a war on two fronts, against Russia and Serbia and against Italy.
1914–18

The Padua armistice (Oct./Nov. 1918) makes Hungary into an independent state, but she suffers huge territorial losses, to the newly-founded state of Czechoslovakia, to Romania and to the Serbo-Croat-Slovene state.

Hungary between the World Wars

After the abdication of Karl IV of Austria as King of Hungary, Hungary is declared a republic under the conservative government of Mihály Count Károly.
Nov. 16th 1918
Republic of
Hungary

In spite of its reform initiatives the government cannot resist the pressure of the revolutionary mood, which gathers momentum as a result of supply problems, unemployment and further territorial losses. A day after the resignation of Károly's government (March 20th), the socialist party in Hungary declares a soviet republic. After the collapse of this republic on August 1st 1919, the country is ruled by the "white terror" of the counter-revolution.
1919

The conservative forces agree to redefine Hungary as a kingdom ("a kingdom without a king") and for the duration of the vacancy on the throne nominate the supreme commander of the fleet, Miklós Horthy, as royal administrator. Through the peace treaty of Versailles-Trianon Hungary loses two thirds of its territory and over half its inhabitants; Bürgenland becomes part of Austria, Upper Hungary and the Carpathian area in Northeast Hungary go to Czechoslovakia, Transylvania to Romania, and Vojvodina to Serbia (June 4th).
Hungary faces the beginning of the new decade with severe economic problems (two thirds of the working population without jobs, a low level of industrial production, etc.).
1920
Beginning of
the Horthy era

The restoration hopes of King Karl IV are dashed; the dethronement of the Habsburgs ends their 400-year domination of Hungary.
1921

István Bethlen, the chief of government between 1921 and 1931, builds up a broad base of support for his government through the newly founded unity party and skilfully manoeuvres between the radical right and the social democrats. Hungary's acceptance into the League of Nations and the foreign credit which that entails paves the way for an economic upturn, albeit spasmodic. In the second half of the 1920s the regime of Bethlen and Horthy is already acquiring autocratic characteristics; the political situation in the country is becoming marked by a right-wing radicalism, anti-semitism and open demands for the restoration of territory.
1921–31

The world economic crisis leads to the fall of Bethlen and his government in 1931. His successor is the defence minister Gyula Gömbös, who actively promotes closer links with Fascist Germany (with the hope of territorial revisions). The two Vienna agreements of 1938 and 1940 reassign parts of the Slovak areas and Transylvania back to Hungary. From 1938 anti-Jewish
1931–39

laws are passed. With the signing of the Anti-comintern Pact of 1939 and the acceptance of the Three Powers Pact of 1940 Hungary renounces its neutrality, but its conduct during the Second World War remains ambivalent.

1941–45

Hungary takes part in the attack on Yugoslavia (1940/41) and joins in the German war against the Soviet Union (1941). After the destruction of the second Hungarian army in 1943 Hungary seeks a truce with the Allies. Hungary is thereupon occupied by German troops on March 19th 1944 with the agreement of Horthy. At the same time the anti-German opposition is arrested and carried off, and Hungarian Jews in the ghettos are rounded up and sent to extermination camps. In October 1944 a second attempt to shake off German shackles also fails and the Fascist Pfeilkreuzler party takes power. At the same time the Red Army is already marching into Hungary and by April 1945 has "liberated" the country. On December 22nd a provisional parliament is elected in Debrecen and a transitional government is formed, with key positions being filled by communists. In March 1945 radical agrarian reform is introduced, with 35% of the country's land area being distributed to landless peasants.

Hungary since 1945

1946

Proclamation of the Republic of Hungary (February 1st). Introduction of the new currency (forint; August 1st).

1947

With Soviet help the communists complete the takeover of power under Matyás Rákosi. The one-party system is introduced, banks and industry are nationalised, a planned economy is set up. The peace treaty of Paris on February 10th 1947 restores Hungary's borders to where they were in 1920 and commits the country to making compensation payments to the Soviet Union amounting to 300 million dollars.

1949

The proclamation of the People's Republic of Hungary. The opposition is decimated by arrests, show trials and emigration. The communist party turns Hungary into a typical Stalinist state.

October 23rd to November 4th 1956 Hungarian national uprising

Inspired and encouraged by the unrest and political changes in Poland, students in Hungary go on to the streets with demands for democracy. When the security forces try to break up a large demonstration, there is a popular uprising. Only the national communist Imre Nagy is considered capable of being able to prevent a general strike and chaos. His government introduces the multi-party system, promises free elections and in defiance of Soviet threats announces Hungary's withdrawal from the War-saw Pact. The Hungarian reform experiment is brutally extinguished, the leaders of the uprising, including Imre Nagy, being executed two years later. The new Soviet-backed government is formed round János Kádár, a former member of Nagy's government.

1956–88

János Kádár dictates politics in Hungary for close on three decades. From the 1960s onwards he allows careful reforms. The gradual replacement of the planned economy with market principles helps Hungary to reach the highest standard of living among the Eastern bloc countries. In addition Kádár's name stands for increasing liberalisation (e.g. freedom to travel) within a socialist regime. He forms links with western governments and raises the international profile of Hungary.

1988

The ageing Kádár stands in the way of growing forces for reform within the Socialist Workers' Party and has to resign his post as general secretary. Government business is first of all placed in the hands of the moderate technocrat Károly Grosz, and then the reform-oriented Miklós Németh (Nov. 24th).

The democratisation process comes to fruition with the founding of opposition parties, trade unions independent of the state, and numerous other interest groups and organisations.

The Soviet leadership under Gorbachev is overtaken in its moves towards reform by developments in Hungary. The reformer Imre Pozsgay triggers off a political avalanche when he no longer refers to the events of 1956 in the official terminology of a "counter-revolution" but as a people's uprising. The rehabilitation of Imre Nagy and his ceremonial state burial (June 16th) represent a massive rejection of the old system. The dismantling of the Iron Curtain along the western border then takes place; East German refugees from the former DDR are now able to travel to the Federal Republic. The Hungarian Socialist Party is now made up of "reform communists" who accept the market economy and the multi-party system. The opposition is able to sit down at the National Round Table and peacefully negotiate the transference of power.
On October 23rd Hungary is proclaimed a republic for the third time in its history. `1989`

In the first free elections (Mar. 25th and Apr. 8th) six political parties are able to qualify for the new parliament. In the Christian-conservative coalition representatives of the Hungarian Democratic Forum (established in 1988 as an opposition assembly) form the majority together with two traditional parties (the Party of the Small Landowners and the Christian Democratic People's Party). The opposition benches are divided between the Union of Free Democrats, the radical democratic Young Democrats and the Hungarian Socialist Party. The head of the government is Jószef Antall. `1990`

Hungary is struggling with the problems involved in modernisation and in remodelling the structure and economy of the country. There has been widespread displeasure over the way privatisation has been carried out, the growing levels of unemployment and inflation. The government and the media are constantly at odds. In the autumn of 1991 over 100 intellectuals circulate a charter signed by thousands in which they demand the continuation of the democratic process and criticise the technocratic and aggressive policies of the government. In October the taxi-drivers of Budapest bring the city's traffic to a standstill as a protest against rises in the price of petrol. `1991/92`

In January 1993 the unity of the governing party is in the balance at the party congress of the Hungarian Democratic Forum. `1993`

Budapest already starts to make preparations for the world exhibition EXPO which is due to be held in the Hungarian capital in 1996.

Famous People

The following alphabetically ordered list includes people who through birth, residence, achievements or death are connected with Hungary and have attained an importance beyond the country's borders.

János Arany (1817–82)

Arany ranks with Sándor Petőfi as a highly important 19th c. poet whose works are a fusion of romanticism and realism. He had his first success in 1845 in a competition for comic epics with "The Lost Constitution". In the following year he wrote the verse epic "Toldi" for a poetry competition, later expanding it into a trilogy, and this brought him to the notice of literary circles, including Sándor Petőfi. During the struggle for freedom he was for a short time a member of the National Guard, but then had to lie low, later working as a private tutor and from 1851 as a teacher at the grammar school in Nagykőrös. His most important poems and ballads were written during this period and he also began to take an interest in questions connected with literary theory and aesthetics. In 1860 Arany moved to Pest, started a newspaper and, as part of a project to produce the works of William Shakespeare in Hungarian, translated several of the plays. In 1865–79 he was secretary, and from 1870 onwards general secretary, of the Hungarian Academy of Science. A late masterpiece of his is the cycle "Meadow Saffron", which is a collection of lyric poems, ballads and sketches.

Árpád (?–c. 907)

Árpád is the progenitor of the first (and only) Hungarian royal dynasty, the Árpáds, which ruled the country from the 9th c. until 1301. The nomadic Hungarian tribes of the ninth century recognised two supreme rulers, the Kende (prince and religious chief) and the Gyula (leader of the army and judge); Árpád held the office of Gyula when he brought his army over the Carpathians (in what is now the Ukraine) and forced his way into the Carpathian Basin, where in the first phase of conquest he seized the land to the east of the Danube. After the death of the Kende in 904 Árpád also took over this role and as prince became absolute ruler. This explains why it is Árpád's name alone which is associated with the legendary conquest of the country and the beginning of the Hungarian state.

Béla Bartók (1881–1945)

Béla Bartók has become famous well beyond the frontiers of Hungary, both as an important composer and as a friend and colleague of Zoltán Kodály. He studied at the conservatoire of music in Budapest and in 1907 was appointed professor of piano there, a post which he held until 1934. Through his friendship with Kodály he developed his interest in Hungarian folk music, into which he carried out research from 1905 onwards both in Hungary itself and in the former Hungarian regions, including Transylvania and southern Slovakia. In 1934 he left the conservatoire in order to devote himself exclusively to composition and the systematic arrangement of the folk songs he had collected. In the 1920s he undertook a large number of foreign concert tours which brought him acclaim and recognition both as composer and pianist. In 1923 he was asked to write a festival composition to celebrate the fiftieth anniversary of the amalgamation of Buda and Pest. This "Dance Suite" was given its first performance together with Kodály's "Psalmus Hungaricus". At the beginning of the 1930s, as a reply to extreme right-wing attacks, he wrote the "Cantata Profana", an oratorical work which embodies sentiments of national brotherhood. After Hitler's seizure of power he no longer visited Germany and protested against the performance of his works in Germany and Italy. Developments in Hungary itself caused him to emigrate to the United States in the autumn of 1940 and he

Béla Bartók   *Ferenc Deák*   *Mór Jókai*

died there in straitened circumstances in 1945. As a composer Bartók was at first very much part of the 19th c. tradition (Liszt, Wagner, Strauss), but then his compositions began to reflect the Hungarian folk music which he was discovering and documenting. His development as a composer can be clearly traced in his six string quartets, the first of which was written in 1908. In 1918 his first and only opera, "Duke Bluebeard's Castle", was given its first performance in Budapest. Bartók's most mature works (written between 1936 and 1943) include the "Music for Strings, Percussion and Celeste", the "Sonata for Two Pianos and Percussion" and the "Concerto for Orchestra". In his "Mikrokosmos" series of 153 piano pieces written between 1926 and 1937, Bartók created a structured teaching manual for the piano.

Deák was a lawyer by training who began his political career as a liberal member of parliament in his home region of Zala. In the spring of 1848 he became justice minister of the Hungarian government, but he later resigned from this post when a rift developed with Vienna during the course of the 1848 revolution. As leader of the nobility's liberal opposition, he became a symbolic figure for the move to use passive resistance against Austrian policies. In his famous "Easter Article" of 1865 he discussed the conditions for renewed negotiations with Vienna and engineered a rapprochement between the two nations. Side by side with Gyula Count Andrássy he worked for a settlement with Austria which in 1867 became a reality, thanks to his brilliant diplomacy (he was called "Hungary's wise man").

Ferenc Deák
(1803–76)

Ferenc Erkel enjoys great popularity in Hungary above all for having composed the national anthem. A trained pianist, he became opera director at the newly-opened Hungarian (later National) Theatre in 1839. While his first opera (he wrote eight in all) "Mária Bátori" still displays Italian and German influences, his second "Hunyadi László" can be considered typically Hungarian, not least for its folk elements, which are derived from "verbunkos" music (see Music).
The arias from "Hunyadi László" and "Bánk Bán", his most important opera, first performed in 1861, today belong to the standard Hungarian operatic reportory.

Ferenc Erkel
(1810–93)

This Budapest-born physicist has entered scientific history as the inventor of holography. In 1934, after studying in Budapest and Berlin he moved to England where from 1949 onwards he was a lecturer at the Imperial College of Science and Technology, and then from 1958 to 1967 Professor of Electrical Physics. The process for producing three-dimensional pictures

Dénes (Dennis) Gábor
(1900–79)

(holography) was developed by Gábor in 1947. The technique of laser light, which he invented in 1960, subsequently achieved great practical importance. In 1971 Gábor was awarded the Nobel Prize for Physics. Other less well known results of his scientific investigations include the holographic microscope and the flat tube for colour television sets.

Miklós Horthy
(1868–1957)

There is no other person who symbolises the turbulent interwar years as well as Miklós Horthy. The political career of this former commander of the fleet began with the removal of the communist soviet republic in August 1919 and the systematic persecution of all left-wing elements in the country (the "White Terror"). Following the electoral rejection of the Social Democrats in 1920 the conservatives became the largest force in parliament and chose Horthy to be the royal administrator of the Hungarian kingdom.
Horthy's regime during the 1930s took on more and more of the characteristics of a dictatorship, pursuing revisionist policies, with the result that Hungary ended up entering the Second World War on the side of Germany. After hopes of regaining old territories failed and the Second World War brought Hungary enormous losses, Horthy attempted, albeit without success, to leave the alliance with Germany. At the end of the war he was taken prisoner by the Americans and from 1949 until his death he lived in Portugal.

Mór Jókai
(1825–1904)

This great national storyteller ranks as one of the most widely read authors in Hungarian literature. In 1846, the same year that he completed his law studies, Jókai published his first novel "The Maze of Life", and launched himself on a career as writer and editor. His novels and stories, which rank among the finest works of Hungarian romantic prose, are characterised by plots full of violent contrasts, characters with extreme personality traits and highly far-fetched situations. His writing is also distinguished by a popularist's sense of humour, a didactic use of anecdote and a magnificent sense of the fantastic. Together with Petőfi he took an active part in the 1848 revolution, but after its collapse he had to go into hiding. An amnesty made it possible for him to return to public life in 1852 and in 1863 he started up the newpaper "Hon". As a writer, however, he was still extremely prolific, but his later output never approached the quality of his early works. Some of his novels have been turned into films and plays.

János Kádár
(1912–89)

As leader of the Communist Party, János Kádár dictated the course of Hungarian politics for over 30 years. By virtue of the relatively high standard of living and the small political freedoms which Kádár was able to make possible through his careful reforms, Hungary earned itself the reputation of being the "happiest" country in the Eastern bloc. Kádár, who joined the Communist Party at the age of 19, was Hungarian Interior Minister from 1948 to 1950 and a member of the revolutionary government of Imre Nagy (1956). After the suppression of the people's uprising, Kádár had Imre Nagy and several others arrested and two years later had them executed. Kádár clung on to the leadership of the Communist Party as long as he could, but eventually, even before the old system was finally displaced, he had to make way for younger reforming elements.

Imre (Emmerich)
Kálmán
(1882–1953)

Kálmán was born at Siófok on Lake Balaton and was the composer of a large number of operettas, inspired by Hungarian folklore, which have a secured a firm place in the repertory of opera houses everywhere. Kálmán won worldwide fame with the "Csárdásfürstin" (Gipsy Princess), as well as with "Der Zigeunerprimas" (Gipsy Fiddler; 1912) and "Countess Mariza" (1924).
His musical works owe their character in equal measure to the carefree elegance of Viennese operetta and the temperament and dark hues of his native Hungary. Until Hitler's invasion of Austria, Kálmán lived and worked in Vienna, whence he emigrated via Paris to the United States, where he remained until the end of the war and earned recognition as a conductor.

Zoltán Kodály   *Lajos Kossuth*   *Ferenc Liszt*

After 1945 he returned to Europe, although not to Hungary, and spent the last years of his life in Paris.

The scion of a rich Hungarian aristocratic family, Károlyi ranks as one of the most distinguished Hungarian politicians of the first half of the 20th c. As president of the Independence Party (1913–16) he pressed for universal suffrage and democratic reforms and disapproved of the militarist politics of the Austro-Hungarian monarchy and their alliance with Germany. In the autumn of 1918, during the bourgeois-democratic revolution, the popular politician was chosen to be the president of the Hungarian National Council of opposition parties and was appointed prime minister by King Karl IV. The aims of his political programme included independence for Hungary, redistribution of land to the peasants (he even set about dividing one of his own estates), measures to create jobs, and press freedom. In the newly founded Republic of Hungary Károlyi took on the office of head of state. Under the pressure of the radicalisation of domestic politics and the possibility of imminent territorial losses, Károlyi resigned in the spring of 1919 and emigrated to Paris, where he organised resistance to the Hungarian Fascists well into the 1930s. At the end of the Second World War he went home to Hungary, returning to Paris in 1947 as ambassador. He lived in France until his death in 1955.

Mihály Count Károlyi (1875–1955)

With the film "Casablanca", shot in 1943 with Ingrid Bergman and Humphrey Bogart in the main roles, the Hungarian-born Michael Curtiz succeeded in writing a piece of cinema history and gained himself an Oscar, the highest accolade of the American film industry. In 1912, when he was only 24, Curtiz shot his first film. After periods in Vienna and Berlin he arrived in Hollywood in 1927 and three years later was already making films in colour. His most famous films include "Robin Hood" (1938), "Virginia City" (1940), "Yankee Doodle" (1942), "Mission to Moscow" (1943) and "The Life of St Francis of Assisi" (1961).

Mihály Kertész (Michael Curtiz) (1888–1962)

The composer and musician, Zoltán Kodály, was born in Kecskemét. He is principally known for his systematic research into Hungarian folk music. He succeeded in defining and describing its special qualities by comparisons with the folk music of other Finno-Ugrian peoples. After his studies at the conservatoire in Budapest he taught theory of music and composition there from 1907, and from 1937 folk music. As a composer (chamber music, choral works, songs, etc.) he won well-deserved recognition during the 1920s. His compositions, which reflect his deep interest in Hungarian folk music, were taken up by conductors such as Toscanini and Furtwängler and made famous abroad. In 1923, for the 50th anniversary of the unification of Budapest, he composed the "Psalmus Hungaricus", using an

Zoltán Kodály (1882–1967)

18th c. psalm text. His close interest in the reform of singing and musical instruction in schools (see Music) was already apparent as long ago as the 1920s but he became even more committed after the Second World War. His teaching methods have gained worldwide acceptance and are still in use today.

György Konrád
(b. 1933)

Konrád is one of the leading representatives of the intellectual opposition in Hungary, who from the 1970s onwards campaigned for democratic reforms in his country. Like many of his fellow writers, Konrád was only able to publish his works abroad or underground (in the "samisdat") until the political changes at the end of the 1980s. The former philosophy student's first novel "Látogató" (The Visitor; 1969) arose out of his experiences as a youth worker employed by the Budapest authorities. In this and in his later novels ("The City Founder", 1975; "The Accomplice", 1980; "Ghost Party", 1986; etc.) he reflects social and political problems in a socialist society.

Lajos Kossuth
(1802–94)

Kossuth, who came from the minor nobility, is important as one of the leading figures in the struggle for Hungarian independence and civil rights in the last century. As the representative of absent magnates he took part in sittings of the Hungarian parliament between 1832 and 1836 and reported about it in newspaper articles, thereby incurring four years' imprisonment. Both as chief editor of the influential liberal newspaper in Pest, "Pesti Hirlap", and as leader of the liberal opposition in parliament, he fought vigorously for independence from Austria, social reforms, the abolition of feudal privileges, universal liability to taxation and the setting-up of a parliament to represent all Hungarians. In April 1849, under his leadership, the rump parliament, which had moved to Debrecen during the revolution, called for Hungarian independence and the removal of the House of Hapsburg, and chose him as head of state. After the suppression of the uprising Kossuth fled first of all to Turkey and from there to other countries in Europe. While in exile he continued his struggle for Hungarian independence and enlisted support on his travels to England and the United States in 1851–52. Although he was granted an amnesty in 1867, he did not return to Hungary, as he stood resolutely opposed to the Austro-Hungarian settlement. In 1880/82 his work "My Writings in Exile" appeared in several volumes. Kossuth, the revolutionary, despite being revered even in his lifetime as a national hero, never returned home and died in his adopted city of Turin in 1894.

Ferenc (Franz)
Lehár
(1870–1948)

This composer of many well-known operettas was born in Komárom in 1870, the son of a kapellmeister (music director). He received his training as a violin virtuoso at the conservatoires in Budapest and Prague and he was encouraged in his composition studies by Dvořak. In 1890 he followed his father's example and worked in several cities in the Austro-Hungarian Empire as a military kapellmeister. From 1902 he lived in Vienna and from 1926 to 1938 in Berlin. After the Second World War he settled in Zürich and only returned to Vienna shortly before his death. After initial attempts at writing full-scale operas, he switched to operetta in which he soon found his own unmistakable style. His most famous works are "The Merry Widow" (1905), "The Count of Luxembourg" (1909), "Gipsy Love" (1910) and "The Land of Smiles" (1929).

Ferenc (Franz)
Liszt
(1811–86)

Franz Liszt was born in the Hungarian province of Raiding (now Bürgenland in Austria) and is today revered as one of the nation's greatest figures. He was only nine years old when he made his début as a concert pianist. He studied in Vienna (under, among others, Antonio Salieri) and then lived from 1823 to 1835 in Paris, where he was influenced by Berlioz, Paganini and Chopin. Concert tours in the 1830s and 1840s took him all over Europe and enabled him to make the acquaintance of all the outstanding musicians of the period, including Richard Wagner, with whom he formed a life-long friendship. During his engagement as kapellmeister at the grand ducal court in Weimar from 1844 to 1861 he gathered a large group of pupils around him, including some who were later to become famous musicians and composers (e.g. Smetana). While in Weimar Liszt composed a total of 12 symphonic poems, the Dante and Faust Symphonies, the Missa Solemnis and a wide range of piano works which can be said to form the foundation of the so-called New German school. From 1861 to 1869 his home alternated between Rome, where he took the lower orders of the priesthood as an "abbé" in 1865, Budapest, where he took over the direction of the music academy which had been founded at his instigation, and Weimar. His connection with Hungary found particular expression in the "Hungarian Rhapsodies", while in 1856 his symphonic poem "Hungaria" received its first performance in Pest. For the consecration of the cathedral in Esztergom he composed the "Grand Festival Mass". Liszt was given the title of Duke of Sachsen-Weimar in 1859 and he died in Bayreuth in 1886.

The literary historian and philosopher, György Lukács, was born in Budapest and became a member of the Communist Party in 1918. After the collapse of the communist republic, in which he had held a political office, Lukács emigrated to Moscow via Vienna. The works that he wrote there, in which he formulated the central theses of Marxist aesthetics and artistic philosophy, had a lasting influence on left-wing European intellectuals. During the 1930s Lukács studied 19th c. European literature, in particular the realistic novel, and arrived at a new Marxist interpretation and evaluation of this literary genre. At the end of the war he returned to Hungary and lectured in aesthetics and cultural philosophy in Budapest from 1945 to 1958. As one of the leaders of the suppressed uprising in 1956 he was subsequently punished by being relieved of his teaching post and had to face additional discrimination. For a number of years Lukács retreated into a private existence, his books being printed in other European countries where they continued to attract a great deal of interest. In the middle of the 1960s he renewed his links with Hungarian intellectual life. He conceived the plan of writing an all-encompassing work about ethics but was never able to carry it out.

György Lukács
(1885–1971)

Matthias I, the son of János Hunyadi, who was chosen to be king in 1458, was one of the outstanding leaders of Hungarian history during the transition from the Middle Ages to the modern period. He was also a historical figure about whom a wealth of popular legend has collected. Supported by the lower nobility and the municipalities, he created a modern state with taxes as a source of income, thereby making possible the creation of a government administration and the maintenance of a standing army of around 10,000 men. While trade and the towns flourished under his government, the main thrust of his foreign policies (apart from aspirations towards the crown of the Holy Roman Empire, an honour which was to remain denied to him) was the safeguarding of his country from Turkish attacks. These he temporarily halted in 1476 with his victory at Szabács near Belgrade. Matthias was married to the Neapolitan princess Beatrice of Aragon. He took a great interest in the arts and sciences, and during his reign the ideas of the Renaissance gained an early foothold in Hungary. He attracted Italian artists to his court and took under his wing humanist scholars such as the Bishop of Pécs, Janus Pannonius. His library, the famous Corviniana, was during his lifetime one of the greatest collections in the world.

Matthias I
(Mátyás)
(1443–90)

Lászlo Moholy-Nagy was born in Bácsbosod in north-east Hungary. A gifted artist in many different media – painting, sculpture, graphics, photography – he is also widely known as an influential teacher at the Bauhaus in Weimar, where he worked from 1923 to 1928. After Hitler seized power he emigrated first to England and then in 1937 to the United States. In Chicago he founded the "New Bauhaus". Moholy-Nagy was the epitome of the modern artist in the first half of the twentieth century who freed himself from traditional forms and uniformity of expression and experimented with new materials, media and techniques, drawing on and influencing

László
Moholy-Nagy
(1895–1946)

Famous People

László Moholy-Nagy

Mihály Munkácsy

Sándor Petőfi

various present-day trends, (dadaism, constructivism, de Stijl). His wide-ranging output includes abstract compositions, collages, stage sets, photograms (pictures produced without a camera) and light sculptures.

Mihály Munkácsy (1844–1900)

Mihály Munkácsy is one of the most important representatives of 19th c. Hungarian painting. After periods of study and residence in Vienna, Munich and Düsseldorf, he settled down in 1872 in Paris, where he lived until his death. His international breakthrough came in 1870 with the picture "Last Day of a Condemned Man" (Budapest, Hungarian National Gallery), which established his reputation as a virtuoso painter of large-scale realistic genre pictures in the Courbet tradition. Even more than these pictures, it was his moving historical paintings which his contemporaries particularly prized, for instance, his wall picture in the Budapest Parliament of "Árpád's Conquest" (1896), as well as his religious works. The intimate landscape pictures which he painted in the 1880s were influenced by the school of outdoor painting of Barbizon.

János (John von) Neumann (1903–57)

Known even in his youth as a genius at calculations, Neumann studied mathematics, physics and chemistry (Budapest/Zürich), qualified as a university lecturer in Berlin and taught from 1933 at the Institute for Advanced Studies in Princeton, New Jersey in the United States. His research activities included quantum mechanics, functional analysis and mathematical statistics. During and after the Second World War Neumann worked with other people on the American atom bomb project; from 1954 he was a member of the US Atomic Energy Commission. In the last years of his life he devoted himself to the development of electronic calculators.

Sándor Petőfi (1823–49)

Sándor Petőfi is revered as one of Hungary's greatest national poets. On leaving school he led an unsettled vagabond existence, serving for some time as a soldier and also travelling around the country as an actor with a theatre troupe. In 1844 he was given a job as an assistant editor in Pest. Two years previously, in 1842, he had had his first volume of poems published and this soon brought him great popularity. His poetry is characterised by his use of colloquial language and the manifestation of very personal feelings, the latter quality very much in evidence in his love poems, but also present in his other writings. In his poems, his heroic and fairy-tale epics, and his songs – the most famous being "Háry János"(1845) – he portrayed the customs and landscapes of the Great Hungarian Plain, depicting the everyday life of the peasants and herdsmen. His revolutionary convictions made him a leading figure in the struggle for freedom. On March 15th 1848 Petőfi led the youth of Pest to the steps of the National Museum and there performed his revolutionary "national hymn". Convinced of the need for armed struggle to secure freedom, he enlisted in the revolutionary army as a captain in 1849 and is assumed to have lost his life in the Battle of Segesvár (today Sighişoara, in Romania).

The revolt of the Hungarians against the absolutist rule of the Hapsburgs in the 17th and 18th c. is indissolubly linked to the name of Ferenc Rákóczi. Rákóczi was a descendant of the Princes of Transylvania, who, while still a child at the age of twelve, was abducted to Vienna and brought up as a courtier of the Emperor. On attaining his majority Rákóczi returned to Transylvania and after some initial wavering took over the leadership of the rebellion (the "Kuruzzen uprising"), which at first was mainly supported by the peasants, but then by a large section of the whole population. In 1704 Rákóczi became Prince of Transylvania, and in the following year was chosen as the ruling Prince of Hungary. The rebellion was brought to an end by an armistice in 1711, all its impetus having been lost because of the lack of support from other European powers. Rákóczki, however, refused to concede defeat and, accompanied by a small retinue, set off across Europe, tirelessly soliciting support at the courts of Russia, Poland and France. In the hope of a resumption of the freedom struggle he finally went to Turkey, where he died in Rodosto (today Tekirdağ) in 1735.

Rákóczi, Ferenc (Franz) II (1676–1735)

Sándor Rózsa, the most famous footpad or "betyár" of the Great Plain was a shepherd who, when in prison for theft, escaped and fled into the wilderness around Szeged. After his amnesty in 1848 he organised irregulars to take part in the freedom struggle, but the troops were disbanded because of robbery and other atrocities. In 1853 a reward was put on his head and four years later he was captured and sentenced to death, although subsequently pardoned. By then he was already a legendary figure and many so-called "followers" pressed for his release. A remission of sentence enabled him to be freed in 1868 and he returned to the familiar world of the heathland peasants where he continued his old way of life. In 1869 he was taken prisoner once more and sentenced to life imprisonment. He died in prison.

Sándor Rózsa (1813–78)

Two of the most famous architectural monuments in Budapest were designed by Schulek: the Fishermen's Bastion, built in 1895–1903 on top of the old castle walls, and the Matthias Church on the castle mound, which was substantially rebuilt for the millennium celebrations in 1896. Frigyes Schulek studied with various teachers in Vienna and from 1870 worked in the construction office of Imre Steindl, the architect of the Budapest Parliament. From 1903 to 1911 he lectured in medieval architecture at the Technical University in Budapest. Under his direction a large number of Hungary's historic buildings were restored in an idealised medieval style. His empathy with the architectural style of the Middle Ages is also expressed in his designs, in which Neo-Romanesque and Neo-Gothic elements are fused with the stylistic features of national romanticism.

Frigyes Schulek (1841–1919)

Semmelweis, who came from Buda, has gone into medical history as the "mothers' saviour". In his work as an obstetrician in a Vienna clinic he recognised that the germs carried by dirty hands, instruments and bandages were a cause of childbed fever, which was one of the commonest and most deadly of childbirth complications. He therefore recommended doctors to disinfect their hands and equipment with chlorine water before treating their patients. In 1850 he returned to Budapest, where he became chief consultant in gynaecology at the Rókus Hospital and taught from 1855 in the Medical University, which today bears his name. Although his methods were highly successful and prepared the way for the aseptic treatment of wounds, during his own lifetime he did not win any real recognition outside the borders of Hungary.

Ignác Semmelweis (1818–65)

Stephan, whose actual name was Vajk, was a member of the Árpád dynasty and followed his father Géza on to the prince's throne. With his conversion to Christianity and his coronation as the first Hungarian king in 1000 (with a crown sent by Pope Sylvester), he laid the foundations of the Christian

(Saint) Stephan I (István) (967–1038)

monarchy in Hungary. By his marriage to Gisela, the daughter of the Duke of Bavaria, he won himself ties of kinship with the west. He turned Hungary, which had been torn apart by external threats and internal power struggles into a state in the West European mould. He divided the country into regions (komitats), organised the administration and justice, and strengthened the structure of the church by creating bishoprics. In addition, two legal treatises, which laid down in writing the laws in force at that time, were produced and handed down during his reign. Hungary celebrates the day when he was canonised (August 20th 1083) as a national holiday,

István Count Széchenyi (1791–1860)

This landowner, who came from a noble family, is one of the key thinkers and one of the most committed politicians during the period of the Hungarian revolution. In his book "Hitel" ("credit"), which appeared in 1830, he brought together the findings he had made about economics during numerous visits abroad. The main impediment to Hungary's economic and social progress lay, in his opinion, in the country's anachronistic economic structure and in the freedom from taxation enjoyed by the landowning nobility. In 1825 he gave a generous donation towards the foundation of the Hungarian Academy of Sciences. He initiated steamer services on the Danube and Lake Balaton, started the merchant bank, forced through the regulation of the Tisza and the lower stretches of the Danube and instituted the building of the Chain Bridge (1836–49). In his politics he took a moderate stance: he wanted reforms but not the overthrow of the political system. In the first accountable government of the revolutionary period he was given the office of transport minister. After the resignation of the cabinet in the autumn of 1849, Széchenyi, his health now highly precarious, entered the Döbling psychiatric hospital near Vienna, where he ended his life in 1860.

Pál Szinyei-Merse (1845–1920)

Pál Szinyei-Merse, the scion of a wealthy noble family, was the forerunner of the school of outdoor painting in Hungary, although for a long time he went unrecognised. His studies in Munich with Piloty had less influence on his later work than the "plein air" paintings of the French artists in Barbizon. Szinyei-Merse very quickly found his way to a new artistic style. Between 1869 and 1874 his main outdoor paintings were created: "The Swing", "Washing drying" (1869), "Couple in Love" (1871) and "Breakfast in the Open Air" (1872/73); Hungarian National Gallery). As his paintings were at that time gaining no real recognition, he returned to his estate, where he remained for more than twenty years, only painting sporadically. In 1896 Szinyei-Merse exhibited "Breakfast in the Open Air" for a second time and now, with Europe having capitulated to impressionism, the work was rapturously received. Szinyei-Merse began to paint again and in addition, as professor at the Budapest Academy of Fine Arts, he brought an influence to bear on the development of the younger generation of artists.

Victor Vasarely (b. 1908)

The famous exponent of Op-Art was born in Pécs in 1908 as Győző Vásárhelyi. His artistic career began in Paris in 1930, where he worked as a commercial artist. In the early stages of his career he was heavily influenced by his no less famous countryman László Moholy-Nagy (see above) and the Dutch de Stijl movement, as well as other contemporary trends which broke away from representationalism in art. Vasarely committed himself to a kind of geometrising abstraction which was very close to constructivism. In the 1950s, after systematic experiments and observations with optical illusions, he came to the conclusion that the contemplation of a work of art and the perception of its shape, colour and space is closely affected by the movement and the (variable) position of the observer. He coined the term "cinetism" for these observations.
Vasarely was also active in other areas of art and one of his collaborations with architects resulted in the project "The coloured town".

Hungarian art nouveau: Kiskunfélegyháza Town Hall ▶

Art and Culture

History of art

Beginnings

The development of Hungarian art is closely bound up with the changing history of the country. In the Roman period the greater part of Hungary formed part of the province of Pannonia. In some places it is still possible, even today, to find the remains of Roman buildings, for instance, in Óbuda (Budapest), the Roman Aquincum, in Sopron (Scarbantia) or to the south of Székesfehérvár, where, near the village of Tác, the Roman camp of Gorsium-Herculia was uncovered. The wall paintings in the underground burial chambers in Pécs are impressive memorials to Early Christian art. After the fall of the Roman Empire, during the migrations of the peoples, the area of present-day Hungary was settled for short periods by Goths, Langobards, Huns and Avars. There are excavation finds to confirm these waves of migration. The Magyars seized possession of the country in the late 9th c. under Prince Árpád, the founder of the first Hungarian royal dynasty. The silver breastplates and gold finds in the History of Art Museum in Vienna and in the National Museum in Budapest provide evidence of the high standard of gold work at this time.

Romanesque

11th c.

The founding of the Hungarian monarchy by Stephen I around the year 1000 was a decisive moment in Hungarian history. Stephen proclaimed his conversion to Roman Catholicism and had himself crowned king with a crown which Pope Sylvester authorised to be sent to him. This crown, known as the Stephen Crown, is still Hungary's most important national symbol. It is stored in the National Museum in Budapest, together with the rest of the ruler's insignia (the sceptre and orb). More recent investigations have indicated that this precious piece was probably not, as originally supposed, made for King Stephen, but for a later ruler in the 11th c. and is the work of a Byzantine craftsman. Hungary's leanings towards the western Church in Rome and to the Christian monarchies of Western Europe also had an influence on the art of the Magyars in the succeeding centuries. Monasteries and churches sprouted up everywhere; King Stephen himself founded several Benedictine monasteries and ten episcopal churches. Unfortunately only a few architectural monuments from the 11th c. have been preserved (the crypt of the former Benedictine abbey at Tihany and fragments of the castle church at Pécsvárad), many buildings being destroyed during the Mongol invasion of 1241/42. The largest building project of the early 11th c. would have been the cathedral of the bishopric of Pécs (founded in 1009). Completely rebuilt in the 19th c., this building acted as a model for a whole series of churches throughout the country. Part of its original sculpturing can still be seen today at the cathedral museum in Pécs.

12th/13th c.

Only a few fragments are still extant of the royal building projects of the 12th and 13th c. Worthy of mention are the (faultlessly restored) chapel at Esztergom Palace, which shows the influence of French Gothic, and the frescoes of the Gisela Chapel in Veszprém (mid-13th c.; thought to be the work of an Italian artist). The "Porta speciosa" is the name of the magnificent doorway which was designed at the end of the 12th c. during alterations to the cathedral at Esztergom. Now only preserved in fragments, it was imitated in numerous churches throughout Hungary (e.g. in Pannonhalma). A style of church belonging to the Late Romanesque and Early

Gothic, particularly widespread in western Hungary, is the ancestral or dynastic church. Its origins are closely connected with the emergence of a landowning nobility in the 11th and 12th c. The nobleman would proclaim his social status and wealth by building his own church, often right in the middle of his estate. The building of such a church generally went hand in hand with the foundation of a Benedictine or Premonstratensian monastery. Large ancestral churches have been preserved in Ják, Zsámbék and Lébény. They all consist of a three-aisled basilica with three semi-circular apses on the east side and two towers on the west side of the church. Another characteristic feature of these ancestral churches is the family gallery situated between the west towers, where the landowner sat when he attended a service. The church doorways at Ják, Karcsa (Northern Hungary) and Csempeskópács (near Szombathely) are evidence of the high quality of the stonemasons' craftsmanship at this time. The ancestral churches of the smaller landowners are also of great interest to the art historian. They are often to be found in remote villages, and their romantic architectural fabric is generally very well preserved (Karcsa, Csaroda, Egregy, Mánfa, etc.). In quite a few of these churches, such as at Feldebrő, Szalonna and Pécsvárad, it has been possible to preserve wall paintings dating back to the time of the church's construction. In these smaller ancestral churches the ground-plan is reduced to a single-aisled nave with an integrated west tower and rectangular choir in the east. The origin of this type of church as a nobleman's private place of worship becomes especially evident in those examples where the central design of the Carolingian palace chapel at Aachen is followed (Szalonna, Karcsa, etc.).

Gothic

In the 13th and 14th c. the Gothic style gained wide currency, having already been anticipated in certain outstanding buildings dating from the end of the 12th c. (the castle chapel at Esztergom). Its origins can be traced on the one hand to the reign of Charles I (1308–42) of the Neapolitan dynasty of Anjou and on the other to the effects of the reforming orders of the Premonstratensians and the Cistercians, originally from France, whose churches heralded the transition to Gothic architecture. Significant examples of the early Gothic style are provided by the churches of Zsámbék, Ócsa and Bélapátfalva, the last named being the only remaining example of a Cistercian church in Hungary. After the Mongol invasion in the middle of the 13th c. many towns were extended and fortified (Győr, Esztergom, Pécs, Sopron) and castles were erected to protect the national borders (e.g. at Buda and Visegrád). The architecture of the late 14th and early 15th c. displays influences of both the cathedral of St Stephen in Vienna and the South German Parler family of artists, which at this time was active in Prague. The preponderant type of building in Germany in the late Middle Ages, the hall church, also spread to Hungary, with examples to be found in Kőszeg, Sárospatak and Miskolc. The fan vaulting in the Gothic Reformed Church in Nyírbátor testifies to the high level of accomplishment in the techniques of vaulting which then existed. The best-known sacred building in the Late Gothic style, the Church of Matthias on the castle hill in Budapest, did not receive the form it has today until it was rebuilt in the Neo-Gothic style at the end of the 19th century.

Architecture

In the 15th c. the importance of wall paintings came second to that of panel paintings, the painted and carved winged altar becoming the main vehicle of religious art. Several regional schools existed, all of which reached a high artistic level. As a large number of paintings were either destroyed or plundered during the Turkish wars, it is mainly works from the north and east of Hungary which have been preserved and these can be admired today in the museums of Budapest and in the Christian Museum in Esztergom. The outstanding artistic figure during the transition to the modern

Painting

Portal of the "family" church in Ják . . .   *. . . and the church in Csempeszkópács*

period was the monogrammist M S, who worked in Hungary around 1500 and left a series of precious altar panels to posterity.

Renaissance

Under the rule of King Matthias I (period of reign 1458–90) and his wife Beatrice of Aragon from Naples, the Italian-influenced Early Renaissance became established in Hungary. The royal residences in Buda and Visegrád and the queen's seat in Diósgyőr near Miskolc became centres of Florentine Renaissance art. Architecture (Visegrád, the palace), sculpture (Visegrád, the Hercules fountain) and books (Biblioteca Corviniana) all flourished during the 15th c. Italian artists, or those who had been schooled in their methods, were employed not only at the royal court, but also at the diocesan towns of Pécs and Esztergom. Besides Visegrád Palace, the outstanding examples of Hungarian Renaissance art are the red marble Bakócz Chapel in Esztergom Cathedral (now on the left of the entrance door), the János Vitéz Hall in the bishop's palace at Esztergom with its humanistically conceived paintings, and the castle in Sárospatak.

The defeat at the hands of the Turks at the Battle of Mohács in 1526 brought an abrupt end to this artistic heyday. In 1541 Buda was conquered and a large part of Hungary remained occupied by the Turks until 1686. Ottoman art and culture became established in the Turkish-occupied areas. Unfortunately, after the reconquest, many of their architectural monuments were destroyed by the Habsburgs or were converted to other uses. Only a very few examples of their civilisation have been preserved, including the two mosques in Pécs and the minaret in Eger. In the Habsburg part of the country many of the remaining castles were fortified with bastions in the style of Italian fortresses, in order to ward off further advances by the Turks (Kőszeg, Sárvár, Mosonmagyaróvár, Siklós).

In Transylvania, the eastern part of Hungary, which had remained an independent principality, significant works of art of all types were produced during the 16th and 17th centuries.

Baroque and Rococo

Baroque and Rococo art in Hungary was fundamentally influenced by the fact that the country was part of the Habsburg empire. Large numbers of Austrian architects and fresco artists worked in Hungary in the 18th c. Large parts of Hungary had been in the hands of the Turks in the 17th c. and even after the Ottomans' withdrawal, the anti-Habsburg freedom struggles kept the country on a knife-edge. It was thus not until the 18th c. that the new style found its full flowering, whereas in other European countries, in particular Italy and France, the transition to Rococo had already been completed long before.

The few Early and High Baroque artistic monuments in Hungary include the banqueting hall at the castle in Sárvár, the Jesuit church in Győr and the Savoy Castle in Ráckeve, which the renowned Viennese architect, Lukas von Hillebrandt designed for the "conqueror of the Turks", Prince Eugene of Savoy. His pupil, Andreas Mayerhoffer, with his designs for the castles at Gödöllő and Hatvan, developed a style of summer residence which the Hungarian landed nobility were to copy. Known as the Grassalkovich type of residence, after the prince who had originally commissioned Mayerhoffer's famous castles, its main characteristics were the U-shaped ground-plan and the domed central section.

The most important secular building of the Hungarian Baroque period is, however, Eszterháza Palace in Fertőd, which was built by the Habsburg loyalist Miklós Eszterházy in 1760 after the model of the Palace of Versailles. Originally this summer residence was surrounded by an enormous park

Baroque church in Szentgotthárd

Altarpiece by Maulbertsch in Sümeg

laid out in the French geometric style and contained its own theatre, Chinese ballroom and many small pavilions.

After the victory of the Counter-Reformation and the extensive recatholicisation of large tracts of their empire by the Habsburgs, the construction of new churches became the most pressing task for architects and builders. There was feverish activity, in particular in the diocesan towns of Eger, Szekesfehérvár, Győr and Veszprém. Here not only did the bishops build their residences in the Late Baroque style, but churches, town houses, public buildings and houses belonging to religious orders were all given a Baroque stamp. When the royal palace on the castle hill in Buda was altered and extended, the Italian architects Fortunato Prati and Antoni Martinelli were involved. In creating the façade of the church in Szentgotthárd, the prolific Viennese architect Franz Anton Pilgram launched a new style of church design, which was copied in numerous Late Baroque village churches (including the Serbian Orthodox diocesan church in Szentendre). He replaced the familiar twin-towered façade (well-known from such examples as the Minorite Church in Eger and the abbey church in Tihany) with an ornamental façade with a single tower in the centre.

Painting

The Baroque period was the age of the art of illusion, and with painting making a major contribution to the total effect of a room, painters were in great demand in 18th c. Hungary to provide frescos and pictures for the churches and palaces. As with architects and stucco artists, they came predominantly from Austria and Italy or had learnt their craft in those countries. The most famous representative is Franz Anton Maulbertsch (1724–96), the virtuoso fresco artist who was born at Langenargen on Lake Constance. Evidence of his brilliant technique can be found in Sümeg, Győr, Vác and Székesfehérvár. The painter Johann Lukas Kracker (1717–79) also worked at various locations in Hungary. With his painted ceiling in the Library Hall in the Lyceum in Eger he left the world a magnificent example of the Baroque art of illusion.

Minhály Munkácsy: "The Village Hero"

In the second half of the 18th c., during the transition to Classicism, what became known as the Mid-18th c. Rococo style developed. The chief exponent of this style was the architect Jakob Fellner, who mainly worked for the Eszterházy family (the former Lyceum in Eger; the castle in Tata, etc.). This Mid-18th c. style is characterised by the marriage of Late Baroque architectural forms with the pseudo-classical ornaments of Neo-Classicism, in particular the plaited garlands which gave the style its German name "Zopfstil" (Zopf = plait).

Mid-18th c.
Rococo

19th century

The Late Baroque plait style had prepared the way for Neo-Classicism with its architectural ornamentation, and this new artistic trend was to determine the course of Hungarian architecture from about 1790 to the middle of the 19th c. One of the earliest ventures into this new style was made by the Viennese architect Isidore Canevale with his reconstruction of the cathedral in Vác (1760/70). Menyhért Hefele followed his example in 1791 with the diocesan church in Szombathely, and in the first half of the 19th c. the great neo-classical cathedrals of Eger and Esztergom were built to plans by the architect Jószef Hild (1789–1867). The city which is most influenced by Neo-Classicism is Debrecen, then a stronghold of Calvinism and anti-Habsburg views. It was these Calvinistic elements that embraced the simple neo-classical style in preference to the prettiness of Rococo, which had associations with Catholicism and the House of Habsburg. Neo-Classicism in Hungary took on the status of the country's first national style and as a result enjoyed great popularity in the Hungarian reform era of 1825–48.

Neo-Classicism

The neo-classical counterpart to Eszterháza Palace in Fertőd is Nagycenk Palace, situated not far away from it, which was the ancestral home of the old Hungarian family of Széchenyi. One of Hungary's most sought after architects of the period, Mihály Pollack (1753–1835), worked on the rebuilding of this palace in the neo-classical style. Several town palaces in Budapest were built using his plans, as were the Evangelical church at Deák Square and the Hungarian National Museum (1837–46), his masterpiece.

The 19th c. in Hungary was a century of nationalism and political reform. The setting-up of the Austro-Hungarian double monarchy in 1867 guaranteed Hungary greater independence than hitherto and its own parliament in Budapest, the building of which was entrusted to Imre Steindl (1839–1902). On the Pest bank of the Danube he designed a monumental set of buildings in the Neo-Gothic style, following the model of the English parliament. These offer a striking contrast to the Royal Palace, which lies further down the river on the castle hill. The new city hall in Pest was also designed by Steindl. After the settlement with Austria (1867) Budapest rivalled Vienna in displays of splendour. Miklós Ybl (1814–91) was one of the architects most in demand in the latter half of the 19th c. He designed many prestigious buildings, even whole streets, in the stylistic forms of the Neo-Renaissance and the Neo-Baroque (e.g. the Budapest State Opera). Many eminent sculptors also played their part in helping Budapest to acquire the identity of a major capital city. Alajos Strobl (1856–1926), the most important representative of this period, produced many fountains and sculptures, including the Matthias fountain on the castle hill, which depicts the legendary love story of King Matthias and the poor peasant maiden Ilonka. A complete picture of a town which grew up in this period is offered by Szeged, which was completely destroyed by floods in 1879 and then rebuilt during the last years of the century.

Historicism,
Architecture

Hungarian painting in the 19th c., in particular in the latter half, produced some notable painters who are scarcely known at all elsewhere. Mihály Munkácsy (1844–1900; see Famous People) is one of the few internationally known painters of this period. His genre and historical paintings can be

Painting

admired both in the Déri Museum in Debrecen and in the Hungarian National Gallery in Budapest, while the parliament building in Budapest is decorated with his frescoes. Laszlo Paál (1846–79) and Pál Szinyei-Merse (1845–1920; see Famous People), who were influenced by the French "plein air" school of Barbizon, paved the way for Impressionism in Hungary. Towards the end of the century a colony of artists grew up in Nagabánya (today Baia Mare in Romania) under the leadership of Simon Hollósy (1857–1918). Among the members of this artistic community were Károly Ferenczy (1862–1917) and Jószef Rippi-Rónai (1861–1927), whose pictures are to be seen in the Hungarian National Gallery in Budapest.

Art Nouveau

The art of the turn of the century, often referred to as "art nouveau", took on different forms in individual European countries, as is clear from the various names it was given: "art nouveau" in France and Belgium, the "modern style" in England and the "secessionist style" in Austria. Hungarian "art nouveau" grew up in the last decades of the 19th c., at a time when nationalism and the politics of magyarisation were reaching their zenith and Hungary was preparing for its millennium celebrations in 1896 with the utmost pomp. In forming a national architectural style (Hungarian "art nouveau" is also referred to as a national style), the wish was expressed for the country to free itself from Austrian and Habsburg domination. Delight in bright colours and a preference for splendour and sumptious ornamentation were regarded as special Hungarian qualities and prized as the supposed legacy of the country's oriental traditions.

Architecture

The architecture of Hungary's art nouveau is characterised by its preoccupation with traditional folk motives, and it has very little in common with the geometric shapes of the Viennese secessionist style or the floral

Post Office building in Pécs   *Dome of an art nouveau house in Szeged*

motives of the Franco-Belgian art nouveau school, even if passing influences of both these styles, as well as Neo-Baroque and Neo-Gothic forms can be observed. Typical Hungarian variants of art nouveau are the façades with their brightly-coloured majolica tiles. The predominantly floral designs on these tiles are derived from the wealth of ornamentation to be found in popular art, which was exploited even more in textile design. The buildings of Ödön Lechner, the foremost exponent of Hungarian art nouveau, can most readily be compared with the designs of the Spaniard Antoni Gaudí.

The majority of buildings in the art nouveau style are to be found in Budapest itself, but there are also examples of architecture from this period in Kecskemét (town hall, Cifra-palota), Szeged (Palais Reök, etc.) and other Hungarian towns. The public baths at the Hotel Gellert in Budapest offer both recreation and artistic enjoyment at the same time, while in Pécs (Hotel Palatinus) and Szombathely (Hotel Savaria) the visitor can spend the night in hotels which have been rebuilt and refurbished in the style of this period.

The main exponent and father of art nouveau in Hungary is Ödön Lechner (1845–1914), who belonged to the generation of the Viennese architect Otto Wagner (1841–1918). Lechner's early buildings are indebted to the Neo-Renaissance, while his main works display borrowings from Persian-Indian motives, the architect wishing to emphasise Hungary's eastern heritage. His most important buildings in chronological order are the town hall in Kecskemét (1890), the Museum of Arts and Crafts in Budapest (1891–96), the Geological Institute (1899) and the Post Office Savings Bank (1899–1901), both also in Budapest. Lechner's later buildings are characterised by their brightly-coloured façade decorations in the form of majolica tiles, which were made in Pécs near Zsolnay. These slabs of pyrogranite, which were weatherproof and could be polished, were developed at Zsolnay expressly for these façade constructions. It is no exaggeration to say that they became the national building material of the period. The products of the Zsolnay ceramics firm, which achieved worldwide renown with their art nouveau vases, are now on show in the Zsolnay Museum in Pécs. At the apogee of the company's success it was producing a third of the entire ceramics output of the Austro-Hungarian Empire.

Lechner's successors also used ornamental ceramic decorations on their buildings. The art gallery at Kecskemét (Cifra-palota), built in 1902 by Géza Márkus (1872–1912), is a particularly decorative example of this style. Lechner's most important pupil was Béla Lajta (1875–1920), who continued his studies in Berlin and with Norman Shaw in London. In 1903 he collaborated with Lechner to design the oriental-looking mausoleum for the Schmidl family at the Jewish cemetery on the Kozma utca in Budapest. His later houses are less colourful and in their form are much more strictly controlled than Lechner's. Lajta prefers façades with red-brick cladding and the sparing use of flat ornamentation. He was responsible for a number of buildings in Budapest, including the commerce school in Vas Street (1910–13). His later work shows a Finnish influence, as are also the buildings of Károly Kós (1883–1977), who discarded Lechner's ornamental style. Kós designed the church in Zebegény (1908–09), the furnishing of which was carried out by the founder of the Gödöllő artists' colony, Aldar Körösfői-Kriesch (1863–1920).

This colony of artists, which is comparable to the Germany artists' community in Worspwede in North Germany, played a central role in Hungarian art nouveau painting and decorative arts. It was formed in 1902, when the painter Aldar Körösfői-Kriesch moved with his family to the small country town of Gödöllő to the north-east of Budapest. Following the English "arts and crafts" model, a community of artists became established here, devoting themselves to a rustic way of life as close to nature as possible, and seeing in popular art an important source of inspiration for their new artistic aims. One of the community's aims was also to create a modern

Ödön Lechner

Gödöllő
Artists' Colony

Hungarian national style. More and more artists started to follow the movement and they are now known as the "School of Gödöllő". Besides painters and sculptors, the movement included the architects István Medgyaszay (1877–1959) and Ede Toroczkai (1869–1945). The most important representative of the Gödöllő School, besides Körösfői-Kriesch, was Sándor Nagy (1868–1950). For Nagy and his wife, István Medgyaszay designed a red-brick house in the middle of an English landscaped garden. It became the quintessential art nouveau artist's villa, closely resembling its English model, the "Red House" of William Morris. In stylistic terms the painters of Gödöllő are closely related to the English Pre-Raphaelites. For content the Gödöllő artists frequently drew on the themes of Hungarian mythology and legend – another indicator of their fervent nationalism. They believed that the foundations for a typical Hungarian style were to be found in the oral tradition of folk tales and legends.

20th century

One of the most famous Hungarian artists of the first half of this century was Lászlo Moholy-Nagy (1895–1946; see Famous People). He mainly worked abroad and was director of the metal workshop at the Bauhaus in Dessau, teaching the introductory course which all students had to follow. After the dissolution of the Bauhaus in 1933 Moholy-Nagy first went to London and then in exile to the USA. From 1937 to 1946 he was director of the "New Bauhaus" in Chicago, now the Institute of Design. He was most of all known for his experiments in the fields of photography and textile production. His compatriot Farkas Molnár, who also worked at the Bauhaus, was first and foremost an architect. In the early 1930s Molnár designed some dwelling houses in Budapest in the Bauhaus style. They are among the few examples in Hungary of such buildings being commissioned from artists.

A return to archaic forms: building by Deszö Ekler in Nagykálló

Famous internationally as the founder of Op-Art was Victor Vasarely (b. 1908; see Famous People), whose works can be seen today in Pécs. Like his famous compatriot Moholy-Nagy, he achieved considerable fame abroad and for many years lived in France. The abstract trend in art known as Op-Art began in the 1950s under his leadership. Vasarely explored in an almost scientific way the physical and psychic processes which make up the perceptions of a person experiencing a work of art and how the work of art makes its effect.

In architecture Imre Makovecz, who designed the Hungarian pavilion at the 1992 EXPO in Seville, became the founder of a new "school", which for a number of years now has enjoyed international recognition. Organic forms mixed with elements of traditional architecture characterise this new Hungarian architectural style, in which, as with other art forms, the desire for national identity and freedom from the shackles of the socialist model of unity finds full expression. Impressive examples of this new "style" can be found in Sárospatak, Nagykálló and Siófok, etc.

Contemporary architecture

Music

At the mention of "Hungarian folk music" we normally think of gipsy music – a misapprehension to which the Romantic composers of the 19th c. fell prey when they added so-called folk music to their canon of forms. One has only to think of the "Hungarian Dances" of Brahms. Of course gipsy music, like paprika and the puszta, is part of Hungary, but it is not synonymous with traditional Hungarian folk music, which since the Middle Ages has only been passed down orally and would never have emerged from obscurity but for the pioneering efforts and research of Zoltán Kodály and Béla Bartók. It consists of songs and dances accompanied by bagpipes and

Folk music

Gipsy music . . .

. . . and folklore dances

73

Music

flutes. When peasant orchestras began to imitate gipsy bands in the 19th c. they started to add the dulcimer and violin. Today Hungarian folk music is once again in good hands in the "táncház" or dance halls, to be found in many towns and villages, particularly in country districts.

Gipsy music

In spite of the fact that gipsies as a minority are afforded little respect in Hungary, their contribution to the creation of a "genuine Hungarian atmosphere" is greatly appreciated, not least by the many foreign tourists who visit the country. From the 18th c. onwards, gipsy bands toured the countryside, providing the music for village celebrations, both large and small, for weddings, burials, fairs and other events calling for a musical backing. In the 19th c. municipal gipsy orchestras were formed, with clarinets, double bass and dulcimer, and the first violinist playing the melody. From the melting-pot of Hungarian folk music emerged the standard type of gipsy music which is well-known the world over for its sad, but also temperamental character. While it can be said that gipsies used to be born with a talent for music in their blood, nowadays musical children in Budapest attend the Rajkó specialist music school, where they are prepared for a career as professional musicians.

Musical beginnings

The oldest Hungarian musical monuments are to be found in the field of church music (the liturgy), and the fact that they were handed down is largely due to the wide use of written script in the cathedral schools. Church song in the vernacular started to become established in the 13th c. In the high and late Middle Ages the royal court was the centre of musical developments. In the wake of the crusaders, who crossed Hungary on their way to the Holy Land, there came itinerant minstrels, bringing western music into the country. At the same time royal Hungarian musicians visited the courts of Europe, where not only Hungarian songs, but also the national dances (ungaresca) in particular, were much admired. King Matthias, the first Renaissance ruler of Hungary, attracted many artists to his court, including Italian instrumentalists. Dutch-Burgundian and German music, however, also exerted a powerful influence on the musical life of the court.

16th–18th c.

The years of Turkish domination which began in 1526, coupled with the division of the country into three, meant a drastic curtailment in the nation's musical life. The highly developed musical culture which had grown up around the bishops' and noblemen's seats and at the royal court temporarily came to an end in the chaos caused by the war and even its permanent records and monuments were destroyed. An exception was Transylvania, which enjoyed a cultural heyday during the 16th and 17th c. and maintained close contacts with Italy in the field of music. The most important forms of musical expression in the 16th c. were chants and epic song. The latter is also referred to as historical song, as it represented historical and contemporary events, in a sung form with an instrumental (often violin) accompaniment. Only the melodies of the songs have been handed down (e.g. in the "Cronica" of Sebestyén Tinódi, which appeared in 1538), not the instrumental accompaniments. One of the most important musicians of the 16th c. was the virtuouso lutenist Bálint Bakfark, who was also very highly thought of abroad. In the 17th c. the maintenance of Hungary's musical tradition was left to the monasteries and the nobility, especially those in the north and east of the country. Many noblemen's courts, both large and small, had an orchestra which provided an accompaniment for balls and other entertainments. At the homes of some of the more important nobility, these ensembles sometimes boasted as many as 15 to 20 members, including violinists, trumpeters, organists, flautists and virginalists. Gamba players, guitarists and trombonists were also employed as court musicians. In the 18th c. this tradition of the court orchestra continued, and it was not uncommon for them to include celebrated musicians among their ranks. The most famous example is probably that of the Austrian composer, Joseph Haydn, who served as kapellmeister to the court orchestra of the Eszterházy family for almost 30 years. Organ and

Historical song

virginal music (the virginal was a Baroque keyboard instrument, rather like a piano) occupied a special place in music of the Baroque period and works for these instruments have been handed down in four important hand-written collections.

One special feature of Hungarian musical history is the Kuruzzen songs, which originated around 1700 in the course of Hungary's struggle for freedom. They are a mixture of folk air and historical song and during the 18th and 19th c. their tunes entered the realms of popular music.

Kuruzzen songs

Verbunkos is the name given to a type of music which has been played since the 18th c. – mainly by gipsy bands – to recruit soldiers. It was originally a lively, often improvised form of instumental dance music, which later came to be sung as well. The "verbunkos style" which developed was considered to be typical Hungarian dance music in the 19th c. and has been used by numerous composers in their works. Although it really counts as a serious music form, the style embodies so many popular elements that its melodies have been recorded by collectors of folk music.

Verbunkos

Hungary's musical culture was not alone in acquiring many bourgeois trappings during the 19th c. Musicians and composers (including Haydn, Berlioz and Beethoven) had their works performed in Buda and Pest , while in the provinces countless music societies were formed. The first copies of printed music were produced in Pest and a musical journal was founded. A forum was created for the new genre of opera or lyrical drama when the Hungarian National Theatre was opened in 1837. Verbunkos, which had been developing as a musical form since the beginning of the previous century, now enjoyed a golden period during the first half of the 19th c. and acquired the status of a national musical style. It was in this music that the csárdás, soon to become the country's national dance, had its roots. Gipsy music was also based on verbunkos melodies, which led Ferenc (Franz)

19th century

Csárdás

State Opera House in Budapest

75

Liszt (see Famous People) and his contemporaries to believe – mistakenly – that it was the repository of genuine Hungarian folk music. This popular misconception was only really rectified when in this century Kodály and Bartók published their folk song collections. The composers of the Romantic tradition latched on to verbunkos melodies and gipsy music and by incorporating them into works conceived in the established forms of western music, they arrived at a synthesis of these two differing musical cultures.

Liszt
Erkel

The most important representatives of Hungarian romanticism were Franz Liszt and Ferenc Erkel (see Famous People). Liszt fell under the spell of Hungarian gipsy music and during the 1840s and 1850s he composed his "Hungarian Rhapsodies", while in his "Hungaria", first performed in Pest in 1856, folk elements are incorporated into a full-scale symphonic work. Ferenc Erkel composed a total of eight operas, including "Hunyadi Lászlo" and "Bánk Bán", thereby ensuring his place in the annals of musical history as the creator of Hungarian national opera. The formation of a genuinely Hungarian national style also owes much to Mihály Mosony, little known nowadays, whose pioneering compositions embraced all musical genres from opera to vocal cantatas. At Liszt's instigation a class was set up in the Budapest Academy of Music (newly opened in 1875) to study Hungarian folk songs. Around the turn of the century, folksong arrangements and operas such as "The Village Rascal" by the music teacher and composer Jenő Hubay enjoyed considerable popularity. Károly (Karl) Goldmark (1830–1915), who was born in Keszthely, achieved great fame, especially for his opera "The Queen of Sheba".

20th century
Kodály
Bartók

Hungarian music saw the advent of two towering artistic figures at the beginning of the 20th c.: Béla Bartók and Zoltán Kodály (see Famous People). Kodály set out for the first time in 1905 to research the wealth of Hungarian folk song and this marked the beginning of a new musical direction which was to supersede the romanticism of the previous century. Together with Béla Bartók, who under Kodály's influence also devoted himself to the collection of folk music, Kodály discovered on his travels an almost inexhaustible repertoire of folk melodies, hitherto unknown and unrecorded, which for generations had been handed down unaltered. Delayed by the First World War, Bartók's folk song collection ("A magyar népdal"), comprising 320 melodies, appeared in 1924, while in 1937 Kodály published his work "Hungarian Folk Music" ("A magyar népzene"), which represented the very first attempt to analyse Hungarian folk music from a stylistic point of view, compare it with the music of neighbouring countries and place it in a historical context. This devotion to their country's songs not only became a lifetime's work for both men, but also had a profound influence on their compositions. As a composer Bartók was able to take his place among the European avant garde of his time, his music being a synthesis of modern musical language and the special distinguishing features of Hungarian folk music. Kodály remained more closely indebted to the musical traditions of his homeland and much of his dynamism went into his duties as a professor of composition at the Academy of Music in Budapest. He influenced generations of Hungarian musicians (e.g. Antal Doráti, Tibor Serly, Sándor Veress) who in turn continued to develop and transmit Kodály's legacy, many of them in far-flung places all over the world. Kodály also devoted himself to the theory of musical instruction with great success.

Contemporary
music

Of the younger generation of composers who emerged after the Second World War, György Kurtág (b. 1926), György Láng (b. 1933) and György Ligeti (b. 1923), the last named living elsewhere in Europe, have achieved international recognition. There is also a long list of Hungarian conductors and soloists who have made their way into the great concert halls of the world (Sir Georg Solti, Ferenc Fricsay, György Széll, etc.).

Operetta

Operetta came to the fore in Hungary in the second half of the 19th c. through the work of Johann Strauss (the father) and others and achieved great popularity. At the turn of the century this genre enjoyed a renaissance which was closely connected with the name of Ferenc (Franz) Lehár (see Famous People). The operetta tradition was maintained in Hungary through the works of Imre (Emmerich) Kálmán (see Famous People), who became famous as the creator of the typical Hungarian operetta ("The Czárdás Princess").

Literature

The Hungarian language, which is of Finno-Ugrian origin, is a minority language in Europe, and the same fate is shared by Hungarian literature. From the 9th c. onwards the Hungarians had to fight for a place in Europe and were faced with the alternative of either measuring up to the might of the ruling powers which surrounded them or going under. This historical imperative had an equally decisive effect on Hungarian literature, manifesting itself in its desire to assert and to defend the national identity. During the long years of Hungary's oppression at the hands of foreign powers, poets and writers took on the role of prophets; in the heroes and martyrs which they portrayed they embodied the conscience and pride of the Hungarian nation. Their work was venerated for the sense of an individual cultural identity which it symbolised.

Even in the 20th c. it has to be said that the only way Hungarian literature can make its way into the ranks of European masters is through translation. Only a small band of specialists was and is in a position to read Hungarian literature in the original. Conversely, even at the end of the last century reputable Hungarian writers were beginning to translate the works of world literature into Hungarian.

With Latin literature holding a position of dominance, the earliest writings in the vernacular which have come down to us were recorded somewhat later than in other European countries. The earliest linguistic monument to have been preserved is a 13th c. Old Hungarian lament to the Virgin, itself an adaptation of a Latin hymn, and also a burial oration, Halottibeszéd. In the 14th c. the early chroniclers narrated Hungary's early history, while court historians described the legends surrounding the royal dynasty. *Middle Ages*

Hungarian literature gained ground during the humanist period. Literature in the vernacular gradually carved itself a place next to the Latin of the church. Janus Pannonius (1434–72) still wrote in Latin, but in contrast to the Latin of the church, his lyrics have a consciously secular quality. It was a sign of the Reformation that the New Testament was translated into Hungarian by János Sylvester in 1541, while towards the end of the century the first translation of the whole of the Bible by Gáspár Károli appeared. Most of these early literary works had as their subject-matter Christian and religious themes, such as sermons and translations of psalms, but these texts were crucial to the formation of a Hungarian literary language. Albert Szenci-Mólnar (1574–1634) not only translated the psalter into Hungarian, but also produced the first Latin-Hungarian dictionary and a Hungarian grammar, in order to make his mother-tongue accessible to the rest of Europe. The first Hungarian poet of real standing was Bálint Balassi (1554–94), who no longer felt impelled merely to deal with religious themes, but also treated chivalry and the arts of love ("ars amatoria") in his sonorous verses. *Renaissance, Reformation*

Secular poetry began to develop, even if to start with its readership was restricted to a small circle of scholarly nobles. In the Baroque epic poem "The Siege of Sziget" Miklós Zrínyi (1620–64) tells the story of the struggle between the old ruling knights and the Turks – a vast battle panorama in which individual experiences come to the foreground. The European Enlightenment also found expression in Hungary. Faced with Austrian domination, which meant that German was elevated to the status of the *17th/18th centuries*

Literature

official language, Hungarians tried to consolidate their sense of national consciousness by creating their own literature. From this resulted a genuinely popular literature, while in the style of Anacreontic poetry there was a blossoming of the most charming love lyrics. One of the most important poets of this period was Mihály Csokonay-Vitéz (1773–1805), who quite deliberately made use of West European Baroque and Rococo traditions and at the same time saw his role as a popular innovator, creating a style of poetry which clearly presages the advent of Romanticism.

19th century
Poetry

The main feature of 19th c. literature is the dominating position occupied by poetry. This was the medium in which the most gifted of Hungarian writers expressed themselves. With the advent of Romanticism Hungarian literature reached its first great peak, having had, in comparison with German and French literature, no real classical period. In the vanguard of the Romantic movement is the lyric and epic poet Mihály Vörösmarty (1800–55) who found in a world of mythical and irrational images the stimulus for a newly-awakened national self-esteem. The pre-revolutionary freedom movement "Young Hungary" took up the ideas of Börnes and Heine, while the epoch as a whole is coloured by the pathos of the freedom poetry which bitterly opposed Habsburg dominance and the power of the nobility. The outstanding figure of the age is the poet Sándor Petőfi (1823–49). Even today Petőfi is still thought of as the national poet of Hungary. The political aspirations and dreams which were left unfulfilled after the failure of the 1848 revolution had already been anticipated by Petőfi in his poetry of liberation which captured the popular mood so closely in its glorification of Hungarian nationhood. János Arany (1817–82) provides an important link between the feudal era and the age of the bourgeois-democratic fight for freedom. In his ballads and poems, the olden times and the modern age are brought together.

The novel

The first great epic works appeared in the second half of the 19th c. Mór Jókai (1825–1904) wrote exotically sprawling light novels with a prolificness worthy of Sir Walter Scott. The ideals which Jókai embodied have spread far beyond the borders of the country, offering a prototype, albeit somewhat sentimentalised, of a way of life which is genuinely Hungarian. The stark wind of realism was blowing through the whole of European literature during this period, but did not have an impact in Hungary until the works of Kálmán Mikszáth (1847–1910). The well-judged descriptive passages in his novels provide satirical portrayals of the life and mores of a threatened society. A considerable sensation was caused by his novel "Strange Marriage", which used the Hungarian "cultural struggle" as a context for a trenchant criticism of official Catholic attitudes to marriage.

The magazine
"Nyugat"

At the beginning of the 20th c. the founding of the magazine "Nyugat" ("West"; 1908) became a focal point for the development of a modern Hungarian avant garde literature, oriented towards Western Europe. At the centre of this movement stands the symbolist Endre Ady (1877–1919), whose fresh lyrical use of language proved a magnet for the young and cosmopolitan men of letters who gathered around him. In contrast to the nationalist writers, Ady stood for the rebirth of Hungarian poetry. After his death the magazine was taken over by the poet Mihály Babits (1883–1941). He was advocate of "pure poetry" and in his own person he united the conflicting trends which were at work in both Hungarian and European literature. The "Nyugat" circle included one of the best known of all writers, the storyteller and dramatist Zsigmond Móricz (1879–1942). His novels ("Behind God's Back", 1922; "The Relations", 1930–32) are mainly set in village or small-town milieus and offer a realistic portrayal of peasant life. In the trilogy "Erdély" (1922–35) Móricz describes life in Transylvania in the 17th century.

20th century
Socialists,
People's writers

Certain writers became leading figures of a movement which displayed involvement at a human level while never allowing itself to be forced into toeing a doctrinaire party line. They include Attila Jószef (1905–37), Tibor

Déry (1894–1977), Gyula Illyés (1902–83) and László Németh (1901–75). They express their convictions in a realistic, at times highly personal style, devoid of any illusions. The poet Attila Jószef, the son of proletarian parents, brings a new tone into his verses. They are motivated by despair and a sense of outrage at the sufferings of the poorest in society. His attempts to reconcile Marx and Freud led to his expulsion from the illegal communist party, but until his suicide in 1937 Jószef remained true to his socialist ideals.

Tibor Déry ("The Answer", 1950–52; "The Unfinished Sentence", 1933, although not published until after the war; "Mr G. A. in X", 1964) was forced to emigrate after the downfall of the Hungarian soviet republic. His first short novel was published in "Nyugat". The age of modern contemporary Hungarian literature is ushered in with Déry. Since the end of the Second World War he has taken his place among the central figures of Hungarian literary life with his stories and novels. In 1956 Déry supported the popular uprising and as a result was imprisoned – the former prize-winning poet finding himself ostracised. As a convinced humanist he refused to have anything to do with one-sided party literature, the theme of his work being the conflict of interests between a subjectively convinced communist and the official party line.

Gyula Illyés ("I Speak of Heroes", 1932; "Petőfi Sándor", 1936; "Luncheon in the Castle", 1962) has also endeavoured to make himself a defender of those who have been marginalised and deprived of their rights. His sociological work on the puszta is a rousing study of the living conditions of the peasant population. His poem "A Proposition about Tyranny", written in the disturbing months of the autumn of 1956, was never able to be published in his lifetime. Unlike Déry, Illyés, who always enjoyed the protection of the party, never dared risking an open split with the authority of the state, even when the contents of his writings amounted to insubordination.

The literature of this century can also boast the realistic novels and dramas of László Németh ("Mask of Sorrow", 1936; "As the Stone Falls", 1947; "The Power of Pity", 1965), whose characters refuse to accept a hostile environment.

Of outstanding merit because of the incorruptibility and self-sufficiency of their new lyrical language are the poets Miklós Radnóti (1909–44) and Sándor Weöres (1913–89). Radnóti was murdered as a Jew in a labour camp, his idealistic search for perfection and purity of language in his poetry being dashed to pieces by the barbarity of the real world. Weöres fascinates by his artificial lingustic experiments and the phenomenal wealth of poetic forms he has at his disposal. He opposes the real world of human experience with a cosmic set of visions.

Outsiders

In the first half of the 20th c. Hungarian literature had made contact with the Classical Moderns of European literature and in so doing went through such a rich development that today it can hold its own against almost any other "minor" European literature. Contemporary Hungarian writers are now being translated into many languages and rewarded with international prizes. Going back to the inter-war years there have been two trends in Hungarian literature which are still felt to this day: on the one hand the "populists", who have elevated village life and Hungarianness to the subject-matter of literature; on the other hand the "urbanists", who consciously see themselves as Europeans and cosmopolitans and whose outlook is shaped by urban living. To this latter tradition belong the magazine "Nyugat" and the journal "Újhold" (new moon), which was founded in 1946 but banned in 1948 because it was incompatible with communist aims. While the "populist" writers were more or less tolerated, because they were prepared to compromise with those in power, the majority of the "urbanists" met with continual censorship, a ban on publication of their writings, and even imprisonment. In spite of these obstructions and intimidations, which were more restrained during the Kádár years than those

Contemporary literature

experienced in other East European countries, post-war Hungarian literature saw the development, particularly after 1956, of an extraordinary
variety and intensity of literary activity, which reached out far beyond the
present borders of Hungary itself. Present-day Hungarian literature is an
extremely vibrant literature, which revels in narrative and linguistic experiment. It can consist of harsh, realistic descriptions, bitterly ironic satire,
surrealist-alienating storytelling methods, gently lyrical prose, and uses
techniques which are both fresh and relevant. The reader will find exciting
narratives full of tension, often couched in a precise pithy style and with an
almost boisterously wild exuberance.

Novelists
Older generation

The "old masters" of contemporary literature are Iván Mándy (b. 1918) and
Miklós Mészöly (b. 1921). Mándy's extensive output of novels and stories
("The Women of the Fabulya", 1966; "On the Edge of the Playing-Field",
1971; "What's the Matter, Old Man?" 1975) are packed with scenes showing the life and people of Budapest. In a style tending towards Neo-Realism
he displays a narrative method which creates its own dramatic flow by
means of gripping dialogue and "cinematic" editing of his material. With
Mészöly ("Torn Map", 1976; "Flashback", 1980; "Winged Horses", 1991)
contemporary Hungarian literature finally achieves the breakthrough to
modernity. Traditional narrative techniques are broken down and a new
perception of language and reality emerges, comparable with the French
"nouveau roman". Experiences are elaborately analysed and then reas-
sembled into new coded pictures, with language itself acquiring its own
iridescent dynamic.

Middle
generation

The outstanding writer of this generation is György Konrád (b. 1933), who
has been showered with international prizes and has been president of the
international P.E.N. since 1990. Through his personal and artistic involvement as a writer, Konrád has become a leading figure of Hungary's democratic opposition. In his novels ("The City Founder", 1977; "The
Accomplice", 1980; "Ghost Party", 1989), which have urban settings, he
takes as his subject the destruction and corruptibility of the individual in the
face of the overweening power of the state. No other writer has exercised
his mind as much over the fate of intellectuals in Eastern Europe, caught
between the conflicting needs of conformity and resistance. No other
writer has expressed this dilemma in words of such tormented eloquence.
In his political essays ("Antipolitics. Central European Meditations", 1985;
"The Melancholy of Rebirth", 1992) Konrád has taken on the role of a
spokesman, initiating discussion on the rebirth of Central Europe as a
cultural area – as opposed to the stark political confrontation of the two
blocks – and he has written passionately against the artificial division of
Europe. The majority of his novels and essays were never able to appear in
Hungary before 1989 and could only be read there by means of Samisdat
publications.

Younger
generation

Central to this generation are two writers, Péter Nádas (b. 1942) and Péter
Esterházy (b. 1950). Both of them describe in a very characteristic way the
state of Hungarian society at the end of the Kádár era.
Nádas is a master at interweaving the smaller family story with the larger
canvas of political history ("End of a Family Novel", 1979). Starting out
from individuals' personal lives and viewpoints he goes on to depict a
whole era ("Book of Memory", 1986). No other Hungarian writer before
him had dealt with the divisions and changes of this century in the same
historical, philosophical and literary way. In powerful complex sentences
he blends a sense of time with the observation of people's feelings, using
subjective experience to achieve a new synthesis in reinterpreting the
history of this century.
Esterházy captivates the reader with the irony and sense of the absurd
which runs through his highly stylised prose ("Small Hungarian Pornog-
raphy", 1984; "Hrabal's Book", 1992). For him language represents an
artistic provocation which deceitfully turns sense into nonsense, order into

disorder and can grotesquely interchange present and past. In a programmatic way Esterházy tries to defend the autonomy of the artist, not politically, but through the freedom of language. There is no other Hungarian writer who stands so clearly in the imperial tradition of satirical-comic literature as Esterházy.

Two other novels are representative of present-day Hungary. In "The Circumcision" (1990) György Dalos (b. 1943) describes the confusion and desperation of a Jewish childhood in the 1950s from an ironically detached viewpoint. In "Satan's Tango" (1985) László Krasznahorkai (b. 1954) uses melancholy metaphors to encapsulate in gloomily ironic pictures the decline of a society which no longer has the strength left to resist its fate. A feature of all Hungarian contemporary literature up to the end of the 1980s has been this fascinating vacillation between irony and melancholy, between resistance and submission.

Whereas the 19th c. was the century of poetry in Hungarian literature, it is the modern novel which has assumed a pre-eminent position in the 20th c. Nevertheless Hungary's thriving poetic tradition has continued without interruption. One of the most impressive poets at the present time is György Petri (b. 1943). In his own highly individual way he incorporates into his verse such themes as powerlessness and rebellion, hope and resignation, struggle and failure, love and hate ("Degenerating into Hope", 1986; "Beautiful and Pitiless Masquerade", 1989). His poetic and political commitment did not please those in power and for many years publication of Petri's work was banned. That there are many other young talents emerging, some with astonishing verbal skills, is attested by the 1990 anthology "Medium Art", in which 50 poets and poetesses presented their work to the public.

Poetry

Film

Hungary can lay claim to a well-established film culture, both in the field of feature films as well as documentaries. The history of this medium began in Hungary in 1896 with the first film showings in Budapest and 1912 saw the opening of the first film studio, producing its own films. The two outstanding directors of the 1920s and 1930s were without doubt Mihály Kertész (see Famous People), who made a career in America as Michael Curtiz, and Sándor Korda (later Sir Alexander Korda), who settled in London in 1931 and started a production company there. One of the classics of the silent film era was his 1931 film "The Private Life of Henry VIII" with Charles Laughton in the leading role. Hungary's own zealously productive film industry was nationalised for the first time during the period of the soviet republic (the second nationalisation followed in 1948). As a result many artists, including Korda, left the country and worked elsewhere in Europe or in America. After the Second World War the Hungarian film industry again achieved international recognition, largely through the offices of Géza Rádványi, whose film "Valahol Euoópaban" ("Anywhere in Europe", 1947) achieved a huge success. The post-war generation of directors was mainly influenced by Italian Neo-Realism, an important theme of their films being the effect of political and social conditions on the day-to-day life of the individual. Important representatives of this period were Zoltán Fábri ("Professor Hannibal", 1955) and Félix Máriássy. The sixties and seventies also saw the emergence of a series of notable directors, many of whom were graduates of the newly-founded film institute. Miklós Jancsó is the leading figure of this generation. Having a key role in his films, such as "Még kér a nép" ("The Red Psalm", is the search for new forms and techniques and his work is characterised by symbolism, uncompromising picture composition and long takes. The examination of a "neuralgic" moment in Hungarian history, the uprising of 1956, is the theme of the 1966 film "Apa" ("Father") of István Szabó. With his film based on the novel

"Mephisto" by Klaus Mann, which was awarded an Oscar by America's film critics, Szabó moved into the international limelight. Among younger contemporary film-makers mention should be made of Péter Bacsó and Márta Mészáros, who achieve artistic results by addressing Hungary's problems, both past and present, with unstinting rigour. The dissolution of the state film company and the economic decline which Hungary has experienced since the political changes of 1989 have had far-reaching consequences for the film industry. A privately financed successor to the state film company, known as "Mafilm", is now responsible for promoting and marketing Hungarian films.

Folk art

Hungary possesses a rich folk tradition, preserved in the numerous small local and folk museums to be found in the provinces, and also kept alive by the various displays of folk song and dance, not to mention souvenir shops, which cater for tourists. A recurring motive in Hungarian folk art is the stylised pattern of flowers, which is to be found in all manner of forms – whether as embroidery or appliqué on coats, jackets, blouses and aprons, as a colour-print on bed and table linen, as a painted addition to furniture and walls and, during the art nouveau period. as a house decoration in the form of majolica tiles. Bright colours such as red, blue, yellow and green predominate, but there is also a long tradition of black or red patterns on a white background or red on black. Centres for the production of textiles using these folk designs include Mezökövesd in the former Matyó region (near Eger), Buzsák (south of Balaton), Kalocsa and Hollókö in the former settlement area of the Paloz, who were also famous for their wood-carving and weaving traditions. The traditional embroidered blouses and aprons for women are the counterpart of the men's traditional leather jackets

An artistic embroidered woman's dress *A shepherd's coat*

(szür), decorated with embroidery and appliqué. The traditional dress of the csikós, or horsemen, can be admired either in museums or at the horse-riding displays in the Bugac and Hortobágy puszta. This dress consists of blue linen breeches, a white shirt, a black waistcoat and over this a long leather coat or a weatherproof sheepskin cape. The dress also included the black broad-rimmed felt hat, which is fastened under the chin with a leather strap.

Beside the production of textiles, which includes the famous Kiskunhalas lace, Hungary also has a long tradition of making pottery, particularly in the Great Plain.

Hungary in Quotations

William Lithgow
(1582–1645?)

Now as for the soil of Hungary , and kingdom itself, and for the goodness of it, it may be termed the granary of Ceres, the garden of Bacchus, the pasturage of Pan, and the richest beauty of Sylvan; for I found the wheat here growing higher than my head, the vines overlooking the trees, the grass justling with my knees, and the high sprung woods threatening the clouds; surely, if I should enter on particulars here, I have more subject to work upon than any kingdom that ever I saw.

Rare Adventures and Painfull Peregrinations, 1614–32

Edward Gibbon
(1737–94)

Arms and freedom have ever been the ruling, though too often the unsuccessful, passion of the Hungarians, who are endowed by nature with a vigorous constitution of soul and body.

The Decline and Fall of the Roman Empire, 1776–88

Edward Daniel
Clarke
(1769–1822)

Budapest
The Danube separates the two cities, in other respects one. Buda is upon an eminence above the western, and Pest below upon the eastern bank. Pest is a very large and handsome city, the streets are full of shops; and there are two theatres: there is also a handsome theatre at Buda. We were quite surprised by the magnificence of these two cities, of which so little is known in other parts of Europe. Pest, situated in a plain, is adorned with public edifices, erected in a style of grandeur and elegance: it also boasts of a University; although as little heeded by the Universities of England, as Cambridge and Oxford are by its Hungarian Professors.

The principal part of the road from Bakabanya to Schemnitz exhibits that grandeur of scenery which is represented by the best pictures of Gaspar Poussin: but some respects of it display the richer and milder dispositions of landscape characteristic of the work of Claude.

Travels in Various Countries, 4th edn. 1818

Matthew Arnold
(1822–88)

Hungarians! Save the world!, Renew the stories
Of men who against hope repelled the chain,
And make the world's dead spirit leap again!
On land renew that Greek exploit, whose glories
Hallow the Salaminian promontories,
And the Armada flung to the fierce main.

Sonnet to the Hungarian Nation, 1849

Karl Baedeker
(1846)

Budapest
Both towns, Óbuda with 30,000 inhabitants, the respected older town with a completely German atmosphere, the seat of the Palatinus and the whole administration, Pesth, the newer blossoming and thoroughly Hungarian town, exclusively devoted to trade and making money, with 75,000 inhabitants, are linked by a chain bridge, the foundation stone of which was laid in August 1842. The Danube here is some 1500ft wide.
A hundred years ago Pest was an unimportant place, but is at present the most heavily populated commercial city in Hungary. The side facing the Danube consists of a long row of beautiful buildings, in the midst of which are the theatre and the Redoutensaal. At the upper end of the wharf is the national casino with reading rooms, a billiard room, and a ballroom. . . .

The Hungarian language is naturally the most common language of the country, but almost as much German can be heard. A knowledge of Latin, even fluency is often found among the middle classes. . . .

The upper part of Óbuda, the fortress, lies on the summit of a hill which dominates the surroundings. The finest building is the palace of the Archduke Palatinus on the south-eastern slope of the hill with a façade 564ft long. It was built in the reign of Karl VI on the same site where the castle of the Hungarian king Matthias Corvinus had stood. In the chapel are kept the Hungarian crown and the other crown jewels.

The surroundings of Óbuda offer an opportunity for many worth-while excursions. From several points of the fortress there are fine views over both towns, the majestic river and the wide plain. In the much-visited garden is a summer theatre, a so-called arena. The Palatinus, or Margaret Island in the Danube is popular as a place of recreation, as are the beautiful and large Palatinus Garden near the royal castle, the Promontorium, or Eugenius Hill, one and a quarter hours from the town, where in a charming vineyard stands a mansion built by the famous Eugene, and the Johannisberg from which a panoramic view can be enjoyed. The hills of Óbuda are covered with vineyards which produce the excellent Óbuda wine about 200,000 barrels a year. Adelsberg and Türkenblut are the best varieties.

A Handbook for Travellers in Germany and the Austrian Imperial Cities,
1846

Suggested Routes

The following suggested routes should be useful for those planning journeys by car through the country, without preventing the traveller from making his own choices as well. The routes given take into account as far as possible the main sights and monuments of the country. The route descriptions also have details of variations and detours. The guide-book also comes with a map which will facilitate detailed planning. Localities, including towns and villages, which are described in the section "Hungary from A to Z" under a separate entry, appear in the route descriptions in bold type, while descriptions of other places mentioned can be looked up using the index.

The distances given in these route overviews are rounded up and refer to the most direct route available. For detours and variations the appropriate additional distances are given.

1. From Mosonmagyaróvár to Budapest 170km/106 miles

Coming from Vienna, the visitor crosses the Austrian-Hungarian border at Nickelsdorf and after almost 15km/9 miles reaches the first town of any size, **Mosonmagyaróvár** (castle, spa). About halfway between Mosonmagyaróvár and **Győr**, some 6km/4 miles south of the main road, stands the Benedictine church of Lébénymiklós, which, with Ják and Zsámbék, is one of the most important Romanesque buildings in Hungary. The town of Győr is famous for its unique historic centre with countless Renaissance and Baroque buildings. From Győr it is well worth making a detour to the Benedictine abbey of **Pannonhalma**, which is the leading abbey of that order in Hungary and is surrounded by fine views (16km/10 miles southeast of Győr; Road 82 as far as Écs and then 3km/2 miles on a country road). The stretch of motorway between Győr and Budapest (M1) goes past the lake town of **Tata**, which owes its Baroque appearance to the Eszterházy family. South of Tata are the Vértes Mountains, which are well worth visiting. The towns of Majk-Puszta (formerly Kamaldulens Abbey) and Csákvár are also interesting. Between Tata and **Budapest**, about 20km/12 miles before the capital and 7km/4 miles north of the motorway (Exit Herceghalom) lies the small village of Zsámbék with the imposing ruin of a Romanesque dynastic church.

Nickelsdorf
Border Crossing

2. From Sopron to Budapest 420km/261 miles

Coming from Vienna (Roads 16 and 332), the Hungarian frontier is crossed at Klingenbach. Only about 10km/6 miles beyond the border is **Sopron**, one of the most beautiful towns in Hungary with a large number of medieval and Baroque buildings. Almost 30km/19 miles to the east of Sopron stands Fertőd, the largest and most famous Baroque palace in Hungary (also known as the "Hungarian Versailles"), the former residence of the Eszterházy family. From Fertőd it is possible to carry on south on minor country roads to **Kőszeg**, which besides Jurisics Castle boasts many pretty and historic squares and houses. Passing through **Szombathely** (24km/15 miles to the south; bishop's palace and Savaria Museum), we come to the river town of **Sárvár** (about 25km/16 miles east of Szombathely), where the castle is worth a visit. From Sárvár Road 84 (going south) provides the most direct link with Lake Balaton (about 67km/42 miles). Following this

Klingenbach
Border Crossing

◀ *Reformed church in the open-air museum at Szentendre*

road, after about 40km/25 miles the visitor should on no account fail to visit the parish church of Christ's Ascension in the little town of **Sümeg**, where Franz Anton Maulbertsch created the most magnificent of all his frescos. 15km/9 miles south of Sümeg and only a few kilometres to the east of the main road in the volcanic scenery of the Balaton hinterland is the little town of Tapolca with a lake cavern which is well worth seeing. After another 10km/6 miles we reach the north shore of **Lake Balaton**. Its varied landscape (volcanic, mountainous outcrops covered with vineyards, bays and beaches, etc.) and mild climate make it a popular place with holidaymakers, both from Hungary and abroad. Following the shore road, the first place we come to on the right-hand side is **Keszthely**, a lively resort at the southernmost point of the lake (beach bathing-pool). Art lovers will wish to see the castle of the Festetics family. Just 6km/4 miles to the north-east of Keszthely is the spa **Héviz**, which is famous well beyond the borders of Hungary because of its unique thermal lake. Returning to Keszthely we follow Road 71, which skirts the northern shore of the lake and passes all the resorts situated there. The main attractions are the scenically beautiful Tihany peninsula, with its famous abbey, and the resort of Balatonfüred, with its long tradition as a watering-place. From Tihany it is worth making a trip to Nagyvázsony (just under 20km/12 miles to the north-west; a pretty village with Kinizsi Castle). After Balatonfüred we leave the shores of Lake Balaton and take Road 73 to **Veszprém** (about 15km/9 miles). On the rocky spur which dominates the town are the buildings which make up the former episcopal and royal residences, many of which are now closed. From Veszprém the fast Road 8 takes us after 44km/27 miles to the old royal town of **Székesfehérvár**, which can also boast some exceptional monuments (the foundation walls of the oldest royal church in Hungary and the marble sarcophagus which for a long time was thought to be the tomb of King Stephen I). Just 10km/6 miles south of Székesfehérvár, in the little town of Tác, is the site of one of the largest Roman towns on Hungarian soil (Gorsium-Herculia) to have been uncovered (it can be quickly reached via

Vineyards in the hinterland of Lake Balaton

the M7 motorway). The shortest route to Budapest is via the M7 motorway, but the route using Road 70, which skirts the southern shore of Lake Velencei, is more attractive. This route also passes through the village of **Martonvásár**. Here, in the Neo-Gothic castle belonging to the Brunswick family, the composer Ludwig van Beethoven was often a guest (small commemorative museum, fine park).

3. From Budapest to the Danube Bend 130km/81 miles

A popular area to visit from **Budapest** is the **Danube Bend**, to the north-west of the capital, where the visitor will find old towns and captivating scenery. We leave Budapest on Road 11 and after passing through a long ribbon of suburban development come to the little artists' town of **Szentendre** on the left bank of the Danube. It is definitely worth making a detour into the Pilis Mountains to visit the largest open-air museum in Hungary, about 3km/2 miles north-west of the town on the Visegrád road. A few kilometres further north from Szentendre, at Tahitótfalu, there is a bridge spanning the western arm of the Danube and leading across to Szentendre Island, which has a ferry connection with **Vác** (beautiful view). The pretty little Baroque town of Vác also makes a good starting-point for excursions into the Börzsöny Mountains and the Cserhát Uplands. From Vác it is best to follow Road 12 as far as Nagymaros, from where there is a ferry to **Visegrád**. The citadel ruins, at the foot of which was excavated the Renaissance palace of King Matthias I, are visible from a considerable distance. The section of the Danube between Visegrád and Esztergom is particularly beautiful because of the wooded slopes of the two mountain ranges which face one another across the river. **Esztergom** is one of the most important episcopal and royal towns in Hungary with an imposing cathedral and the former royal and diocesan palace. Those not wishing to proceed directly back to Budapest can take the route through the Pilis Mountains (Esztergom – Pomáz – Budapest).

4. From Budapest to northern Hungary 260km/162 miles

We leave Budapest in an easterly direction on the E 71, the great transport axis leading to northern and eastern Hungary, which runs through the area connecting the southern foothills of the North Hungarian Mountains and the Great Plain. The first stop after Budapest is **Gödöllő**, famous as the former summer seat of the Hungarian queen and Austrian empress Elisabeth "Sissy" (Grassalkovich Palace). About 30km/19 miles beyond Gödöllő the E 71 passes the little town of Hatvan; from here detours can be made to **Jászberény**, centre of the Jazygen population, and, going north, into the Cserhát Mountains, where at Hollóko an old Palozen village has been classified as a historical monument and opened to visitors as a museum village (just before Pásztó on Road 21, then along the side road to Szécsény). **Gyöngyös**, 25km/16 miles east of Hatvan, is the gateway to the Matra Mountains and enjoys great popularity with holidaymakers. On Road 24 the visitor will come to the main tourist centres of Mátraháza and Parádfürdő; it is possible to travel further along this road to **Eger** (alternatively use the well maintained, if less interesting E 71). In this Baroque town (Lyceum, former Minorites church) with its massive neo-classical cathedral the visitor is recommended to make the ascent to the castle, which was one of the most important border fortifications in the country during the Turkish Wars (view). Between Eger and **Miskolc** we can either take the fast E 71 or alternatively a less direct route through the wooded **Bükk Mountains** (via Bélapátfalva and Szilvásvárad; toll road from Szilvásvárad), which boast highly attractive scenery. From Miskolc the **Aggetelek National Park** can be reached, either by Road 26 (a country road from Putnok onwards) or by the Road 27 (a minor road) through the Bódva Valley. The national park's

Typical scenery in the Great Plain

unique karst landscape is a very popular place with visitors, most of all on account of the enormous dripstone caves at Baradla (conducted tours), but also because it offers excellent opportunities for walking and rambling.

5. Circular trip through the east of Hungary 300km/186 miles

Starting point
Miskolc

From **Miskolc** we take Road 37 to **Sárospatak**, a small peaceful town on the Bodrog with an interesting Renaissance castle (museum). In order to reach **Tokaj**, it is necessary to return along Road 37 for about 25km/16 miles; the little wine town is situated at the confluence of the Bodrog and the Tisza in the centre of the wine-producing region of Tokaj-hegyalja. In the Rákóczi cellar (tour of the old wine cellar) it is possible to taste the famous Tokaj wine. From Tokaj we follow Road 38 in a southerly direction and after about 30km/19 miles reach **Nyíregyháza**. The town itself has little to offer the tourist, but in contrast the Tisza countryside to the north and east of Nyíregyháza is full of delightful discoveries (with a good network of small country roads). As a starting-point for shorter excursions the visitor can use either Kisvárda (about 45km/28 miles north-east of Nyíregyháza on the E 77) or Vásárosnamény (about 50km/31 miles north-east on Road 41). In Nyírbátor, about 35km/22 miles east of Nyíregyháza, there are two superb churches.

Just under 50km/31 miles to the south of Nyíregyháza lies the former Calvinist stronghold of **Debrecen**, which still retains the character of a small town even in its urban centre. The former Heiduc settlement of Hajdúszoboszló, 22km/14 miles south-west of Debrecen, is today one of the most famous Hungarian spas. To the west of Debrecen stretches the **Hortobágy** (puszta), a visit to which must be an indispensable part of any holiday in Hungary (Nine Arch Bridge, horsemanship displays, herdsmen's museum, etc). Road 33 leads through the Hortobágy National Park and at Tiszafüred crosses the Tisza. Here a recreational area has grown up during the past few years around the artificial reservoir called Tisza-tó and it is steadily gaining in importance. 37km/23 miles beyond Tiszafüred Road 33 joins the E 71, the main connecting road between Budapest and Miskolc.

6. From Budapest to the south of Hungary 630km/391 miles

Leaving by the E 5 the first destination on the route is **Kecskemét** (about 90km/56 miles), a popular town of cultural interest in the centre of the fertile area between the Rivers Danube and Tisza. The art nouveau town hall by Ödön Lechner is especially interesting. 27km/17 miles south of Kecskemét lies **Kiskunfélegyháza** (town hall!), which is also a good place for a trip into the **Bugac**. Here there are also horser-riding displays, coach rides and organised excursions. From Kiskunfélegyháza to **Szeged** it is best to take the alternative road through Csongrád (36km/22 miles; Road 451) and **Ópusztaszer** (about 27km/17 miles south of Csongrád). The appearance of the lively university town of **Szeged** is defined by its late 19th c./early 20th c. architectural styles. In the summer months its attractive squares and the pedestrian areas in its old centre really come to life.

Anyone wishing to discover the charms of the south-eastern province of Hungary should make an excursion through Hódmezovásárhely, a typical agricultural town of the Great Plain and **Békéscsaba** to the charming little spa town of Gyula (about 110km/68 miles).

Going in a westerly direction from Szeged Road 55 crosses the flat, sparsely populated area between the Danube and the Tisza. In **Baja** the route crosses the Danube and then at Bátaszék turns off southwards to **Mohács**, which has entered the history books because of the battle which was lost there against the Turks in 1526 (memorial park about 5km/3 miles south of the town near the village of Sátorhely). From Mohács it is better not to proceed directly to Pécs but instead at Szajk, 9km/6 miles west of Mohács, turn off southwards in the direction of Siklós and spend some time travelling through the gently undulating vine-growing area of Villány, where the local wine can be sampled and bought in the comfortable surroundings of the many wine-cellars. The best-known wine-producing village in the region is Villánykövesd, 3km/2 miles north-west of Villány. **Siklós** is worth a visit for its important and well-preserved border fortress. At the spa town of Harkány, 5km/3 miles west of Siklós, a detour can be made into the Ormánság region (interesting examples of folk architecture). Road 58 leads to the southern Hungarian town of **Pécs**, which has a Mediterranean climate. With its wealth of architectural monuments the town repays a visit of several days. The Roman (Early Christian) tombs and the architectural legacy of almost 150 years of Turkish rule are of particular interest. Returning to Budapest on the E 6, we come to the villages of Pécsvárad and Mecseknádasd, where today the descendants of 18th c. German settlers still live ("Danube Swabians"). After passing through **Szekszárd** a choice can be made between the direct route using Road 6 and the alternative Road 63. This latter route enables visits to be made to the impressive Roman town of Tác (Gorsium-Herculia) (about 10km/6 miles south of Székesfehérvár) and the royal town of **Székesfehérvár**.

Hungary from A to Z

Aggtelek National Park (Aggteleki Nemzeti Park) F 1

Region: Borsod-Abaúj-Zemplén
Altitude: 300–600m/930–1850ft

Covering an area of 20,000ha/78sq.miles on the Slovak-Hungarian border, some 70km/44 miles north of Miskolc (see entry), lies Aggtelek National Park, with some unique flora and fauna and several hundred limestone caves and underground passages. A network of signposted paths and roads attract many walkers to this nature reserve. The chief attraction is the Baradla Cave; it is 25km/15½ miles long (of which 7km/4 miles lie in Slovak territory, where it is known as the Domica Cave), making it one of the largest and most impressive dripstone caves anywhere in Europe.

Situation and Characteristics

There are entrances to Baradla-barlang (as the cave is known) near Jósvafő, at Vörös tó (Red Lake) and the main entrance, with a small natural history museum, is near the town of Aggtelek. One-hour guided tours (with commentary in Hungarian only) start from here – stout shoes and a warm sweater are recommended, as the temperature in the caves is only about 10°C/50°F. Tours lasting several hours can also be made by prior arrangement.

**Baradla Cave*

The main tunnel of the Baradla Cave is 7km/4 miles long, with several side passages averaging 10m/33ft in width and 7–8m/22–26ft in height. They were formed over many thousands of years, as rain and melting snow penetrated fine cracks in the limestone to form underground streams which in turn carved out long tunnels and giant caves. The water dripping through the chalk has carved bizarre shapes, stalactites like giant icicles hanging from the roof and stalagmites in all colours of the rainbow towering up from the floor. Quite often their shapes are reminiscent of familiar animals or objects, as reflected in the fantasy names which have been given to many dripstones (Turtle, Pheasant, Eagle, Tiger, Father Christmas, etc.) or to whole sections of the caves (Fairyland, Hall of the Giants). The rock formations increase in size by one millimetre every 15 to 20 years so, for example, it has taken 250,000 years for the giant dripstone in the Cave of Peace (see below) to attain its present height of 13m/42½ft. As it possesses superb acoustics the giant underground "hall" has been equipped as a concert hall. The guided tour will include a ten-minute "son et lumière" show with Pink Floyd providing the background music!

More and more visitors are discovering the cave known as Béke-barlang near Aggtelek; first discovered in 1952, it commences in the Aggtelek valley, extends as far as Komlós Spring at Jósvafő and boasts even more dripstone formations than the Baradla Cave. The high humidity proves most beneficial to a large number of asthma sufferers.

Cave of Peace

Sights

This National Park in the extreme north of Hungary can be approached along several roads. Those with ample time at their disposal who wish to see the Bükk Mountains should take the Eger–Szilvásvárad–Putnok–Kelemér road. Road 27 leads northwards from Miskolc through charming countryside, including the pretty Bódva Valley.

◀ *Former Jesuit church and Cathedral in Esztergom*

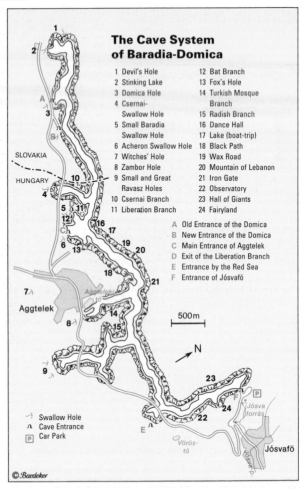

The Cave System of Baradia-Domica

1 Devil's Hole
2 Stinking Lake
3 Domica Hole
4 Csernai-Swallow Hole
5 Small Baradia Swallow Hole
6 Acheron Swallow Hole
7 Witches' Hole
8 Zambor Hole
9 Small and Great Ravasz Holes
10 Csernai Branch
11 Liberation Branch
12 Bat Branch
13 Fox's Hole
14 Turkish Mosque Branch
15 Radish Branch
16 Dance Hall
17 Lake (boat-trip)
18 Black Path
19 Wax Road
20 Mountain of Lebanon
21 Iron Gate
22 Observatory
23 Hall of Giants
24 Fairyland

A Old Entrance of the Domica
B New Entrance of the Domica
C Main Entrance of Aggtelek
D Exit of the Liberation Branch
E Entrance by the Red Sea
F Entrance of Jósvafö

SLOVAKIA
HUNGARY
Aggtelek
500 m
N

⌐ Swallow Hole
∩ Cave Entrance
P Car Park

Jósva forrás
Jósvafö
Vörös-tó

© Baedeker

Edelény	30km/19 miles along this road lies Edelény. At the end of a beautiful avenue and surrounded by a large park stands the Baroque Palace, built in 1727–30 by Giovanni Battista Carlone for Colonel L'Huillier and one of the largest in Hungary. Unfortunately the visitor can go no further than the wrought-iron park gates, as the palace is not open to the public. Nevertheless, a walk round the walls of the park will provide some excellent views of the building, particularly impressive because of its sheer size, in spite of the many renovations that have been necessary over the years.
Szendrő	14km/9 miles beyond Edelény lies the township of Szendrő, dominated by a castle. Formerly a border fortress, this was built in 1590 by an Italian master and fortified with five bastions.
Szalonna °Village church	This idyllic and sleepy village some 6km/4 miles beyond Szendrő is an historical gem which is well worth a brief visit. Standing close to the main

Karst landscape in Aggtelek National Park   *Village church in Szalonna*

road and surrounded by a rough stone wall, the small Reformed Church has a separate bell-tower. (The key can be obtained from the house opposite.) The church was a gift from the Ors family in the 11th c. Like that at Karcsa (see Sárospatak, Surroundings), it was originally a simple round church, to which a single-aisle nave was added in the early 13th c., the basic building being converted to a chancel. In 1598 the church was taken over by the Reformed Assembly and the wooden bell-tower built. The interior church boasts some beautiful 13th c. frescos portraying in four scenes the martyrdom of its patron saint, St Margaret of Antiochien (the heathen governor wants to marry Margaret; he has her brought before him in chains; she is whipped and executed). The paintings in the nave and triumphal arch date from the 15th c.

About 8km/5 miles through Szalonna there is a turning to the left from where it is a further 18km/11 miles to Aggtelek.

Baja

D 3

Region: Bács-Kiskun
Altitude: 99m/325ft
Population: 40,030

The tranquil summer resort of Baja, 160km/100 miles south of Budapest and 20km/12½ miles from the Serbian border, is surrounded by water – by the Danube, the Kamarás Danube (called Sugovica by Croatian settlers known as the Bunyevaz) and a further small arm of the Danube. The bridges over the Danube make Baja an important rail and road centre and a flourishing commercial town. The town has a long tradition of weaving, and the more modern meat factory processes about one thousand pigs every day; electrical and furniture industries also play an important role.

Situation and Importance

95

Baja

The town shows many signs of the influence of the Serbs and Croats who settled here after the Turks had been driven out. In addition to the Bunyevaz a considerable number of "Danube Swabians" from south-west Germany live here, and one of the six high schools is German-speaking.

Sights

Szentháromság tér, Town Hall

The centre of Baja, the Szentháromság tér, opens onto the Sugovica with Petőfi Island beyond it; of the buildings on the other three sides (18th c. town houses in the 18th c. plait style), particular mention must be made of the Town Hall (No. 1), an 18th c. Baroque palace built for the Grassalkovich family and rebuilt in the Neo-Renaissance style in 1896. On the square in front of it stands a Late Baroque Trinity Column with figures of the four evangelists.

István Türr Museum

This museum (Deák Ferenc utca 1; open: Tue.–Sun. 10am–6pm) is devoted to life by the Danube together with modern Hungarian art. It was named after a famous son of the town (1825–1908) who fought with General Garibaldi in the struggle for a unified Italy and later made a name for himself as an hydraulic engineer, assisting in the construction of the Panama and Corinth canals and others in the Hungarian lowlands. A statue of him stands at the entrance to the museum which is built in the neo-classical style.

Franciscan church and convent

The Franciscan church of St Anton and the convent at the corner of Bartók Béla utca 1 were built in the Baroque style in the 18th c. In the garden of the church (Déri Garden) stands a statue of the agonised Virgin Mary as well as busts of famous men born in Baja.

Great Serbian church

The Late Baroque Greek-Orthodox Serbian church in Táncsics utca was built in 1790 with donations from worshippers. The holy paintings on the chancel screen are by the well-known Serbian artist Arsenije Teodorovich (1768–1826).

Former synagogue

The magnificent Synagogue (Munkácsy utca 7) was built in the neo-classical style in 1845, that is to say, prior to the emancipation of the Jews in Hungary in 1867. In the Second World War most of the Jewish population were killed; since 1985 the building has housed the regional library and the interior decoration has been carefully restored.

Nagy Gallery

The István Nagy Art Gallery (Nagy István Képtár, Arany János utca 1; open: Tue.–Sun. 10am–6pm) was built in the early years of this century in the neo-classical style as a mansion for the respected Vojnich family, and now houses an important collection of Hungarian art. The major artist represented is István Nagy (1873–1937), who painted landscapes and rural subjects in the constructivist realist style and who worked in Baja for a number of years and bequeathed his pictures to the gallery.

Petőfi Island

Petőfi Island (Petőfi-sziget) is the town's tourist centre, containing a stadium, swimming-pool, the Sugovica Hotel and a beautifully situated camp site; walks through the forest are most relaxing, and this is also a favourite spot with anglers and sailing and rowing enthusiasts.

The viewing tower at the confluence of the Danube and the Sugovica provides a fine view over the countryside. Also worth a visit is the Bunyevaj local history museum in Bajaszentiván, a suburb of Baja.

Bakony

See Veszprém, Surroundings

Balassagyarmat   E 1

Region: Nógrád
Altitude: 148m/486ft
Population: 19,700

On the border with the Slovak republic, 75km/47 miles north of Budapest, lies Balassagyarmat, formerly the capital of the region and now its administrative, commercial and cultural centre, with much industrial development. Lying on the Ipoly river, the town was soon occupied by the invading Magyars, as witnessed by the second part of its name – Gyarmat. In the 15th c. the name of the aristocratic Balassa family, who owned the town, was added.

Situation and
Characteristics

The town still boasts some Baroque and neo-classical buildings, of which the old council building (1832–35) on Köztársaság tér with its projecting central ressaut and mansard roof deserves special mention. The two poets Imre Madách and Kálmán Mikszáth worked here as employees of the regional council.

Sights

The Palocs, whose origin has never been definitely established, were a group of peoples who settled in northern Hungary and who, in the seclusion of their villages, succeeded for a long time in pursuing an individual life-style with their own customs, a common dialect and special building styles. They also became very skilled in many forms of handicraft, such as woodcarving, ceramics and embroidery. In the Paloc Museum on Palócliget 1, about 100m/110yds from Köztársaság tér, the visitor will find many examples of the rich artistic skills of the Paloc people – embroidery, weaving, carved wooden objects and many more (open: Tue.–Sun. 10am–6pm). The ethnographic collection is supplemented by a Paloc house (Palócudvar),complete with stable and barn, which has been erected in the museum courtyard. It came originally from the village of Karancskeszi in 1932, and was the first historical building to be transported to a museum in this way.

Paloc Museum

Surroundings

This region of flat-topped hills lying between the Börzsöny and the Mátra is a part of the central mountain range of northern Hungary, but can scarcely be said to possess mountainous characteristics, its highest peak being that of Naszály (652m/2140ft); gently undulating hills, meadows, fields and small areas of mixed woodland dominate the landscape. The Cserhát remains a thinly populated and mainly agricultural region as yet scarcely opened up to tourism, and the home of the Palocs (see above). Hidden in the valleys or lying in sheltered positions on a hillside and linked only by narrow roads can be found small, idyllic villages where time seems to have stood still. A particularly beautiful route through this rural area is that leading from Balassagyarmat by way of Szécsény to the pretty Paloc village of Hollóko, where the visitor can see examples of their traditional forms of building.

Cserhát
(Uplands)

This little provincial township (pop. 7000) lies 18km/11 miles east of Balassagyarmat, on the way to Salgótarján (Road 22). It was here, during the struggle for freedom from Habsburg rule, that Ferenc Rákóczi II was chosen

Szécsény

97

as ruler by parliament in 1705. The Kubinyi Ferenc Museum is now housed in the Baroque palace which once belonged to Count Forgách. It contains mainly archaeological finds from the region as well as a small natural history collection and a separate department devoted to hunting exhibits. The sacristy in the Franciscan church is well worth a visit; the church itself has been rebuilt several times.

Salgótarján

Some 25km/16 miles east of Szécsény, on Road 22, lies the mining and industrial town of Salgótarján (altitude 255m/837ft; population 50,000), which extends along the banks of the Tarján rivulet and into its side valleys. It is also the administrative centre of the Nógrád region. It received its name from the neighbouring castle of Salgó and from the Magyar tribe known as the Tarján which settled here at the time of the Hungarian conquest. Although man is known to have lived in the neighbouring hills as long ago as the Early Stone Age, and there was a settlement here during the Bronze Age, Salgótarján remained a village of little importance with a population of only 1000 until the early 19th c. In 1821 a devastating fire destroyed the whole town. When rich deposits of brown coal were discovered, however, and a rail-link was built in 1867, it rapidly developed into an important industrial centre. The mining of brown coal received a further impetus after the Second World War, but has declined considerably in recent years, whereas the steel works and a sheet-glass factory have gained in importance. This young industrial town has no historical monuments of any note.

Mining Museum

However, it is worth paying a visit to the Mining Museum (Bányamúzeum) in the former József mine at Bajcsy Zsilinszky utca 1, where everything from trucks to large mining machinery of various kinds is on display (open: May–Sept. Tue.–Sun. 9am–4pm; Oct.–Apr. Tue., Thur, and Sat. 9am–4pm).

Local History Museum

Since 1980 there has been a local history collection housed in the Helytörténeti Múzeum on Múzeum tér, with an extensive collection devoted to industrial history and the background of the labour movement (open: Tue.–Sun, 9am–5pm).

Hollókő

This famous Paloc village, which is included in the UNESCO world cultural and natural heritage list, lies south of Szécsény in the Cserhát mountain range. After travelling some 16km/10 miles along the main country road the visitor will find a narrow road branching off to the right; Hollókő lies hidden among the hills 3km/2 miles along this side road.

Castle ruins

On approaching Hollókő the visitor will first of all see the ruins of the once proud castle high above the village. Built in the 13th/14th c. and the scene of fierce battles during the wars with the Hussites and Turks, the castle was destroyed by the Habsburgs in 1701. From the round north bastion there is a beautiful panoramic view over the surrounding countryside.

**Museum Village (Ófalu)

The old centre of Hollókő contains 54 houses, some of them under a protection order, which have survived almost unchanged since the Middle Ages in spite of a number of fires; some of these buildings are also rented out as tourist accommodation. The simple little church marks with a wooden tower the centre of the village. Characteristic of these houses is the cellar with access from street level, its rough stone finish contrasting with the whitewashed walls of the front of the house, and also the pergola leading from the courtyard side and often extending all the way around the house. A narrow hipped roof covers the pergola on the gable side, and wooden railings and balconies are artistically carved – a Paloc speciality. Everyday objects and furnishings from years gone by are exhibited in three rooms in the little museum at Kossuth Lajos utca 82. The women's costumes are particularly beautiful; a number of short dresses are worn one

Palozen houses and . . .   *. . . the village church in Hollókő*

on top of the other, then a blouse with very wide sleeves followed by a shawl. A wide black apron is worn to protect the dresses, and on the head sits a bonnet of several layers, decorated with pearls. In cold weather an embroidered fur jacket or waistcoat may also be worn.

Balaton

Lake Balaton covers an area of 598sq.km/230sq.miles, making it the largest inland lake in Central Europe, and together with its surrounding country-side it has become Hungary's major tourist region. It lies west of the Danube between the hilly region and the Bakony Forest, about 95–190km/60–120 miles south-west of Budapest. The many opportunities for bathing and leisure pursuits, areas of natural beauty and places of interest all serve to attract more than 600,000 holidaymakers to the region every year.

**Situation and Importance

The name "Balaton" comes from the Slavonic word "blatno", meaning marsh or moor.

Name

From Budapest Lake Balaton can quickly be reached by rail (South Station; Déli pályaudvar), by bus (Erzsébet tér) or by car along the M 7 motorway (E 96).

Access from Budapest

Measuring 77km/48 miles in length and up to 14km/9 miles in width, and fed mainly with water from the Zala river and the karst springs in the Tapolca region, the lake was formed at the end of the Pleistocene period, some 20,000–22,000 years ago, as the result of structural sinking of the earth's crust. With an average depth of 3–4m/10–13ft, the bed of the lake is comparatively flat (measuring only 12·4m/41ft at its deepest point, near the

Characteristics

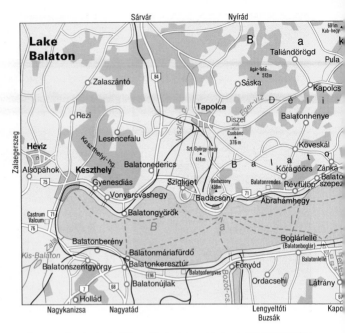

Tihany peninsula, in the Tihany Spring), has dried out completely twice during its existence, mainly because of the relatively small amount of water it contains, i.e. approximately 1·8 billion cubic metres/2·35 billion cubic yards. Being so shallow the water in the lake warms up very quickly; as early as May it reaches a temperature of 15°C/59°F and does not fall below that level until late autumn. In the summer months the average temperature is over 20°C/68°F and quite often will reach 27°C/81°F, especially near the flat south bank. When the lake freezes over, as it usually does in winter, it provides excellent opportunities for ice-sailing and skating.

The climate on and near the lake is very pleasant. From early June to the end of August the average day temperature is over 20°C/68°F. Every year there are about 830 hours of sunshine, more or less equally divided over the three summer months. During these months the thermometer averages 25°C/77°F on 70 days, while the nights cool down to a pleasant 20°C/68°F or just under. The relative humidity is 70–75%. The soft water, being sweet and slightly alkaline, has a high calcium, magnesium and hydrocarbonate content, and can be described as a heavily diluted mineral water.

Nature reserve

At the mouth of the Zala river, in the south-west of the Balaton region, lies Little Balaton (Kis-Balaton), a humid area covering 40sq.km/15½sq.miles, with many rare plants and animals. Protected species of birds which have already died out in other parts of Europe include the great white egret (*egretta alba*). The Tihany peninsula is also a nature reserve, because of its interesting geology and unique topography, and so is the Badacsony volcanic mountain on the slopes of which flourish vines producing top quality grapes.

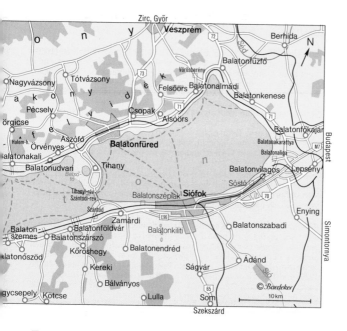

Tour around Lake Balaton

North bank of Lake Balaton (going from east to west)

After driving along the M 7 motorway from Budapest for some 90km/ 56 miles the visitor will reach Road 71, which branches off to the lake and links all the towns and villages between Balatonkarattya and Keszthely on the north bank.

*Topography

The north bank of Lake Balaton, with its charming landscape dominated largely by the foothills of the Bakony Mountains and many extinct Pliocene volcanoes, is often described as the "Hungarian Riviera". Favourite excursions from here include those to the southern edges of the Bakony Forest, the Balaton Uplands and extinct volcanoes in the Tapolca Basin.

On leaving the motorway, the first place arrived at is Balatonakarattya on the north bank (3km/2 miles from the motorway). Beyond the 25km/15 mile officially protected area near the bank lies the Akarattya Lido with its large beach. A legend from the days of the Wars of Independence has grown up around the remains of a mighty 400 year-old elm tree some 800m/880yds from the railway station. The saying goes that Prince Ferenc II Rákóczi (1676–1735), the famous leader of the independence fighters, tied his horse to this tree before issuing the historical proclamation stating that Hungary had broken away from Habsburg rule.

Balatonakarattya

Balatonkenese immediately adjoins Balatonakarattya. This district, the population of which now numbers 3600, was inhabited before Roman times but, like many another village, completely disappeared from the map during the period of Turkish occupation. At the beginning of the 20th c. it began to develop as a holiday resort. The largest and most modern resort

Balatonkenese

101

complex on the north bank, known as Adám Béri Balog, covers an area of 28ha/70 acres.

Sights

Places of interest in Balatonkenese include the Reformed Church (1568–70), which was rebuilt in the Baroque style after the Turkish period, and a number of pretty houses listed as historical monuments. The pleasant Zsindely Csárda restaurant at Táncsics utca 25 is popular with visitors both for its fine cuisine and its historical atmosphere; dating from the 18th c. it is a typical arcaded house built in the rural Baroque style. A walk on the nearby Partfő (180m/590ft above sea-level) is also worthwhile for the fine view it offers over the Tihany peninsula. The caves in the Partfő wall are popularly known as Tartar Holes or Turkish Holes (Tatárlikak, Töröklikak), as the inhabitants of the village are said to have hidden in them at the time of the Mongol attacks in 1241–42 and during the period of Turkish occupation.

Balatonfűzfő

This little town 5km/3 miles north of Balatonkenese, at the north-east tip of Lake Balaton, has a population of some 550 and, being the site of the Nitrókémia chemical factory, has little to attract the tourist. There is, however, a beach near the bank of the lake.

Balatonalmádi

After Balatonfüred and Keszthely, Balatonalmádi is the third largest holiday resort on the north bank. First mentioned in the records in 1082, it was until the middle of the 19th c. just a tiny vine-growing village. As beach holidays became fashionable, however, the quiet life in Balatonalmádi came to an end, and since 1877 it has been a popular bathing resort. In the 1920s and 1930s it developed rapidly and soon absorbed the former vineyards and spread up into the hills. The local red sandstone is the material used to build most of the villas and holiday homes.
As well as being popular for its beaches Balatonalmádi is also a good base for excursions – by car into the Balaton hinterland, on foot into the nearby surrounding countryside (see Viewing Points below) or by ship on Lake Balaton (almost all the shipping companies berth in Balatonalmádi).

Sights

The railway station and its immediate surroundings form the centre of Balatonalmádi. From here the villa quarter extends north to the slopes of Mount Öreg (Öreg-hegy), while to the south lies one of the largest and most beautiful beaches to be found on the north bank. The twelve-storey Hotel Aurora towers above all the other buildings in the town. In its grounds stands the Csárda Cockerel (Kakas csárda), decorated with Hungarian folkart motifs. From the hotel a bridge leads over the main street into the park and to the hotel's private beach. Seventy years ago a park was laid out behind the beach, containing statues of Sándor Petőfi, Lajos Kossuth and Ferenc II Rákóczi.

Vörösberény district of the town

On a chain of hills north of the beach lies the village of Vörösberény, which forms part of the municipality of Balatonalmádi and which was mentioned in local records back in the 12th c. The local sandstone, coloured red as a result of its high iron content, is excellent for growing grapevines. On a hill above the main street in Vörösberény stands the Reformed Church, once a fortified church with embrasures, a stocky tower and an encircling wall. Built in 1290 in the Romanesque/Gothic Transitional style, it was taken over by the Calvinists at the end of the 17th c. and was given a tripartite capped vault in the course of rebuilding at the end of the 18th c.
The former Jesuit church, now the Catholic parish church of St Ignatius, at Veszprém út, is worth a visit especially for the historically important frescos. Dating from c. 1780 and gloriously built, they are attributed to the Baroque artist Franz Xaver Bucher from Schaffhausen in Switzerland. The Jesuit monastery near the church is a Baroque building with some superbly executed stonemasonry at the entrance. The monastery also owns the 60m/200ft long granary which, like the monastery itself, was built in the 1770s.

A peaceful spot on Lake Balaton

In the Káptalanfürdő district, situated to the west on Road 71, stands the former Csárda Torgyöpi (now a private house). The regional boundary between Veszprém and Zala runs right through the balcony of this house. On either side of the table below robbers from the Bakony Forest would cheerfully drink wine with police officers from the adjoining region, knowing they had no powers to arrest them.

Káptalanfürdő district of the town

From the railway station in Balatonalmádi a path marked in blue leads via Batthyány utca to the Wesselényi Viewing Tower on Öreg-hegy (132m/433ft); after the half-hour climb to the top the visitor will be rewarded by a wide view over the eastern half of Lake Balaton. An even more beautiful panoramic view as far as the hills of the Bakony Forest can be obtained from the Szabadság Viewing Tower (283m/929ft), which is about an hour's walk from the town centre along another path also marked in blue.

Viewing Points

Alsóörs is charmingly situated on a lakeside terrace, at the foot of Somló-hegy (200m/656ft), which is covered in vineyards and forest. This little resort has moorings for boats and a sandy beach. The Reformed Church with a west tower dates originally from the 13th c., but underwent marked changes during a rebuilding programme in the 18th c. A road known as Petőfi köz – on which stands the "Turkish House" (Török ház), a 15th c. Late Gothic manor house – leads up to Somló-hegy. The building gets its name from its rather unconventional turban-shaped chimney.

Alsóörs

3km/2 miles inland from Alsóörs lies the little village of Felsőörs, which so far has remained unspoiled by mass tourism. The church of St Mary Magdalene is a pretty Romanesque building in red sandstone which was later rebuilt in the Baroque style. The west tower and the richly decorated recessed doorway are original, dating from the 12th c., whereas the nave

Felsőörs

103

and west wall are 13th c. The interior decoration including the high altar, gallery and beautifully carved pulpit are in the Baroque style and were installed in the mid-18th century.

Csopak

Between Alsóörs and Balatonfüred lies the old wine-producing village of Csopak which has now become a holiday resort.

*Balatonfüred

Balatonfüred (106m/348ft; pop. 14,200) is a resort which is steeped in tradition and an important spa for heart and circulation disorders. The healing properties of the carbonated waters were recognised back in the 1730s; in 1743 the monastery in Tihany acquired the town and built a bath-house near the streams, In 1772 Balatonfüred was officially declared a spa town. Between 1825 and 1848 it became the meeting-place of the Hungarian intelligentsia of the Reform Period, and in 1831 the town council presented it with the first permanent theatre to perform plays in the Hungarian language. It was from Balatonfüred harbour that the first steamship sailed on Lake Balaton in 1846.

Sights

Surrounded by parks and historic buildings and containing the pump room built around the Lajos Kossuth stream in the 19th c., Gyógy tér (Spa Square) forms the centre of this bustling spa town. The most splendid building on Gyógy tér is Horváth House, built c. 1790 and now forming part of the sanatorium, the main façade of which is graced by an oriel window with columns and by wrought-iron railings. The "Balatonfüred Pantheon" contains an arcade decorated with plaques in memory of famous people who have visited the spa. In the hall of the former Horváth hotel, a late 18th c. plait style building (1802–10) on the west side of the square, the well-known "St Anne's Ball" has been held on the last Sunday in July every year since 1825. On the west side of the square, too, is the street known as Blaha Lujza, formerly Balatonfüred Corso, where Mór Jokai had his summer residence. It leads to the Classical round church dating from 1841–46, modelled on the church of St Anne in Esztergom. On the main front of the church is an attractive open portico, the triangular gable of which is supported by three Ionic columns.

South of Gyógy tér lies a park filled with plane and lime trees. Stretching right down to the lake, it is the resort's favourite meeting place. The promenade is named after the world-famous Hindu author Rabindranath Tagore, who found here a cure for his heart condition here and planted a lime tree in the park in 1926 as a token of his gratitude. Since then it has become the custom for renowned visitors or patients to do the same. From the park a long mole leads down to the harbour and to the beautiful sculpture "Balaton Wind" by Miklós Borsos.

Along the bank to the west of the mole are a row of hotels, former nursing homes, offices of sailing clubs and the largest camp site by Lake Balaton – each with its own beach.

On the other side of the railway line, in that part of the town which is north of the spa and the holiday homes, the mansion belonging to the Gombás family will be found at Arácsi utca 94; it is a pretty dwelling of rural character built at the end of the 18th c. in the 18th c. plait style and with an extension housing a wine-press.

Wine-cellars

A visit is also recommended to the cellars of the Badacsony state wineries, where 12,000hl/264,000 gallons of wine can mature at a constant temperature. An excellent Riesling is produced from the fine grapes grown in the Balatonfüred vineyards.

The Baroque Abbey Church, a landmark of Tihany

**Tihany

The Tihany peninsula is one of the most popular holiday resorts on Lake Balaton. Originally an island, today it covers an area of 12sq.km/ 4·6sq.miles and extends 5km/3 miles into the lake, terminating 1·5km/ 1 mile from the opposite shore. Here, where the lake is at its narrowest, the only car ferry operates between Tihany and Szántód on the south bank. As a result of its extraordinarily charming and geologically interesting scenery Tihany has been designated a nature reserve since 1952; the south-western section of the peninsula has been closed to traffic and can be explored only on foot along well-marked paths. The tourist centre is the little township of Tihany, with its 2000 inhabitants, nestling around the famous Benedictine abbey. On the steep east coast lies the "Inner Harbour" for passenger ships, while at the southern tip will be found the car ferry to Szántód mentioned above.

During the Late Tertiary and Quaternary periods of geological history the peninsula was the scene of much volcanic activity. At that time geysers at temperatures of about 100°C/212°F forced their way up through the hard basalt tuff and formed "geyser humps". Subsequently the centre of the peninsula sank to leave two hollows surrounded by "geyser cones". In the deeper southern hollow a stretch of water formed, not unlike a crater lake. The Belső-tó, or "Inner Lake", as it is known, lies 26m/85ft above the level of the Balaton and today is an anglers' paradise; numerous waterfowl nest on the "Outer Lake", which is overgrown with reeds. The landscape is particularly beautiful in spring, when the almond trees are in bloom, and in summer, when the fields are a sea of deep-blue lavender.

Topography

Tihany was inhabited in prehistoric times. Impressive evidence of a Bronze Age settlement is provided by the massive earth-fort (Óvár) in the north-

History

Balaton

east of the peninsula, which was later also used by the Slavs. Archaeological finds have also confirmed the presence of Celts, Romans and Avars. Andreas I, one of the first Hungarian kings, founded a Benedictine abbey on Tihany in 1055. Five years later the abbey was sufficiently finished for its founder to be able to find his last resting place there. The foundation charter, written in Latin, in fact contains some one hundred Hungarian words and suffixes and is thus the oldest known document in the Hungarian language. Today it is housed in the parent Benedictine monastery in Pannonhalma, with a copy in Tihany. In Andreas' wake immigrant Russian monks settled on the peninsula in the 11th c. Near the Cyprian Stream (Ciprián-forrás) under the Bronze Age earth-wall they carved out cells in the rock which can still be seen today. The monastery had already been fortified against Mongol attacks as early as the 13th c., and with the advance of the Ottoman armies it was converted into a fort, and the monks moved elsewhere. After the withdrawal of the Turks the Habsburgs razed the building to the ground so that it should not fall into the hands of the insurgents. The present monastery complex was built between 1740 and 1754, and a small fishing village grew up around it. It was only in the early 20th c. that Tihany first attracted tourists.

*Abbey

Visible from afar is Tihany's symbol and landmark, the towers on the front of the Baroque abbey which was built by Abbot Ágoston Lécs between 1740 and 1745 on the foundations of the original church dedicated in 1060. Although it may appear somewhat plain from the outside, the Late Baroque interior is quite magnificent. The pulpit, which portrays the personification of the Christian virtues of Faith, Hope and Charity between the seated figures of the four Fathers of the Church, is particularly worthy of note. The high altar is decorated with carved figures of St Benedict and St Scholastika, as well as of saintly kings Stephen and Ladislaus. Like those of the pulpit and the side-altars, these are the work of the cabinet-maker Sebastian Stuhlhoff. a lay brother in the monastery. His excellent reputation and the esteem in which he was held are reflected in the fact that he is buried in the crypt next to the abbots. More high quality carvings by him can be seen in the sacristy. The crypt under the raised choir formed part of the original Romanesque church. This gloomy, sombre room with its heavy round pillars hewn from blocks of stone contrasts sharply with the jubilant Baroque style of the church above.

The patron of the abbey, King Andrew I, lies interred in the central aisle beneath a marble slab adorned with an abbot's cross. In the cellar of this former Benedictine abbey is a lapidarium containing Roman, Early Christian and medieval memorials in stone, and on the upper floors is the Tihany local history museum.

Village, open-air museum

The plateau behind the abbey sees the beginning of Pisky sétány (Pisky Promenade), offering a beautiful view over Lake Balaton. Here, too, is the historical centre of the old fishing village (open-air museum) with some lovely old peasants' cottages. Some particularly well-preserved buildings are to be seen in Csokonai, Batthyány and Kossuth utca. Typical of the style of buildings found on Tihany are the bare walls of local volcanic basalt tuff and the thatched roofs. In the "Potter's House" (Fazekasház) some beautiful examples of traditional ceramic art are on display. The guild-houses once occupied by fishermen and the small folk-museum are also worth a visit.

"Inner Harbour"

From the village of Tihany two winding roads lead down to the "Inner Harbour", the bustling business centre with moorings for passenger ships and a promenade along the bank of the lake, guest-houses and a neighbouring bathing beach. The former summer residence of the Grand Duke of Habsburg, now with a modern extension wing, has been made into a first-class hotel. Large numbers of rare plants and many beautiful conifers are grown in the hotel park.

Since time immemorial there has ben a ferry plying between the southern tip of the peninsula and Szántód harbour on the south bank of the lake. In recent years hotels, a holiday club, a sailing marina, restaurants, a swimming pool, a riding school, a mini-golf course and other leisure facilities have sprung up in the beautiful surrounding countryside.

Ferry centre

Remains of a Roman villa have been uncovered on the edge of this little village. The old water-mill was in use from about 1800; today it is a museum.

Örvényes

There was a settlement in Balatonudvari back in Roman times. Pretty farmers' houses with gable fronts and some very individual gardens adorn the village street of this holiday resort which has grown rapidly in recent years.

Balatonudvari

Balatonudvari cemetery, on the eastern edge of the village, is under a protection order aimed at preserving the heart-shaped gravestones dating from the first half of the 19th century.

Cemetery

Balatonakali and Balatonszepezd are old wine-producing villages which only recently have become holiday resorts. In Balatonakali a famous muscatel is produced, which can be sampled in the Csárda on Road 71. Balatonszepezd grew up around the Catholic church on a small hill. The building of this 18th c. Baroque church displays both Romanesque and Gothic features.

Balatonakali,
Balatonszepezd

See Vesprém, Surroundings

Nagyvázsony

Near Révfülöp the bank protrudes into the lake in the form of two small peninsulas and forms an excellent harbour site, from where ships regularly sail to Boglárlelle. Close to the harbour the foundations of a 13th c. single-aisled Romanesque church in red sandstone were uncovered in 1962. In

Révfülöp

A heart-shaped tombstone in the Balatonudvari cemetery

recent years many villas have sprung up in the vineyards and along the banks of the lake there is a modern holiday development. On Road 71 in the direction of Balatonrendes can be seen remains of another Romanesque church, known as Ecser church.

Balatonrendes, Ábrahámhegy

These two places – once separate but now merged into one – are quiet holiday villages in the middle of a rich wine-producing area. Ábrahámhegy wines, produced in a valley on either side of a winding stream (Burnót), are particulary popular.

*Badacsony

Visible from afar is the imposing 438m/1438ft high Badacsony, an example of a volcanic mountain with steep basalt sides and the characteristic flat top. From its top there is a splendid panoramic view over the charming countryside with its vineyards and forests, the western Balaton and the Tapolca Basin. On the gradual south slopes of Badacsony grow the grapes used to make such well-known white wines as Badacsony Riesling, Blaustengler and Furmint, Buda Green and Grey Monk (Szürkebarát), which visitors can sample in the vineyard cellars and purchase direct from the producer. In addition to the professional wine-growers more and more amateurs are growing vines in their gardens as a paying hobby, using existing or homemade presses to produce the wine. Badacsony together with its fertile surroundings so reminiscent of Mediterranean regions forms one of the most beautiful stretches of land on the banks of Lake Balaton and attracts large numbers of visitors and holidaymakers during the summer and autumn months. At the foot of the mountain, on the promontory between the towns of Badacsonytomaj and Badacsonytördemic, an extensive holiday complex has grown up in recent years, with guest-houses, a string of bazaars, snack-bars and a mooring for ships. Near the railway level crossing (Egry sétány 12) stands the former home and studio of the artist József Egry (1883–1951), which is now a museum and open to the public from May–Oct. Tue.–Sun. 10am–7pm. His paintings portray perfectly the scenic beauty of Lake Balaton.

*Climbing Badacsony

The climb up to the mountain begins at the railway station in the Badacsony holiday complex (look for the yellow signs). Those who prefer not to tackle the first stretch on foot can, during the main holiday season, take a group taxi from the railway station to the car park at Kisfaludy House. The basalt stone path – known as Római út because legend has it that it was laid down by the Romans – leads through vineyards with small wine-presses scattered here and there. Almond, fig and poplar trees give the landscape an almost Mediterranean appearance. Halfway up the mountain is a Late Baroque wine-merchant's house built in 1790. This thatched building with an arbour around the upper floor belonged to the Hungarian author Sándor Kisfaludy (1772–1844) and his companion through life Rózsa Szegedy, for

Badacsony, a hill of volcanic origin

whom a small museum has been set up here. From the terrace of the nearby Kisfaludy House guest-house there is a fine view over the lake. Anyone wishing to be able to see further afield should climb either the Kisfaludy or the Páholy viewing tower.

The Szigliget peninsula, 4km/2½ miles beyond Badacsonytördemic, was (like Tihany) originally surrounded by water. Anyone visiting the village of Szigliget cannot fail to be captivated by its picturesque centre and the beautiful thatched cottages which are now listed buildings. Fortunately, it is as yet unspoilt by tourists. The most impressive building on the village square (Fö tér) is the former Eszterházy Palace, a Classical 19th c. edifice surrounded by parkland, which now provides working accommodation for Hungarian writers. Of the 13th c. church of All Saints (Avasi templom) on the former ferry mooring in the east of the peninsula only the Romanesque basalt tower still stands; this is being converted from a square to an octagonal design. The climb up the 280m/920ft high castle mound is worthwhile just for the magnificent view. At the top can be seen the remains of the 13th c. castle which at times was owned by the king and was razed to the ground by imperial troops in the early 18th century.

Szigliget

12km/7½ miles north of Szigliget, in the Tapolca Basin between the Bakony Forest and the Keszthely Mountains, lies the up-and-coming industrial town of Tapolca (415m/1362ft, pop. 17,000), where large basalt and bauxite deposits have been found in the surrounding countryside. The town developed from a medieval settlement of which the first records are dated 1272; from the 19th c. it was a trading centre for the wine-producing regions round about, and more recently has become a popular spot with tourists in the Balaton region. Its main attraction is the "Tavasbarlang" underwater grotto, part of an extensive network of limestone caves. The cave can be visited by rowing-boat daily between May 15th and August 20th, from 8am to 4pm; the entrance lies in Kisfaludy utca (No. 5). Also worth a visit is the Catholic parish church on the church mound, which embraces styles of building ranging from Romanesque to Baroque. Fragments of 15th c. frescos can be seen on the outer walls of the Gothic choir. All around the church lies a "Garden of Ruins" with remains of a Roman estate. Later a manor house was built on the same foundations, and in the second half of the 15th c. this was extended by Carthusian monks into a castle and surrounded by walls and fortifications. Remains of the castle walls can still be seen. The school at the foot of the church mound as well as the "choir-house" nearby , which now houses the municipal museum, are basically medieval buildings. Near the mill-pond (Malom tó) the wheel of a 200 year-old water-mill still turns.

Excursion to Tapolca

*grotto

See entry

Keszthely

See entry

Hévíz

South shore of Lake Balaton (going from east to west)

The scenery on the flat south shore is somewhat less attractive and varied than that on the north side, but on the other hand its wide beaches (though unfortunately only a few are still sandy beaches, many having been grassed or concreted), the somewhat warmer water which deepens very gradually, and the numerous facilities for water-sports combine to make it ideal for a lakeside holiday – sun-worshippers, those who love the water and families with children will find all they seek here. Covering a length of some 70km/44 miles, all the various places along the south coast have merged almost completely to form one holiday complex.

Siófok

Situated at the mouth of the little Sió river, Siófok is the regional centre and the largest town on the south bank; in recent years it has become a favourite spot with holidaymakers, mainly because of its excellent infrastructure (good restaurants, shops, hotels, etc.) and beaches; in the summer months the population of Siófok increases fivefold.

History

Back in Roman times attempts were made to put the mouth of the little Sió river to good use, and a canal was built. The town of Fok, mentioned in 1055 in the Tihany town charter, was seized by the Turks in 1541. They took up positions in a castle built in the water and from there they ruled the whole of the south bank area. In 1863 the Sió Canal was built, through which the Balaton fleet of ships could find its way to the Danube. Siófok has the building of the Budapest–Fiume rail link in 1861 to thank for its development into a tourist resort; five years later the park and promenade came into being and hotels and restaurants shot up after Budapest society had "discovered" the resort.

Sights

The town centre of Siófok lies south of the railway line between Kálmán Imre sétány and Tanácsház utca, with the extensive and partially lawned Fő tér (town square) in the very centre. The square is dominated by the South Balaton Cultural Centre, opened in 1976, with a theatre seating 500, conference and exhibition rooms and a municipal library. The Beszédes-József Museum on the bridge of the same name over the Sió (Sió utca 2) provides information on the history of Lake Balaton, including archaeological finds, economy, navigation and folk-art. In the house in which the great composer of operettas Imre Kálmán was born, at Kálmán Imre sétany 5, some of his personal possessions are displayed in a small exibition in his memory. The Evangelical Church built by Imre Makovecz, situated outside the town in Fő utca, just before it joins Dózsa György utca, looks more like

Yacht harbour on the southern shore of Lake Balaton

some mythical creature than a church. Makovecz, who also designed the Hungarian pavilion at the 1992 World Exhibition in Seville, was the founder of a new alternative form of architecture in Hungary which has already earned international recognition (see also Sárospatak). The Balaton Navigation Company has had its head office at this busy port since 1889. East of the harbour Petőfi sétány forms a promenade along the bank of the lake, and on it will be found Siófok's largest hotels – some six-storied, some twelve – with their own swimming pools, sports facilities and restaurants. Adjoining the line of hotels is the well-known beach resort of Aranypart (Golden Beach); the beach west of the harbour is called Ezüstpart (Silver Bank). Both beaches offer both public bathing areas and others reserved for hotel guests.

The motorway M 7 ends before it reaches Zamárdi, and Highway 7 then continues along the south bank. North of the railway line there is a 10km/6 mile stretch of holiday homes one after the other, and on the other side of the line lies the old village centre. Visitors should visit the local museum at Fő utca 83, a typical arcaded house with a pergola, thatched roof and barn. One room and the kitchen are fitted out with country-style furniture and everyday items from days gone by.

Zamárdi

Beyond Zamárdi there is a turn-off from Highway 7 to a former 18th/19th c. estate, which was once owned by the Tihany monastery and today serves partly as a museum but is used mainly for tourist purposes, with a riding school, horse and carriage rides, wine-tasting, restaurants, overnight accommodation, etc. The oldest buildings are those comprising the magnificent country seat dating from 1741, now occupied by the administrator of the estate, together with its adjoining wine-cellar where 5000hl/110,000 gallons of wine are stored and which visitors are invited to taste. There is also a bailiff's house, stables where typical Hungarian animals such as longhorn mountain sheep are kept, servants' quarters, and on the hill the chapel of St Christopher built in 1735 (open: May–Sept. 9am–7pm). The old kermis, a traditional annual fair with craft-markets, performances of folk-dancing, etc., has recently been revived and is held in the last week in July each year.

Szántód-puszta

On the narrowest part of the lake (1·5km/1 mile) will be found the landing stage for the ferry to Tihany, the only ferry across Lake Balaton. The trip to the north bank takes only about ten minutes. The friendly inn known as Rév-csárda (Ferry csárda) has stood near the jetty since 1839.

Szántód

The small town of Balatonföldvár (alt. 108m/355ft; pop. 2200) can look back on a long tradition as a bathing resort. Beautifully situated and criss-crossed with parks, this holiday centre boasts a sizeable bathing beach and the largest marina on Lake Balaton. Remains of the ditch around the Iron Age earth fortifications (Földvár) – from which the town gets its name – can still be seen. Carbonated water bubbles forth from a fountain near the railway station. In the harbour bay, between the breakwaters of the 246m/270yd long mole, lies the little island of Galambsziget (Dove Island), a sun-worshippers' paradise.
In the evenings people like to stroll along the mile-long promenade lined with plane trees. The promenade is named after the great Hungarian hydraulic engineer Jenő Kvassay.

Balatonföldvár

In Köröshegy, 3km/2 miles south of Balatonföldvár, the Franciscans built a church with an east tower in 1460; today the church is known mainly for its organ concerts. The exterior is reminiscent of Gothic fortified churches. The reredos of this single-aisled church (now a parish church) with its portrayal of Christ on the Cross is the work of the Viennese artist Johann Hofbauer (1803–46). In Köröshegy's little wine-vault it is possible to try the local wines.

Excursion to Köröshegy and Zala

Balaton

In Zala, some 20km/13 miles inland from Köröshegy, is the house in which Mihály Zichy (1827–1906), the court painter of the Russian Czars, was born.

Balatonszárszó

In the autumn of 1937 the great Hungarian poet Attila József (1905–37) tragically committed suicide in the quiet holiday resort of Balatonszárszó. In the boarding-house at József Attila utca 7 where he spent his last days there is a museum in his memory.

Balatonszemes

Situated more or less in the middle of the south bank, Balatonszemes has developed into an impressive bathing resort. The old village centre lies on a hill, the more exclusive residential quarter is on a slope above the railway line and the modern holiday complex, harbour and swimming pools lie on the bank of the lake. At Bajcsy Zsilinszky út 36, at the upper end of the village, visitors will find the Postal Museum, housed in what used to be the post office on the Székesfehérvár–Nagykanizsa stretch of road. "Owl Castle" (Bagolyvár), near the railway station, was built at the beginning of this century as an extravagant folly. During the Turkish period there was actually a castle here, known by the name of "Fools' Castle" (Bolondvár); some remains can still be seen.

Boglárlelle

The communities of Balatonlelle and Balatonboglár merged to form that of Boglárlelle. Like most of the townships on the south bank of Lake Balaton, the core of the old town lies south of the railway line and main highway, while the modern holiday area is on the very banks of the lake. The House of Culture (Muvelodési ház) at Kossuth Lajos utca 2 in Lelle, a former Classical manor house built in 1838, is renowned for the exhibitions of craft and folk-art held there every summer. On August 20th (Constitution Day) the Antal Kapoli Prize is awarded to the best woodcarver. There is a fine view over the lake to be had from the 162m/530ft high castle mound with its forest parkland which has been designated a nature reserve.

Excursion to
Buzsák

Some 20km/13 miles south-west of Boglárlelle (approach by way of Lengyeltóti and turn right there), Buzsák has earned a reputation as a stronghold of folk-art and crafts in the Somogy region. Even today the ladies of the town still embroider blankets and rugs, cushions and costumes with colourful ethnic patterns or decorate them with *appliqué* flowers and leaves made from red material. In the Museum of Arts and Crafts their work can be admired and, of course, purchased. The old costumes are still worn in the village procession on the occasion of the traditional kermis or fair held on the second or third Sunday in August of each year.

Somogyvár

From Buzsák it is worth making a detour to Somogyvár, 11km/7 miles south of Lengyeltóti on the road to Kaposvár. The royal Benedictine monastery, the uncovered ruins of which are open to visitors, was built in 1091–95 on the site of a Bronze Age rampart.

Fonyód

The second largest holiday town on the south bank stretches as far as the ancient settlement area at the foot of the extinct Fonyód volcano, the highest elevation on the south side with the two peaks of Sipos-hegy (207m/680ft) and Vár-hegy (233m/765ft). When the railway line was built along the south bank in the 19th c. the town soon grew into a popular resort. Four holiday centres lie along the 8km/5 mile stretch along the bank from Fonyód – Sándortelep, Bélatelep, Fonyódliget and Alsó-Bélatelep.

Balatonfenyves

This comparatively recent lakeside resort was wrested from the Nagyberek marshes in the 1950s, when land was needed for agricultural purposes. The resort grew up north of the railway line. Large and small holiday homes and villas are scattered over the wooded terrain.
A miniature railway runs to the neighbouring Csiszta-puszta, where the warm springs supply water at 42°C/108°F to a thermal bath with three basins.

The township of Balatonmáriafürdő extends for 10km/6 miles along the bank. It is only since the 1960s that it has grown into a holiday centre. The railway station and the adjacent public beach form the centre of Balatonmáriafürdő. This is a good place for anyone seeking a quiet and restful holiday.

Balatonmáriafürdő

This, the last resort before reaching the mouth of the Zala river and the Kis-Balaton nature reserve, was a popular holiday destination around the turn of the century. The old village at the foot of Bokros-hegy (153m/502ft) still boasts a number of the beautiful rural houses so typical of the region (especially the building at Csillagvár utca 68) and a Gothic church at Kossuth Lajos utca, converted to Baroque in the mid-18th c. From Bokros-hegy, too, there is a beautiful view of Lake Balaton and the surrounding countryside.

Balatonberény

See Facts and Figures, Lakes and Rivers

Kis-Balaton

Békéscsaba   G 3

Region: Békés
Altitude: 90m/295ft
Population: 70,150

Békéscsaba, the capital of the Békés region, lies 210km/130 miles southeast of Budapest in the centre of Hungary's most fertile wheat-growing area. There are indications that it was inhabited back in the year 1300, but the town died completely during the turmoils of the Turkish wars. In 1718 the great landowner Baron Harruckern arranged for Slovaks from Upper Hungary to settle here, as a result of which Békéscsaba is still the focal point of the Slovak minority living in Hungary. In addition to Slovaks, Germans came here from the Rhineland and Romania. This region is also known as "Stormy Corner", because at the turn of the century the rural population resorted to large-scale strikes and demonstrations in support of their struggle for rights.

Situation and Characteristics

Sights

The building at Kossuth tér, built between 1807–24 in the classical 18th c. plait style, is the largest Evangelical church in Hungary. It has galleries on two levels, providing seating for a congregation of 2900. The church tower is 70m/230ft high.

The great Evangelical Church

The house at Garai utca 21, built in 1818 in the rural neo-classical style, gives an insight into the lives of the Slovaks in and around Békéscsaba (open: Tue.–Sun. 10am–6pm).

Slovak local museum

The major 19th c. Hungarian painter (1844–1909; see Famous People), was apprenticed to a cabinet-maker in Békéscsaba, and later lived and worked in Vienna, Munich, Düsseldorf and Paris. Munkácsy, whose real name was Lieb and who was descended from a Bavarian family who had settled in Hungary 200 years earlier, became famous for his realistic genre scenes and still lifes. Some of his works and personal effects are on display in the museum at Széchenyi utca 2 (open: Tue.–Sun. 10am–6pm) together with some beautiful and rare specimens of the local fauna as well as folklore items. In front of the museum stands a statue of Munkácsy by Miklós Borsos.

Mihály Munkácsy Museum

Békéscsaba

Árpád Baths | The right bank of the Elúvíz Canal – lined with sculptures of famous men born in the town – leads to the Árpád fürdő baths, with alkaline water containing hydrogen carbonate which reaches temperatures of 74°C/165°F.

Open-air museum | A farmstead and a windmill 4km/2½ miles outside Békéscsaba on the road to Gyula (open: April 4th–Oct. 31st, Tue.–Sun. 10am–4pm) also provide an insight into the culture of this region in days gone by.

Surroundings

Mezoberény | This town (pop. 12,000) 18km/11 miles north of Békéscsaba, a commercial and industrial centre of this mainly agricultural region, was also populated by Baron Harruckern with Germans, Slovaks and Hungarians. The German-Protestant tradition is still very much alive – for example, there is a German-speaking grammar school here – and this is strengthened by links with the German town of Münsingen. The mid-18th c. Evangelical church is Late Baroque, and the reredos by Soma Petrich was installed in 1854.

Szarvas | See entry

Orosháza | The agricultural town of Orosháza (91m/300ft; pop. 37,000) lies 38km/24 miles south-west of Békéscsaba on the main road to Szeged, and the surrounding region is a centre of poultry production in Hungary. Industrial development commenced with the discovery of natural gas, and foodstuffs and glass are now manufactured here. The modern glassworks in Orosháza accounts for 40% of the country's glass production. In the early years of this century the town was a stronghold of socialist agricultural movements and the radical peasants' party.
Apart from the Evangelical church on Győry Vilmos, Orosháza boasts no historical monuments. The church authorities were granted permission to build a church only on condition that the tower, which they began to erect in 1777, was kept separate. It was 1830 before a start was made on building the main body of the church. In the Rágyánszki Arboretum in Gárdonyi Géza utca thrive more than 2000 species of tree, including many conifers and exotic plants.

Gyopárosfürdő | 5km/3 miles north of Orosháza lies the resort of Gyopárosfürdő near Lake Gyopáros, into which flows thermal spring water containing soda.

*Gyula

Characteristics | Gyula (pop. 35,000), a nostalgically pretty and popular spa town, lies near the Hungaro-Romanian border 16km/10 miles south-east of Békéscsaba on an arm of the White Körös river. The town was first officially recorded in 1214 as a monastery; its castle was captured by the Turks in 1566 and until they were driven out in 1695 it was the capital of a *sandchak*, or administrative district. The new lord of the manor, the Austrian Baron Harruckern, built a palace near the castle in 1720 and imported German workers who established themselves with their own town administration in what is now known as "German Gyula" to the left of the present-day avenue Béke sugárút. To its right lies Hungarian Gyula. Later on Harruckern invited Romanians into the country, and today Gyula is still the centre of the Romanian minority.

"Gyulai kolbász" | From the meat factory in Gyula comes "Gyulai kolbász", a richly-spiced sausage.

Castle | The massive square castle at Gyula (near the thermal baths), the only medieval brick-built castle on the lowland plain, was built in phases between the 14th c. and 1480, and was restored in the 1950s. It was 1802

Gyula Castle

before a proper bridge was built across the ditch. The red stone of the castle provides a perfect backdrop for the boats sailing on the pond. Inside the walls the Gyula Castle Theatre puts on performances every summer. Objects and documents illustrating the castle's history are on display in the castle museum (open: Tue.–Sun. 10am–5pm).

The large Várfürdő baths in a 30ha/75 acre park on Kossuth Lajos utca, provide everything the visitor to the spa can wish for. The waters, with a temperature of 70°C/158°F at source, contain sodium and hydrated sodium carbonate and have proved beneficial especially in the treatment of joint problems and gynaecological complaints. The old baths were built in 1833 by converting a former riding school. The complex also includes a sanatorium and a spa hotel with 800 beds.

Castle baths

The Late Baroque church (Belvárosi plébánia templom) on Harruckern tér was built in 1777. In the choir can be seen the tomb of its founder, Baron Harruckern; it dates from 1777 and was the work of the Viennese artist Martin Schmidt. The main altarpiece by Hubert Maurer shows the Assumption of the Virgin Mary.

Parish church

In a corner of pretty Erkel tér (at No. 1) stands a house built in 1801 in the classical 18th c. plait style. Here the Százéves cukrászda, famous throughout Hungary, sells tempting coffee and cakes, a pleasant experience made all the more enjoyable by the 1840 Biedermeier furnishings. The old cooking utensils are also of interest.

One hundred year-old café and cake-shop

The neo-classical house at No. 6 Apor Vilmos tér, built in 1795, is where Ferenc Erkel (1810–93) was born; he was the founder of the Hungarian National Opera and composer of the National Anthem. An exhibition (open: Tue.–Sun. 10am–5pm) portrays his life and work. On the wall of the

House commemorating Ferenc Erkel

house facing Dürer Albert utca there is a plaque pointing out that Albert Dürer was Hungarian by birth. The Ajtóssy family from the nearby village of Ajtós-falva ("Doormaker Village") lived here. Antal Ajtóssy later became a goldsmith, emigrated to the Netherlands and in 1455 went to Nuremberg in Germany where he took the name of "Türer". His son was the brilliant painter and engraver Albrecht Dürer. In Kossuth utca 17, near the castle, is the Dürer Room (Dürer terem), in which temporary exhibitions are held of work by contemporary artists.

Budapest   E 2

Region: Budapest
Altitude: 97–529m/318–1736ft
Population: 2.2 million

Note

The description of Budapest in this guide has deliberately been kept comparatively brief, as a more detailed guide to the city is separately available in this series.

Metropolis

Budapest, capital of the Republic of Hungary, is considered by many visitors to be the "Paris of the East" because of its particular charm; it is the most densely populated and culturally the most important metropolis of Eastern Central Europe.

Situation

Budapest is situated at a favourable spot for communications across the Danube, leading from the Hungarian Central Uplands to the Great Hungarian Plain. Topographical contrasts are a feature of the unique townscape. The territory of the city on the right of the Danube includes the river terraces of varying heights and extends far into the Buda Upland, which is composed of dolomite and chalk and which was articulated by a tectonic disturbance into a higher northern part and a lower southern part.

The Danube separating Buda from Pest

The plain of Pest on the left bank of the Danube is far better suited to settlement.

The present Hungarian capital formally came into being in 1872, with the amalgamation into one of three previously independent towns, Old Buda (Óbuda), Buda, strategically placed on a hill, and Pest, a densely inhabited and rapidly developing township on the other side of the Danube. The new city very quickly became the administrative, commercial and industrial centre of Hungary.

The emergence of the city

The city covers an area of 525sq.km/203sq.miles. About 173sq.km/67sq.miles of the city area are on the right bank of the Danube and about 352sq.km/106sq.miles on the left bank. Budapest extends from north to south approximately 25km/16 miles and from east to west about 30km/19 miles.

Area and city districts

The city is divided into 22 districts. The commercial quarter (District V), which was not dissimilar to the central business district of a Western city even before the fall of the "Iron Curtain", extends along Pest's Danube bank. Before the fall of Communism all the government and administrative offices, financial and commercial institutions as well as important cultural and scientific establishments were concentrated in this area, and indeed this is still the case under the new democratic regime. There are more than 600,000 jobs in District V alone. The population density amounts to 4000 per sq.km/1540 per sq.mile, and another 500,000 or more commute daily from elsewhere.

The fringe districts comprise the outer domiciliary and working districts. More than 200,000 jobs have been set up here, mainly created by modern industrial concerns. Most people in these areas live in dull high-rise flats and on housing estates, although there are now larger areas of mostly privately-owned houses with pretty gardens.

The richest mineral springs in Europe are to be found in the area of the city of Budapest. 123 registered thermal springs provide curative waters of varying temperatures. Some of these springs have been used for therapeutic purposes since Celtic times.

Spa town

Traces have been found of settlements dating back as far as the Old Stone Age. People lived on both sides of the Danube, where Budapest now stands, in the second millennium B.C. Bronze Age urn sites have also been uncovered. In the 6th c. B.C. Scythians from the Black Sea region settled here, and there are signs of Celto-Illyrian tribes having been here in the 4th/3rd c. B.C.

History

A decisive factor in the town's development was the building of a Roman fort in what is now Óbuda. The Roman base of Aquincum, separated into civilian and military districts, was the capital of the province of Pannonia and flourished during the second half of the 2nd c. B.C.

In the 5th c. A.D. the Huns swept across the country, and King Attila set up a great new kingdom in what is now Hungary. From the 6th to the 9th c. the Avars settled where Budapest now stands. About 896 the Magyars led by Prince Árpád settled in the area of present-day Óbuda.

Around the year 1000 Stephen (István) I, King of Hungary, organised a feudal state on the Central European model and introduced Christianity. A few years later merchants from central and western Europe settled in Buda and Pest and helped both places to develop rapidly. In 1241–42 Mongols stormed the Danube cities of Buda and Pest. A few years later the construction of the Castle of Buda ordered by King Béla IV was completed. From then on Buda became a royal town, while Pest developed into a prosperous trading centre. In the second half of the 15th c. Matthias Corvinus extended the Royal Palace and Buda, together with Visegrád, became a centre of Renaissance culture.

In 1526, after their victory at Mohács, the Turks took Buda and Pest. Under

Buddapest

Budaer Bergland

Royal Baths
Kacsa u.
Margit körút
Market Hall
Bus Station
Retek u.
Varsányi t. u.
Csalogány u.
Vitéz u.
Fő u.
Bem rakpart
Balat...
Stollár
Markó u.
Moszkva tér
Hattyú u.
Batthyány u.
Moszkva tér
Batthyány u.
St. Elisabeth
Ethnographisches Museum
Kálmán
Duna (Danube)
Parliament
Kossuth L. tér
Batthyány tér
St. Anna
Batthyány tér
Széchenyi rakpart
LIPÓT-
Báthori u.
Szilágyi D. tér
Iskola u.
Szabó Ilonka u.
Donáti u.
Kossuth tér
Szabadság tér
National Bank
VÁROS
War Museum
Magdalen Tower
Hotel Hilton
Fishermen's Bastion
Corvin tér
Széchenyi u.
Arany J. u.
VÁR
Matthias Church
Szenth tér
Old Town Hall
Hunyadi J. út
Fő u.
Bem rakpart
Academy of Science
Október 6. u.
Zrínyi u.
Déli pu.
South Station
Disz tér
Roosevelt tér
Krisztina körút
Castle Theatre
Clark Á. tér
Széchenyi lánchíd
Chain Bridge
József nádor tér
Busba
Erzs
Dorottya u.
Vörösmarty tér
Christian Town Parish Church
Krisztina tér
Szt. György tér
Palota út
Buda Castle
National Gallery
Forum-Hotel
Belgrád rakpart
Café Gerbeaud
Vigadó
Becsi u.
D. F. u.
Váci u.
Alkotás u.
Márvány u.
Győri u.
Tigris u.
Avar u.
Naphegy u.
Attila út
Széchenyi Library
Histor. Museum
Groza Péter rakpart
Duna Inter-Continental
Duna (Danube)
Sports Academy
Naphegy tér
Semmelweis-Museum
Apród u.
Petőfi tér
TABÁN
Tigris u.
Krisztina körút
St. Katharina
ELTE
Márc. 15. tér
Inner Cit Parish C
Alkotás u.
Hegyalja út
Raizen Baths
Hegyalja út
Erzsébet Railway Bridge
Rudas Baths
Otthon u.
Urania Observatory
Orom u.
Bérc u.
Bodaörsi u.
GELLÉRT-HEGY
Citadel, Freedom Monument
Szt. Gellért rk...
Kelenhegyi út
Ge...
Budapest
St John the Baptist
Somlói u.
Kelenhegyi út
Minerva u.
300 m
© Baedeker
Ménesi út
Gellért Baths

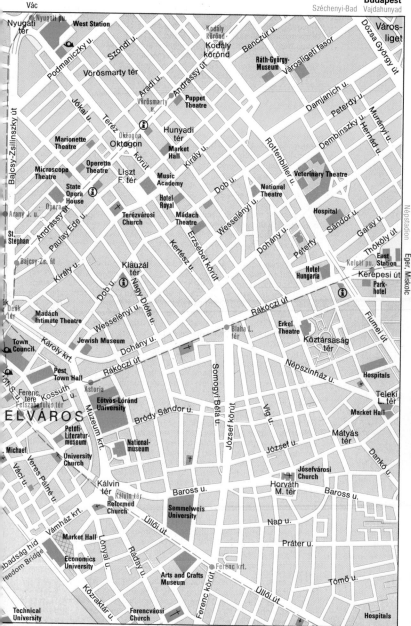

Budapest

Sultan Süleyman I (the Magnificent) many churches were converted into mosques, fine bath-houses constructed and defensive works modernised. Buda became the seat of a Grand Vizier.

It was 1686 before Charles of Lorraine was able to retake Óbuda, Buda and Pest for the House of Habsburg. Various measures taken during the reign of Empress Maria Theresa led to a further economic upsurge in Buda and Pest, largely brought about by an influx of German-speaking settlers. In 1777 Buda was made a university town but lost this title to Pest a few years later. The left bank of the Danube soon became the intellectual and political centre of the country. In 1848–49 there was a civil revolution led by liberal nobles.

The Chain Bridge was opened in 1849, with the aim of helping Óbuda, Buda and Pest to merge more quickly. In 1867 Emperor Franz Joseph I and Empress Elisabeth ("Sissi") were crowned in Matthias Church. The Austro-Hungarian monarchy of the Danube came into being. In 1872 Óbuda, Buda and Pest were combined into one city with a population of more than 150,000, and a great economic upswing followed, and continental Europe's first underground railway was opened in 1896. At the outbreak of the First World War many well-known industrial firms established themselves in the Budapest region.

As a result of the war Budapest suffered severe economic setbacks which continued in the years between the wars. Towards the end of the Second World War, in the autumn of 1944, Budapest became a front-line town and suffered severe damage, especially in the castle quarter where units of the German army were barricaded in.

From February 13th 1945 onwards Soviet troops controlled the whole of Budapest and thereafter it was ruled along strict Soviet lines. In the autumn of 1956 political turmoil and economic hardship fuelled popular uprisings which were savagely put down by Hungarian and Soviet forces of law and order. The inner city presented a picture of devastation.

In the 1960s and 1970s much inner-city building and reconstruction took place, such as the opening to traffic of the Elisabeth Bridge, extension of the underground network, renovation of the old city centre. especially the castle quarter, and the building of large luxury hotels both in the castle quarter and on the Pest bank of the Danube. What soon became known as "goulash communism" encouraged an upsurge in tourism, and visitors from both East and West Germany, Austrians, Italians and Americans in particular visited the city in ever-increasing numbers.

In the 1980s Budapest joined other large cities in becoming the venue for important sporting events (e.g. the world gymnastic championships in 1983) and other large functions, such as the KSZE-Culture forum which was held in Budapest in 1985. In 1986 an important COMECON conference was held here which heralded the start of far-reaching changes in world politics. In 1989 the events of 1956 could be viewed in a fresh light, and on June 16th hundreds of thousands paid homage to the former prime minister Imre Nagy who had been disgraced and executed 31 years previously. These political changes led to the Iron Curtain on the Hungaro-Austrian border being pulled down, and several thousand East Germans took advantage of the situation to flee to West Germany and other western countries.

Trade and industry

Budapest is the economic, industrial and communications centre of Hungary, and since the fall of the Iron Curtain in 1989 in particular foreign money has poured in and it now boasts a stock exchange as well as branches of foreign banks and insurance companies. A considerable part of Hungarian industry is concentrated in Budapest, including the manufacture of motor cars and machinery, chemicals, pharmaceuticals, textiles and clothing, foodstuffs and luxury goods, building firms, the printing and paper industries and publishing firms. Csepel harbour with its free port area is at present the most important port on the Danube. Ferihegy Airport in Budapest has grown within just a few years to become the most prestigious airport in Eastern Europe outside Russia.

Furthermore, Budapest is currently a leading centre of international tourism, as it can equally meet the needs of the business traveller or of those seeking cultural fulfilment or just a relaxing holiday. There is much to see, historical sites, 64 museums and art galleries, some famous educational institutions (over 20 colleges including the Semmelweis University of Medicine and the Franz Liszt Academy of Music, to name but two), extensive exhibition and conference centres, excellent health facilities, including at least five well-known spa establishments, gambling casinos, massive sports halls and stadiums and even a Formula 1 race-track.

About a fifth of Hungary's total population lives in Budapest. However, for some years now significant changes have been noted in the city's population statistics. Population growth has slowed down considerably, and people are tending more and more to move from the inner city to the outskirts; more than 16,000 people have left District V, for example, since the mid-1970s.
The vast majority of the inhabitants of Budapest are of Magyar descent. As well as Sinti and Romany gypsies, other important minorities include Germans, Slovaks, Serbs, Croats and Romanians.
Well over a half of the population of Budapest are Roman-Catholics, and about a quarter are Protestants.
The political troubles in Romania and the civil war conditions in the former Yugoslavia have resulted in floods of refugees, and Budapest has felt the effects of this. Unconfirmed reports at present indicate that there could be between 100,000 and 200,000 refugees living in the Budapest area. In addition, large numbers of immigrants, some describing themselves as "tourists", are entering the country from the Ukraine, Russia and Poland as well as from many Far East and Middle East countries .

Population

Sights in Buda

Most museums in Budapest are open from Tuesday to Sunday inclusive (closed on Mondays), from 10am to 6pm.

Note

In the 13th c. the Hungarian King Béla IV recognised the importance of the wedge-shaped hill (168m/550ft) standing alone on the right bank of the Danube. He built a castle on its south-eastern spur and soon this was extended to become the royal residence of the kings of Hungary. At the same time a royal town grew up on the plateau of Castle Hill, and over the years this became the glittering capital of Hungary.
The settlement known as Buda quickly spread down the hill and in the course of time merged with the neighbouring settlement of Óbuda. The old centre of Buda, now pedestrianised, has been able to retain its ancient charm. After suffering severe damage in the Second World War its historical monuments have been lovingly restored and now attract thousands of visitors every year. Buda and the adjoining section of the River Danube have been designated areas of great cultural value by UNESCO.

Situation and Importance

**Castle Palace (Vár-palota)

The first castle was built in the 13th c. on the south spur of Castle Hill. Its purpose was to provide protection from attacks by Mongols and Tartars. Unfortunately nothing remains of this building.
Under King Karl Robert a smaller palace was erected. King Sigismund, who made Buda his residence, had a Gothic castle built, which was considerably extended, in Renaissance style, under Matthias Corvinus.
Although the Castle Palace survived during the time of Turkish occupation, it was nevertheless almost completely ruined during the Siege of 1686. Therefore, in the 18th c. a new castle was built, which in the time of the

History

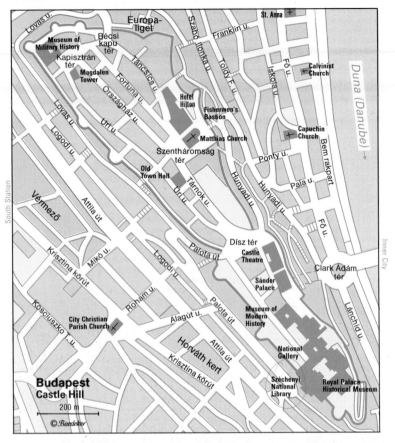

Budapest
Castle Hill
200 m
© Baedeker

Empress Maria Theresa had more than 200 rooms. The Castle Palace, from now on the residence of the Palatine (the representative of the Habsburg overlords), was rebuilt by the architects Alajos Hauszmann and Miklós Ybl in Neo-Baroque style. A symmetrical layout was created which is focussed on the central dome (62m/203ft high) facing the Danube.

The extensive buildings were badly damaged in the Second World War. After decades of restoration work, in the course of which it was possible to preserve many medieval and Renaissance structures, individual sections are gradually being opened up to the public.

Remains of the medieval castle

At the southern end of the complex, parts of the medieval castle have been reconstructed. The Buzogány Tower (buzogány means flail or club) near the Ferdinand Gate is impressive. Outside stands the South Tower, which was in existence in the 15th and 16th c.

Outside the walls of the castle a number of Turkish tombstones can still be seen.

*Hungarian National Gallery

The Hungarian National Gallery (Magyar Nemzeti Galéria) is housed in the main wing of the castle facing the Danube. A wide cross-section of Hungar-

ian sculpture and painting is on display, ranging from the time of the
Magyar invasion through the Gothic, Renaissance and Baroque periods to
the richly productive 19th and 20th centuries. The sculptures and panel
paintings from the medieval and Renaissance periods are of particular
interest, as are the Late Baroque works and 19th c. paintings and sculptures
by Bálint Kiss, Mór Than, László Pál, Mihály Munkácsy, Alajos Stróbl and
György Zala.
Also very worthy of study are pictures painted in the 20th c., including
works by Béla Czóbel, József Egry and József Rippl-Rónai.

The Budapest Historical Museum (Budapesti Történeti Múzeum; City
Museum; Castle Museum) is housed in the south wing of the castle. It
contains highly interesting documents, ceramics, wrought-iron work, textiles, household utensils and other objects which provide a comprehensive
picture of life in the independent towns of Óbuda, Buda and Pest up to 1872.
In the Renaissance Room is a picture showing Matthias Corvinus and
Beatrice of Aragon, his second wife. In the Gothic Room are fine sculptures
dated between 1370 and 1420, which were discovered during excavation
work in 1974.
Other Gothic sculptures can be seen in the lower chapel. A beautiful 15th c.
triptych has been set up in the choir of the chapel.

*Budapest
Historical
Museum

The Széchenyi National Library has been housed in the south-west wing of
the palace since 1985. This institution, founded by Count Ferenc Széchenyi
in 1802, contains about 6 million documents, including well over 600,000
manuscripts and more than 180,000 maps. The highlight of the collection is
the "Budapest Manuscripts", some of the oldest known medieval illuminated scripts.

*Széchenyi
National Library

Restored house façades in the Castle Quarter

| Museum of the Hungarian Workers' Movement | The Museum of the Hungarian Workers' Movement (Magyar Munkásmozgalmi Múzeum) is housed in the northern wing. |
| Equestrian statue of Prince Eugene | In front of the domed building, on the side facing the Danube, stands a bronze equestrian statue by József Róna (1900), representing Prince Eugene of Savoy who opposed the Turks. |

**Castle Quarter

Szent György tér (St George's Square)	Between the Castle Palace and the former Upper Town lies St George's Square, where jousting tournaments and other equestrian games were held in the Middle Ages. On the south side of the square, near the castle, stands a beautiful ornamental fountain (1904) designed by Alajos Stróbl; it shows King Matthias Corvinus hunting.
Sándor Palace (Sándor palota)	On the north-east side of the square stands Sándor Palace, built in 1806 in the neo-classical style.
*Castle Theatre (Vársinház)	From St George's Square Szinház utca (Theatre Street) leads north to Disz tér (see below). On its east side an old Carmelite monastery was converted to the Castle Theatre (Vársinház) following its dissolution in the 18th c. The theatre was designed by F. Kempelen in 1787. The building was damaged in the Second World War but was renovated and re-opened a few years ago in glittering new splendour.
Disz tér (former Parade Ground)	Disz tér stands more or less in the middle of the Castle Quarter. This square, surrounded by several Baroque and Classical buildings, has in the past been a market place, place of execution and parade ground. In the centre stands a pleasing Honvéd statue by György Zala (1893) which commemorates the War of Liberation of 1848–49.
Úri utca (Gentlemen's Street)	Úri utca (Gentlemen's Street) leads north from the north-west side of the square. Baroque and, above all, Gothic architecture (see No. 40) are features of Úri utca.
Cave system in the Castle Hill	From No. 9 Gentlemen's Street there is access to the vast system of caves and underground passages which were dug in the castle hill in days gone by. This subterranean network covers about 24km/15 miles in all. The German army was able to hold out here for a long time towards the end of the Second World War. A waxworks (panopticum) has been installed in part of the cave-system, portraying important events in Hungarian history.
Tárnok utca (Treasurer's Street)	Tárnok utca leads north to Szentháromság tér (Trinity Square) from the north-east side of Disz tér. Along this bustling street are a number of historically important buildings, which still display medieval, Baroque and neo-classical elements.
Arany Sas (Golden Eagle) Arany Hordó	The Arany Sas-patika (Golden Eagle Pharmacy; No. 18), dating from the 18th c., is now furnished as a pharmaceutical museum. The Arany Hordó guest-house (Golden Barrel; No. 14) retains its medieval painted façade.
*Szentháromság tér (Trinity Square)	The central square in the Castle Quarter is Szentháromság tér, with a large Baroque plague column designed by Barbier and Ungleich (1714). A number of particularly noteworthy buildings are grouped around the square.
*Matthias Church (Mátyás-templom)	The Matthias Church (Church of Our Lady, Coronation Church) in Buda is one of the principal sights of the Hungarian capital. It is the successor to a 13th c. church built in the time of King Béla IV, which has since been rebuilt and extended on several occasions. During the period of Turkish rule it was converted into a mosque. In 1867 Emperor Franz Joseph I of Austria and his

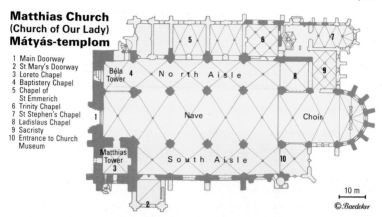

**Matthias Church
(Church of Our Lady)
Mátyás-templom**

1 Main Doorway
2 St Mary's Doorway
3 Loreto Chapel
4 Baptistery Chapel
5 Chapel of
  St Emmerich
6 Trinity Chapel
7 St Stephen's Chapel
8 Ladislaus Chapel
9 Sacristy
10 Entrance to Church
  Museum

10 m

© Baedeker

Empress Elisabeth ("Sissi") were crowned here; Franz Liszt (see Famous People) composed his famous Coronation Mass for the occasion.
The church was rebuilt in its present form at the end of the 19th c. by Frigyes Schulek.
Behind a grille enclosing the Chapel of the Holy Trinity in the north aisle can be seen the sarcophagi of King Béla III and his wife; they were originally buried in the Cathedral at Székesfehérvár and were reinterred in the Matthias Church in 1848.
The crypt, the Royal Oratory, the Oratory of the Knights of St John, and St Stephen's Chapel now serve as the church museum. In the Royal Oratory the standards which were raised at the Coronation of King Charles IV and Queen Zita on December 30th 1916 still hang. In the museum can be seen reliquaries and other ecclesiastical treasures, as well as a replica of the Hungarian royal crown.

On the south-west corner of Trinity Square (Szentháromság tér) stands the former Town Hall of Buda, now the home of one section of the Hungarian Academy of Science. This magnificent building was erected at the end of the 17th c. from plans by the Italian architect Ceresola. The oriel balcony, small towers, courtyard and staircase are of considerable architectural and historical interest. Below the east oriel window can be seen "Pallas Athene", by Carlo Adami (1795).

*Old Town Hall

Szentháromság utca leads from Szentháromság tér to the west wall of the Castle Quarter. A visit is recommended to Ruszwurm Café (Ruszwurm cukrászda; No. 7); steeped in tradition, it has stood here since 1827 on the site of its medieval predecessor.

Szentháromság utca (Trinity Street)

On Castle Hill, at the spot where in the Middle Ages the fishermen had their defence installations, the Fishermen's Bastion was built behind the Matthias Church between 1895 and 1902. Its towers, colonnades and embrasures, which were designed in Neo-Romanesque style by Frigyes Schulek, were renovated a few years ago. From the bastion there is a magnificent view over the city and the Danube.

**Fishermen's Bastion (Halászbástya)

In the south courtyard of the bastion stands a bronze equestrian statue of St Stephen (Szent István); dated 1906, it is the work of Alajos Stróbl. On its base are reliefs showing scenes from the saint's life.

St Stephen

In the north courtyard of the bastion stand two pleasing statues of the monks Julianus and Gellért, by Károly Antal (1937).

Julianus and Gellért

125

Above the Danube: Fishermen's Bastion . . .   . . . and the Matthias Church

Hess András tér
(Andrew Hess
Square)

This square is named after Andrew Hess, the first printer of books in Buda (1473). Medieval remains on the east side of the square were cleverly incorporated a few years ago into the architecture of the highly modern luxury hotel the Budapest Hilton. Among these important remains is the St Nicholas Tower (Miklós torony), a relic of the Late Gothic Church of St Nicholas of the Dominicans who had a monastery here.

The monument to Pope Innocent XI was the work of J. Damko (1936). Behind the monument is the architectural complex known as "Vörös sün" (the Red Hedgehog), which dates from the 17th–18th c. and which was later remodelled in Classical style.

Fortuna utca
(Fortuna Street)

At the north-west corner of Andrew Hess Square is Fortuna utca, characterised by some very beautiful buildings in the Baroque and plait styles. The street is named after the Fortuna Inn (No. 4; now the Museum of Commerce and Catering).

Táncsics Mihály
utca

Táncsics Mihály utca, the street where large numbers of Jews once lived, leads from the northern end of Andrew Hess Square to Bécsi Kapu (Vienna Gate). A prayer-house of the Jewish community of Buda was founded here in the 15th c.

Országház utca
(Parliament
Street)

Országház utca is the principal street of the northern Castle Quarter, and Baroque and Classical architecture predominate here.

The former Monastery of St Clare (No. 28), founded in the Middle Ages, was rebuilt by Franz Anton Hillebrandt in the 18th c. Thereafter it was the home of the State Parliament and the High Court of the Hungarian capital. The great hall of this building has been splendidly restored, and highly-valued cultural functions are held here from time to time.

The Saturday Market was formerly held in this square by the north gate (Vienna Gate) of the Castle Quarter. Nearby will be found the Lutheran Church, the huge National Archive (Országos Levéltár; 1917) in Neo-Romanesque style, and the Anjou Bastion (Anjou-bástya).

Bécsi kapu tér (Vienna Gate Square)

Kapisztrán Square is situated in the north-west of the Castle Quarter. It is named after a companion of the Turkish conqueror János Hunyadi. On the north-west side of the square stands the Museum of Military History (Hadtörténeti múzeum). On the south-east side there stood, until it was destroyed in the Second World War, the Church of St Mary Magdalene (Mária Magdolna templom; 13th–15th c.); unfortunately only the Gothic tower now remains.

Kapisztrán tér

On the south-west side of Castle Hill run the battlements named after Árpád Tóth. From here there is a fine view of the western parts of Budapest and the Buda Hills.

Tóth Árpád sétány (Battlements)

*Víziváros

Víziváros, the "Water Town", occupies a narrow terrace between Castle Hill and the Danube. Right up until the Turkish period it was fortified. The Turks installed baths in that part of the town which was chiefly inhabited by fishermen, handworkers and merchants, and they turned the existing churches into mosques. A great deal of building went on in the Baroque period, and this was when St Anne's Church was built. Since the end of the last century the townscape has altered considerably as a result of the building of multi-storeyed blocks of flats.
This district was often flooded in the past when the Danube overflowed its banks. The river was widened in an attempt to alleviate the problem, but unfortunately this in turn led to a sinking of the water-table. As a consequence some of the older buildings subsided and could only be preserved by means of expensive technology.

Location

The twin-towered St Anne's Church, which was built between 1740 and 1758 to plans by Christoph and Michael Hamom and Matthäus Nepauer, is one of the most beautiful Baroque buildings in present-day Hungary. The magnificent High Altar, portraying St Anne with her daughter Mary in the Temple of Jerusalem, dates from 1773 and is by Carlo Bebo, who also designed the pulpit.
The side altars contain fine sculptures by Anton Eberhard and splendid paintings by the Viennese artist Franz Wagenschön.

*St Anne's Church (Szent Anna-templom)

This square in front of St Anne's Church is named after Count Lajos Batthyány, and has always been the centre of Víziváros and was once the market-place. There are many notable buildings around the square. These include the former White Cross Inn (No. 4). dating from 1770, mainly Baroque with a Rococo front, Hickisch House (No. 3), built in 1795 in the Mid 18th c. plait style, and a 19th c. Franciscan monastery on the north side.

Batthyány tér

This Baroque church, erected in 1757 on the foundations of a Turkish building, originally belonged to the Franciscans. In 1785 it was transferred to the Order of Elisabeth, who ran a hospice here.

St Elisabeth's Church (Szent Erzsébet-templom)

The König Baths have nothing to do with kings. They were the property in the 19th c. of a family named König and are among the most interesting establishments of their kind in Budapest. The oldest part of the building is the Hamam (Turkish for bath) built in 1570 under Mustafa Paşa. In the Baroque period the baths were considerably enlarged, and a wing and courtyard added in the 19th century.

*The König Baths (Király-fürdő)

St Florian's Chapel (Szent Flórián-kápolna)	This little church at Fő utca 88 was designed by the architect Matthäus Nepauer in 1760. On the façade of St Florian's are fine statues of St Nicholas, St Florian and St Blaise. There were once pictures and sculptures by Franz Wagenschön and others inside the church, but these are now housed in the Historical Museum on Castle Hill.
Former Café Friedl (Friedl cukrászda)	This once famous café at Fo utca 20, with origins going back to the 15th c., was rebuilt in the 18th c. and in 1811 received its neat Mid 18th c. plait style façade and corner oriel. The Biedermeier furnishings are well worth seeing.
Corvin tér	Around Corvin Square, with a fountain by Holló (1904), will be seen a number of notable 18th c. buildings. On the south side of the square stands the former Capuchin monastery with a church which still shows considerable Turkish influence in its architecture and ornamentation. On the north side of the square stands the former Buda Redoubt.
Foundry Museum (Öntödei Múzeum)	The iron-foundry at Bem József u. 20, built in the middle of the 19th c. by Abraham Ganz, is the core of the Ganz industrial complex (locomotives, cranes, wagons) which has become well known far beyond the boundaries of Hungary.
**Chain Bridge (Szécheny-lánchíd)	Chain Bridge, one of the landmarks of the Hungarian capital, was constructed between 1838 and 1849 by the British engineers William Tierny Clark and Adam Clark. The bridge, 375m/410yd long and almost 16m/18yd wide is supported by chains fixed to 48m/158ft high towers at either end. At the end of the bridge stand stone lions by Marschalkó. The bridge was destroyed in the Second World War and was finally rebuilt in 1949.
Clark Adam tér	At the Buda end of the bridge lies the square known as Clark Adam tér. In 1971 the 0-km-stone by Miklós Borsos was placed here. This is the point from which distances along main roads in Hungary are measured.
Alagút	From Clark Adam tér the Alagút, a road tunnel about 350m/380yd long which was constructed in 1857, leads to Kristinaváros (Christina Town).
Sikló	From the Buda end of the bridge tourists can also take the "Sikló" funicular railway up to the Castle Palace. This railway was built as long ago as 1870. After having "slumbered" for decades it was restored a few years ago.

Tabán

Location	The district of Tabán lies in the depression between Castle Hill and Gellért Hill. During the time of the Turkish occupation Tamils in particular were settled here. In the 18th c. there was an influx of Serbian refugees. In 1810 a fierce fire devastated the area. Extensive parks and traffic layouts are features of the modern district.
*Tabán Parish Church (Tabáni plébánia-templom)	This Baroque church was completed in 1740, and replaced a medieval church which the Turks had converted into a mosque. One of the treasures of the Tábán Parish Church is a carved figure known as the "Tabán Christ", dating from the 12th c., which is now housed in the Castle Museum.
Rác Baths (Rác-fürdő)	The Rác Baths which are situated on Hadnagy utca to the south of Tabán Parish Church, were established and extended in the Turkish period, but the medicinal springs were known long before that.
Semmelweis Museum	At the foot of Castle Hill on the south-east side, at Arpród utca 1–3, stands the 18th c. house in which the famous Hungarian doctor, Ignáz Philipp Semmelweis (see Famous People) was born. It is now furnished as a museum of the history of medicine.

This famous old inn in Szarvas tér is built in the plait style of the 19th c. From here steps lead up to the castle.

Golden Stag
(Arany Szarvas)

North of the Semmelweis Museum lies the square named after the famous architect Miklós Ybl (1814–91). Around the square stand buildings designed by Ybl, who was also responsible for the splendid flight of steps (1882) leading up to the castle.

Ybl Miklós tér
(Miklós Ybl Square)

The 310m/340yd long castle bazaar always attracts many tourists to its shops, artists' studios, inns and terrace.

Castle bazaar
(Várbazár)

*Gellért hegy (Gellért Hill)

Probably the most striking feature of the landscape of Budapest is the panoramic Gellért Hill (235m/771ft): a block of dolomite, the east flank of which falls steeply down to the Danube, while the west side consists of terraces which were formerly vineyards. Along its geological fault several medicinal springs emerge which supply the Gellért Baths, Rudas Baths and Rác Baths.

Situation and Importance

The hill is named after St Gellért (St Gerald of Csanád), a Benedictine monk who did good works during the time of King Stephen I. He was made the first Magyar bishop, but died a martyr's death in 1046. On the north-east slope of Gellért Hill, above a man-made waterfall, stands a statue of St Gellért by Jankovits (1902).

St Gellért

The Citadel, built by the Austrians on the summit of Gellért Hill after 1851, is still in good repair. Parts of the fortifications are open to the public.

Citadel

On the south-east point of Gellért Hill stands the Liberation Monument, commemorating the victorious Soviet Army in the Second World War; it was designed by the artist Zsigmond Kisfaludy Stróbl (1947). On the limestone plinth is a female figure, 14m/46ft high, bearing a palm branch.

Liberation Monument

Jubilee Park, on the southern slope of the hill, was laid out to celebrate the 40th anniversary of the October Revolution. Charming walks, flower-beds and valuable artistic sculptures, including "Budapest" by István Kiss, attract many visitors.

Jubilee Park
(Jubileumi Park)

At the north-east foot of the hill are the interesting Rudas Baths. The thermal springs were already in use in the Middle Ages, and the first bath-houses date from that period. The installation was extended during the Turkish period, and a typical domed building with its octagonal main room has been preserved from that time. In the pump-room near the steam (Turkish) baths, medicinal water from the Juventus and Hungaria springs is available.

*Rudas Baths
(Rudas-fürdő)

The modern Elisabeth Bridge, 378m/413yd long and 37·5m/40yd wide, spans the Danube to the north of Rudas Baths. It is a suspension bridge designed in 1964 by Pál Sávoly.

*Elisabeth Bridge
(Erzsébet híd)

On the south-eastern slope of Gellért Hill can be found the famous medicinal baths and hotel complex of Gellért-fürdő.
There was a spa here as early as the 13th c., when the thermal waters of Gellért Hill were used for medicinal purposes. The Turks extended the establishment and converted it into a luxurious spa. The hotel was built in Secessionist style between 1912 and 1918 and many well-known personalities have fallen under its spell. The therapeutic bathing and treatment facilities were completely modernised in 1983 to provide a thermal bath with wave-making equipment, jacuzzis and saunas.

**Gellért Hotel
and Thermal
Baths

The steel Freedom Bridge over the Danube near Gellért was opened to traffic in 1896. The plans for this 331m/360yd long and 20m/22yd wide bridge were drawn up by J. Feketeházy.

Freedom Bridge
(Szabadság híd)

Buda Ring (Budai körút)

Route	The semi-circular Buda Ring encircles Castle Hill like a crescent moon. The road leads from the western end of Elisabeth Bridge and sweeps northward in a long arc to the western end of Margaret Bridge. The most important stretches of this ring road are Krisztina körút/Attila út and Margit körút.
Parish church of Christinatown (Krisztinavárosi plébánia templom)	The interesting church of Christinatown (Krisztinavárosi) stands to the west below the Castle Palace. It was built in the Baroque style at the end of the 18th century.
Museum of Theatrical History	A little to the north of the church the visitor will find the interesting Budapest Museum of Theatrical History (Színháztörténeti Múzeum) which is well worth a visit.
Vérmező (Meadow of Blood)	Next comes the Meadow of Blood (Vérmező), where the instigators of the Hungarian Jacobin Movement were executed in 1795.
South Station (Déli pályaudvar)	This is followed by the very modern South Station, opened in 1977. In the semi-circular station forecourt is a very impressive work in enamel by Viktor Vasarély.
Moskva tér (Moscow Square)	Further north lies Moscow Square, one of the most important traffic hubs of the inner city. The square is dominated by the brick building topped with a crown, which houses the postal administration.
Városmajor (Municipal Park)	West of Moscow Square lies Városmajor Park, about 10ha/25 acres in extent. This welcome green area is nearly 200 years old and was once used for hunting. The old trees are a charming feature and these, together with the attractive tennis-courts and games areas, attract many citizens on fine days. On the north-west side of the park stands the Hotel Budapest, an imposing circular tower block of 18 storeys. A cog-wheel railway nearby ascends to Széchenyi-hegy.
Széna tér (Hay Square)	To the north-east of Moscow Square is Széna tér (Hay Square). with the former shooting-range, built in 1826, and remains of the medieval town fortifications.
*Rose Hill (Rózsadomb)	Rose Hill, to the north above Margit körút, has long been an exclusive residential area, with elegant villas, large gardens, avenues and footpaths.
*Türbe of Gül Baba	In the grounds of an old villa on Mecset utca can be found the Türbe (mausoleum) built in the 16th c. for a Muslim Dervish Gül Baba (Turkish for "rose father"). Gül Baba died during a festival in the Matthias Church which had been converted into a mosque. The mausoleum, a plain octagonal domed building, is now a museum with memorials of Gül Baba and the Bektazi Order.
Bem Jószef tér	On the banks of the Danube further to the north-east lies a square named after the Polish General Jószef Bem (1794–1850), who was a successful leader of the Honvéd troops in the Hungarian War of Liberation.
Margaret Bridge (Margit híd)	Margaret Bridge is in two sections; the first connects the Buda Ring with the southern tip of Margaret Island, and the second continues on to provide a link with the Outer Ring (Szent István körút). It was constructed in 1876, making it the second oldest bridge over the Danube. The bridge was destroyed during the Second World War, was rebuilt in 1948 and extended to measure almost 640m/700yd long and 25m/28yd wide.
*Lucas Baths (Lukács-fürdo)	Just to the north of the Buda end of Margaret Bridge are the famous Lucas Baths, a spa establishment which has been extended several times since 1760. The spacious pump-room and the adjoining treatment room are visited by large numbers of patients every day.

Adjoining the Lucas Baths is the well-known Budapest Institute of Physio-therapy and Rheumatology.

Rheumatism
Institute

To the north of the Lucas Baths and sharing some of its open-air facilities are the Emperor Baths, one of the oldest spa establishments in Budapest. It can trace its history back to a Turkish bath (Hamam) built during the reign of Sokollu Mustafa Paşa, and an octagonal dome building from that time still remains. In 1806 the baths were re-built in the Classical style.

*Emperor Baths
(Császár-fürdő)

In 1976 a sports swimming pool was opened in the wing facing the Danube, with seating for 2000 spectators.

Swimming pool

Opposite the two thermal baths lies the "Mill Pond", the water level of which corresponds with that of the neighbouring thermal springs. On its northern side stands St Stephen's Chapel, designed by Lószef Hild in 1844, with a fine reredos.

"Mill Pond"
(Malom-tó)

Margaret Island (Margit-sziget)

Margaret Island, barely 2.5km/1½ miles long and up to 0.5km/550yd long, is undoubtedly the main local recreation and recuperative centre for the people of Budapest. Thermal springs, feeding the medicinal and swimming baths, space for sports and games, carefully tended gardens and paths, and not least the remains of buildings which play a significant part in the history of the town all serve to attract many visitors every day.

**Situation and
Importance

The island gets its name from the canonised Princess Margit (1252–71), daughter of the Hungarian King Béla IV; as the result of a vow made by her father she became a nun in the Dominican convent on the island.

Name of
the island

The Romans utilised the supply of thermal water in the north of this island in the Danube. In the 12th and 13th c. monasteries and churches were built here. At the end of the 18th c. the Habsburg Archduke John, Palatine of Hungary, had the island landscaped.
At the end of the 19th c. a thermal bath with a pump-room was built, but this was damaged in the Second World War and after the war a modern spa centre was established including the fashionable Hotel Thermál, opened in 1979.

History

In the south of the island stands a metal sculpture by István Kiss (1972) in the form of a flower. It was unveiled on the occasion of the centenary of the union of Óbuda, Buda and Pest. On the inside surface of the "leaves" are symbols depicting the modern history of Budapest.
Near the Union Monument is a large fountain.

*Union
Monument

The Alfréd Hajós Sports Bath on the south-west side of the island is named after the double Hungarian champion of the first of the modern Olympic Games held in 1896. It was constructed in 1931 and boasts several pools.

Alfréd Hajós
Sports Bath

Only scant remains have survived of the church of the Franciscan Monastery which was built in the 13th/14th centuries.

Franciscan Church
(ruins)

The comprehensive facilities of the Palatinus Baths include a bath with artificial waves, various medicinal pools and swimming and children's pools, and can accommodate up to 20,000 at any one time.
Opposite the baths can be found the pretty Rose Garden with an animal enclosure.

*Palatinus Baths

Along Artists' Promenade (Művészsétány) can be seen busts of celebrated Hungarian personalities of the art world.

Artists'
Promenade

Dominican Convent (ruins)	After serious flooding of the Danube which occurred in 1838, remains were discovered of the Dominican convent which had decayed during the Turkish occupation. The most celebrated nun was Princess Margarete (see above), the daughter of King Béla IV. Traces of Romanesque and Gothic architecture have been detected.
Water-tower	The 52m/170ft high water-tower, built in 1911, was recently restored and given a viewing platform. Temporary exhibitions are held inside the tower. Close by lies an open-air theatre (seating 3,500) which is very popular.
Premonstratensian Monastery (ruins)	A few remains of the 12th c. Premonstratensian Monastery can still be seen. Some years ago the church of this foundation was rebuilt in Romanesque style.
*Spa Hotel Thermál	This hotel, completed in 1979, is extremely modern and has become well-known far beyond the borders of Hungary. It was designed by the architect G. Kéry and is equipped according to the most recent balneological ideas.
Musical Fountain	The so-called "Musical Fountain" in the north of the island is a copy of one built in 1820 in Tirgu Mures in Romania by the Transylvanian artist Bodor. The water-driven mechanism was unfortunately destroyed in the Second World War.

Óbuda

History	Until its union with Buda and Pest in 1872, Óbuda was a somewhat sleepy little town, and in spite of considerable rebuilding and modernisation it has still managed to retain something of its former atmosphere. This old settlement, where evidence of prehistoric culture has been discovered and where shortly after the birth of Christ the Romans founded their camp of Aquincum, was according to tradition the residence of the Hunnish king Attila in the 5th century. Under the Árpáds the place experienced enormous prosperity. In the Middle Ages there was a palace of the Hungarian queens here; in the days of the Turkish occupation the little Danube town fell into complete decay, as a result of the increasing importance of the neighbouring royal city of Buda. Not until the 17th c. was life restored to the town by German-speaking settlers.
Óbuda Parish Church	This Baroque church at Lajos utca 17 was built in the 18th c. In front of the church can be seen some fine figures by Károly Bebó.
Former Synagogue	The former synagogue at Lajos utca 16, which since the Second World War has been used as a cultural centre, was built in the Classical style by A. Landherr between 1820 and 1825. Six pillars and a tympanum with the tablets of the law enhance the main façade.
*Zichy Castle	Commissioned in the middle of the 18th c. by Count Nicholas Zichy, this Baroque castle at Fő tér 1 has undergone lengthy restoration. It houses a local museum and mementoes of Lajos Kassák (1887–1967), the versatile representative of the Hungarian avant-garde. Works by Viktor Vasarely are also on display. From time to time excellent concerts are held here. Nearby are Óbuda Town Hall, the ethnographic collection of Zsigmond Kun and a number of very pleasant inns.
Flórián tér (Florian Square)	Flórián tér is an important traffic junction. On its north side can be seen ruins of the baths of the Roman legion; the actual hot baths themselves are well-preserved. A small museum provides information about the baths and medicine in Roman times. At the south edge of the square are the remains of the medieval Queens' Palace and the Reformed Church of Óbuda, which was built in the 18th century.

The oval building of the former silk-mill (1785) is now of importance as an   Filatorigát
historic industrial building. It commemorates textile production in Óbuda,
which began as a result of a demand by Emperor Joseph II.

Kiscell, a part of Óbuda, owes its name to a copy of the miracle-working   Kiscell
statue of the Virgin Mary of Mariazell. Here there is a branch of the Histor-   Museum
ical Museum, housed in rooms of the recently restored Trinitarian monastery (18th c.; architect J. Entzenhoffer). Of particular interest are the
pictures and accounts of the recovery of Buda by the Austrians in 1686.

The remains of an Early Christian graveyard, laid out in the second half of   Cella trichora
the 4th c. on a clover-leaf plan and known as "cella trichora", are very
interesting from an historical point of view. It is situated at the corner of
Raktár utca and Hunor utca.

In the 1950s and 1960s the ruins of a magnificent Roman villa (probably   *Villa of
dating from the 3rd c. A.D. were excavated. The mosaics discovered here,   Hercules
which are among the finest ever found in Hungary, depict scenes from the
Hercules myth and the Dionysus saga. The sarcophagi exhibited in the
garden of the archaeological museum were probably made in the 3rd and
4th centuries.

In 1950 the remains of the military camp belonging to the Roman town of   *Roman
Aquincum were discovered to the south of Flórian tér. As well as remains of   Military Town
buildings dating from the 2nd to the 4th c. tools, various vessels and
sarcophagi were also found. Also of interest are the remains of an under-
floor hot-air heating system.

**Aquincum

The remains of the Roman town of Aquincum, founded in the 1st c. A.D. on   Situation and
the west bank of the Danube – now on Szentendrei utca – have been   History
systematically excavated since the 1870s. A considerable part of the former
"municipium" is now accessible as an open-air museum.
About the year 10 B.C. the Romans occupied the territory of their later
province of Pannonia. A few years after the birth of Christ they built within
the boundaries of Óbuda a military camp (see above), around which a civil
town soon grew. The flourishing settlement of Aquincum became, as early
as the beginning of the 2nd c., the principal town of the province of
Pannonia Inferior. The Emperor Septimus Severus raised it to the status of
a "colonia" in A.D. 194.
After the defeat of the Pannonian legions at Hadrianopolis in the year 378
Aquincum declined, and this decline was accelerated by increasing and
violent attacks by the Barbarians.

In the rooms of the Archaeological Museum, opened in 1894, are exhibited   Archaeological
cult objects, sculptures, vessels, coins and jewellery. Among the most   Museum
valuable exhibits are a water-organ of A.D. 288, which has become celebrated, a Jupiter column, a marble Diana and a marble Minerva, as well as
gems and ivory-carvings.
In the Pillared Hall and in the Lapidarium can be seen some fine stone-
carvings (altars, gravestones, reliefs).

The ruins around the museum give an impression of the Roman civil town,   Ruins
some 400m by 600m/440yd by 660yd in area, which was laid out according
to a plan. As well as numerous and generally one-storeyed private houses
it boasted several large bathing establishments, a market-hall, a Mithras
sanctuary and a forum.
The provision of water and the sewage system – water-pipes, disposal
pipes and heating installations – will also be of interest.

The archaeological museum at Aquincum

Amphitheatre of the Roman military town

In the 2nd c. A.D. the Romans built a large amphitheatre for their military camp at Aquincum. The ruins on the present-day Korvin Ottó utca were excavated in 1940. The arena, constructed on an elliptical plan, was 131m/143yd long and 107m/117yd broad, and had room for several thousand spectators who could enjoy battle games here as well as other spectacles.

Some historians are of the opinion that the Magyars used this theatre as a fortress in the 9th and 10th c. when they occupied the country.

Amphitheatre of the Roman civil town

In 1880 and 1937 the remains of the amphitheatre of the civil town of Aquincum were uncovered diagonally opposite the main excavation site. It originally occupied an area of about 80m by 90m/87yd by 98yd.

Ancient fortifications

On the opposite side of the road can be seen a restored section of the ancient town fortifications.

Pest

Centre

Situation and Importance

Until its union with Buda and Óbuda in 1872 Pest was an independent town, but for a long time it was overshadowed by the neighbouring royal town and development was difficult. Nevertheless, for many years Pest has had close links with Buda. The Romans maintained a "castrum contra Aquincum" here, the purpose of which was to protect the Danube crossing. The Hungarian rulers who resided in Buda visited Pest from time to time to attend services in what is now the Inner City Parish Church (see below). By the 15th c. Pest had become prosperous.

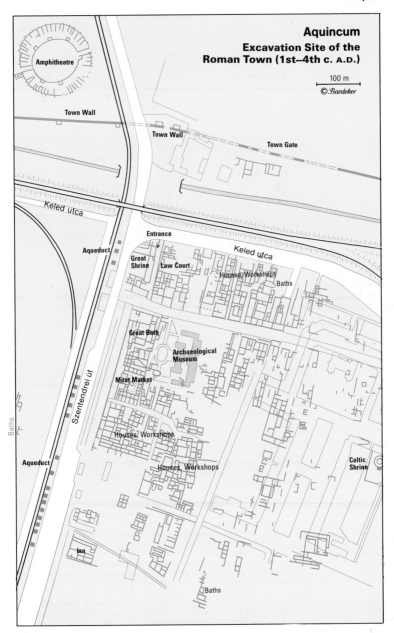

Aquincum

Excavation Site of the Roman Town (1st—4th c. A.D.)

100 m

© Baedeker

Amphitheatre

Town Wall

Town Wall

Town Gate

Keled utca

Aqueduct

Entrance

Keled utca

Great Shrine

Law Court

Houses, Workshops

Baths

Great Bath

Archaeological Museum

Szentendrei út

Meat Market

Houses, Workshops

Aqueduct

Houses, Workshops

Celtic Shrine

Baths

Inn

Baths

It was in the 19th c. that Pest attained its greatest prosperity as the town of craftsmen, traders and merchants; this is revealed by the numerous fine buildings which are still standing today. At that time the principal focus of population shifted from the Buda to the Pest side of the Danube. As early as 1830 there were more than 60,000 people in Buda, the majority of them living in the rapidly growing suburbs. The inner city forms the central business district of the Hungarian capital. Pest is the headquarters of the most important organs of government, parliament, ministries, etc., as well as leading cultural institutions such as universities and museums.

*Inner City
Parish Church

The twin-towered Inner City Parish Church (Belvárosi plébánia-templom) is the oldest church in Pest. It stands on the remains of the Roman Castrum Contra Aquincum at the Pest end of Elisabeth Bridge. As early as the 11th c. there was a small church here in which Bishop Gellért was buried in 1046. Extensive rebuilding in the Gothic manner took place under King Sigismund. The side chapels were added in the 15th c. During the Turkish occupation the church functioned as a mosque. On the south-west wall of the choir remains of a Turkish *mihrab* (niche showing the direction of Mecca) can still be seen. During the siege and retaking of the town by Austrian troops in the 17th c. the church was considerably damaged, and later rebuilt in Baroque style. In the late 19th c. it was refashioned in Gothic style by the architect Imre Steindl. In 1949 work began on rebuilding the church which had been severely damaged in the Second World War.
The juxtaposition of Baroque and Gothic styles is very impressive. The 18th c. side-altar of John the Baptist is a jewel of historical art. Also notable are the two Renaissance epitaphs in red and pale yellow marble and the pulpit constructed in 1808 by Ungnad.

*Elisabeth
Bridge

The modern Elisabeth Bridge (Erzsébet-híd) replaces a predecessor built at the turn of the century which, for many years, was the largest arched bridge in the world and which was destroyed in the Second World War. The modern suspension bridge, built between 1961 and 1964 to plans by Pál Sávoly, is 378m/413yd long and 27m/30yd wide.
There is a sculpture by György Zala of the earlier Hungarian Queen Elisabeth, who was murdered in Geneva in 1898.

Petőfi tér

North of the Pest end of Elisabeth Bridge lies Petőfi tér (Petőfi Square), named after the great Hungarian lyric poet Sándor Petőfi. The bronze Petőfi monument in the square is by Adolf Huszár (1882).

Greek church

On the east side of Petőfi tér stands the three-aisled Greek church (Ortodox Egyházi templom), erected in 1789 and rebuilt in the 19th c. to plans by the famous architect Ybl. Inside this large church are fine works of art by Nikolaus Jankovits, Anton Kochmeister and others.

Szabad
Sajtó útja

The Street of the Free Press (Szabad Sajtó útja) links the Elisabeth Bridge with busy Franciscan Square, on the southern edge of the Pest shopping centre.

Ferenciek tere

Ferenciek tere, the busiest square on the southern part of the "shopping centre", has several architectural styles and is one of the most charming squares in the town.
On the side facing the Danube are two pleasing buildings protected by towers, Klothild Palace and Mathild Palace, built in 1902 in Eclectic style.

*Paris Court

On the north side of the square lies the attractive complex of buildings known as Paris Court (Párizsi udvar), built in the most beautiful art nouveau style with elements of Italian and Turkish architecture.

*Franciscan
Church

The Franciscan Church (Ferenciek templom) dominates the north-west side of Ferenciek tere. This church, which was renovated a few years ago, dates from the 18th c. It is built in Baroque style and is the successor to a

church which Franciscan monks had founded on this site in the 13th century.
The façade facing the square is adorned with statues of saints as well as the arms of the Franciscan Order above the doorway. On the north-west exterior wall can be seen a bronze relief commemorating Baron Wesselényi, who saved numerous people from drowning during a flood in 1836.

The artists J. Fessl and F. Uhrl (1835) were responsible for the pretty Naiad Fountain outside the church.

Naiad Fountain

The bank of the Danube on the Pest side of the river between Chain Bridge and Elisabeth Bridge is locally known as the "Danube Corso" (Dunakorzó). From here, especially when illuminated at night, there is a fantastic view of the Fishermen's Bastion, Matthias Church, Castle Palace, the Gellért Monument, the Citadel and the Freedom Monument on Gellért Hill. The large luxury hotels Duna Inter-Continental, Fórum and Atrium Hyatt stand along the Danube Corso.

°Danube Corso

This square, lying in the very heart of the city of Pest, commemorates the writer Mihály Vörösmarty (1800–55); there is a marble monument (1908) to the poet. Around the square stand some faithfully restored commercial offices.

Vörösmarty tér

On the north side of Vörösmarty tér can be found the renowned Café Gerbeaud, which has been a popular meeting-place since the beginning of this century.

°Café Gerbeaud

On the west side of Vörösmarty tér will be seen the rear of the Pest Redoubt ("Vigadó"). Intended for festival occasions and all kinds of musical entertainment (Liszt, Brahms and Bartók all appeared here), the Vigadó was built between 1859 and 1864 to plans by Frigyes Feszl (1821–84), and is one of the most remarkable creations of Hungarian Romanticism. It was severely damaged at the end of the Second World War, but after very many years of careful restoration it was again opened in 1980.

°Vigadó
(Pest Redoubt)

In the Vigadó Gallery are exhibitions of works by famous artists.

Vigadó Gallery

The world-famous shopping precinct of Váci utca leads from Vörösmarty tér south-eastwards to Szabad Satjó út and the eastern end of Elisabeth Bridge, and thence to Fővám tér. Here there is a succession of boutiques, footwear and leather shops, jewellers, arts and crafts shops, offices of leading airline companies and branches of various commercial and service industries.

°Váci utca

The Pest Theatre (Pesti Szinház; Váci utca No. 9) occupies the former Hotel of the Seven Electoral Princes, where the twelve-year-old Franz Liszt gave his first concert in Pest in 1823. The foyer of the theatre with its beautiful dark mosaic work is very impressive.

Pest Theatre

The new Town Hall (Uj Városháza; Váci utca 62–64) was built by the architect Imre Steindl in Neo-Renaissance style between 1869 and 1875. There are wonderful mosaics by Károly Lotz in the Council Chamber.

New Town Hall

The Serbian church (Szerb templom), on the corner of Veres Pálné u. and Szerb u., was probably designed by the famous architect Andreas Mayerhoffer in the 18th c. The three-aisled nave is separated from the choir by an iconstasis painted in a manner which shows the influence of the Italian Renaissance.

Serbian Church

The large square at the Pest end of Chain Bridge commemorates the former US President Franklin D. Roosevelt. At the beginning of the last century markets were held here and Danube freighters discharged their cargoes. On the northern side of the square stands a memorial to Count István Széchenyi (see Famous People) by J. Engel (1880), and on the south side is one to Ferenc Deák (see Famous People) by A. Huszár (1882).

Roosevelt tér

*Gresham Palace | On the east side of Roosevelt tér can be seen one of the masterpieces of the Secessionist style in Budapest, Gresham Palace (Gresham palota) built in 1907. It was originally a traditional insurance office, but between the two world wars it became the Café Gresham, a well-known meeting place for artists.

*Hungarian Academy of Science. | The north side of Roosevelt tér is dominated by the monumental building of the Hungarian Academy of Science (Magyar Tudományos Akadémia); built in Neo-Renaissance style and founded on the initiative of Count István Széchenyi, it was completed in 1864. The plans were drawn up by the Berlin architect F. A. Stüler. The Academy, with which are now associated a number of research institutes, has a scientific library which enjoys world-wide renown, especially the Oriental Department. In the restored Festival Hall are some fine frescos by Károly Lotz.

Akadémia utca | In Akadémia utca, behind the Academy, there are two notable Classical buildings: at Akadémia utca 1, a house completed in 1835 with a fine façade and Corinthian wall pillars, where the Polish General József Bem (a renowned freedom fighter) once lived, and at Akadémia utca 3, an imposing building dating from 1836 and designed by the great architect József Hild.

Eötvös tér | Adjoining Roosevelt tér on the south lies the small Eötvös tér, with a monument to József Eötvös. On the south side of Eötvös tér stands the luxury hotel Atrium Hyatt.

**Parliament Building | Parliament Building (Országház) was constructed between 1884 and 1904 to plans by the famous architect Imre Steindl. It stands north of the Pest end of Chain Bridge along the Danube (Széchenyi rakpart) and is one of the landmarks of Budapest. The building, with no less than 691 rooms, 10 courtyards and 27 doorways, is 268m/820ft long and up to 118m/387ft wide, and consists of a central range with a dome 96m/315ft high, two 73m/240ft high towers on the loggia facing the Danube, and two side wings; the southern one is the Chamber of the House of Representatives and the northern one is Congress Hall. Each of these beautifully decorated rooms is crowned by a roof bearing four turrets.

The imposing façade on the bank of the Danube is embellished with no fewer than 88 statues including Hungarian hereditary princes, military leaders and kings. On the east side a flight of steps leads up to the main doorway which is flanked by two stone lions.

On the ceiling of the stairwell are some fine frescoes by Károly Lotz. On the first floor is the magnificent domed Hall (height 27m/88ft), with the dome supported on sixteen pillars; today the Hall is used mainly for official functions. To the south of it will be found the Conference Hall used by the cabinet. In the Hunting Room can be seen some fine paintings. Behind this, in the Gobelin Room, hangs a colossal wall tapestry which depicts an assembly of Magyar princes at the time when they occupied the country. In the Munkácsy Room can be seen the great painting by M. Munkácsy, "Conquest of the Country" (by the Magyars).

The building also contains the offices of the President and Prime Minister as well as those of several government bodies.

The Parliamentary Library has a comprehensive stock of legal, governmental and historical literature; it is reached by the south door on the side of the building facing the Danube.

*Kossuth Lajos tér | On the northern edge of the centre of Pest lies Kossuth tér, surrounded by monumental buildings. On the west side stands Parliament Building and on the east side the Neo-Renaissance Ethnographical Museum (see below) and the neo-classical Ministry of Agriculture and Food building.

On the northern lawns of the square stands a monument commemorating Lajos Kossuth (see Famous People) by Zsigmond Stróbl (1952); on the

Parliament building on the Danube bank at Pest ▶

The former Palace of Justice, now the Folklore Museum

southern lawn is an equestrian statue of Count Ferenc Rákóczi by János Pásztor (1935). On the square in front of the north front of the Parliament Building the famous sculptor Imre Varga unveiled a statue in 1975 of the politician Mihály Károlyi (1875–1955).

To the south of Parliament Building stands a pleasing statue of the great lyricist Attila József by László Márton.

*Ethnographical Museum

The Ethnographical Museum is housed in the former Palace of Justice, which had been built in 1896 to the designs of Alajos Hauszmann.

Over the tympanum, which is supported by six tall columns, can be seen a troika with the Goddess of Justice by K, Senyei. The frescos in the entrance hall are by K. Lotz.

The museum's extensive Hungarian collection includes articles of rural life, implements for handwork and craft, as well as unusual examples of craft and textiles. Special exhibitions are concerned with ethnic groups from central Asia and Siberia who are related to the Magyars, as well as with the development of various cultures.

Also of interest are the New Guinea collection of Biró and Fenichel, the African collection of Teleki and Torday and the more recent exhibits from Central Asia, Siberia, South America and, most importantly, those from the South Pacific.

Szabadság tér

Freedom Square (Szabadság tér), laid out in the last century after the demolition of a barracks where many Hungarian freedom fighters of 1848/49 were executed, forms with the surrounding buildings one of the most charming architectural ensembles of Budapest.

On the west side stands the Exchange Building, on the east the Hungarian National Bank (Magyar Nemzeti Bank). Both of these buildings were designed by the architect Ignác Alpár and date from 1905. The former Exchange is in Secessionist style, while the National Bank is a first-class example of a Late Classical building. The northern arc is lined by buildings

St Stephan's Basilica, in pure Neo-Renaissance style

in the Neo-Romanesque-eclectic manner. Near the bank, but oriented towards Hold utca, is the former Post Office Savings Bank (No. 4) by Ödön Lechner, who was here anxious to create a new Hungarian architectural style. The building, which was opened in 1901, is characterised by variegated majolica decoration.

St Stephen's Basilica (Szent István bazilika), in Neo-Renaissance style, is one of the most imposing ecclesiastical buildings of the Hungarian capital. The church is of monumental proportions with a central dome 96m/315ft high, and two 80m/262ft high towers at the west end. Building began in 1851. The plans were largely the work of Jószef Hild, the great exponent of Classical architecture. After Hild's death and the collapse of the dome in 1868, Miklós Ybl proposed new plans for the church. After Ybl's death in 1905 Josef Kauser completed the work.

°St Stephen's Basilica

Magnificent works of art adorn the interior, including figures by Alajos Stróbl and János Fadrusz. The mosaics on the dome were produced in the Salviati workshop in Venice. At the magnificent High Altar is a statue of St Stephen made of Carrara marble by Alajos Stróbl.

Of particular note is the painting on the second side-altar to the right of the main entrance; it is a work by Gyula Benczúr and shows St Stephen offering the Hungarian crown to Mary.

The sacristy, which has been converted to a chapel, contains the "Holy Laws" drawn up by the great Hungarian ruler.

The Fessler statues are one of the special features of St Stephen's Basilica. On the exterior wall of the apse the Twelve Apostles can be seen; the Four Evangelists stand in niches on the outside of the dome; in niches on the towers of the main façade are likenesses of the Fathers of the Church, while in the tympanum of the narthex can be seen the Patrona Hungariae, surrounded by Hungarian saints.

Almost 2ha/5 acres in extent, Erzsébet tér (Elisabeth Square; formerly known as Engels tér) was once the site of a cemetery. In the centre of a lawn

Erzsébet tér

stands the Danubius Fountain, designed by Ybl in 1883 and originally set up on Kalvin tér. The figures on the fountain, by Fessler, symbolise "Mother" Danube and her "Daughters", the three main tributaries, the Drau, the Tisza and the Save.
Of considerable architectural merit are the buildings in the classical manner in József Attila utca on the north side of the square.

Deák Ferenc tér

Deák Ferenc tér adjoins Erzsébet tér on the south-east, and is one of the most important inner-city traffic junctions. Three Underground lines meet here. Anker Palace on its east side, formerly the head office of an insurance company, should not be overlooked.

*Evangelical
Church

Of special merit is the Evangelical Church (Evangélikus templom; Lutheran Church), which was built at the beginning of the 19th c. to plans by Mihály Pollack. The main façade was rebuilt by József Hild in 1856. Visitors will find much to admire in the copy of Raphael's "Transfiguration" on the altar.
The church is at present the home of the Evangelical National Museum (Evangélikus Országos Múzeum). It contains some very interesting exhibits of church history and some valuable gold work. Martin Luther's testament is also kept here.
Near the church stands the minister's house and the former Evangelical secondary school, both fine neo-classical buildings.

Underground
Museum

The Underground Museum (Földalatti Vasúti Múzeum) occupies a tunnel dug in 1896 for the then first Underground railway in continental Europe. Various exhibits, especially some early Art Nouveau-style carriages, illustrate the development of this mass transport undertaking which was to prove so important for the Hungarian capital.

József Nádor tér

A short distance west of Elisabeth Square lies József Nádor tér. This square commemorates Archduke Joseph of Habsburg who was elected Palatine of Hungary in 1796 and who did so much for Budapest. Johann Halbig created this monument to him in 1859. The buildings around the square still retain something of the atmosphere of the last century, especially No. 1 which was designed by J. Hild.
Nearby stands the tall and modern administration building of the Ministry of Finance.

*Martinelli tér

Martinelli tér was still in use as a market-place in the last century, but today it has become a busy traffic intersection in Pest. Two well-restored office and business premises are deserving of mention; these are the former Török Bank (No. 3; 1906 by Hegedüs and Böhm) and Béla-Lajta House (No. 5, built 1912), with a noteworthy glass façade and rich ceramic decoration.

Servit Church

Of architectural interest is the Servit church (Szerviták templom), on the south-east side of the square. Built in the 18th c. and rebuilt in the 19th., it has a very fine Baroque interior.

Biermann István
tér

Nearby lies Biermann István tér, with a beautiful Danaid fountain by Sidló (1933).

City Hall of
Budapest

This Baroque building, which is now the home of the Municipal Council of Budapest, was built between 1716 and 1728 to designs by Anton Erhard Martinelli. Its first use was as a home for those wounded in the Austro-Turkish campaign. Above the doorways of the main façade are two fine reliefs, commemorating Emperor Charles IV (Hungarian King Charles III) and Prince Eugene of Savoy.
In the south entrance gateway on Kossuth Lajos utca there is a statue of Pallas Athene by Adami (1785). At the southern end of the building can be seen a relief by M. Kovács (1949) commemorating the rebuilding after the Second World War.

On Kamermayer tér stands an aluminium monument by the artist   Kamermayer tér
B. Szabados in memory of the first Mayor of the newly formed city of
Budapest in 1873.

To the south are the Regional Council Offices, a building with three inner   Regional
courtyards. It was built mainly in the 19th c., and it is where the elected   Council
members of the nineteen Regional Councils hold their meetings. The archi-   Offices
tects responsible were János Hild and, in particular, Mátyás Zitterbath jnr.
In the first courtyard, which is surrounded by arcades, can be seen memorial tablets honouring the freedom fighters of 1848/49 and the victims of the
Uprising of 1956.

*Inner Ring (Kis körút)

The Inner Ring (covering Fovám tér at the eastern end of Freedom Bridge–   Situation
Kálvin tér–Múseum körút–Károlyi körút–Deák tér–Erszébet tér–Bajcsy-Zsi-
linsky út) encircles the old town centre of Pest and follows the former town
walls.

Károly körút (Charles Ring, formerly known as Tanács körút, or Councillors'   Károly körút
Ring) leads south-east from Deák tér. In recent years it has become an
important business street. On its north-east side stands Madách House
(1937), the home of the Madách Studio Theatre. Nearby is the exhibition
hall of the City Council (No. 4) together with the Budapest Film Museum
(Film-múzeum; No. 3) in which performances are given mostly of old films.

Further east, at the beginning of Dohány utca, stands the Pest Synagogue,   *Synagogue
built between 1854 and 1859 to the plans of the Viennese architect Ludwig
Förster. The romanticised Moorish-Byzantine style of this three-aisled temple is very pleasing to the eye; Frigyes Feszl was responsible for the fine
interior.
The Jewish Museum (Orságos Zsidó Vallási és Történeti Gyüjtemény) is
housed in an annexe of the synagogue. In 1944/45 the garden, surrounded
by arcades, was made into a cemetery for the victims of the Budapest
ghetto.

In Museum Ring, further to the south-east, two leading Hungarian cultural   Múzeum körút
institutions are located: the National Museum and the Neo-Renaissance
buildings of the Faculty of Natural Science of Eötvös-Lóránd University,
which were designed by Imre Steindl.

The National Museum (Magyar Nemzeti Múzeum, at Múzeum körút Nos.   **National
14–16) was founded in 1802 by Count Széchenyi and is housed in a large   Museum
neo-classical building erected in 1847 to the plans of Mihály Pollack. The
portico of the building is very impressive, with Corinthian pillars supporting a triangular gable adorned with allegorical figures.
In front of the building stands a monument to the famous Hungarian poet
János Arany (1817–82; see Famous People), which was the work of Alajos
Stróbl in 1893. In the park-like museum garden other busts and monuments of notable personalities can be seen.
In the wide foyer of the museum are many interesting objects from Roman
and medieval times. Much emphasis is placed on the history of Hungary
from the occupation by the Magyars until the year 1849. A specially
guarded room houses the Crown of St Stephen and his sceptre, orb and
sword, together with the coronation robe.
As well as portraying the country's history, the museum also devotes itself
to the natural history of Hungary. The collections of geological and zoolog-
ical specimens are most informative.

Just to the west of the National Museum lies the little garden known as   Károlyi Palace
Károlyi-kert (Charles Garden), which adjoins the historic Károlyi Palace,   Károlyi-kert
built in the neo-classical style and named after its former owner, Mihály

143

Károlyi (1875–1955), politician and Hungarian President from 1918 to 1919. In 1848/49 the Austrian General Julius Haynau, who was to defeat the freedom fighters, resided here.

*Petőfi Museum

Károlyi Palace houses this museum which contains memorabilia, texts and sound archives of the leading Hungarian poet and author Sándor Petőfi (see Famous People).

*University
Church

South of the palace stands University Church, probably the most beautiful Baroque building in Budapest. It was built between 1725 and 1742 to plans by Andreas Mayerhoffer for the Pauline Order established in Hungary. Its two mighty towers were not completed until 1771.
The fine frescos on the ceiling are the work of J. Bergl (1776), the choirstalls and some further sculptures are by Josef Hebenstreit. The copy of the "Black Madonna of Czestochowa" was probably completed about 1720.

Former
Pauline
Monastery

This 18th c. monastery near the University Church has housed since 1805 the Theological Faculty of the first Hungarian University which was transferred to Pest in 1784.
The library, finished in 1775, has richly decorated bookcases, a gallery running round it and a wonderful ceiling fresco by Pietro Rivetti (1803). Visits to the library are by prior arrangement only.

Kálvin tér

Kálvin tér (Calvin Square), on the southern edge of the centre of Pest, is now an important traffic junction. A few years ago, during building work, the remains of a medieval city gate were uncovered. There are some interesting buildings around the square, including the former inn, The Two Lions (No. 8), dating from 1818. A little to the east is Baross tér is the Ervin-Szabó Library in a 19th c. Neo-Baroque building by A. Meining.

Reformed Church

This single-aisled church in a severe Classical style was designed by József Hofrichter and József Hild and built between 1816 and 1859. The four columns of its notable portico support a tympanum. The interior has a good coffered ceiling and contains the funerary monument of Countess Zichy. The church treasury houses valuable articles of goldsmiths' work dating from the 17th, 18th and 19th centuries.

Vámház körút

Vámház körút (Department Store Ring; previously named Tolbuhin körút, or Tolbuhin Ring) leads from Kálvin tér to the Danube, and in recent years has become a busy shopping street. This is largely due to the proximity of the central market hall at the Pest end of Freedom Bridge (Szabadság-híd). The University of Economics stands nearby.

Freedom Bridge
(Szabadság-híd)

The steel Freedom Bridge, which links Gellért tér on the Buda bank of the Danube with Fővám tér (formerly Dimitrov tér) on the Pest side, was opened to traffic in 1896. The bridge, which is 331m/362yd long and 20m/22yd wide, was destroyed during the Second World War but was the first bridge to be rebuilt, and it was reopened to traffic in 1946.

*Outer Ring (Nagy körut)

Situation

The 4km/2½ mile long Outer Ring starts at the east end of Margaret Bridge in the north and then continues in a semi-circle, almost parallel to the Inner Ring, around the city of Pest to the east end of Petőfi Bridge. It consists of the following sectors: Szent István körút–Nyugati tér–Teréz körút–Oktogon–Erzsébet körút–Blaha Lujza tér–József körút–Ferenc körút–Boráros tér. The Ring, which was opened to traffic in 1896 and along which can be seen many imposing buildings dating from the end of the last century, follows the course of an arm of the Danube which has been filled in although, in 1867, proposals had been put forward to make it navigable for ships.

Svent István körút (St Stephen's Ring) is the most northerly sector of the Outer Ring. Note the Theatre of Comedy (Vigszínház; No. 14), which was designed in the 1890s by the Viennese architects Fellner and Helmer. The theatre was destroyed in the Second World War but has now been completely rebuilt.

Svent István körút

Nyugati tér (formerly Marx tér), which from 1978 was redesigned and extended at considerable expense, is also the busy forecourt of the West Station (Nyugati pályaudvar), a protected building which was erected in the 1870s by the Parisian firm of Eiffel. The first trains on Hungarian territory were run in 1846 from this site.
Opposite the station stands the famous "Skala" department store, around which in recent years "grey" and "black" market trading has developed to a degree unequalled elsewhere.

Nyugati tér
*West Station

Terz körút (Theresa Ring) leads south-east from West Station to the "Octagon", with its unique Neo-Renaissance buildings. Here the Outer Ring is crossed by the boulevard known as Andrássy út (see below).

Teréz körút
Octagon

Batthyány Palace, built by Alajos Hauszmann in 1884 for Count Batthyány, is worthy of note; it is an exact copy of the Palazzo Strozzi in Florence.

Batthyány Palace

Erzsébet körút (Elisabeth Ring) forms part of the Outer Ring to the southeast. Along it will be found such interesting buildings as the Hotel Royal, built in the 1890s by the architect Ray, Madách Theatre (Madách Színház; Nos. 29–33) with wall mosaics by Eszter Mattioni, and the Café New York.

Erzsébet körút

The Café New York (formerly Café Hungária), a favourite rendezvous of writers, publishers and various well-known personalities during the first thirty years of this century, is on the ground floor of the Palais New York built by A. Hauszmann, K. Giergl and F. Korb. The Neo-Renaissance building was severely damaged during the Second World War but has been restored. The Late Eclectic interior architecture is much admired.

*Café New York

This square, situated where the Outer Ring crosses Rákóczi út, is named after the famous Hungarian actress Lujza Blaha (1850–1926), who had great success in the National Theatre which was formerly situated here.

Blaha Lujza tér

József körút (Joseph Ring) now continues southwards through the suburb of Joseph Town. To the east of the junction of József körút and Baross utca stands the imposing twin-towered Joseph Town Parish Church. It was built at the end of the 18th c. in Late Baroque style, in accordance with plans drawn up by J. Thalherr. Fine examples of ecclesiastical art are the High Altar by József Hild and the reredos, the "Apotheosis of St Joseph", by the famous Viennese painter Leopold Kupelmaier.

József körút
*Joseph Town
Parish Church

In front of the church stands a monument to Péter Pázmány, the famous Archbishop of Esztergom and founder of the first Hungarian university.

Pázmány
Monument

*Andrássy út

This Budapest boulevard, which is 2·5km/1½ miles long, was laid out from 1872 and leads in a north-easterly direction first to the "Octagon" and thence to Hosök tere (Heroes' Square). Grand palaces, important cultural buildings and fine old villas line this imposing thoroughfare which since 1896 has also been the course of one of the oldest underground lines in Europe.

Location

The Museum of the Hungarian Post Office (Posta Múzeum; No. 3) is housed in a most unusual building which was designed by György Czigler in the 1880s. Highlights of the collection include the telephone used by Emperor Franz Joseph I and a 1919 transmitter.

Postal Museum

*State Opera

Miklós Ybl drew up the plans for the prestigious Hungarian State Opera (Allami Operaház), which was built between 1875 and 1884 in Neo-Renaissance style. It was renovated a few years ago at considerable expense.

The interior boasts a magnificent foyer with a double marble staircase. The auditorium possesses unusually good acoustics. The ceiling frescos by Károly Lotz and the wall-paintings by Mór Than are masterpieces of their kind. The statues of Franz Liszt and Ferenc Erkel, the first Director of the Opera, are by Alajos Stróbl.

Nagymezo utca "Pest Broadway"

Nagymezo utca crosses Andrássy út near the State Opera, and for a long time has been known as the "Pest Broadway". Its reputation is due not only to the various night-clubs, such as the Moulin Rouge, but also to the number of theatres in this street, such as the Municipal Operetta Theatre and the Thália Theatre.

Jókai tér, Liszt Ferenc tér

Pest Broadway is followed by Jókai tér (with a monument by Alajos Stróbl on the left) and Liszt Ferenc tér (Franz Liszt Square on the right) with the Franz Liszt Academy of Music (see below).

*Franz Liszt Academy of Music

The Academy of Music established by Franz Liszt is housed in a building designed by Flóris Korb and Kálmán Giergl between 1904 and 1907.

The Grand Hall on the ground floor occupies two levels and has room for an audience of 1,200; it boasts exceptionally good acoustics. Most concerts are now held in the Small Hall on the first floor.

Musical Academy, Puppet Theatre, Academy of Fine Art

Other buildings of note along Andrássy út include the former Musical Academy (No. 67; architect A. Lang, 1879; at one time the residence of Franz Liszt), the State Puppet Theatre (Allami Bábszínház, No. 69; architect A. Lang, 1877) and finally the Academy of Fine Art (Kepzőművészeti Főiskola, No. 71; architect L. Rauscher, 1875).

Kodály köröND

Kodály köröND, a beautifully laid-out circular open space, is named after the great Hungarian composer Kodály. This square is bounded by statues of Hungarian freedom fighters.

Kodály House

The former residence of Zoltán Kodály at No. 89 is now a museum and open to the public. Opposite stands a neat Neo-Renaissance palace designed by G. Pertschacher.

*Ferenc-Hopp Museum of East Asian Art

This museum at No. 103 occupies the house of the art collector Ferenc Hopp (1833–1919), and the interesting collection comprises Japanese, Korean and Indian *objets d'art*, including lacquer and bronze work, porcelain, jewellery and book illustrations. There is also an archaeological collection and sculptures in the museum garden.

The museum's Chinese collection has been transferred to the China Museum in the Ráth villa at Gorkij fasor 12 further south.

Heroes' Square/City Woodland Park (Hosök tere/Városliget)

*Heroes' Square

At the northern end of Andrássy út lies the extensive Heroes' Square (Hosök tere), which also forms the western edge of City Woodland Park (Városliget; see below). The layout of the square is chiefly the work of the architect Albert Schickedanz, who was also largely responsible for the huge buildings of the Museum of Fine Art (see below) and the Art Gallery (see below) which flank the square.

Millennium Monument

The Millennium Monument (Millénniumi emlékmű), unveiled at the end of the 19th c., is the dominant feature of the square. The 36m/118ft high column is crowned by a figure of the Archangel Gabriel by György Zala. Around the plinth can be seen a group of horsemen in bronze representing the conquering Magyar Prince Árpád and six of his fellow warriors.

Heroes' Square, laid out by Albert Schickedanz

On either side of the column colonnades extend in a semi-circle. Between the individual pillars stand statues of Hungarian rulers, and above the corner pillars are beautiful works in bronze by Zala. In front of the Millennium Monument stands a memorial to the Unknown Soldier.

This splendid building in Classical-eclectic style, which was designed by Albert Schickedanz and completed in 1895, serves as an exhibition gallery for various artists.

Art Gallery
(Műcsarnok)

The Budapest Museum of Fine Arts is one of the major European art museums. Its collection of Italian masters of the Renaissance enjoys an international reputation.

**Museum of
Fine Arts

The neo-classical monumental building was completed in 1906 to the designs of Albert Schickedanz and Fülöp Herzog. The portico is very impressive; its huge Corinthian columns bear a tympanum with a relief inspired by one on the gable of the Temple of Zeus in Olympia.

Exhibited on the ground floor are Egyptian and Greco-Roman antiquities, including statues and statuettes, gravestones, reliefs, gold and bronze work, vases and terracotta. In the nearby Department of Modern Sculpture will be found works such as Rodin's "Eternal Spring" and "A Mother's Sorrow" by Meštrovič. Also on the ground floor are some incredibly rich drawings and engravings by Raphael, Tintoretto, Dürer, Cranach, Altdorfer, Rembrandt and others.

The museum's real treasures are to be found in the twenty-three rooms which make up the Art Gallery. The following are some of the most outstanding works on display: Tuscan painting of the 13th–15th c. (including Giovanni da Ponte and Taddeo di Bartolo), works of art of the 14th–16th c. from central and northern Italy, (including some by Giovanni Santi, Domenico and Rodolfo Ghirlandaio, Gentile Bellini. Michele Pannonio, Tintoretto, Veronese, and Raphael's "Eszterházy Madonna"), Italian Baroque artists (including Bernardo Bellotto, Bernard Strozzi, Giovanni

147

Vajdahunyad Castle in the City Woodland Park

Battista Tiepolo), Dutch and Flemish masters of the 16th and 17th c. (including works by Hans Memling, Jan Brueghel the Elder, Rembrandt, Frans Hals, Jan van Goyen, Rubens), 16th and 17th c. Spanish masters, including El Greco, Esteban, de Ribera, Goya ("Portrait of Señora Bermúdez") and Velázquez ("Farmers at Table"). Also of note are various German and Austrian masters of the 15th–18th c., such as Lucas Cranach, Hans Baldung Grien, Albrecht Dürer and Franz Anton Maulbertsch. 19th and 20th c. works include those by Cézanne, Gauguin, Leibl, Manet, Monet, Toulouse-Lautrec, Waldmüller, Arp, Chagall and Picasso.

*City
Woodland Park

The Városliget (City Woodland Park) in the north-east of Pest was laid out in the 19th c. in accordance with the ideas of the French landscape-gardener Nebbion. Over the years the park has become a major public attraction through its cultural and recreational facilities, as listed below.

*Castle
Vajdahunyad

Castle Vajdahunyad was built by Ignác Alpár in 1896 on the occasion of the millennium festival. In his work Alpár tried to combine several architectural features which are characteristic of Hungary. The greater part of the building complex was based on the castle of the Turkish conqueror Hunyadi, which can be seen in the present-day Romanian town of Hunedoara.

Agricultural
Museum

The Agricultural Museum (Mezőgazdasági Múzeum) is housed in the Baroque palace of Castle Vajdahunyad. The interesting exhibits include those covering the raising of animals, the production of wine, fishing and hunting. There are also special temporary exhibitions.

Anonymus
Monument

In the south-eastern courtyard of Castle Vajdahunyad stands a memorial by Miklós Ligeti (1903), honouring Anonymus, an unknown historical scribe of the 12th/13th c. who, it is believed, composed the first Hungarian chronicle.

Zoological-
Botanical Garden

The Budapest Zoological-Botanical Garden (Fővárosi Állat-és Növénykert) lies in the north-west part of Városliget. It was laid out in the 1860s and ever since has been very popular with the citizens of Budapest. Among the attractions are the birds of prey cage, the rock garden, the polar bear and sea-lion pool, the children's zoo, the palm house and the aquaria.

The Civic Circus on the eastern edge of the zoo area (Fővárosi Nagycirkusz) is one of the most popular institutions of its kind in Europe. The circus tradition here goes back to 1891, when the first performances were staged.

Civic Circus

Every year thousands of visitors come to the "Budapest Tivoli" in the north-eastern corner of the park.

Pleasure Park
(Vidám Park)

Széchenyi baths (Széchenyi-fürdő) in the northern part of Városliget comprises an open-air bath and a covered bath in Neo-Baroque style with steam and normal baths; it is one of the largest buildings of its kind in Europe. The warm water (over 70°C/158°F) comes from a spring discovered in the previous century. The baths are visited by up to two million people a year.

*Széchenyi Baths

South-east of the park lies the Budapest "Sports Town" with the Népstadion (People's Stadium) as its centre. This arena, built in 1953 to the plans of K. Dávid, can accommodate 70,000 spectators.

Népstadion

Around the stadium are other sporting facilities: the Kisstadion (Small Stadium; 1962; 15,000 seats), which has already served as a stage for many show-business artistes; the Millenáris Cycle Race-track (1896), the Testnevelési és Sport múzeum (Museum of Physical Culture and Sport), the ultra-modern Új Sportscarnok (New Sports Hall; 1981; 12,500 seats) and a number of other sports halls.

Along both sides of Ifjúság útja (Youth Street) stand sculptures in praise of sport.

Ifjúság útja

On returning from the stadium to the city centre the visitor will pass East Station (Keleti pályaudvar). A main terminus, the station was completed in 1884 to the plans of J. Feketeházy and G. Rochlitz and has been renovated several times since. The main façade, in Neo-Renaissance style, is adorned with two statues of James Watt and George Stephenson. Murals by Károly Lotz and Mór Than embellish the prestigious station concourse.

East Station

In the square outside the station stands a memorial by A. Szécsi (1898) in honour of the former Trade and Transport Minister Gábor Baross.

Baross Memorial

The Kerepesi Cemetery (Kerepesi temeto; Pantheon Cemetery) just south of East Station is one of the largest in Budapest. Since the 1950s it has been a cemetery of honour in which notable people are buried. The Munkásmozgalmi Pantheon (Pantheon of the Workers' Movement) is a monumental building by József Körner, with artistic details by Zoltán Kiss. The mausoleums of Lajos Kossuth, Lajos Batthyány and Ferenc Deák have places of honour; they were designed by Gerstl and Stróbl, Schickedanz and Gerstner respectively.

Kerepesi Cemetery

Üllői út leads from Kálvin tér (Inner Ring) along an arterial road to the south-east. The section near the centre is flanked by a number of very well-maintained neo-classical buildings. Of especial note is the former residence of the composer Ferenc Erkel (No. 17; architect Miklós Ybl) as well as some of the older buildings of Semmelweis University.

Üllői út

The Budapest Museum of Applied Arts (Iparművészeti Múzeum), one of the oldest of its kind, dates from 1872; it is housed in a three-storey building erected between 1893 and 1896 to the designs of Ödön Lechner and Gyula Pártos. With its domed projecting ressaut it is an outstanding example of the Oriental-Hungarian Secessionist style.

**Museum of
Applied Arts

The red granite facing of the exterior (prepared in the Zsolnay porcelain factory of Pécs) and the ceramic work which beautifies the roofs and corners are particularly fine.

The collection is on five floors and includes furniture, textiles, work in precious metals, glass, ceramics and carved ivory, jewellery and leather-work. The items of goldsmith's work from the Eszterházy treasure chamber, which have been lovingly restored after being damaged in the Second World War, are of very high quality.

Ludovika tér

Further south lies the triangular Ludovika tér, an open space forming part of the campus of Semmelweis University. The University's twenty-three storey building makes it one of the tallest landmarks in the city.

Botanical Garden of the University

To the north off Ludovika tér are the Botanical Gardens of the University (Fuvészkert), laid out in 1847 and now containing more than 7000 different species of plant.
The Early Classic administration building dating from 1802 is also worthy of note.

* Népliget

With an area of 112ha/277 acres Népliget (People's Park) to the south-east is the largest park in Budapest. It was laid out in the 1860s, and was refurbished some time ago in accordance with the latest horticultural ideas. Its old trees, flower-beds, greenswards, fountains and playing areas make it extremely popular.

Planetarium

The Planetarium, opened in 1977 in the south-east part of Népliget, is one of the most modern of its kind in eastern Europe. In the dome-room visitors can see an astro-show made possible by the use of Zeiss-Jena projection equipment.

*Danube

Boat trips

During the warm months of the year these depart daily from the landing-stages at Vigadó tér (on the Pest bank) and Bem József tér (on the Buda bank).

Course of the river

The Danube (Hungarian "Duna") flows through Budapest from north to south; within the city boundaries its widest part (640m/700yd) is in the north of the city just below the junction of the two arms which enclose the island of Szentendre (Szentendrei-sziget). The river is at its narrowest (283m/310yd) below Gellért Hill; here it is about 9m/30ft deep.

Flooding

Until the late 19th c. rises in the water level caused major problems in the districts near the Danube. At such times the width of the river could exceed 1000m/1100yd, and in the lower lying parts of the city considerable damage could result. Therefore, in the second half of the last century, measures to regulate the flow of the water were urgently put in hand.

Waterway

With the expansion of industry in Budapest and in locations further upstream, the Danube became of increasing importance for the movement of goods and the capacity of the port installations of the island of Csepel (Csepel-sziget) was considerably increased. Along the Danube Corso on the Pest bank landing stages for national and international passenger ships were built and these were heavily used.

Bridges

The Danube is at present spanned by two railway bridges (the New Pest Bridge and the South Rail bridge) and by six road bridges (Árpád Bridge, Margaret Bridge, Chain Bridge, Elisabeth Bridge, Freedom Bridge and Petőfi Bridge).

Surroundings

*Buda Upland

The Buda Upland forms the natural western boundary of the Hungarian capital. The hills, consisting of dolomite, chalk, clay and marl are, for the most part, wooded and have long been very popular with the inhabitants of Budapest as a local recreation area. A close network of paths, fine scenery, games and sports facilities, a pioneer railway, cafés, etc., testify to the attractions of this beautiful upland area.

Three Frontier Hill (Hármashatár-hegy; 497m/1631ft) rises to the north within the boundary of Budapest. From its almost bare summit there is a fine view of Óbuda.

Three Frontier Hill

Below the top of the hill to the north-east can be seen the strangely-shaped Guckler Rock (Guckler-szikla).

Guckler Rock

2km/1¼ miles north-west of Three Frontier Hill rises Csúcs-hegy (445m/1460ft), from which there is a beautiful view.

Csúcs-hegy

Below to the south in charming Paul's Valley is a stalactitic cave (Pálvögyi cseppkőbarlang) which is well worth visiting.

Paul's Valley Caves

János-hegy rises in the west of Buda. It is the highest eminence in the Hungarian capital (529m/1736ft), and there is a magnificent view from the almost 24m/79ft high observation tower built in 1910. János-hegy has also been made attractive for winter-sports enthusiasts by the installation of a chair-lift, a ski-jump, a piste and a ski-lift.

János-hegy (John's Hill)

In the west of the city stands Szabadság-hegy (Freedom Hill), once known as the Swabian Mountain. During the Turkish Wars there was an army camp here. Over the years well-to-do inhabitants of Budapest have settled here, and today it is a smart area with fine villas, the result of the industrial boom, and some architecturally interesting, ultra-modern bungalows.

Szabadság-hegy

From Városmajor Park a cog-wheel railway, which was planned back in the 19th c., ascends Szabadság-hegy and Széchenyi-hegy (439m/1441ft; Hungarian Television transmitter). Up here are several tourist hotels and nursing homes.

Széchenyi-hegy

A narrow-gauge pioneer railway, opened in 1951 and staffed by children and young people under the supervision of adults, provides an excursion into this especially charming and scenic part of the Buda Upland.

Pioneer railway

*Budafok (formerly Promonter)

The scenically charming district of Budafok in the south of the Hungarian capital on the right bank of the Danube was famous up to the second half of the 19th c. for its viticulture. A maze of wine cellars and subterranean tunnels still bear witness to its former reputation.

Situation and Importance

A particularly charming Baroque church, completed in 1756, stands in the old village square. Features of the interior include an altar-painting by Altomonte and a pulpit in Rococo style. Also of note are sculptures dating from the time when the church was built. Near the church, Péter-Pál utca climbs up the hill, and along it a number of buildings from previous centuries have been preserved.

Baroque church

In Budafok cemetery, south-west of the church, there are some beautiful Baroque and neo-classical tombstones.

Cemetery

The headquarters of the National Wine Producers (Állami Pincegazdaság; Kossuth Lajos utca 84) and the Budafok Wine Producers (Budafoki Pincegazdaság) still make use of part of the considerable network of cellars and tunnels. A wine-cellar furnished in the traditional manner is the "Borkatakomba", at Nagytétényi út 63.

Many of the cellars were lived in at one time.

Wine Cellars (viewing by appointment)

Csepel

Situation and Importance
Csepel (Csepel-sziget), District XXI of the Hungarian capital, is situated on an island in the Danube and is the headquarters of the Csepel Vas-és Fémművek (Csepel Iron and Metal Works). This undertaking, which produced goods ranging from steel pipes to bicycles, once employed many thousands of workers; today, however, it finds itself in the middle of a serious financial crisis.

Free Port
On the west side of Csepel lies the largest Free Port anywhere on the Danube, with an annual turnover of more than 3 million tonnes.

Swimming-bath
The riverside swimming-bath at Csepel, fed by a thermal spring, is the third largest of its kind in Budapest. It is situated on the Soroksári Duna, a branch of the river on the east side of Csepel Island.

Érd

Situation
The Budapest suburb of Érd (106m/348ft; pop. 44,000) lies on the right bank of the Danube 20km/12½ miles downstream from the city centre. There were settlers here in the Middle Ages. The town has developed rapidly following the great wave of industrialisation in the early 20th century.

Parish church
The Parish church (Ófalu, Mecset utca), originally built in the 15th c. in Gothic style and later converted to Baroque, is well worth a visit.

Church of Our Lady Érdliget
The Church of Our Lady in Érdliget (Tálya utca 4) is a very fine example of modern Hungarian church architecture. It was built in 1983 to the plans of István Szabó. The front and rear glass fronts are asymmetrically offset, thereby providing the interior with floods of light.

Hungarian Geographical Collection
The comprehensive Hungarian Geographical Collection at Budai út 4 (open: Tue.–Fri. 2pm–6pm, Sat./Sun. 10am–6pm) is housed in a neo-classical mansion designed by J. Hild. The collection includes documents and other items belonging to Hungarian geographers and globetrotters.

Ferihegy Airport
Ferihegy Airport, 16km/10 miles south-east of the city centre, is Hungary's only international airport. It is also used by the national airline Malév.
Even before the political changes which took place in 1989 it was becoming clear that the old terminal (Ferihegy I) was bursting at the seams and could no longer cope with the increasing numbers of tourists and businessmen flying to Hungary. To meet these new demands the airport has recently been extended and modernised and Ferihegy II terminal built. It can now handle 4 million passengers a year.

Hungaroring

Situation and Importance
Situated 16km/10 miles north-east of the city centre, near Mogyoród, the Hungaroring motor racing circuit was opened in 1986. In August every year important Formula I races are held here. In addition, highly-rated motor cycle and trucking competitions take place, such as the "Truck Trophy".
Technical details: total length 4014m/4390yd, maximum gradient 7%, longest straight 700m/766yd. There are 25,000 seats and 150,000 standing places for spectators.

Kispest (Little Pest)

Situation and Importance
Kispest has existed only since 1871 and is now part of District XIX. It is the headquarters of a number of large industrial concerns, including engineering works, the Ganz industrial combine , textile factories, etc.

Wekerle Settlement
Of particular interest from the town-planning point of view is the so-called "Wekerle Settlement", which was methodically laid out on a chess-board pattern between 1908 and 1925. It comprises more than 1000 dwellings.

Kobánya

Kobánya (= quarry) forms District X of Budapest. Its name indicates that, until late into the last century, building stone was quarried here. In the lengthy tunnels various beers are now stored and mushrooms grown.

Situation and Importance

In the centre of Kobánya stands the Church of St Ladislaus (Szent László-templom), which was designed by Ödön Lechner and built at the turn of the century. The architecture combines elements of Neo-Gothic and Secessionist styles. There is some fine Zsolnay ceramic work to be seen on the altars and pulpit.

Church of St Ladislaus

Rottenbill Park is named after a former Burgomaster of Pest. Zoltán Kiss created the impressive red granite statue of Don Quixote.

Rottenbill Park

The Greek-Catholic Trinity Chapel (Kápolna) is one of the oldest buildings in Kobánya. This little Baroque church dates from *c.* 1740 and has a very fine Baroque altar.

Kápolna

The Budapest Fire Brigade Museum (Tuzoltó Múzeum; Martinovics tér 12; open: Tue.–Sun. 9am–4pm) contains not only documents about the history of the fire brigade but also a collection of rare historic fire-fighting equipment.

Fire Brigade Museum

The Budapest HUNGEXPO exhibition grounds are situated in the north of Kobánya. International fairs are held here every year (May and September/October) and there is also a tourism exhibition in March which is well attended. Every five years one of the largest agricultural shows in eastern Europe is held here.

HUNGEXPO

In the most easterly part of Kobánya lies the vast New Cemetery (Új köztemető) with several thousand burial plots. Many of the victims of the 1956 uprising are buried here.

Új köztemető (Cemetery)

On June 16th 1989, the 31st anniversary of his execution, the body of Imre Nagy, prime minister in 1956, was reinterred in burial plot 301, together with those of his comrades.
This national memorial is open to the public daily from 8am to 8pm.

Burial plot 301

Nagytétény

Nagytétény is the most southerly part of Budapest (District XXII) on the Buda side of the Danube and is largely an agricultural region. From the 2nd to the 5th c. there was a Roman military camp here.
In Nagytétény, which was probably named after a Magyar leader, viticulture played a major role from early times, but in the last few decades this has gradually declined in importance.

Situation and Importance

The major place of interest in Nagytétény is the Baroque castle (Kastély; Csókásy Pál utca 9–11; open: Tue.–Sun. 10am–6pm) , which now houses a branch of the Museum of Applied Arts. This great country house was built in the 18th c., using remains of its 15th c. predecessor.

*Castle Museum

Of interest are some finely constructed items of 15th to 19th c. furniture, (predominantly of Hungarian and German origin), and a collection of stove tiles and stoves. Displayed in some of the rooms are valuable paintings, carpets, china and clocks dating from the 18th and 19th c. In the castle stables are some interesting Roman finds.

Exhibits

See entry

See Ráckeve

See entry

Danube Bend (Danube Knee)
Ócsa

Ráckeve

Bugac (Puszta)

Region: Bács-Kiskun
Altitude: 122m/400ft. Population: 4000

Situation and Topography

Bugac-Puszta, covering an area of 10,000ha/ 40sq.miles, forms the major part of Kiskunság National Park (see Practical Information, National Parks and Nature Reserves). It lies some 30km/19 miles south-west of Kecskemét. Sand-dunes, marshes, meadows covered in wild flowers, areas of reeds and freshwater lakes are the main features of the ever varying landscape. Like the Hortobágy-Puszta (see entry), this strange land form came about during the period of Turkish occupation as the result of good farming land being ravaged and deserted and allowed to fall into decay. After that time Hungarian shepherds used the region as pasture for grey cattle, mountain sheep, crossbred horses and woolly boar. While in the 19th c. most of Kiskunság, especially the area around Kecskemét, was restored to fertile agri-

Riding display in the Bugac

cultural land, some strips of land were kept as *puszta* and designated as nature reserves. Today the typical *puszta* animals are bred only as tourist attractions.

Tourism

The entrance to the national park lies a few miles beyond the town of Bugac, about 16km/10 miles west of Kiskunfélegyháza. As an alternative to taking the car, buses run to Kecskemét and Kiskunfélegyháza and a narrow-gauge railway operates between Bugac and Kecskemét. Those who wish to ensure that they can enjoy horse-riding demonstrations or trips in horse-drawn coaches should book the one-day programme (including the journey there) offered at the offices of Bugac Tours in Kecskemét (see Practical Information, National Parks), as this item on the agenda is subject to sufficient people being interested. Covered waggons bring visitors to the herds of grey cattle and mountain sheep, the working *csárda* and the stud farms. In the little Herdsmen's Museum can be seen the costumes, folk-art and utensils of the *csikós*

Bükfürdő

See Kőszeg, Surroundings

Bükk Mountains (Bükk hegység)

This central mountain range in north-eastern Hungary is bounded by the River Sajó, the streams named Eger and Bán and the Great Hungarian Plain. The highest mountains are Istalló-kő (959m/3147ft) and Bálvány (956m/3138ft). The centre of the range forms a plateau some 20km/ 12½ miles long and 5km/3 miles wide, with dense mixed woodland and beech forests, the home of many kinds of animals including deer, wild boar and some rare species of birds.

Situation and Characteristics

In the Bükk Mountains over 300 caves have been discovered, some showing evidence of prehistoric settlement. The most valuable archaeological finds were made at Szeleta Cave near Lillafüred (see Miskolc, Surroundings), which provided men with shelter during the Ice Age.

Since 1976 the scenically most beautiful part of the mountain range, especially the plateau covered with dense beech forests, has been designated a National Park. In summer in particular, large numbers of holiday-makers and day-trippers visit the National Park, seeking rest and relaxation in the seclusion of the mountainous countryside. The tourist centre of Bükk National Park is the holiday resort of Szilvásvárad (see below), which offers plenty in the way of accommodation (often in former state nursing homes), restaurants and snack bars.

**Bükk National Park (Bükki Nemzeti Park)

Highly recommended is a trip from the Szalajka Valley near Szilvásvárad to Lillafüred (journey time about 1½ hours; subject to toll charges), an opportunity to become acquainted with the natural beauty of the mountains. The narrow road winds its way up to the top of the Bükk Range, from where there are magnificent panoramic views over the mountain landscape.

Trip through the Bükk Mountains

Bükk mountains: scenery and . . .

. . . Lipizzaner horses

Szilvásvárad

Szilvásvárad lies nearly 30km/19 miles north of Eger in beautiful surrounding countryside on the western edge of the National Park. Before 1945 this resort was owned by Count Pallavicini, who had a palace built here in 1860 by the famous architect Miklós Ybl; it is now a nursing home.

Lippizaner Stud

Szilvásvárad is known to horse-lovers above all because of the Lippizaner stud farm which was opened here in 1952. Visitors can see the horses in their stables, study documents describing the stud's history, watch riding demonstrations, ride out themselves or enjoy a trip in a horse-drawn carriage.

Szalajka Valley

A walk or a ride on the narrow-gauge railway in the romantic Szalajka Valley (Szalajka-völgy) is a very popular pastime, to the extent that at weekends the valley becomes rather crowded. A few yards down from the railway terminus, near the little waterfall with steps cut out of the limestone, a Forest Museum (forest-workers' huts, tools, etc.) provides interesting information about the lives of the woodcutters. A fifteen-minute walk along a signposted path will take the visitor to the cave in Istálló-kő mountain, in which prehistorical finds including tools, animal bones, etc. have been made. From this cave the path continues steeply up to the highest peak in the Bükk Range, Istalló-kő (959m/3147ft). The path is difficult to negotiate, but is well worth it for the panoramic view.

Bélapátfalva *Cistercian Church

On the road to Eger, 8km/5 miles south of Szilvásvárad, lies the somewhat uninspiring industrial town of Bélapátfalva. An untarred but signposted road leads from the town up to the foot of the imposing Bélkő Mountain, where the Late Romanesque monastery church stands on a plateau in the middle of the wooded slopes. It is Hungary's sole surviving Cistercian church. The secluded position and simple solemnity of the church give this spot its own special charm. In 1232 monks from the Pilis monastery in Esztergom settled here. The construction of the church and monastery was interrupted as a result of the Mongol attacks, and they were not finally completed until the 15th c. By the 18th c. the buildings had gradually decayed, and finally only the external walls remained. About 1730, after coming into the possession of the seminary of Eger, the buildings were restored, using the old materials. A further restoration programme between 1953 and 1966 again brought to light the original Cistercian building and the foundations of both monastery and church.

The severe exterior of the church, together with the flat end to the choir, the façades almost devoid of decoration of any kind and the lack of a tower are all in accord with the strict building regulations laid down by the Order. The only adornment on the west front is the recessed doorway with beautifully carved capitals and the Early Gothic rose window. This impression of marked restraint can also be seen in the mainly Baroque interior of the triple-aisled church. A typical feature of most Cistercian monasteries is the reading cell, which adjoins the south transept and is accessible from the cloister.

Cegléd

See Szolnok, Surroundings

Cserhát (Mountain region)

See Balassagyarmat, Surroundings

Cistercian church in Bélapátfalva

Danube (Duna)

A 1–D 4

The Danube, Europe's second largest river, is 2840km/1765 miles long overall; 417km/260 miles of that is in Hungary, 142km/88 miles forming the frontier with the Slovak Republic. The source of the river is near Donaueschingen in the Black Forest; from there it flows through South Germany, Austria, the Slovak Republic, Hungary, Croatia, Serbia, Bulgaria, Romania and the Ukraine, and then enters the Black Sea. The major tributaries which either flow through or touch Hungary are Lajta, Rába, and Drava, as well as Váh, Hron, Ipel' and Tisza. On average the Danube in Hungary carries 2200cu.m/2875cu.yd of water per second. From the Hungaro-Austrian border as far as Komárom the fall is still relatively marked. The giant masses of detritus deposited by the river over thousands of years divide it into two arms; the Mosoni Duna flows around the Small Deposit (Szigetköz) to the north-west of Győr, while in Slovakia the Great Deposit lies between the Danube and the Malý Dunaj. From Komárom to Esztergom the Danube winds its way between terraced banks. It then continues through the Hungarian Central Mountain Range to Vác, turning south at the Danube Bend (see entry). Between Vác and Dunaújváros it again divides into two arms and forms islands, like that near Szentendre, Margaret Island in Budapest and Csepel-sziget south of Budapest. From Budapest the Danube flows south, its rate of fall reducing rapidly, into a wide valley part of which is very marshy and divides Hungary into the regions known as the Transdanubian Highlands (Dunántúl) to the west and the Great Hungarian Plain (Alföld) to the east. The river then flows on past the industrial towns of Dunaújváros, Dunaföldvár, Paks and Baja and leaves Hungary some 15km/9 miles south-east of Mohács.

Course of the river

Throughout Hungary the Danube is properly controlled and navigable. It is extremely important as a transportation route, because it links the land

Economic importance

157

The Danube near Ráckeve

with the sea and – by way of the Rhine–Main–Danube Canal – with western Europe. Along its route numerous hydro-electric power stations have been built in Germany, Austria, at the Iron Gateway in Romania and in the former Yugoslavia. The power station near Gabčíkovo/Nagymaros, which was planned in co-operation with the then Czechoslovakia and which is now already partially built, has been deemed to constitute such a threat to the environment that the Hungarians have withdrawn from the project (see Facts and Figures, Rivers and Lakes). The Danube towns of Dunaújváros, Dunaföldvár and Paks are important centres of heavy industry in Hungary.

Tourism

The Danube naturally attracts a lot of tourists. After Vienna, Budapest is the most popular cruise destination on the Danube and many shipping companies operate there; there is also a quick hydrofoil link with Vienna. The countryside around the Danube Bend and where it breaks through the threshold of the Hungarian Central Uplands, one of the most delightful scenic reaches of the whole course of the river, is often referred to as the "Hungarian Wachau". The Szigetköz region, too, has good prospects of equalling the Danube Bend and Budapest in attracting tourists. South of the capital, near Soroksár, the river becomes a veritable angler's paradise. Its lower reaches near Baja and Mohács (Mohácsi-sziget) are also becoming increasingly important from a tourism point of view.

Danube Bend (or Danube Knee; Dunakanyar)   D/E 2

**Situation and Topography

The Danube Bend is one of the favourite recreational and excursion spots around Budapest. The name is applied to the extremely charming section of the Danube between Esztergom and Szentendre, where the river winds its way through the Visegrád Mountains and then turns sharply south (the river's "knee") towards Budapest. Because of the wooded hills which

The Danube Bend (or "Danube Knee")

border it this section has become known as the "Hungarian Wachau". The main tourist centres are the beautiful towns of Esztergom, Visegrád and Vác, together with Szentendre, the little town so popular with artists (see entries). Walkers and nature-lovers will be attracted to the region lying behind the Danube Bend, in the Pilis Mountains (see Esztergom, Surroundings) and the Visegrád Hills to the south, as well as the quieter Börzsöny Mountains (see Vác, Surroundings) or the Cserhát mountain region (see Balassgyarmat, Surroundings) to the north and east of the Danube.

The well-maintained Highways 11 and 2, as well as a railway line, lead directly along the Danube; Highway 10 crosses the Pilis Mountains between Budapest and Dorog. At those places in the mountains where the roads become fewer and of inferior quality, as for example in the Börzsöny Mountains, visitors can explore the countryside from a narrow-gauge railway. Szentendre is linked with Budapest by the HÉV suburban railway. Alternatively, visitors may prefer to view this picturesque stretch from the promenade deck of a pleasure cruiser or from a hydrofoil. Pleasure cruisers ply regularly between Budapest (Vigadó tér) and Esztergom; the trip takes five hours going upstream and four hours downstream.

Transport

Debrecen

G 2

Region: Hajdú-Bihar
Altitude: 121m/397ft. Population: 215,000

Debrecen, the third largest town in Hungary after Budapest and Miskolc, lies in the lowlands east of the Tisza, on Highway 4; it is the traditional cultural and economic centre of the region and, since 1950, its capital. In

*Situation and Importance

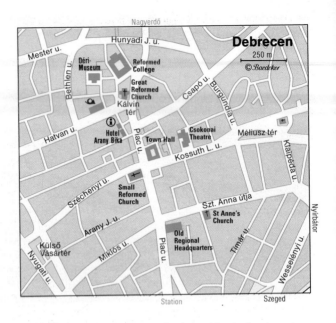

spite of having developed into a modern industrial and college town, away from the centre Debrecen has managed to retain its rural, small town atmosphere. The Great Reformed Church and the Reformed College serve as a reminder that Debrecen proudly bears the title of "Calvinist Rome", the stronghold of Protestantism in Hungary.

History

Following the merging of several smaller settlements in the Middle Ages, the place where Debrecen now stands became a regional trade centre for livestock and agriculture, and in 1361 it was elevated to the status of a town. In the 16th c. fifty craftsmen plied their trades here, and formed themselves into fourteen guilds. When the Reformation spread to Hungary Debrecen became a stronghold of Calvinism; those of other religious persuasions were prevented by the townsfolk from settling here or were forced to leave. In 1538 the Reformed College was founded and the town became a spiritual centre for Calvinistic teachings. This prosperous trading town also enjoyed special status under the Turks, who took over Debrecen in 1535 but allowed the people to continue to practise both their businesses and their Calvinistic religion. It was a different story with the Catholic Habsburgs, who freed the town from Turkish rule in the 17th c. but encountered resistance from the good people of Debrecen when they tried to introduce the Counter-Reformation, meeting a barrier of nationalist aspirations and religious convictions. During the 1848 Revolution Lajos Kossuth made the town the headquarters of the freedom fighters and the seat of his government. It was in the Great Reformed Church that he issued the declaration of Hungary's independence from the House of Habsburg. A century later, in 1944, Debrecen was once again the scene of historic events: on December 21st that year the Provisional National Assembly met here and Debrecen became the capital of those parts of Hungary which had by then been liberated. It retained this status until March 1945, when the Government was able to return to Budapest.

Every year on Constitution Day (August 20th) Debrecen becomes the scene of a colourful procession with floats bedecked with flowers in the form of animals, fairytale figures, coats of arms and so on.

Flower Carnival

Sights

A main arterial road passes through the centre of Debrecen, from the "Great Forest" in the north to the railway station in the south. The middle section of the road is known as Piac utca, or Market Street. As well as the buildings described in the following pages the visitor will find here and also in some of the side streets (especially in Kossuth utca) a number of interesting houses dating from the transitional period leading up to the art nouveau style.

Townscape

The very emblem of Debrecen is the imposing Great Reformed Church (Református Nagytemplom), at the end of Piac utca. As well as being the town's dominant feature it is also its most important building from an historical point of view and the largest Calvinist church in Hungary. A church has stood here since the 12th c. The Church of St Andrew, a Gothic basilica built in the 13th c. and burned down in the 16th., was rebuilt but again reduced to ashes and rubble in a town fire of 1802. Remains of the walls from this church have been uncovered at the north end of the present building. This was built between 1807 and 1819 (the interior having been completed somewhat later) to the design of Mihály Péchy and Josef Tallherr. It is in Classical style with a tympanum above and towers either side of the entrance which is on the south side, The centrally-arranged interior is also somewhat cold and severe. The bell from the previous church, weighing 5600 kilos/5½ tons, was preserved and recast in 1873; it is rung only on special occasions. The Transylvanian Prince György II Rákóczi originally had the bell cast from melted-down cannons used in the Thirty Years' War.

Great Reformed Church

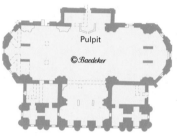

Pulpit

© Baedeker

Since 1914 the monument to Lajos Kossuth has stood in front of the church; behind the church, between the oratorium and the college, lies the Garden of Remembrance with a memorial to those departed souls whom the Habsburg Court of Justice despatched into slavery for preaching the Calvinist doctrine. A bronze statue erected here in 1906 is in memory of Prince István Bocskai (1557–1606) and his contribution to religious freedom in Hungary.

Garden of Remembrance

On Kálvin tér stands the building of the Reformed College (Református Kollégium). Once a school of Latin for Dominican monks, the college was formed here in 1568 and became known far and wide as a seat of Calvinist learning. The college owned 100 elementary schools and 40 senior schools, which it provided with teachers, school-books and curricula. Built in 1675, the college building was severely damaged in the town fire of 1802 and rebuilt between 1802 and 1816 in Classical style by Mihály Péchy, who was also entrusted with the plans for the Great Reformed Church (see above). The side wings were added between 1870 and 1874. The gable-end with the main entrance is decorated with portraits of famous students. The college library boasts 526,000 volumes, including an extremely comprehensive collection of Bibles, valuable manuscripts (36 codices) and 146 early printed books (incunabula).

Reformed College

Debrecen

Debrecen: Great Reformed Church . . .   *. . . and Déri Museum*

In the oratorium the Revolutionary Parliament met in 1849 under the leadership of Lajos Kossuth and decided on the deposition of the Habsburgs; it was here, too, that the provisional Hungarian government assembled in 1944.

*Déri Museum

One block further west, on the square of the same name, stands the Déri Museum, named after the industrialist Frigyes Déri, whose art collection forms the basis of the museum's exhibits. Its extraordinarily rich stocks include art treasures from Eastern Asia, ancient finds from Egypt (mummies, sarcophagi), Greece and Italy, as well as a collection of local folk-art (shepherds' cloaks from Hortobágy, decorated earthenware and porcelain vessels), together with 15th–20th c. art, such as the large painting "Ecco Homo" by Mihály Munkácsy (1844–1900). The four bronze figures in the museum courtyard, the work of the Debrecen sculptor Ferenc Medgyessy (1881–1958), symbolise the four spheres of the museum's collections, namely archaeology, history, art and ethnography. The sculptor was awarded the Grand Prix at the World Exhibition in Paris in 1937 for this work of art. In Péterfia utca (No. 28) is a small museum with more of his work.

Hotel Arany Bika

On returning to Piac utca the visitor will be attracted by the art nouveau building of the Hotel Arany Bika, built in 1914 at Pica utca 11–15, near the Reformed Church. There was an inn here as long ago as the end of the 17th c., which came into the possession of János Bika (John Bull) in the early 19th c. His inn sign portrayed a golden bull – hence the name Arany Bika (Golden Bull).

Town Hall

At the corner of Piac utca and Kossuth utca stands the Town Hall, built in 1842/43 in Classical style to the design of Ferenc Povolny. The central ressaut has five windows and is divided up by Corinthian columns; the arms of the town of Debrecen with the Paschal Lamb are carved on the tympanum.

The Small Reformed Church (Kistemplom) at the corner of Piac utca and Széchenyi utca is a little 1726 Baroque building renovated in 1870. The original onion dome of the massive west tower was destroyed in a storm and replaced in 1907 by crenellations, thus emphasising the fortified nature of the church. Since then the church has been affectionately known by the local people as "Stumpy Church".

At Széchenyi utca 6, a few yards behind the Small Reformed Church, stands the former postmaster's house (Old Post Inn), which can lay claim to having had a famous guest; in November 1714 the Swedish King Charles XII spent the night here when fleeing from the Csar of Russia. A notable example of Hungarian historical architecture is the Csokonai Theatre (1861–65) at Kossuth utca 10. Continuing along Kossuth utca in an easterly direction the visitor will come to the Neo-Gothic brick-built church on Méliusz tér. In Szent Anna útja stands the Baroque church of St Anne, built in 1721–46 to plans by the Milanese architect Giovanni Battista Carlone. The small church was originally used by the Piarists (the former Piarist convent is nearby), then by the Catholic community of Debrecen. The main altarpiece is by Karl Rohl and portrays St Anne, the patron saint of the church. At Piac utca 54 are the old regional council offices (Régi Megyeháza), built in 1911–12 in Secessionist style. The stained glass windows in the festival hall are by Károly Kernstok (1873–1940) and represent the seven princes who conquered Hungary.

The Nagyerdő is the recreational area in the north of the town which can be reached by tram. In the 2300ha/5750 acres of forest and parkland (which also contains the University and the Central Cemetery), there are plenty of sports and recreational facilities, including a pond for rowing and sailing, a stadium, a small zoo and a pleasure park. In a 9ha/22½ acre park will be found the thermal baths (Nagyerdei körút 9/11), supplied by two mineral springs at a temperature of 63°C/145°F. There are four thermal baths in the domed hall, where alternating hot and cold and orthopaedic underwater baths can be taken. The three open-air pools have a total water area of 5000sq.m/5500sq.yd, and one of them has artificially induced waves. These medicinal baths are open daily from 8am to noon and 1pm to 6.30pm, and the open-air pool daily May–Sept, 8am to 7pm.

In the Central Cemetery (Köztemető; Ady Endre út) the mortuary designed by József Borsos in 1932 is a building worthy of note.

The main building of the University Clinic (Nagyerdei Körút 98) was built by Flóris Korb in 1918; the individual departments are housed in pavilions all linked by a 3km/2 mile-long system of underground passages. Korb also designed the main building of Lajos Kossuth University (Egyetem tér 1), which was built in 1928–32 in Neo-Baroque style in the western part of the park.

Surroundings

In the immediate vicinity of Debrecen the visitor will come across a number of small towns and villages whose name begins with the syllable "Hajdú" (Haiduks). The Haiduks were originally cattle-drovers and farmers who served as mercenaries in the border regions after the 15th c. and were known for their courage and warlike mentality. Some of the Haiduks fought in the 17th c. for the Transylvanian Prince István Bocskai against the Habsburgs. After victory over the Habsburgs in 1604 he granted them land around Debrecen on which to settle (hajdúság = land of the Haiduks). Their villages were mostly in the form of rings of buildings protected by a palisade fence or a wall, as seen in the present-day town of Hajdúböszörmény.

163

Dunaújváros

Hajdúböszörmény	The town of Hajdúböszörmény (pop. 30,000), 18km/11 miles north-west of Debrecen, was the centre of Haiduk country and after 1699 the headquarters of the Haiduk leader. The home of the former Haiduk leader at Kossuth utca 1 now houses the Haiduk Museum (Hajdúsági Múzeum). In 1870 a neo-classical north wing was added to this Baroque building. The extensive archaeological, ethnographic and local history collections are complemented by an exhibition of works by members of the local artists' colony.
Hajdúdorog	A further 16km/10 miles north lies Hajdúdorog (pop. 10,000), since 1912 the only Greek Catholic bishopric in Hungary. The Baroque Greek Catholic church at Tokaji út 2 with its defensive wall dates from 1770 and was renovated in 1869. The iconostasis, with 54 paintings, is mainly Late Baroque in character.
Hajdúszoboszló	One of the best-known spa towns in eastern Hungary is the former Haiduk township of Hajdúszoboszló (pop. 24,260), situated 20km/12½ miles southwest of Debrecen. After boring down 1091m/3580ft, water with a temperature of 73°C/163°F was discovered in 1925, and as a result the sleepy little town found itself transformed within a few years into a popular spa resort. Today some 1½ million visitors every year flock to the baths on the 30ha/75 acre site at József Attila utca. The waters, which contain sodium, iodine, bromide and bitumen, are used in the treatment of rheumatic complaints, slipped discs, tendovaginitis and inflammation of the muscles as well as degenerative complaints. The indoor and outdoor baths together have a water area of 8500sq.m/9350sq.yd and can also be used for sporting events. A well-designed infrastructure also awaits the visitor.
Hortobágy	See entry

Dunaújváros   D 3

Region: Fejér
Altitude: 116m/380ft
Population: 62,000

Situation and Importance	The town of Dunaújváros, situated some 70km/44 miles south of Budapest on the right bank of the Danube 50m/160ft above the river, is one of Hungary's major iron and steel-producing towns. In the 1st c. A.D. the Romans settled in the region of Dunaújváros and set up the military camp of Intercisa, which developed into a flourishing town in the 2nd and 3rd c. The village of Dunapentele, which grew up here during the Middle Ages, was deserted during the period of Turkish occupation but people gradually moved back in during the 17th and 18th c. After the Second World War the region was selected for industrial development and the town of Stalinváros (Stalin Town), designed in "chess-board" fashion, was built around the new iron-foundries; it was later renamed Dunaújváros (Danube New Town). Apart from the 17th c. Rác Church (Rác templom) in Dunapentele and the Intercisa Museum, part of which houses some high quality finds from the Roman camp of that name, Dunaújváros can boast little of interest in the conventional sense. It is interesting only as an example of urban industrial development during the Socialist era, with its dreary tenements and gigantic industrial complexes. From the viewing terrace on the river bank, however, there is a beautiful view of the Danube and the wide *puszta*.

Surroundings

Dunaföldvár	Dunaföldvár, situated 20km/12½ miles south of Dunaújváros, is also an important industrial town and traffic hub with a bridge over the Danube.

The "Turkish Tower" (Töröktorony) dates from the time of the Turkish wars and is a square defensive tower built on a hill overlooking the Danube for the protection of a nearby fort. In one of its six prison cells can still be seen paintings made on the walls by a condemned prisoner, describing the story of his capture. On the top floor of the tower is a café with a good view. The restaurant known as the Fisherman's Csárda (Halászcsárda), in the old buildings on the landing-stage, is renowned for its speciality fish cuisine.

Eger

F 2

Region: Heves
Altitude: 180m/590ft
Population: 63,920

Eger, lying in the Eger valley on the southern slopes of the Bükk Mountains, is the gateway to northern Hungary and one of the most beautiful Baroque towns in the whole of the country. The radioactive springs to the south-east of the Old Town were known and highly valued during the time of the Turkish occupation. The grapes used to make Egri Bikavér (Eger Bull's Blood) and other well-known wines grow on the mountain slopes near Eger. As the regional capital and home to a number of schools and a teacher training college, Eger makes an important contribution to the administrative and educational needs of the surrounding area.

*Situation and Importance

Eger came to prominence in the 11th c. when King Stephen I founded a diocese here. In 1241 the still young diocesan town was almost completely

History

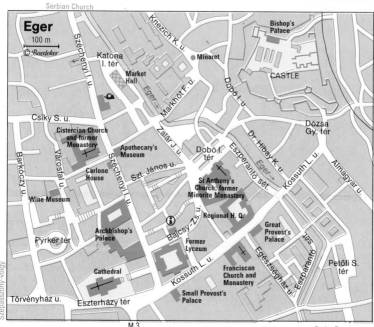

destroyed by the Mongols, but after being rebuilt it developed to become a centre of Hungarian Renaissance. Twice the Turks attempted to invade the town; the first time, in 1552, their army numbering some 80,000 men came up against the legendary resistance offered by the fort's commander István Dobó who – with only 2000 soldiers and the support of the courageous women of the town – successfully defended it. However, the Turkish siege of 1596 was successful, and Eger remained under Turkish rule for 100 years and became the chief town of the newly founded Ottoman province of Wilajet. Public baths, mosques and other oriental buildings, of which only a minaret remains, were the dominant features of the town at that time. When the Turks were forced to leave Eger in 1687 the population numbered a mere 3500. In the 18th c. Eger again flourished and, now once again the see of a bishop, blossomed into a rich Baroque town. The presence of bishops and monastic orders led to much building taking place, which in turn heralded an influx of well-known artists and craftsmen. The vineyards around Eger grew rapidly and the thermal springs brought many visitors to the town. After the Second World War a number of industries set up here, and its schools made Eger the education centre of the region.

Sights

*Cathedral

From the hill on which the medieval church of St Michael once stood the massive Classical Cathedral (Főszékesegyház) now looks down on the town. It was built in 1831–37 to the design of the Hungarian architect József Hild, who reversed the usual scheme of things whereby the entrance area is on the west side, and transferred the main doorway to the east side, facing the Lyceum and the Old Town. The two towers at the west end are counterbalanced at the east end by a portico with a wide flight of steps leading up to it. The three large statues above the tympanum portray the three heavenly virtues of Faith, Hope and Charity; those on either side of the steps are of the Apostles Peter and Paul and the holy kings Stephen and Ladislaus.

Eger: the Cathedral

They are the work of the Italian sculptor Marco Casagrande (1804–80), who also created the façade reliefs in the columned entrance hall (Pietá, or the Virgin Mary holding the dead body of Christ on her lap, Jesus in the Temple, Expulsion of the Traders). This artist was also responsible for the interior decoration; special note should be taken of the painting of SS Stephen and Ladislaus 1773 on the side-altar by the Baroque artist Johann Lukas Kracker, and of the high altar (1834), the paintings on which are by the Viennese artist Josef Danhauser.

Opposite the Cathedral, on Szabadság tér, stands the building of the former archiepiscopal Lyceum, now the teachers' training college. Built around a rectangular inner courtyard, the building dominates the square and is one of the most important examples of the mid 18th c. plait style. Bishop Károly Eszterházy actually intended it to be a Catholic university when he initially instructed F. A. Pilgram and J. I. Gerl to draw up the plans in 1763. However, by the time the building was completed in 1765 – Jakob Fellner, the Eszterházys' own architect, having meanwhile taking over the designing of it – the climate of the time tended to be against a church university of any kind, so this educational establishment had to be content with being ranked as a lyceum, or lecture hall. *Former Lyceum*

The entrance area lies in line with the Cathedral entrance, and is accentuated by the central protruding ressaut. On the first floor above the entrance lies the banqueting-hall, decorated with frescos by the Baroque artist Franz Sigrist; it can be seen by prior arrangement only.

The most imposing room in the whole building is the Library in the south wing; founded by Károly Eszterházy in 1793, it boasts an impressive ceiling fresco painted in 1778/9 by the Austrian artist Johann Lukas Kracker. The fresco contains a total of 132 figures and represents the meeting of the Council of Trent (1545–63) to discuss the consequences of the Reformation and the revival of the Catholic church. In the four corners of the room the resolutions drawn up by the Council are illustrated – ordination of priests, ***Library*

Fresco in the library of the former Lyceum

censorship of books, last sacraments and worship of relics. The architectural aspects of the same event are duplicated in the Late Gothic chapel, which gives an illusionistic impression of height without actually imitating Trento Cathedral in Italy, where the Council met. A *trompe l'oeil* painted "ledge" which appears to project well out from the wall represents the transition from feigned architecture to more realistic interior furnishings. Some 130,000 books, including 34 medieval codices, are kept in the oak cupboards which were made by the Eger cabinet-maker Thomas Lotter in 1778–80, to designs drawn up by Jakob Fellner. Some particularly valuable examples are displayed in showcases (open: Tue.–Fri. 9.30am–1pm, Sat., Sun. 9.30am–noon).

In the 53m/174ft high tower in the east wing is the Observatory with its revolving dome (fine view) and an Astronomical Museum (open: Tue.– Sun. 9.30am–1pm).

Széchenyi utca

The road leading away from the Lyceum is Széchenyi utca. This busy shopping street in the heart of Eger still boasts a number of 18th c. buildings.

Archbishop's Palace (Érseki palota)

In the immediate vicinity of the Cathedral and the Lyceum stands the Archbishop's Palace, at Széchenyi utca 1–3. This horseshoe-shaped Baroque edifice was built in 1764/66 to the plans of Jakob Fellner and renovated in the 19th c. It retains its original stairwell, which is worthy of note. The wrought-iron gateway opening on to the street is by Lénárd Fazola, the younger brother of Henrik Fazola.

Wine Museum (Bormúzeum)

The little street named Városfal utca runs parallel to Széchenyi utca. In No. 1, a simple Baroque building, equipment used by local wine-producers is exhibited. Some very old wine can be tasted in the cellar.

Cistercian Church

The largest building in Széchenyi utca is the twin-towered Cistercian Church (Cisztercita templom) built, like the Franciscan church, on the foundations of a Turkish mosque. Although work was started in 1699 after the Turks withdrew, it was 1733 before the building was complete. Although it may appear rather unprepossessing from the outside, the interior furnishings are of extremely high quality. The artistically sculpted group in Rococo style on the high altar made the name of Johann Anton Krauss from Moravia famous throughout Hungary. The six side-altars are decorated in beautiful stonework.

The modern sculpture "Daidalos" (1964) in front of the church is by György Segesdi (b. 1931).

Carlone House

The architect Giovanni Battista Carlone, a member of the famous Italian family of artists who lived and worked in Eger, built the corner house at Széchenyi utca 13 for himself in 1725.

Apothecary's Museum

The gabled Baroque building at Széchenyi utca 14 was built in 1763 to plans of Jakob Fellner. Visitors can admire the equipment used by the Jesuit apothecary in 1710 (open: Tue.–Sun. 9am–5pm).

Rác Church

At the end of Széchenyi utca (No. 59) will be found the Serbian Orthodox Church. It was designed in the 18th c. plait style by János Povolni in 1799. The interior furnishings, including the richly embellished iconostasis and pulpit, are in the Byzantine/Southern Slavonic style.

Dobó István tér

The market place below the castle, named after the legendary leader Dobó István, forms the centre of the town of Eger. After walking through the narrow lanes of the Old Town the visitor will be surprised by the scale of the market place, with its harmonious mix of beautifully renovated town houses and the impressive parish church of St Anthony (see below). The group of figures in front of the church, the work of Zsigmond Stróbl, is in memory of the defender of the castles on the south Hungarian border,

Church of St Antonius

Minaret

while the statue of Dobó István by Alajos Stróbl (1906) adorns that side of the market place which faces the castle.

The main feature of the market square is the former Minorite Church (Minorita templom), now the Parish Church of St Anthony, one of the most outstanding Baroque edifices in Hungary. The Minorite Order of monks had been resident in Eger since the 13th c. and built a monastery here which fell into decay during the period of Turkish occupation and was later rebuilt. The Bohemian architect Johann Ignaz Dientzenhofer, schooled in Viennese Baroque by Lukas von Hildebrandt, drew up the plans for the church, which was commenced in 1758 but not completed until 1773. Baroque dynamism is already evident in the twin-towered front, in the centre of which the overall alignment changes to form an elegantly rounded contour. In the centre of the gable stands a statue of St Anthony of Padua, and phases in his life are portrayed on the ceiling fresco inside the church – the work of the Bratislavan artist Márton Raindl. The paintings on the side-altars are also valuable Baroque/Late Baroque works. To the right of the church stands the plain, three-storey monastery building.

**Parish Church of St Anthony

It is just a short walk from Dobó tér to the slender, 40m/130ft high Minaret at the end of Markhot utca. This place of prayer is the most northerly Ottoman edifice in Europe and a reminder of almost 100 years of Turkish rule. The mosque which went with it was initially used as a church and then pulled down in the 19th c. Visitors are not allowed inside the minaret for technical reasons.

Minaret

Kossuth Lajos utca, where the senior echelons of the priesthood lived, is reached either through Jókai utca or along the Eger river. About 1775 Jakob Fellner, the architect of the Lyceum, designed the Great Provost's Palace (Nagypréposti palota) at Kossuth Lajos utca 16, a building which is in

The Great Provost's Palace

delightful contrast to the Regional Council Offices opposite. Today it houses the Municipal Library.

Regional
Council Offices

The Regional Council Offices (Megyeháza) at Kossuth Lajos utca 9 were built between 1748 and 1756. Note in particular the decorative grilles and lattice-work by the immigrant German metalsmith Henrik Fazola (1730–79) – the decorative grille above the entrance with the gilded wooden figures – symbolising the three virtues of Faith, Hope and Charity, and the magnificent gates on either side of the great archway. The left-hand one is embellished with flowers and tendrils, and that on the right with the stork coat-of-arms of the Heves region and the coat-of-arms of Archbishop Barkóczy who commissioned the building. These two gates rank as Fazola's masterpiece.

Franciscan
Monastery

The former Ferences kolostor, a simple building diagonally opposite the council offices at Kossuth Lajos utca 14, was built in the 18th c. on the site of a mosque. The monastery church, with its twin-towered front, was designed by the Eger architect Giovanni Battista Carlone in 1736–55. The interior is worth seeing for its uniform Late Baroque furnishings.

The Small
Provost's Palace

Where Kossuth Lajos utca enters Szabadság tér, at No 4 opposite the Lyceum, stands the former Small Provost's Palace (Kispréposti palota), dating from 1758. The balcony grille on the first floor was the work of Henrik Fazola, who also built the oldest preserved iron-foundry in Miskolc. The banqueting-hall is decorated with frescoes by Johann Lukas Huetter and Johann Lukas Kracker (1774).

Bath Quarter

South-east of the Old Town, on the far side of the river, lies the Bath Quarter with radioactive springs which have been in use ever since the 14th c. Visitors can still see the ruins of an old Turkish bath (Török fürdő) on Dózsa-tér below the castle. As well as the thermal baths there is also an open-air bath surrounded by old trees. As the water from the Eger river mixes with the medicinal waters the effects of the springs are felt there too.

Valley of the
Beautiful Lady

On the western edge of the town lies the best-known row of wine-cellars in the Eger region, known as Szépasszony völgye. Wine has been pressed and stored here since the Middle Ages. The cellars penetrate deep into the mountainside, and many of them are fitted out as wine-bars or lounges. The most popular wine of the region is Eger Bull's Blood (Egri bikavér), followed by Medoc-noir, while Egri Leányka is a delightful sweet white wine.

**Castle

History

From the 11th c. onwards the bishop and canon of the cathedral resided on Castle Hill, which afforded protection to the town and allowed it to develop. There had been a fortified building here since the time of the Mongol attacks, and in the 16th c. Péter Perényis gave instructiuons for the castle to be extended to withstand Turkish onslaughts; the work was supervised by the Italian architect Giovanni Maria de Specia Casa and was based on the designs of contemporary Italian fortresses. After the Turks had succeeded with their second attack in 1596 in capturing both castle and town, they repaired the castle once again. In 1702, on instructions from Emperor Leopold I, the castle – like many others – was blown up. In 1783 it became the property of Bishop Károly Eszterházy, who used the stone for his new buildings. Nationalism and a growing sense of history during the 19th c. led to the fortress being seen in a new light as something to be preserved for posterity.

Tour of
the Castle

Although the castle towers high above the town, large parts of it are nothing but ruins. Nevertheless, these remains do give an idea of the

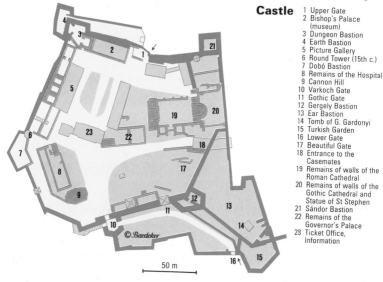

Castle

1. Upper Gate
2. Bishop's Palace (museum)
3. Dungeon Bastion
4. Earth Bastion
5. Picture Gallery
6. Round Tower (15th c.)
7. Dobó Bastion
8. Remains of the Hospital
9. Cannon Hill
10. Varkoch Gate
11. Gothic Gate
12. Gergely Bastion
13. Ear Bastion
14. Tomb of G. Gardonyi
15. Turkish Garden
16. Lower Gate
17. Beautiful Gate
18. Entrance to the Casemates
19. Remains of walls of the Roman Cathedral
20. Remains of walls of the Gothic Cathedral and Statue of St Stephen
21. Sándor Bastion
22. Remains of the Governor's Palace
23. Ticket Office, Information

50 m

© Baedeker

former size and strength of this great fortress, and there is a fine view from here of the town of Eger. Those who, instead of taking their car to the North Gate, climb up from the Old Town on foot (the ascent from Dózsa György tér is beautiful) will enter the castle through the southern Varkoch Gate. The relief by István Tar and Gyula Illés (1952) is in memory of the heroic defence of the castle in 1552. To the left lies the Dobó Bastion, while uphill to the right is the Handsome Bastion.

The central courtyard of the medieval castle complex is now surrounded by administrative buildings such as the ticket office, museum, etc. On the north side of the courtyard stands the former Bishop's Palace, built in 1470 for Bishop Johann Bekensloer; its ground floor has a beautiful arcaded walkway with a ribbed vaulted ceiling. This building was later to be the residence of the lord of the castle and in the 18th c. it served as a corn store and dungeon. Today it houses the Dobó István Museum with exhibits relating to the castle's history. The high ground to the right (east) of the Bishop's Palace is where the first Romanesque Eger Cathedral once stood. The remains of three massive pillars in the east of the choir give some idea of the dimensions of the extension; begun in the 15th c. but never completed, which would have converted this building into a Gothic hall church. The Cathedral was completely gutted by fire in the siege of 1552 and was later demolished. On one of the former pillars stands a statue of King Stephen, the work of the sculptor Marco Casagrande in the first half of the 19th c.; Casagrande was also employed in the rebuilding of the Cathedral. A Gothic tower containing a flight of stairs leads up to the battlement walk, from where there is a fine view. Here, too, will be found the casemates built within the east wall (admission free). In the south-eastern part of the castle lie bastions built in the 16th c. – the Ear Bastion (with the grave of the writer Géza Gárdonyi, who died in 1922), the Turkish Bastion, the Gregory Bastion and the Handsome Bastion. The coat-of-arms of Bishop Ippolito d'Este adorns the Gothic gate-tower of the Gregory Bastion.

The bishop's palace

Memorial of Dobó István

Surroundings

Mezőkövesd

This little town of 20,000 inhabitants, lying 20km/12½ miles south-east of Eger on the main highway between Budapest and Miskolc, is the traditional focus of the Matyós, a group of people who have long lived in Mezőkövesd and the neighbouring villages of Kövesd, Tard and Szentistván. Their name can be traced back to King Matthias (Mátyás), who in the 15th c. raised Mezőkövesd to the status of regional town. As in other ethnic enclaves (for example, the Palóc villages in the Cserhát Mountains), much emphasis is laid on preserving traditional crafts and skills. The colourfully embroidered flowers, based on old patterns, with which the women adorn their blouses, fabrics and aprons – red on a white or black ground being particularly popular – produce some of the most beautiful articles in Hungarian folklore. Those wishing to take home a souvenir of their visit to the Matyó region are recommended to pay a visit to the Matyó House at Béke tér No. 2, which contains the workshops and salerooms of the Folk Art Society.

Matyó Museum

In the Matyó Museum at Béke tér 3 (open: Tue.–Sun. 9am–5pm) visitors can admire embroidered traditional costumes from the Matyó villages. These include a long, bell-shaped dress and a colourfully-stitched apron worn by both men and women. Other colourful embroidery work can be seen in the Bori Kis Jankó Museum, in a thatched house in Bori Kis Jankó street.

Local Museum

The house at Mogyoró köz 4, dating from the second half of the 19th c., has been furnished in its original style. Similar houses can be found at Kis Jankó Bori utca 12 and 21, in Anna Köz, Diófa utca and Kökény köz.

These spa baths lie in a well-tended park on the edge of the town. Medicinal waters, containing carbonic acid, iodine and sulphur, surge to the surface from a depth of 875m/2870ft at an incipient temperature of 71°C/160°F, and then cool down to about 40°C/100°F.

Zsóri Baths
(Zsóri fürdő)

See entry

Bükk mountains

See entry

Szilvásvárad

Feldebrő

About 20km/12½ miles south-west of Eger (take the road to Verpelét, from where it is a further 4km/2½ miles to the south) lies the little town of Feldebrő which boasts something of an historical rarity. In the 11th c. a Romanesque church, based on a Byzantine model, was built here, its ground plan being in the shape of a Greek cross. The patron of the church was Aba Sámuel, who tried to steal the Hungarian throne from King Peter (the heir to Stephen's throne and the protégé of both Pope and Emperor) and in so doing sought protection from Byzantium. He died in 1044 while fighting against King Peter's supporters and was buried in the church crypt, beneath the High Altar.

*Parish Church of St Martin

The church soon fell into decay and was finally destroyed by the Mongols; in the 13th c. a Romanesque church in the form of a Latin cross was constructed on the site, and this in turn underwent changes during the Baroque period. The Romanesque crypt underneath the church came to light again in the course of excavations in the 1920s. The church is divided into two naves by clustered columns hewn from stone. It derives its special quality from 12th c. ceiling vault

Frescos in the crypt

frescos, fragments of which have been preserved and which are remarkable because of the vivid manner in which the figures are depicted (Christ in the apse, the apostles, prophets, Abraham and a crucifixion group in the nave).

Both church and crypt are open Mon.–Sat. 9am–noon and 1–5pm; the key to the crypt can be obtained from the presbytery behind the choir.

Érd

See Budapest, Surroundings

Esztergom

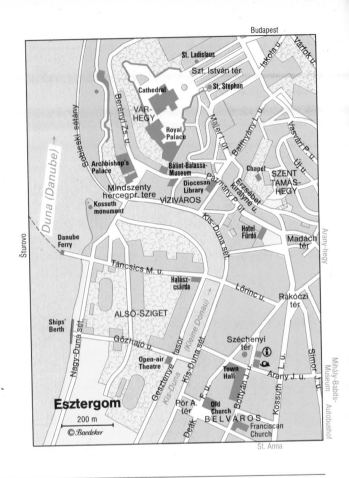

Esztergom

Region: Komárom-Esztergom
Altitude: 103m/338ft
Population: 31,800

Situation and
Importance

Esztergom is one of the oldest towns in Hungary. It lies about 60km/
37 miles north-west of Budapest, on the terraces of the right bank of the
Danube at the place where the river breaks through the Hungarian Central
Uplands ("Hungarian Wachau"). The old residence of the Hungarian
Princes and Kings has, since 1715, been the seat of the Catholic Prince
Primate of Hungary and, thanks to its many historical buildings, an impor-
tant tourist centre.

History

The castle hill was inhabited back in Neolothic times. After the Celts, the
Romans settled here and maintained the military camp of Solva Mansio. In

the 9th c. the Magyars occupied the region. Grand Prince Géza chose it as his place of residence and built what was probably the oldest stone castle in Hungary. His son Vajk was born here c. 973 and some 25 years later, in 997, was crowned King Stephen I, the first King of Hungary, in the church founded by Géza and dedicated to St Stephen. Esztergom, together with Székesfehérvár, became the most important palatinate in Hungary, and it was here too that the archbishop had his see. Contrary to the normal custom among western European rulers, it was in Esztergom that King Béla III (reigned 1172–96), who had been brought up in Byzantium, established his seat of government and had the castle made into a magnificent residence. Among the guests he received there was Emperor Frederick I. Barbarossa, who stayed in Esztergom on his way to the Third Crusade in 1189. In 1241 Mongols destroyed the flourishing town, the royal court moved to Buda and the palace became the property of the archbishop. After having been captured by the Turks in 1543 the town became the scene of constant attacks and sieges during the 16th and 17th c.; the castle palace was filled with rubble and covered over by a military fort. Many houses in the town were destroyed. Having been won back in 1683, Esztergom became the archbishop's residence in 1715 and also the seat of the Prince Primate of Hungary, whereafter it blossomed into a spiritual centre. In 1856 the newly-erected Cathedral, the largest and most magnificent church in Hungary, was consecrated. After the Second World War a number of large industrial firms established themselves here.

Sights

The most important historical buildings in Esztergom are concentrated on the Castle Hill, along the Danube and on Széchenyi tér.

Esztergom Cathedral, on the top of the Castle Hill

** Cathedral (Foszékesegyház)

History

The Cathedral, of monumental proportions (118m/130yd long and 48m/52yd wide) and with an imposing dome, dominates the skyline of Esztergom. Until the 18th c. the Primate Church stood in the centre of the densely built medieval town on the 156m/512ft high Castle Hill; this church had been founded in 1010 by King Stephen I and was dedicated to Stephens's tutor, Bishop Adalbert of Prague. In the course of rebuilding in the 12th c. the church was given the legendary door known as the Porta Speciosa, which has now been reconstructed from the original parts and is housed in the Castle Museum. Badly damaged in the Turkish wars, the church was demolished in the 18th c. A modest Baroque church built on the site in 1767–74 soon proved to be insufficiently grand for the country's highest church dignitaries, and it was decided to build a more imposing new cathedral. The draft plans for this were drawn up by the architects Paul Kühnel and János Páckh, who envisaged a massive cathedral with a broad semi-circular space in front of it on which the archiepiscopal administrative buildings would stand. To fit in with this scheme the level of part of the castle hill had to be lowered by up to 11m/33ft. Work commenced in 1822, but János Páckh died in 1839. In his place came József Hild, a busily employed architect who two years before had made his name with his designs for the cathedral in Eger (see entry). The leading advocate of Classicism in Hungary, he worked mainly in Budapest, where he left his unmistakable stamp on the Pest district in particular. In 1856 Esztergom Cathedral was completed, although somewhat smaller than first envisaged and without the open space in front of it. During the celebrations at the dedication festival Franz Liszt (see Famous People) conducted his "Esztergom Festival Mass" which had been specially composed for the occasion.

Description

Across the open Szent István tér lies the east front of the Cathedral, which is where the entrance is located. Two projecting towers flank the entrance hall, with 22 Corinthian columns giving it the appearance of a Greek temple. Over the crossing rises a central dome, 102m/335ft high, borne on twenty-four pillars. The architect put the entrances on the east side, facing the town, just as he did in Eger. The grey marble interior exudes Classical coolness and sublimity. The sculptures and wall-reliefs are by Johann Meixner and Marco Casagrande, while the High Altar is the work of Pietro Bonnanis. The altarpiece portraying the "Assumption of the Virgin Mary" by the Venetian Michelangelo Grigoletti imitates an "Assunta" by Titian.

* Bakócz Chapel

The historically important burial chapel of Archbishop Tamás Bakócz, commissioned in the first half of the 16th c. as a part of the old Cathedral, was demolished in 1823 and then reconstructed to form part of the new Cathedral, to the left of the main entrance. An artist from the circle led by Giuliano da Sangallo built this little chapel of red marble between 1506 and 1510. The white altar, decorated with an original relief showing the Annunciation, was created by the Florentine artist Andrea Ferrucci in 1519. The archbishop is portrayed for posterity in the shape of a kneeling figure near the right-hand pillar; the walls are emblazoned with the arms of King Vladislav II (reigned 1490–1516) as well as those of Archbishop György Szathmáry, Bakócz's successor. The altar-piece, the figures in the niches and the canopied niche are 19th c. additions.

Crypt

The massive crypt is in Egyptian style; some superbly carved sarcophagi of the Archbishops of Esztergom are well worth seeing. In the summer of 1991 the remains of Cardinal József Mindszenty, who died in 1975 while in exile, were moved from Mariazell in Austria to their last resting place here in Esztergom. The two large angel figures were the work of the Viennese sculptor Andreas Schroth (1826).

* Treasury

In the north-eastern corner of the square room below the dome lies the entrance to the Cathedral Treasury, in which is kept one of the richest

Castle Hill
Várhegy

1 Entrance Hall
2 North Tower
3 South Tower
4 St Stephen's Chapel
5 Bakócz Chapel
6 Treasury
7 Meeting Hall
8 St Stephen's Hall
9 Jeanos Vitéz Hall
10 Castle Chapel

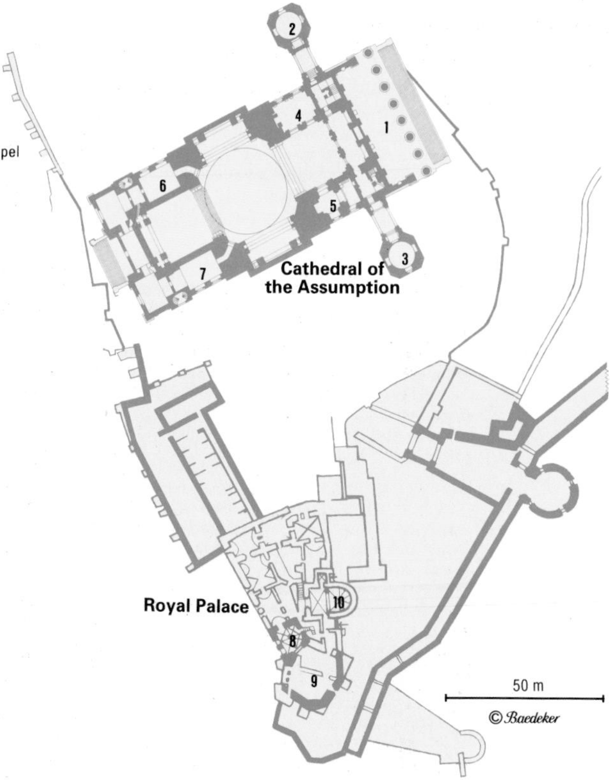

Cathedral of
the Assumption

Royal Palace

50 m

© Baedeker

collections of sacral art (9th–19th c.) in Hungary. Containing numerous liturgical vessels, valuable chasubles and relics, the collection has been repeatedly plundered throughout its history, and during the Turkish period it was removed from the Cathedral to various castles in Upper Hungary and Austria in order to keep it safe. The oldest piece in the collection is an oval piece of rock-crystal dating from the 9th c. carved with the Crucifixion scene. Other outstanding items include a 12th c. Byzantine tablet, a 13th c. Hungarian coronation cross and three Gothic goblets. Outstanding examples of the goldsmith's art include the Transylvanian Suki Goblet of 1440 and the golden "Hill of Calvary" Cross owned by Matthias Corvinus, which on its own makes a visit to this museum worthwhile. The upper half of the "Hill of Calvary" Cross was made in Paris in 1402, while the lower section was made in Florence in the 1580s.

*Royal Palace (Királyi palota)

The remains of the oldest Hungarian Royal Palace are situated on the southern promontory of Castle Hill, to the left of the Cathedral. It was reputed to have been built under Grand Duke Géza in the 10th and 11th c., and towards the end of the 12th c. King Béla III ordered that a two-storey west wing and a residential tower at the southern end should be added, and

History

177

that it should be lavishly furnished. Later renovations were carried out in Renaissance style by the archbishops of Esztergom, who were the sole residents here after 1256. The Palace was sacked and filled with rubble during the Turkish siege; some of it was uncovered during excavations in the 1930s and 1960s, and the major rooms have now been opened up as museums (open: Tue.–Sun. 10am–6pm).

Tour of
the Palace

The first rooms contain remains of the walls of St Adalbert's Church (11th/12th c.), which once stood near the Palace, as well as a model of its magnificent Romanesque doorway, the "Porta speciosa", which has been frequently copied (for example, in the monastery church at Pannonhalma – see entry). The visitor will then enter the long chamber which was once a casemate, which now houses the Lapidarium with some original carved stonework from the medieval castle. In the 19th c. it was believed that the groin-vaulted room at the south-west end of the Palace was where King Stephen I was born. The marble central pillar and the carved niche with twin windows are 19th c. additions, made when the room was converted to a chapel. A staircase leads to the upper floor and a Romanesque room with two beautiful portals, the larger of which leads to the János Vitéz Room beyond, which is divided into two by a wall. In the second half of the 15th c. János Vitéz, the eminent humanist, archbishop and tutor of King Matthias, had this, his study, painted with a fresco cycle modelled on some found in Italian Renaissance palaces, and which included the horoscope of the person who commissioned the frescos and a triumphant procession of heavenly bodies (fragments can still be seen on the arch and on the dividing wall) as well as some beautifully-restored female figures between the painted arcades – personifications of the four cardinal virtues of Prudentia (Wisdom; holding a mirror as a symbol of self-knowledge), Temperantia (Temperance; diluting wine with water), Fortitudo (Fortitude; holding a cudgel) and Justitia (Justice; with scales and a sword). It seems probable

A decorated capital in the castle chapel

that Vitéz commissioned Italian artists from the Florentine circle led by Filippino Lippi, who also worked at the court of King Matthias.

From the János Vitéz Room a narrow medieval staircase leads back down to the ground floor. Here the foundations of a round palatinate chapel from the oldest building (10th/11th c.) have been unearthed.

After having returned to the János Vitéz Room, the visitor should take the narrow corridor to the magnificent Castle Chapel.

Not only is the Castle Chapel of Esztergom Palace one of the pinnacles of ecclesiastical art in Esztergom, it is also one of the most beautiful of all the Hungarian buildings which mark the transition from Romanesque to Gothic. Above all, this is the result of extremely careful reconstruction work, in which the concealed sections of the original walls were incorporated into modern brickwork in such a way that they stand out clearly yet subtly, thus preserving the original impression of space.

**Castle Chapel

Above a plain and simple base – an almost square main nave, with a semi-circular apse joining it at the east end – rises a place of prayer which originally was luxuriously appointed with sculptures and paintings and is spanned by a high groin-vaulted roof. Two doorways with Norman dog-tooth decoration and superbly carved capitals lead to side chapels (the south one being also the entrance to the chapel itself). On the west side the wall above the doorway has a beautiful rose-window, while the south and north walls are broken up by means of niches with seats. The portraits above the niches were commissioned by Archbishop Csanád Telegdi c. 1340. The Norman double-pillars in the apse are an early indication of the Gothic style to come; the Romanesque wall on which they stand is disintegrating. In the 1930s some authorities suggested that two of the male figures on the capitals (one with a beard and one without) were meant to be likenesses of the French master-builder and his assistant, but since then further research has led to the conclusion that they are more likely to be medieval representations of Good and Evil. The walls of the Chapel were originally almost completely covered with paintings, but now only a few fragments remain in the choir remain.

The west front of the Castle Chapel has also been restored. From the small square in front of it one door led into the Chapel, the other into the Palace.

In the south and west of the Royal Palace remains of the walls of 14th and 15th c. defensive structures have been preserved, such as the Leopold Bastion (Lipótbástya) on the south side and the castle gate with pipes carrying drinking water on the Danube side (open: Tue.–Sun. 10am–6pm).

Defensive structures

From the Riverside area to Széchenyi tér

The Palace of the Primate of Hungary at Berényi Zsigmond utca 2 was completed in 1882. It is now the Christian Museum (open; Tue.–Sun. 9am–4.30pm). This provincial museum has become known far and wide and – apart from those in the Budapest museums –its collections of works by old Hungarian and early Italian Renaissance artists are beyond compare. It came into being largely as a result of the collecting passion of Archbishop János Simor, who allowed the public in to see his paintings as early as 1875. His collection was complemented by the purchase of the Bertinelli Collection of early Italian sacred art and also that of medieval work owned by Alexander Schnütgen of the Cologne cathedral chapter, together with an inheritance from Bishop Arnold Ipolyi who had systematically tracked down and purchased Late Gothic panels by Hungarian masters which had become scattered abroad.

**Christian Museum (Keresztény Múzeum) (Archbishop's Palace)

The highlight of the collection is the Picture Gallery, where the main paintings on view are by Italian masters of the 13th to 18th c., including Filippo Lippi, Duccio di Buoninsegna and Lorenzo di Credi. The main Hungarian Late Gothic work comprises the four tablets portraying Our Lord's Passion on a Lady altar (1506) with the monogram "M. S.". 15th to

Picture Gallery

Altarpiece in the Ecclesiastical Museum

The former Jesuit church

18th c. Austrian and German artists include Franz Anton Maulbertsch and Lucas Cranach the Elder. Outstanding among the Early Dutch works is "Man's Suffering" by Hans Memling.

Sculptures, Applied Arts

In addition to the superb Picture Gallery the museum also boasts a high-quality sculpture collection with Hungarian and German work from the 14th–18th c. The most beautiful Hungarian wood-carving is the "Holy Sepulchre of Garamszentbenedek", a 15th c. reliquary carried in processions. The exhibits in the Applied Arts department include gold and silver work, ceramics, tapestries and textiles.

Former Jesuit Church

Close to the Archbishop's Palace stands the pretty Baroque church in which Jesuits worshipped between 1728 and 1738. The towers were not built until the end of the 18th c., the spires being added in the 19th c. The Baroque interior was destroyed in the Second World War. After having been spared the ravages of plague in 1740 the citizens of Esztergom gave thanks by paying for a Lady Column to be erected in the square in front of the church.

Bálint Balassi Museum

This museum at Pázmány Péter út 63 is named after Bálint Balassi, the Hungarian poet who fell while fighting against the Turks near Esztergom in 1594. It houses an interesting collection of archaeological and local historical material illustrating the history of Esztergom, including finds dating from the Middle Ages and the Turkish era. It is open Tue.–Sun. 10am–6pm.

Diocesan Library

József Hild, the architect who designed the Cathedral, also drew up the plans for the Diocesan Library (1853), which stands near the river not far from the Archbishop's Palace. The valuable collection of books is in two rooms which are open to visitors (open daily 10am–6pm).

Hotel Fürdő Thermal baths

The Esztergom baths have been well known since Roman days. Adjoining the Hotel Fürdő, an imposing early 19th c. Classical building, are a thermal bath and outdoor baths, recommended for the treatment of rheumatism and gynaecological disorders, etc. They occupy the same site as the country's first public baths, opened by the Knights of St John in the 12th c.

Esztergom's former market-place, surrounded by a number of 18th and 19th c. buildings, is still the very hub of the town's life. The building styles range from Baroque and Late Historicist to colourfully painted more modern houses, all combining to give this wedge-shaped open space its graphic appearance. On the south side of the square stands the arcaded Town Hall (Városháza; 1770) with its particularly fine Rococo façade.

Széchenyi tér

Built during the 1760s on Pór Antal tér, the so-called "Old Church" (City Parish Church) replaces a 13th c. Franciscan church. The reredos of the High Altar by the Hungarian painter János Vaszary (1867–1937) is exceptionally fine.

Old Church
(Öreg templom)

The island of Alsó-sziget, which is linked to the mainland by three bridges over the Kis-Duna, has in recent years been developed as a recreational park. Landing-stages, sports grounds, an open-air theatre and the well-known inn, the Halász-csárda, provide for all kinds of leisure activity.

Danube Island
(Alsó-sziget)

From St Thomas' Hill, the second highest hill in the town, there is a fine view of Esztergom and the Danube.
On the hill stands a chapel dating from 1823, which contains a notable "Way of the Cross" with 18th c. statues.

St Thomas' Hill
(Szent Tamás-hegy)

St Anne's Church on Hősök tere (Heroes' Square) was built between 1828 and 1835 to plans by János Páckh. The artist had in his mind the great model of the Roman Pantheon. His church served as a model for the new Cathedral of Esztergom. The interior of the main building with dome above is clad in Carrara marble. The Classical church in Balatonfüred (see Lake Balaton) and others elsewhere are clearly based on that of St Anne's.

St Anne's Church

Surroundings

An excursion into the Pilis Mountains, which lie between Esztergom and Budapest in the loop formed by the Danube Bend, is highly recommended. This chain of mountains, an official nature reserve, covers an area of some 23,000ha/90sq.miles, with the coffin-shaped Pilis tető being its highest point (757m/2485ft). There is little in the way of lakes or other waterways, but there are large numbers of caves with fossils and other signs of life from the geological past. Mountain slopes covered mainly in forests of beech and oak mingle with steep and picturesque chalk cliffs. Because so many wild animals roamed the region and it was close to the royal residences at Esztergom, Visegrad and Buda, it was a favourite hunting-ground with the Hungarian kings, who built a number of hunting lodges here (such as that at Pilisszentlászló). Today the beautiful Pilis Mountains, being so near to the town, are a popular spot with day-trippers. Favourite places from which to set out on walks include the villages on the narrow chain of hills between the Pilis Mountains and Visegrad Hills, especially Pilisszentkereszt, where the road leads up Dobogó-kő, which is 700m/2300ft high and offers a superb view of the Danube Bend (see entry). The health resort which is also named Dobogó-kő is very popular in both summer and winter (winter sports).

*Pilis Mountains
(Pilis-hegység)

Fertod · Eszterháza Palace

See Sopron, Surroundings

Gödöllő

Ceiling painting in the Great Hall of Aszód Castle

Gödöllő   E 2

Region: Pest
Altitude: 180m/590ft
Population: 29,240

Situation and Importance

This little town lies in the middle of the Gödöllő Highlands 29km/18 miles east of Budapest, to which it is linked by a high-speed railway. Its many visitors are attracted especially by the Palace, once the summer residence of Empress Elisabeth. After 1956 the quiet town began to flourish economically, and today several large industrial plants are established here as well as agricultural research institutes.

Grassalkovich Palace

On Szabadság tér, in an extensive park in the centre of Gödöllő, lies this famous Baroque stately home (kástely), designed by Andreas Mayerhoffer in 1744–48. It is named after its first owner, Prince Antal Grassalkovich, a favourite at the court of Empress Elisabeth. In the 19th c. it was rebuilt by the famous Hungarian architect Miklós Ybl. After accommodation had been reached between Austria and Hungary in 1867 Hungary bequeathed the palace to the royal couple as a summer residence. The gift was no doubt intended mainly for Empress Elisabeth ("Sissi"), who enjoyed great popularity among Hungarians and used Gödöllő as her favourite escape from the rigours of Viennese court life.

Her former summer residence is now an old people's home and visitors are not allowed inside. The palace chapel in the right-hand wing now serves as the Parish Church of Gödöllő. Following many years of neglect the buildings are at present being renovated; on completion of this work they will probably be put to a different use. The buildings comprise three wings surrounding a courtyard; in the middle wing the dominant feature is a high, domed central ressaut embracing the ground floor entrance and the banqueting-hall above it. The projecting gable on the front of the central ressaut is emblazoned with the royal coat-of-arms. Although badly weathered, the characteristic "Schönbrunn Yellow" favoured by the Habsburg monarchy can still be detected on the façades of the side wings to the palace.

In the centre of the campus-like complex stands the two-storey Neo-Baroque building of what was once a Premonstratensian school; in front of it lies a well-tended park with a number of rare plants. The various institutes and other university buildings are grouped around this main building. Of interest is the bronze relief on the wall of the university assembly hall by the artist Amerigo Tot, who was born in Hungary in 1909 and died in Italy in 1984; he called it "The Apotheosis of the Atom".

University of Agricultural Science

Surroundings

This church lies about 2km/1¼ miles from the centre of Gödöllő, on a hill above Road 30 to Hatvan. A "Way of the Cross" leads up to the Late Baroque Chapel (Kegytemplom), built in 1759–70, together with its lower and upper churches.

Máriabesny Pilgrimage Church

14km/8¾ miles along Road 30 towards Hatvan lies the little town of Aszód. The Eger architect Giovanni Battista Carlone drew up the plans for the stately home which the Pomaniczy family built here c. 1730. Side wings were added by the Counts of Széchenyi in 1770, forming a horse-shoe shaped complex with a beautiful double staircase in the centre.
Although the former residence (now a boarding-school) is not officially open to the public, a polite enquiry will usually result in a tour of the great banqueting hall, which was decorated in 1776 by Johann Lukas Kracker and Joseph Zach, who also worked in Eger and painted the fresco in the Lyceum library. The wall-frescos with *trompe l'oeil* architectural features culminate in a fake dome with allegorical figures in the centre.

Aszód, Stately home

16km/10 miles beyond Aszód lies Hatvan, an important traffic hub in the foothills of the Mátra Mountains and extending to both sides of the River Zagyva. Its 25,000 inhabitants are engaged mainly in the food industry, especially in sugar refineries and canning factories.

Hatvan

As well as having a stately home in Gödöllő the Grassalkovich family also built a fine Baroque palace in 1754–63 a short distance away in Hatvan; with its U-shaped ground plan and domed central ressaut, it was the family's favourite style of residence. Situated on the Hatvan through-road, at Kossuth tér 18, the building has been sadly neglected and can be viewed only from the outside.

Grassalkovich Palace

The onion tower with its clock and the architrave above the main entrance are features of the 1757 Baroque Catholic Church on Kossuth tér. The pulpit, altars and stalls are also Baroque in style.

Catholic Church

In 1974 the newly-built Hatvan Thermal Baths, surrounded by a park, were officially opened. The water is at a temperature of 40°C/104°F and is said to benefit diseases of the digestive organs as well as joint problems.

Thermal Baths

It is worthwhile making a small detour to see the Baroque palace of the Counts of Teleki-Degenfeld, which is about 30km/19 miles north-west of Hatvan in the southern foothills of the Cserhát Mountains (see Balassagyarmat, Surroundings). It is now a hotel. To find it take Road 21 to Pásztó, and turn left at Jobbágyi, from where it is a further 13km/8 miles to Szirák.

Excursion to Szirák Palace

Gyöngyös   E 2

Region: Heves
Altitude: 171m/561ft
Population: 37,600

Situation and
Importance

Lying on the southern slope of the Mátra Mountain, 80km/50 miles north-east of Budapest, the industrial town of Gyöngyös is the centre of the historic but little known wine-producing region of Mátraalja. The popular resorts of Mátraháza and Mátrafüred also form part of Gyöngyös; the town's name means "Rich in Pearls", possibly because a lot of mistletoe used to grow around here.

Sights

St Bartholomew's
Church

The 14th c. St Bartholomew's Church (Szent Bertalan templom), one of the largest Gothic chuches in Hungary, was rebuilt first in the Renaissance style and later, following a fire in the early 18th c., in the Baroque by Giovanni Battista Carlone, whose major work was done in Eger. The towers are early 19th c. A large number of 15th c. sacral masterpieces are kept in the Treasury. Near the church, on Fő tér, stands a modern sculpture by Pál Kő (born 1941) of King Charles Robert of Anjou, who reigned in the early 14th century.

Mátra Museum

This museum at Kossuth utca 40 (open: Tue.–Sun. 9am–5pm) found a home in Orczy Palace, which was rebuilt in the Classical style in the mid-1800s. The local history collection is enriched by classic exhibits telling the story of viticulture past and present; on the upper floor is a display documenting the geology, fauna and flora of the Mátra. Near the Palace lies the beautiful Dimitrov Park.

Church of the
Franciscan
Monastery
(Ferences
kolostor)

The late 14th c. church on Nemecz József tér was destroyed during the Turkish occupation and rebuilt in 1701–27 in Baroque style, to designs by Giovanni Carlone. The doorway and interior are very beautiful; note the statues by the Austrian Josef Hebenstreit on the side altars. On the keystone of the choir-vault can be seen the coat-of-arms of the Báthori family, who endowed the church.

Surroundings

*Mátra Mountains
(Mátra hegység)

Together with Lake Balaton and the Danube Bend, this central mountain range rising to more than 1000m/3300ft is one Hungary's most popular regions with both day-trippers and holiday-makers; Budapest is only 80km/50 miles away. 50km/30 miles long and covering an area of 1000sq.km/390sq.miles, it forms a part of the North Hungarian Central Range. There are good roads and a total of 400km/250 miles of trails and paths, as well as ski-slopes – snow can be expected on between 100 and 120 days in the year on the upper slopes.

Mátrafüred

Mátrafüred, a picturesquely situated climatic health resort 340m/1115ft above sea-level and six miles north-east of Gyöngyös, can be reached by a narrow-gauge railway if desired (the station is near the Mátra Museum), which first passes through vineyards. There are also a number of marked trails, such as that leading up to the Hanák observation tower (584m/1917ft. Above the town is a beautifully situated camp site.

Mátraháza

Mátraháza (8.5km/5¼ miles north of Mátrafüred, 715m/2347ft) is another health resort on Road 24. A TB sanatorium has been built here, to benefit from the mountain air and sheltered position. A small but interesting local

Palóc-Múzeum in Mátraháza

Coach Museum in Parádfürdő

museum (Palóc-Múzeum) has been installed in three rooms of the Bérc Hotel.

From Mátraháza it is 3km/2 miles to the north-east up a steep mountain road to the highest mountain in Hungary, Kékes Mountain (1015m/3330ft); note that the road is sometimes blocked. There is a large car park with restaurant. The sanatorium treats metabolic disorders and anaemia. A 2·4km/1½ mile ski-slope leads down to Mátraháza.

Kékestető

10km/6¼ miles north-west of Mátraháza lies Galya, at 965m/3167ft the second highest peak in the country. The Grand Hotel and convalescent homes were built here in order to benefit from the mountain air.

Galyatető

The spa and health resort of Parádfürdő lies 13km/8 miles north-east of Mátraháza, 240m/788ft above sea-level on the twisting Road 24. The first baths were built here in the late 18th c.; the waters are said to be particularly beneficial in treating digestive problems. A beautiful 80ha/200 acre park surrounds the sanatorium and baths. There is also an open-air bath on the lower edge of the town.

Parádfürdő

The Coach Museum in the Cifra Stables in the upper part of the town, with both simple wagons and very elegant carriages from various eras, is of considerable interest; it is open daily 9am–5pm.

The Gothic Church of the Virgin Mary in Gyöngyöspata (11km/7 miles west of Gyöngyös) is well worth a visit. It was built in the 15th c. on the foundations of a 13th c. Romanesque church and was renovated and extended several times in the 17th/18th c. The tower, which is square at the base but octagonal higher up, is military in appearance. Inside the church will be found Gothic frescos and a magnificent Early Baroque high-altar, with wood-carvings portraying Christ's genealogical tree.

Gyöngyöspata

185

Győr

C 2

Region: Győr-Moson-Sopron
Altitude: 118m/387ft
Population: 130,000

Situation and
**Importance

Győr, 123km/76 miles west of Budapest and 51km/32 miles from the
Austro-Hungarian border town of Hegyeshalom, lies at the confluence of
the Mosoni-Duna (Danube), Rába and Rábca rivers, in the middle of the
Little Hungarian Plain. It is the administrative capital of the Győr-Moson-
Sopron region and a major industrial, transport and cultural centre.
The Old Town, with Cathedral Chapter Hill (Káptalan domb) and the Royal
Town, is one of the most beautiful Renaissance and Baroque townscapes to
be found anywhere in Hungary; 170 old buildings and other monuments
are officially listed.

History

Founded by the Celts and named Arrabona, the original settlement developed under the Romans to become one of the major towns in the province
of Pannonia. It remained of importance during the Magyar period, and King
Stephen made it a diocesan town. After a conflagration in 1566 it was
rebuilt on Italian Renaissance lines. During the Turkish Wars its citizens
held out until the castle governor betrayed them to the Turks in 1594, and
for the next four years it remained in Turkish hands and was allowed to
deteriorate. In the 17th c. the town blossomed once again; mainly because
of its port on the Danube it was an ideal centre for trade in cattle and corn
between Hungary and the Austrian Empire. The beautiful Baroque buildings date from this period. From the mid-19th c. Győr developed to become
the major industrial town in northern Transdanubia; the "Rába" engineering combine, which manufactures railway engines and trams, is well
known, and there are also some important textile and leather factories.

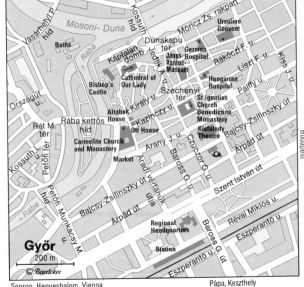

Sopron, Hegyeshalom, Vienna   Pápa, Keszthely

Sights

Anyone entering the town on Road 1 from the west or 83 from the south will be greeted by the grandiose Neo-Baroque Town Hall (Városháza). U-shaped in plan and built in 1896–98, it boasts a tower 58m/190ft high. Concerts, such as the Győr Musical Summer programme, are often performed in the magnificent festival hall.
There are a few parking places in front of and near the Town Hall, and the Old Town is within easy walking distance.

Town Hall

This open area on the Rába, formerly known as "Republic Square", is one of the most beautiful Baroque squares in Hungary. Lying between Káptalan Hill in the north and the impressive façade of the Carmelite church, the Baroque and 18th c. plait style houses bear witness to the town's great past. On the square stands a memorial to Károly Kisfaludy (1788–1830), the well-known Hungarian dramatist.

**Bécsi kapu tér*

The most striking houses along the east side of the square are Altabak House (No. 12) and Ott House (No. 13). The first was built in 1620 on the framework of a medieval house (the Gothic corbel has been preserved), and the corner oriel window and the elaborate stucco front were added in 1767. The pillars and arcades in the inner courtyard are Late Renaissance. Ott House can also trace its history back to medieval dwellings which were converted in 1778–82 for the Győr Bishop Francis Count Zichy. The attic-like upper floor of the 18th c. plait style front covers the gable of the house.

*Altabak House
Ott House*

The magnificent Baroque edifice of the Karmelita templom (1721–25) on the southern edge of Bécsi kapu tér is the work of Martin Athanasius from the Austrian Tirol. It is modelled on the Carmelite church in Rome, and thus is one of the few examples of Italian Baroque to be found in Hungary. In a chapel-niche to the right of the main doorway can be seen what is probably the best known Hungarian sculpture of the Virgin Mary, by the Venetian sculptor Giovanni Giuliani (1663–1744), who lived in Austria. The pictures on the high altar are of SS Stephen and Emmerich paying homage to the Virgin Mary. Those on the side-altars (1726–27) are by the Neapolitan Martino Altomonte, a major Austrian Baroque artist, and depict the Fall of St John Nepomuk into the River Vltava, the Death of St Joseph and the Death of St John of the Cross and Teresa of Avila, both Carmelite mystics. The sculptures in the church are the work of Franz Richter, also a Carmelite monk.

Carmelite Church

Király utca leads off from the north-east corner of Bécsi kapu tér. No. 4 is the former Eszterházy Palace; on the first floor can be found the art gallery owned by the János Xantus Museum. Today the house is called either after its owner or alternatively Napoleon House, the Emperor having stayed here on August 21st 1809.

Napoleon or Bezerédy House

Bishop's castle in Győr

Győr

Bishop's Castle
(Püspökvár)

To the north of Bécsi kapu tér rises Káptalan Hill, surmounted by the Bishop's Castle. Nothing remains of the first castle, built in the 11th c. during the reign of King Stephen; in the centre of the present range of buildings stands the tower which was the 14th c. residence of Bishop Kálmán, son of King Charles Robert of Anjou; the Bishop's coat-of-arms adorn the front of the tower. The Gothic chapel, near the tower, which bears the name of the the Győr Bishop Orbán Dóczy, forms part of additions built in 1481–86. After 1537 eight large bastions were added, on the lines of Renaissance fortresses; a part of the buildings was blown up by the French in 1809. Baroque and Historicist extensions were added in the 18th and 19th century.

The Castle Museum and Lapidarium are to be found in the Sforza bastion (entrance in Káptalan domb; open: Apr.–Oct. Tue.–Sun. 10am–6pm). A Diocesan Museum with some valuable religious utensils from the 14th–19th c. is housed in a former seminary dating from 1765. Below the bastions, on the walkway, stands an equestrian statue of King Stephen by Ferenc Medgyessy (1940).

∘Cathedral of
the Virgin Mary
(Székesegyház)

Opposite the Bishop's Castle, on Apor vilmos püspök tere, stands the town's most important historical building. The Cathedral dates back to an 11th c. triple-aisled Romanesque building, which was rebuilt after having been destroyed by the Mongols (13th–15th c.; north side-apse, St Ladislaus Chapel). The Early Baroque interior was added after the Turkish period; this includes the barrel vaulting with engraved coping 1639–45 by the Italian master Giovanni Battista Rava. The exterior is dominated by the west façade and tower, built in 1803–23 in a mixture of 18th c. plait style and Classicism by Jakob Hendler. The ceiling frescos and the main altarpiece (Assumption of the Virgin Mary) are masterpieces by Franz Anton Maulbertsch, painted between 1772 and 1781.

The Ascension can be seen depicted in the central aisle, in the north aisle the Transfiguration of Christ, in the south aisle scenes from the life of St

Ladislaus Reliquary in Győr Cathedral

Stucco detail in Apothacary's Museum

Stephen, and in the choir Hungarian saints. The contrast between light and dark used by Maulbertsch in his paintings in the side-aisles in particular – the Crucifixion, Christ on the Mount of Olives – illustrate the power of expression he was able to achieve in his work.

The revered image above the north side-altar shows Mary with the Infant Jesus; it is Irish in origin and was brought to Győr in the 17th c.

From the south side-aisle the visitor enters the early 15th c. Gothic Chapel of St Ladislaus (also known as the Héderváry Chapel, in honour of its founder); on its altar stands a masterpiece of Gothic art, a reliquary bust of St Ladislaus, King of Hungary from 1077 to 1095, who was canonised in 1192. It dates from 1405, stands 65cm/26in high, and is made of gilded silver with *cloisonné* decoration (enamel patterns separated by strips of wire). On the breast can be seen the Hungarian coat-of-arms. The crown is a later addition, made in Prague c. 1600.

* Ladislaus Reliquary

On the south side of the Cathedral stands a Rococo statue of St Michael (1764), based on that of the Archangel Michael above the porch of St Michael's Church in Vienna.

In the former Bishop's Palace in the southern corner of Apor vilmos püspök tere (No. 1) can be seen a collection of work by the great modern sculptor Miklós Borsos (1906–89).The exhibition is open Tue.–Sun. 10am–6pm.

Miklós Borsos Exhibition

This 8m/26ft tall Baroque monument (Frigyláda emlékmű) on Gutenberg tér to the east of the Cathedral was constructed in 1731, at the request of Emperor Charles III (1685–1740), by the Viennese court sculptor Antonio Corradini to a design by Joseph Emanuel Fischer. The monument shows two angels holding the Ark of the Covenant in their upstretched hands; legend has it that the Emperor ordered it to be made as an act of atonement for the violation of the Blessed Sacrament: during a Corpus Christi procession a soldier who was chasing a criminal is said to have knocked the Ark of the Covenant out of the hands of a priest and smashed it.

* Ark of the Covenant Monument

The figure standing on Duna kapu tér on the bank of the Mosoni Danube is the town's emblem – a cockerel on a double cross with a crescent-moon base. There is also a legend attached to this: when Győr fell into the hands of the Turks the victors are said to have erected a weather-cock on top of a pavilion here, saying that it would crow if the Hungarians ever succeeded in re-conquering the castle. The original cockerel is now in the János Xantus Museum.

The Iron Cockerel (Vaskakas)

Between Gutenberg Square and Széchenyi Square, on Jedik Anyos utca, some prettily restored town residences in Baroque and 18th c. plait styles provide an "old town" atmosphere.

* Széchenyi tér

Since Roman times Széchenyi tér has been the centre of Győr, and it was here that weekly and annual markets, public meetings and festivals were held. In the middle of the square stands a Lady Column which commemorates the liberation of Buda from the Turks in 1686; there are also statues of saints. The houses on the square are 17th–18th c.

Dominating the square is the Early Baroque former Jesuit Church, built in 1634–41, the work of the Florentine architect Baccio del Bianco (1604–41). He modelled the single-aisled church on the Jesuit church of Il Gesù in Rome, the first Baroque church to be built anywhere in the world. Originally the relatively plain façade had no towers – these were added by Martin Witwer in 1726. The niches contain statues of St John Nepomuk, St John the Evangelist, St Andrew and St Francis of Borgia; above the entrance is one of the Madonna and in the tympanum the founder of the order, St Ignatius Loyola.

Church of St Ignatius

The superb frescos which decorate the church were painted in 1744 by the Austrian artist Paul Troger. He was also responsible for the Transfiguration of St Ignatius Loyola which can be seen on the high altar. Mention must

Győr

Széchenyi tér, the central square of Győr

also be made of the statues of saints by Johann Josef Rössler from Vienna, and the lavishly decorated pulpit by Ludwig Gode from Bratislava.

Benedictine Abbey Museum of Medicine

St Ignatius' Church forms a part of the Baroque abbey of Bencés rendház, which was built by the Jesuits and, following the dissolution of their order in 1773, passed to the Benedictines in 1802; the latter installed a grammar school here. The vaulted ground floor, which is decorated with ceiling

Church of St Ignatius

Romanesque church in Lébénymiklós

frescos and stucco work, was used by the Jesuits for the sale of medicines as early as the 17th c., and has now been made into a Museum of Medicine (open: Tue.–Sun. 10am–6pm).

In the 1580s several small buildings grouped on the west corner of Széchenyi tér were made into a Baroque mansion for the Italian merchant Angarano. In 1770 Gábor Count Eszterházy had it rebuilt, and today its most striking features include the lattice-work arch over the door and the oriel window with its elaborate wrought-iron grille.

Angarano House

The late 17th c. Baroque house at Széchenyi tér No. 4 was once the residence of the town's magistrates. It takes its name from a tree-trunk into which in 1833 a timber merchant drove iron nails and then used as his shop sign. After the fashion of the "Stock im Eisen" (Iron Trunk) in Vienna, itinerant journeymen and apprentices used to carve their initials on it.

Iron Stump House

The Győr Municipal Museum is housed in the 1741 Baroque "abbot's house" on the north side of Széchenyi tér (No. 5). The Benedictine abbot of Pannonhalma had several medieval houses converted into a palace for himself; the present banqueting hall was once the refectory, The beautiful Rococo oriel window above the door is framed by sculptures of St Benedict and King Stephen. The ceiling frescos by Stephan Schaller (1708–79) from Győr depict scenes from the legend of the founding of Pannonhalma. The museum, named after János Xantus, a 19th c. Hungarian naturalist, contains local history, ethnographic, natural history and applied art collections, as well as coins, pictures, etc. It is open Tue.–Sun. 10am–6pm.

János Xantus Museum

Old people still spend their twilight years here at Rákóczi utca No. 6, where in 1666 György Széchenyi, Bishop of Győr, had a number of old houses made into a hospice (Magyar ispita) for Hungarian citizens.
The two arcaded courtyards with Tuscan pillars are suggestive of the Late Renaissance style. In the rear courtyard stands a decorative fountain by Miklós Borsos (1961). Adjoining the hospice is St Anne's Church, originally dating from 1730 and rebuilt in the second half of the 19th c. The painting by Stephan Schaller in the left side-altar is all that remains from the contents of the original building.

Hungarian Old People's Home

In Czuczor Gergely utca, to the south-east of the Benedictine monastery, stands the modern Kisfaludy Theatre (Színház), built in 1978. One wall is covered with ceramics by the world-famous artist Victor Vasarely (see Famous People).

Kisfaludy Theatre

Surroundings

This little town (pop. 3400), in the Little Hungarian Plain 24km/15 miles east of Győr, was first mentioned in official records in the 13th c.; in 1789 Emperor Joseph II established an estate here; it is now a stud for thoroughbred and crossbred Arab and Lippizaner horses and has a worldwide reputation. After the Second World War Bábolna became an agricultural combine (horse-breeding and poultry-keeping).
In front of the main buildings stands an equestrian statue by Iván Szabó (born 1913), erected in memory of the horses which were killed during the First World War – probably the only such memorial anywhere in the world.

Bábolna

See entry

Pannonhalma

About 32km/20 miles west of Győr lies the little town of Csorna (alt. 117m/384ft; pop. 12,530). In the 13th c. the Osl family founded a Premonstratensian monastery here. The medieval church was rebuilt in Baroque style in 1774–86; in the porch is a 13th c. Romanesque relief of St Michael. The 16th c. monastery was destroyed in a fire and rebuilt in Baroque style at

Csorna

the end of the 18th c. Today it houses a collection of folk-art and local history exhibits from the János Xantus Museum (open: Tue.–Sun. 10am–6pm).

** Lébénymiklós Romanesque Church

In Lébénymiklós, 22km/14 miles north-west of Győr, stands one of Hungary's major Romanesque edifices, the massive St James' Church, built c. 1210 by a rich and noble family from Győr as the abbey church of a small Benedictine monastery. As the oldest church of its kind in western Hungary it became the model for other similar buildings, such as the church in Ják (see entry). During the Turkish wars it was badly damaged and rebuilt several times. In 1631 Jesuits replaced the ruined medieval ribbed vaulting with Baroque barrel vaulting. Finally, the church was restored between 1862–65 and 1872–79 under the guidance of the director of the German National Museum in Nuremberg.

The west front, flanked by two massive towers (with 19th c. Rhenish roofs), has a magnificent, richly carved door. The painting in the tympanum dates from 1879 and is by the Viennese artist Klein. The south door, used mainly by the monks, is also lavishly carved in Norman Romanesque style. The three east apses are decorated with frescos around the arches; the choir has semi-circular columns.

Cluster-columns surmounted by bulb-shaped capitals separate the three aisles. The stained glass windows by Lili Sztéhlós date from 1953.

Gyula

See Békéscsaba, Surroundings

Hajdúszoboszló

See Debrecen, Surroundings

Hatvan

See Gödöllő, Surroundings

Hévíz   C 3

Region: Zala
Altitude: 132m/433ft
Population: 5700

** Situation and Importance

This health resort 7km/4½ miles north-west of Keszthely, is one of the leading traditional Hungarian spa towns. Hévíz owes its international reputation to its thermal bath, the largest natural warm-water lake in Europe. As long ago as the late 18th c. articles were already being written about its healing properties, and in 1795 the first wooden bath-house was built.

Warm-water lake

The lake, which covers an area of 47,500sq.m/52,000sq.yd, is fed by radioactive water containing sulphur. The water comes from a spring lying 36m/120ft down in a funnel-shaped trough and which pours between 60 and 80 million litres/13 and 18 million gallons of water a day into the lake, thus completely changing the water every 28 hours. In summer it reaches a temperature of 33–34°C/91–93°F, and in winter never falls below 26°C/79°F, so the waters can be enjoyed even when it is quite cool outside. On the bed of the lake is a layer, several yards thick, of greyish-brown, coarse-grained

Héviz: the largest thermal lake in Europe

mud which can be very effective in treatments involving the use of mud-packs. The pools in the spa hospital and hotels are also filled with water from the lake, and these establishments also provide additional medical treatment facilities. Those visitors who have come to Hévíz simply to enjoy the baths rather than for any specific medical reason are recommended to use the open-air baths at the northern end of the lake, where large numbers of water-lilies are in flower from April to October. The thermal bath and treatment facilities here lie in the midst of a nature reserve, surrounded by a beautiful park with lots of walks.

See Practical Information, Spas and Health Resorts

Treatment
information

Surroundings

A trip out to the little village of Egregy 2km/1¼ miles north of Hévíz, will be found rewarding largely because of its Romanesque church of Mary Mag-dalene, built in the second half of the 13th c. on the village cemetery. It is a simple church with a short nave, west tower and choir. Inside can be seen remains of painted decoration in rural Baroque style.

Egregy

Hódmezővásárhely

See Szeged, Surroundings

Hollókő

See Balassagyarmat, Surroundings

Hortobágy (Puszta)

Region: Hajdú-Bihar
Altitude: up to 88m/289ft

Situation and Characteristics

Between the Tisza river and the eastern Hungarian town of Debrecen (see entry) stretches the Hortobágy, a lowland prairie covering an area of 2300sq.km/888sq.miles, at one time the flood plain of the Tisza. The countryside is composed mainly of barren land with relatively infertile soil, wide areas of grass-covered steppes and pasture. Large herds of cattle and sheep and horse-paddocks bring to mind romantic pastoral tales of the Puszta of old.

History

During the period of the migration of Indo-European peoples the Hortobágy was relatively thickly populated. Attacks by tribes from eastern Europe and Asia (especially Tartars and Turks) caused many to flee the Puszta, with only spasmodic growth in the few towns and villages. From the 14th c. onwards the region – especially that part which enjoyed the protection of the town of Debrecen –developed a pastoral system involving

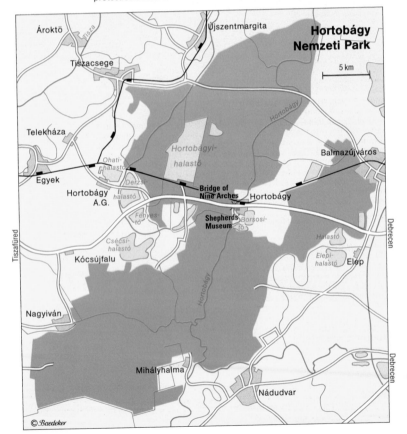

the rearing of grey cattle and sheep, together with the breeding of horses. When the course of the River Tisza was changed a part of the Hortobágy region became noticeably barren and depopulated now that the land no longer benefited from the deposits of natural fertiliser previously found in the mud deposited when the river flooded its banks every year.

In the late 19th and early 20th c. attempts were made to develop the Hortobágy to meet the needs of large-scale agriculture. After the Second World War various melioration measures brought at least localised improvements in soil quality. Two canals running parallel one to the other and working in conjunction with the little Hortobágy river helped to irrigate fields.

Traditional pastoral life has gradually disappeared from the Hortobágy and now remains only in the form of folk-lore and simple tourist attractions. Large agricultural combines, formerly state-owned, which are concerned with the production and sale of greenstuffs and the rearing of livestock (mainly Hungarian cattle and sheep) as well as the breeding of horses, are gradually being returned to private ownership following the collapse of Communism. In some places rice-cultivation and fish-farming are playing an ever-increasing role.

Present situation

**Hortobágy National Park (Hortobágyi Nemzeti Park)

In 1973 the central region of the Hortobágy Puszta, an area of 690sq.km/266sq.miles, was declared a nature reserve, in an attempt both to safeguard the varied fauna and flora and to preserve the traditional farming and pastoral methods which have been employed on the Hungarian Plain since the 14th c. Extensive areas of grassland interspersed with clumps of oak and maple trees, and large expanses of reeds dominate the landscape. Water-lilies, floating motherwort and other aquatic plants are nearly as common as camphor, camomile, mugwort and aster. In spring and autumn the Hortobágy provides a resting-place for vast numbers of migrant birds, including various species of heron, spoonbills, white geese, reed-warblers, waders, rare black storks, falcons and eagles. Also frequently seen are wild boar, otters and ground-squirrels. Descendants of many hundreds of years of animal rearing include the Hungarian Steppe cattle, the long-horned sheep, the nonius horse and the komondor and puli dogs so beloved by the shepherds. The occasional water-well and shepherd's dwelling complete the picture.

In the middle of the nature reserve lies the town of Hortobágy. There was a *csárda* (country inn) here at the end of the 17th c. (see below).

Hortobágy (Town)

The first *csárda* was built here in the 1690s. The west wing, in rural Baroque style, was added in 1781, and the Classical east wing in 1815.

Hortobágy Csárda

Behind the *csárda* there is a gallery displaying works of art mainly on the "puszta" theme, including some by Mihály Munkácsy, János Pásztor, Ferenc Medgyessy and László Holló. Open: Apr.–Oct. Tue.–Sun. 9am–5pm, Nov.–Mar. 9.30am–4pm.

Hortobágy Galéria

Near the *csárda* a bridge with nine arches spans the River Hortobágy. 167m/183ft long, this road bridge was built between 1827 and 1833 to designs by the architect Ferenc Povolny. After 1850 a Bridge Market was established here and became well-known throughout the land. Carrying on this tradition, a very colourful market is held here every year on Constitution Day (August 20th).

*Nine Arch Bridge (Kilenclyuku híd)

Bridge Market

Near the bridge is a Pastoral Museum, housed in an old wagon shed. Here the visitor can learn something about the life of the "csikós", the horse-riding shepherds of the puszta (cattle rearing, everyday life of the shepherds and cattlemen, pastoral art, etc.)

Pastoral Museum (Csikómúzeum, Pásztormúzeum)

195

In the "Körszín", a round building with a thatched roof, there is an exhibition providing information on the Hortobágy Puszta region.

On the first week-end in July every year international horse shows are held in the Hortobágy Puszta. Events include riding and jumping contests, carriage-driving competitions and traditional equestrian games.

Anyone visiting the Hortobágy Puszta has the opportunity to participate in various excursions which provide an insight into rural life, with exhibitions, riding displays and visits to stud farms. In addition, there is the opportunity to observe grey cattle, buffalo and long-horned sheep "in the wild".

Hortobágy Nemzeti Park Igazgatósága, Sumen u. 2, H–4024 Debrecen. Tel. 52 19–472, 52 49–922.

Ják

Region: Vas. Population: 220

The village of Ják, 12km/7½ miles south of Szombathely, is a treat in store for all those interested in art and church architecture, as the massive edifice standing on a hill above the village is one of Hungary's outstanding Romanesque churches.

**St George's Church

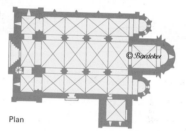

Plan

In the early 13th c., probably *c.* 1214, the influential Hungarian nobleman Márton Ják, known as "the Great", laid the foundation stone of a dynastic church on a hill in the centre of his extensive estates. At the same time he called upon some Benedictine monks and invited them to found a modest monastery near the church. By the time of the Mongol attacks of 1241 the triple-aisled nave, the choir and the twin-towered façade had been built, but only the most westerly bay under the gallery and the square choir had been covered with the Early Gothic groin-vaulted roof – the remaining parts of the church were roofed over in a simple way after the interruption in the building work. It was finally consecrated in 1256. During the Turkish wars the monks left the abbey, and it was burned down a few years later. The church retained the Late Renaissance gateway (1663) in the church wall dating from the time when it was renovated by Abbot Ferenc Folnay; the door is embellished with the abbot's coat-of-arms. The famous architect Frigyes Schulek undertook an extensive restoration of the church in 1896–1904, shortly after he had completed the rebuilding of the Gothic Matthias Church in Budapest. He removed the Baroque additions, rebuilt the towers on the lines of the church in Zsámbék (see Tata, Surroundings), replaced numerous sections of the building and erected a groin-vaulted roof over the central and south aisles.

Passing through Abbot Folnay's Late Renaissance gateway the visitor will find himself facing the imposing west front, where his attention will immediately be drawn to the magnificent recessed doorway. Surmounted by a

◀ *Impressions of Hortobágy-Puszta*

Ják: a "family" church

triangular gable, it stands forward of the wall between two massive towers which have double campanile arcades in their two upper floors. The doorway is richly decorated with geometric patterns, human figures and plant ornamentation in the Norman Romanesque style. Extremely important examples of Late Romanesque art in Hungary are the almost life-size figures of Christ (in the centre) and ten of His Apostles which stand in the recessed niches above the door and in the two niches in the fronts of the towers. These almost true to life, *avant-garde* figures are modelled on the architectural sculptures in Bamberg Cathedral (Germany) and in the "Giant's Doorway" of St Stephen's Cathedral in Vienna. The heads of Christ and the two Apostles on either side of Him are original, whereas the others were torn down by the Turks and replaced in the 18th c. A Madonna on her throne (head missing) and a representation of Samson and the Lion embellish the two niches level with the tops of the door columns. The relief on the tympanum is a modern copy of the original which is now in the Savaria Museum in Szombathely. There is also some remarkable architectural sculpture to be seen on the other sides of the church. On the east side there is a pleasing statue of a young king with his sceptre on the north apse, and on the main apse a sculpture of Androcles and the Lion. The south door is surmounted by a simple tympanum with the Lamb of God between two Dragons.

Interior

The fact that this was originally a dynastic church for the use of the family and relatives is clearly shown inside; above the west porch can be seen the characteristic gallery used by the senior members of the family, fitted with three niche-seats (entrance above the spiral staircase in the south tower). The rich sculptural decoration on the outside was at one time complemented by expensive interior paintings, only fragments of which still remain. The frescos in the porch show the founder Márton Ják and his family together with angels bearing the souls of the departed up to Heaven. In the roof-panels the faithful are shown praying to saints whose identity has not yet been established. The fresco in the choir, showing St George and the Dragon, is sadly very much the worse for wear. The 15th c. carved wooden figure of the Virgin Mary on the side-altar in the choir has considerable rarity value, because very few medieval Hungarian sculptures have been preserved. A further major medieval work of art came to light during restoration work in the summer of 1991 – a unique Gothic winged altar dating from about 1400 was found hidden under a Baroque altar painting of 1705. Some individual sections have already had the overpainting removed to reveal the apostles Peter and Paul and John the Baptist.

Opposite the west front of the church, on a quartered ground plan, stands the small, two-storey St James' Chapel, built c. 1260. It served the local community as a parish church where baptisms, weddings and funeral services were performed, these not being allowed in the main church. The rounded decorations on the double-windows of the upper floor complement the motifs on the windows of the abbey church. The relief on the tympanum above the south door depicts the Lamb of God between two Dragons. The interior furnishings of the chapel are Rococo. Note the mid-18th c. altar, which was originally in the main church. St James' Chapel

Jászberény E 2

Region: Jász-Nagykun-Szolnok
Altitude: 100m/330ft
Population: 30,900

This former small market town on the bank of the River Zagyva, 79km/49 miles east of Budapest, is the "capital" of the Jászság region, where the Jazygians traditionally settled. This nomadic people, originally from what is now Iran, reached the Carpathian Basin in the 13th c. and – like the Cumans from the steppes of southern Russia (see Karcag) – were allowed by the King of Hungary to settle in certain areas and retain their tribal structure. In return for this favour they agreed to fight on the side of the Magyars in the event of war. Some of the Jazygians emigrated from the Great Hungarian Plain during the confusion of the Turkish wars; those who did not do so soon lost their special status and mingled with the Hungarian people. Situation and Importance

Sights

The Classical building at Tánesius utca 3 is the home of the Jazyg Museum (Jász múzeum), which was founded in 1874 and boasts an extraordinarily rich collection of exhibits. It includes an archaeological department, with finds ranging from ancient times to the Middle Ages, local history items and some beautiful furs made by the Jazygians. The most valuable piece in the collection is a Byzantine ivory horn, known as the "Lehel Horn". According to legend, it is said to have belonged to the Magyar tribal prince Lehel, who was taken prisoner in 955 after being defeated in the battle of Lechfeld. Prior to his execution he asked to be allowed to blow his horn just once more, only to use it to strike down the Hun Emperor Konrad with the words "Thou shalt enter Eternity before me and there be my servant". As he spoke these words a splinter is said to have sprung from the horn. As there is no historical data to support this legend the true origin of the horn remains a mystery. Jazyg Museum

In 1742 the Franciscans, who had succeeded in converting the Jazygs to Christianity, built a Gothic church and monastery in Jászberény. After the Turkish occupation the church was rebuilt in Baroque style in 1723–55, but some Gothic features remain, such as the supporting pillars and an ogival doorway. Franciscan Church

Kalocsa

Lehel Horn

Catholic
Parish Church

The Parish Church of the Virgin Mary on Köztársaság tér was built in 1774–82, also on Gothic foundations. The spire of its elegant tower, designed by Andreas Mayerhoffer in 1759, is adorned with a replica of the crown worn by the Hungarian Kings.

Thermal baths

The hot spring discovered in 1959 produces 600 litres/130 gallons of water every minute, at a temperature of 45°C/113°F, which flow into a covered pool. The neighbouring open-air pool in Hatvani út is also filled with warm water.

Kalocsa

D/E 3

Region: Bács-Kiskun
Altitude: 97m/318ft. Population: 19,600

Situation and
Importance

* Folk-art

This town, situated on the east bank of the Danube, on a wide plateau stretching between the Danube and Tisza rivers, is known mainly for the cultivation of paprika, but its name is also synonymous with high-quality folk-art, especially in the form of the colourful embroidery to be found on textiles, walls and furnishings, the most beautiful example being at Kalocsa railway station. In the 11th c. King Stephen I made Kalocsa the diocesan town for this bank of the Danube. The first archbishop, an abbot by the name of Astrik, delivered to the king the crown which was a gift from the Pope. From the 19th c. onwards the area around Kalocsa developed into a fertile agricultural region, and its produce still supplies the local food-processing factories.

Sights

* Cathedral

The historical centre of Kalocsa is Szabadság tér, the site of its two major buildings, the Cathedral and the Archbishop's Palace. The first episcopal church was built in the time of King Stephen, but was destroyed and rebuilt several times over the centuries. The plans for the new Baroque building, which was erected between 1735 and 1754 on the medieval foundations, were probably drawn up by Andreas Mayerhoffer, a pupil of the famous Austrian Baroque architect Johann Lukas von Hildebrandt. The twin-towered west front boasts a gable with statues of the Virgin Mary between the Apostles Peter and Paul. The interior was completed *c.* 1770 and restored following a fire in 1816. Italian masters were responsible for the stucco reliefs in the roof vaulting, while the painting of the Assumption of the Virgin Mary on the high altar was by Leopold Kupelwieser of Vienna. The figures in front of the choir represent Kings Stephen and Ladislaus. The relief on the south side of the cathedral is a likeness of the first archbishop of Kalocsa, the abbot Astrik.
Valuable examples of religious art are housed in the oratory near the choir and in the cathedral treasury. The oldest bishop's sarcophagus in the crypt dates from the early 13th century.

This Baroque palace was built in 1776, to plans by the Piarist monk Gáspár Oswald, on the walls of a 14th c. castle. The wall-paintings in the festival hall and the ceiling frescos in the chapel are the work of the famous Austrian Baroque artist Franz Anton Maulbertsch (1724–96). The east wing houses the library, which contains some 100,000 volumes, including 56 codices and 508 incunabula. The most valuable books include a Martin Luther Bible.

Archbishop's Palace

As well as local history exhibits, this museum at István Király utca 25 houses the collection formed by the ethnographer Károly Viski, which illustrates by means of some particularly beautiful examples the development of folk-art in the Kalocsa region, especially in the field of embroidery. Note also the collections of minerals and coins. Open: Tue.–Sun. 9am–5pm.

Károly Viski Museum

The sculptor Nicolas Schöffer was born in Kalocsa and lived in Paris from 1937. He left to his home town a collection of sculptures which can be seen in the house in which he was born, at István Király utca 76 (Schöffer gyűjtemény; open: Tue.–Sun. 9am–noon and 2–5pm).
Not far from the house, in front of the bus station, stands his huge space sculpture "Tower of Light".

Nicolas Schöffer Collection

Kalocsa's major product and an important export item is paprika, a sweet, golden-red condiment obtained from the capsicum plant, the fruits of which, red peppers, can be seen hanging up to dry on houses everywhere in the region. In the Paprika Museum on Marx tér the visitor can learn a lot about the history of this pepper which was introduced from Central America, as well as its cultivation and processing. The museum is open May–Oct. Tue.–Sun. 10am–noon and 1–5pm.

Paprika Museum (Fűszerpaprika Múzeum)

In a typical lowland farmstead with an arbour and furnished in true period style, at Tompa Mihály utca 7, the Local Crafts Society displays its products

Folk-art Museum

Typical folk-art of Kalocsa . . .   *. . . and red peppers*

(Tajház). The flower patterns which have been handed down from generation to generation are incorporated by means of a special technique into embroidered costumes, blankets, table-cloths and sheets, and also in the form of painting on the walls and furnishings in the house. Beautiful souvenirs may be purchased in the museum shop. Open Tue.–Sun. 10am–6pm.

Kaposvár   C 3

Region: Somogy
Altitude: 141m/463ft
Population: 73,900

Situation and Importance

Kaposvár, situated on the River Kapos 190km/118 miles south-west of Budapest, was documented as long ago as 1009, but has only effectively made its mark in modern times as an industrial town. The castle after which the town is named (Kaposvár means "Kapos Castle") was an important fortification but nevertheless unable to resist attacks by the Turks. After the construction of the Danube–Dráva railway link in the second half of the 19th c. Kaposvár became the administrative and industrial hub of Somogy, the hilly region south of Lake Balaton which was once covered in marshland and steppe meadows, but is now home to the food and textile industry. 80% of the houses in Kaposvár were built during this century, so it does not possess many historical monuments, and its claim to the title "Town of Flowers" (because of its many parks) has been considerably weakened in recent years.

Former regional Town Hall

The main street (a pedestrian precinct) is Május 1. utca. No. 10 is the old Town Hall, a Classical building (1829–32) with a beautifully structured façade; it houses the Museum of the Somogy Region (including the folklore of the Dráva fishermen and the Somogy shepherds) and a valuable art collection, with paintings by well-known sons of the town and the surrounding region. These include József Rippi-Rónai (1861–1927), János Vaszary (1867–1939), Mihály Zichy (1827–1906). Open: Tue.–Sun. 10am–6pm.

Dorottya House

The Baroque house at Május 1 utca No. 1 was chosen by the writer and poet Mihály Csokonai Vitéz (1773–1805) as the setting for his light-hearted epic poem "Dorottya". The Shrovetide celebrations described therein are the subject of a Carnival and Dorottya Ball which take place in Kaposvár every year.

"Golden Lion" Pharmacy

Május I utca No. 19, built in 1774, was the town's first two-storey house. The fittings and equipment of the old pharmacy where the painter Rippi-Rónai worked as a chemist have been preserved.

Catholic Church

The present Catholic Church on the main square, Kossuth tér, was built in 1734–44 on the site of an old clay church. It was renovated in Neo-Romanesque style by Ottó Tandor (1852–1913). A striking feature are its many towers – one large, four smaller and two smaller still.

Film Museum

The only Film Museum (Mozimúzeum) in Hungary can be found at Kossuth Lajos utca 37. Temporary exhibitions are held on the ground floor, with an historical film collection on the upper floor. 6000 films are stored in the archives, with regular showings in the cinema (open: Tue.–Sun. 10am–noon and 3–5pm).

Leisure Park

In the north of the town, at the end of Kossuth Lajos utca, lies Szabadság Park, with herbaceous borders, decorative shrubs and sculptures.

Open-air swimming pool

In the Jókai Grove to the south, by the side of the River Kapos, lies a spacious thermal bath complex with both covered and open-air baths. The alkaline water is at a temperature of 43°C/110°F. The baths are tastefully decorated with ceramics, copper-reliefs and aluminium sculptures.

The castle was built in the Kapos floodplain, and the marshland proved almost to be a better form of defence than the walls. Remains of the walls can still be seen on the western edge of the town, on the old market place (Vár utca). In 1555 the Turks captured the castle and retained possession of it for almost 113 years. On orders from Vienna it was razed to the ground in the early 18th c., and it was 1931 before the remains were discovered and brought to light.

Castle ruins (Várromok)

Karcag
F 2

Region: Jász-Nagykun-Szolnok
Altitude: 87m/286ft
Population: 25,100

This town 60km/37 miles south-west of Debrecen was once the main seat of the Cumans, a nomadic people from the steppes of southern Russia. Like the Jazygs (see Jászberény) the Cumans reached Hungary in the 13th c. They agreed to serve in the armies of the Magyar king, and in return were given land and the right to self-government. In the 16th c. the Cuman language and culture tended to become swallowed up, but it was 1876 before their settlements finally lost their autonomy and were merged into the regional administration. The syllable "kun", which is still found in some place-names (Kiskunhalas, Kiskunfélegyháza), as well as in the regional names of Kiskunság ("Little Cumania") and Nagykunság ("Greater Cumania"), provides evidence of the earlier Cuman occupation.

Situation and Importance

Two museums in Karcag will serve to acquaint the visitor with the way of life and culture of the Cuman people; these are the typical Cuman farmhouse in Jókai utca, with an exhibition of Cuman folk-art, and the Great Cuman Museum, housed in a neo-classical manor house (1830) at Kálvin utca 4 and named after the ethnologist István Györffy (1884–1939), a native of Karcag.
In the house formerly owned by the potter Sándor Kántor (1894–1984) at Erkel Ferenc utca 4 some of his finest work is on display and there are also pottery-making demonstrations. Kántor was responsible for reviving pottery skills in this region and for developing them as an art form.

Sights

9km/5½ miles north-east of the town lie the Berekfürdő baths, where the warm water containing iodine and bromine leaves the ground at temperatures of 55–57°C/130–135°F.

Berekfürdő

Kecskemét
E 3

Region: Bács-Kiskun
Altitude: 122m/400ft
Population: 105,300

Kecskemét is the capital of the Bács-Kiskun region as well as the cultural and economic centre of the area lying between the Danube and Tisza rivers. The home of the famous apricot liqueur known as "Barack Pálinka", it has few really old buildings but does boast some fine art nouveau style edifices and an extremely attractive town centre. The billy goat which appears in the town's coat-of-arms is explained by the name Kecskemét, which roughly translated means "goat walk". Kecskemét is within easy reach of Budapest and a good setting-out point for excursions into the Bugac puszta (see entry), the tourist-favoured region of the Kiskunság National Park (Kiskunsági Nemzeti Park).

*Situation and Importance

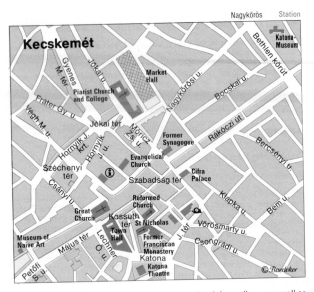

Boasting an impressive number of schools and training colleges as well as three university colleges, Kecskemét has become an educational stronghold. The Institute of Musical Education housed in the former Franciscan Priory (see below) promotes the new teaching methods devised by the musician and composer Zoltán Kodály (1882–1967; see Famous People), a native of Kecskemét. The Institute's reputation has now spread far and wide.

History

The area now covered by the town of Kecskemét was already settled *c.* 3000 B.C. (Bronze Age urnsite). During the migration of the peoples Scythians, later Sarmatians, Goths and Avars and finally the invading Magyars all settled here. The earliest documented record of Kecskemét as a town is dated 1368. The medieval settlement had no walls, being defended solely by moats and ditches in a ring round the town (now the route followed by the E5 road). Being owned by the Pasha of Buda and subsequently by the Sultan the town enjoyed the privilege of self-government during the period of Turkish rule. The basis of its economic prosperity was cattle-rearing and trading, and this was followed by other prosperous trades such as those of furrier, shoemaker and specialist metalworker. After the Turks withdrew, Kecskemét came under Habsburg rule in 1710. In 1834 a redemption treaty freed Kecskemét from its loan burdens and enabled it to boost its economy through the cultivation of fruit, vegetables and vines. In the early 19th c. 7 million young trees were planted around Kecskemét in an attempt to bind the sandy soil, which had lain fallow for centuries. On July 8 1911 a heavy earthquake lasting 25 minutes caused great damage to the town and the surrounding area.

Economy

As a result of the intensive system of viticulture and the growing of fruit and vegetables the area around Kecskemét has been named "The Garden of Hungary". Its horticultural products are processed in the factories in Kecskemét. Far less important are such other branches of industry as prefabricated buildings, engineering, shoe manufacture and printing.
As well as the famous "Barack Pálinka" liqueur, Kecskemét also produces some good table wines.

Sights

Kecskemét has all the characteristics of a market town on the Hungarian Plain: scattered around the periphery of the town are a number of individual farmsteads, which give way to rustic dwellings with fruit gardens (and now unfortunately some sad-looking satellite estates too) as one gets nearer to the town centre. The atmosphere in the medieval quarters, with their typical cobbled streets lined with acacia trees, is typical of that usually found in a small town and only the centre itself is a reminder of Kecskemét's size. The main places of interest will be found within a comparatively small compass and in one of the three large squares, Kossuth tér, Szabadság tér and Katona József tér.

Townscape

On Kossuth tér stands the imposing Town Hall (Városháza), which was built in 1893–96 to plans by Ödön Lechner (1845–1914) and Gyula Pártos (1845–1916), and is an important example of the Hungarian art nouveau style. Varying architectural features, especially the Gothic ogival arches, round columns and artificial pillars mingle with traditional majolica ornamentation and contemporary extensions to form a unique and unconventional whole. The entrance hall decoration reflects the way the town saw itself during its halcyon days in the 19th c. The stairwell with its wide almost Baroque-like staircase obtains its special effect as a result of the light shining through the brightly-coloured stained-glass windows.

**Town Hall

Visitors are also allowed into the magnificent, wood-panelled council chamber on the first floor. The frescos by Bertelan Székely (1835–1910) depict famous scenes from Hungarian history, ranging from the treaty with the tribal princes being signed in blood to the coronation of the Emperor Franz Joseph.

Every hour the carillon above the main door plays a melody from the "Háry János" Suite, written by the composer Zoltán Kodály, a native of Kecskemét, and at 12.05pm, 6.05pm and 8.05pm other popular tunes are played.

Kecskemét: Town Hall in national style

Great Church

Kecskemét

Memorial stone to Jószef Katona

In front of the Town Hall stands a memorial marking the spot where the dramatist József Katona (1791–1830) died of a heart attack. Born in Kecskemét, he spent the last ten years of his life working in his native town. His play "Bánk ban", which takes as its theme the murder of the wife of King Andreas II of Hungary, has assured him a place in Hungarian literary history.

Great Church

The church with the contrasting yellow and white façades near the Town Hall is known as the Great Church (Nagytemplom); work on it commenced in 1774 to plans by Gáspár Oswald, but it was 1806 before it was completed. The group of figures above the entrance shows Christ handing the Keys of Heaven to Peter. The faces on the niche-sculptures on the front of the building are those of SS Stephen and Ladislaus, Peter and Paul. The Hungarian artist József Ferenc Falkoner was responsible for the painting of the Ascension on the high altar.

József Katona Theatre

The south side of Kossuth tér merges into Katona József tér, on which stands the Neo-Baroque Theatre (1896), which has been renovated and has regained its original charm. It was designed by the Viennese architects Fellner and Helmer, who were among the busiest builders of theatres of their time. The front of the Kecskemét theatre has the triangular gable and pillars to the side, a feature so typical of these architects, with the large rounded arch reaching down into the main entrance.

Plague Column

The sculptor Leopold Anton Conti carved the figures on the Baroque Plague or Trinity Column in front of the theatre; the cost of the column was met by public subscription in 1742.

Church of St Nicholas

On the east side of Kossuth tér stands Szent Miklós, the oldest church in the town, dating from the 13th c. Entrance is by way of a walled forecourt with Rococo wrought-iron tracery of the highest quality on both entrance gates.

The Neo-Baroque József-Katona Theatre

In the 15th c. the church was extended eastwards and the St Anne Chapel added in the side-aisle. The Franciscans, who took possession of the church in 1647, renovated it in Baroque style and in 1799 built the tower in the 18th c. plait style. The only remaining vestiges of the original Gothic are to be seen on the pillars supporting the tower and on the plinth in the side-aisle. Excavations carried out to the north of the church revealed the foundations of the medieval St Michael's Chapel.

The Calvary sculpture in front of the church wall was the work of an unknown artist in 1790.

In 1975 the Institute of Musical Education (Kodály Zoltán Zenepedagógiai intézet) was opened in the former Franciscan priory (built in 1702–36) on the pedestrian walk called Két templom köz. Its aim was to preserve the name of Zoltán Kodály as a teacher of music and to develop further the instruction methods he had devised. Concerts are regularly performed in the old refectory and in the cloister courtyard. A permanent exhibition in the cloisters documents the life of the composer.

"Zoltán Kodály" Institute of Musical Education

Built in 1683–84 and extended in the late 18th c., the Reformed Church stands on the remains of a medieval church. The choir is Classical in style whereas the pulpit shows Rococo characteristics.

Reformed Church

Surrounded by beautiful houses and with lush green swards, Szabadság tér is like a small oasis in the very heart of the town. In the famous Café Szabadság the visitor can relax with a cup of excellent coffee while enjoying the view of this spacious square. On its south side stands the massive art nouveau building of the New College (1911), which also houses the Library and the Ráday Ecclesiastical Museum.

Szabadság tér

Géza Márkus, a pupil of Lechner and one of the second generation of Hungarian art nouveau architects, was responsible for designing this remarkable building at the beginning of Rákóczi Ferenc utca. In the manner of Belgian and French art nouveau style buildings, the façades carry flat, mainly floral decoration, here in the form of majolica ceramic tiles from the Zsolnay factory in Pécs. Originally intended as a commercial casino, it has been used as an Art Gallery since 1963. The collection concentrates on Hungarian artists of the last hundred years or so, but there are also works by the colony of artists domiciled in Kecskemét (open: Tue.–Sun. 10am–6pm).

*Cifra Palace (Cifra Palota) Kecskemét Art Gallery

Directly opposite the Citra Palota stands the former Synagogue, built in 1871 in the Moorish style to the designs of János Zitterbarth. Since 1973 it has been the "House of Science and Technology" (Tudomány és technika háza). The onion tower was destroyed in the 1911 earthquake, and the building suffered further damage during the Second World War. Extensive renovations in 1973 to plans by József Kerényi helped to restore it to its former glory. In the foyer stand copies of fifteen Michelangelo sculptures.

Former Synagogue

As well as his extensive work in Budapest, the architect Miklós Ybl designed the Evangelical Church (1861–63) at Arany János utca 1. Its ground plan is in the form of a Greek cross. Built in Neo-Romanesque style, the church contains two beautiful late 19th c. tiled stoves made in the Zsolnay factory in Pécs.

Evangelical Church

In addition to the church, this complex of buildings at Jókai utca 1 embraces a priory, a college and a school in Classical style. Built c. 1730, the Baroque church is the work of the well-known architect Andreas Mayerhoffer. The front is embellished with statues of SS Stephen and Ladislaus, as well as with figures of the Virgin Mary and the founder of the order, St Joseph Calasanz. Inside can be seen some beautiful original altars. Note also the paintings on the pastoral side-altar in which the figures display the traditional hairstyle and clothes of the Cuman settlers.

Piarist Priory and College

Kecskemét

Other museums

Kecskemét can offer a number of interesting museums. As well as the Art Gallery in the Cifra Palace (see above) a visit is recommended to the József Katona Museum in the park of the same name at Bethlen utca 1. It provides detailed information on the history of the region (archaeology, ethnology, local art) and is open Tue.–Sun 10am–6pm.

Unique in Hungary is the rich collection of naive Hungarian art housed in the pleasant surroundings of the rural Baroque mansion at Gáspár András utca 11 (open: Tue.–Sun. 10am–5pm).

"Sorakatenus" is the name given to the Toy Museum founded some ten years ago at the corner of Gáspár utca and Hosszú utca. The special thing about it is that it combines a museum and a workshop – not only are toys dating back to the early 19th c. exhibited but also children and young people can try their hand at making toys in the workshop, under the guidance of skilled teachers (open: daily 9am–5pm).

An old 19th c. distillery at Serfőző utca 9 now houses the Museum of Local Arts and Crafts. Its exhibits include pottery, carvings in wood and ivory, weaving and crochet work from about 1960 onwards (open: daily except Mon. and Tue. 9am–5pm).

The Hungarian Photographic Museum at Katona József tér 12 first opened its doors in 1991. Its collection is still being built up and concentrates on Hungarian photography (open: Wed.–Sun. 10am–6pm).

Leisure Centre

An area of some 57ha/143 acres on the western edge of the town is equipped with an open-air pool, sports pitches, an aboretum and much more.

Surroundings

Nagykőrös

Characteristics and History

Nagykőrös, a town of 28,000 inhabitants 16km/10 miles north-west of Kecskemét on Road 441 to Cegléd, is the centre of a fruit and vegetable-growing region and makes a considerable contribution to the country's agricultural produce. The food-canning industry in Nagykőrös is also of great economic importance.

First documented in 1266, the community developed in the Middle Ages to become a small market town; during the Turkish period it – like Kecskemét and Cegléd – was elevated to the status of a "khas" town, thus enjoying the special protection of the Sultan and remaining immune from pillage and destruction, so that it actually grew in size and importance under Turkish rule. Finally the region's borders reached from Pest as far as the River Tisza, and 8000–10,000 cattle grazed on the meadows. The school founded in 1553 grew into a famous grammar school in the 19th century.

János Arany Museum

In the Cifrakert, a small park on the main street (Ceglédi út 19) are the former Hussar Barracks (1836–38), which now house a collection of municipal memorabilia as well as the Arany Memorial Museum. On the entrance side of the long. single-storey building there is a tympanum resting on Doric pillars, and on the courtyard side an arcaded walkway. The great Hungarian writer János Arany (1817–82; see Famous People) taught at Nagykőrös Grammar School for nine years, from 1851 to 1860. The most beautiful of the exhibits include old hand tools, personal items owned by the Arany family, burial plaques and the first document in which the name Kőrös appears (open: May–Sept. Tue.–Sun. 10am–6pm; 9am–5pm at other times of the year).

Church of St Ladislaus

When Nagykőrös became Protestant in 1688 all the Catholics left. Ninety years passed before a new Catholic community was formed; Queen Maria Theresia donated 8000 pieces of gold to assist it in building this new church. The painting on the Baroque altar shows King Ladislaus fighting against the Cumans.

Decorated façade of the Cifra Palais

Synagogue

The Town Hall at Szabadság tér 5 dates from 1710. The tower with its collar-like oriel window is original.

Town Hall

This church on Szabadság tér was built as a Catholic church in the 15th c.; when the Catholics left the town the members of the Reformed Church took it over. Its present appearance is largely the result of changes made in 1811 and 1847; the front with its impressive tower was rebuilt in 1907. Visitors will appreciate the beautiful interior, with the gallery running all the way round, the Baroque pulpit and organ and the gilded metalwork in the little treasure-chamber.

Reformed Church

See entry

Bugac (Puszta)

See entry

Kiskunfélegyháza

See Szolnok, Surroundings

Cegléd

Keszthely

C 3

Region: Zala
Population: 22,500

Situated on the west bank of Lake Balaton the holiday centre of Keszthely, with its population of 22,500, is the largest town on the lake, rich in tradition and offering a sandy beach, hotels and ample leisure facilities. György Festetics built Europe's first agricultural college here (now the University of Agriculture), which helped to confirm Keszthely's importance as a cultural and educational centre. Keszthely was the birthplace of Károly Goldmark, the composer of the opera "The Queen of Sheba".

*Situation and Importance

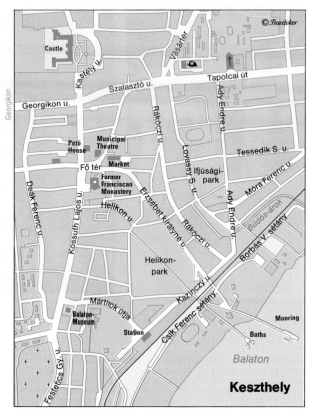

© Baedeker

Keszthely

Neolithic man settled in this region, to be followed later by Celts, Romans, Lombards, Avars and Magyars. Benefiting from its position at the intersection of important trade routes, Kesthely became a thriving market town in the Middle Ages and a provincial town from 1421. It found itself unable to avoid being taken by the Turks and later by Habsburg troops, after lending its support to the Rákóczi uprising. After 1739 Kesthely came into the ownership of the Festetics family, who possessed large estates in the surrounding countryside and made the town the centre of their cultural activities. The great landowner György Count Festetics (1755–1819), a patron of the arts and sciences, founded the Helikon literary circle and the Helikon Festivals, and laid the foundation-stone of the Helikon Library. His most important contribution to the country's cultural development, however, was the founding of the Georgikon (1797), the first agricultural college in Europe (now the University of Agriculture). Since the mid-19th c. Kesthely has become a fully-fledged holiday resort.

Sights

*Festetics Palace

In a large park to the north of the town centre lies the Palace which was the residence of the Festetics family for two hundred years. The first palace,

Festetics Castle, the exterior . . .   *. . . and interior*

built for Kristóf Festetics in 1745, was a comparatively modest affair with "only" 34 rooms and a French Baroque garden. The enlarged and changed building we see today was the work of the Viennese architect Viktor Rumpelmayer, carried out between 1883 and 1887 on the instructions of the future Duke Tasziló Festetics. The result is a spacious, horseshoe-shaped complex with 101 rooms. The uniform Neo-Baroque façade, built on the lines of French palaces, is accentuated by the tower in the central wing. The garden at the rear was designed by the English landscape gardener E. H. Miller, and a wall with a gateway separates the palace from the town.

The Palace Museum in the south wing takes in several rooms with their original furnishings, including the Chapel, the great Dining Room, which is now used for concerts and other events, and the famous Helikon Library (see above), with its 80,000 volumes. | Palace Museum

From 1808 the students of the Agricultural College received their tuition in the single-storey building near the Palace (Georgikon utca 20). Adjoining it to the south is the former Festetics family estate which was later used to provide practical instruction for the students; it includes three yards, a dairy, office buildings, stables and workshops. On the ground floor of the old corn-store there is an exhibition on the history of the Festetics family, while the upper floor and attic house a Dairy Farming Museum with old tools and equipment and machinery used in viticulture and farming in the Lake Balaton region (open: May–Oct. Tue.–Sun. 10am–5pm). | Georgikon House, Dairy Farming Museum

In 1386 the Franciscans built a single-aisled, groin-vaulted church on Fő tér; in 1550 a priory was added on the north side. During the Turkish occupation it was converted to a fortress and linked with Lake Balaton by a canal so that boats could sail right up to it. The Turks besieged the fortified church but were unable to take it. The Neo-Gothic tower on the front was added in 1878. In 1896 the Baroque furnishings were removed to reveal the original | Former Franciscan Priory, Parish Church

Gothic. During the restoration work some fragments of frescos of remarkable quality were uncovered; these show the influence of late 14th c. Italian painting. The coat-of-arms of the architect István Lackffy adorn the keystone of the choir ceiling; his tomb is also in the choir.

Balaton Museum

The magnificent 1928 Neo-Baroque building at Múzeum utca 2 (entrance in Kossuth Lajos utca) now houses an extremely informative and rich collection of exhibits devoted to the natural history and culture of the "Balaton" region. On the ground floor is a lapidarium with Roman and medieval stone finds, while the second floor documents a range of subjects including flora and fauna, unique aspects of folk-lore and traditional forms of work, shipping and tourism on Lake Balaton (open: Tue.–Sun. 10am–6pm).

Pethő House

The plain Baroque building at Kossuth Lajos utca 22, one of the town's oldest houses and with a medieval cellar, is where the composer Károly Goldmark was born.

Helikon Park

Helikon Park, an extensive area reaching as far as the promenade along the bank of the lake, is Kesthely's modern leisure centre. It has shops, sports facilities and a large beach.

Surroundings

Fenékpuszta

In the Fenékpuszta, 7km/4½ miles south of Kesthely, visitors can still see the Classical-style stables of the Festetics stud as well as remains of the Roman camp of Valcum.

Zalavár

In the 9th c. the Carolingians gave to the Slavonic Prince Privina the region around Lake Balaton as his feudal due; 18km/11 miles south-west of Kesthely, on the banks of Kis Balaton, is the spot where he built his castle, in the middle of his lands near the present-day village of Zalavár. As the region became converted to Christianity a number of churches were built here, including the basilica to the west of Zalavár. It originally had three aisles, a west porch and three apses, but only the foundations have survived.

Zalaapáti

In the town of Zalaapáti, 13km/8 miles west of Keszthely (Road 75) stands the Late Baroque abbey of St Adrian (c. 1780), with altarpieces by the Austrian Johann Schmidt (1718–1801). The abbey was originally founded in the 11th c. by King Stephen on the site of Prince Privina's castle (see above), and was rebuilt on its present site in the 18th century.

Zalakaros

See Nagykanizsa, Surroundings

Hévíz

See entry

Kiskunfélegyháza

E 3

Region: Bács-Kiskun
Altitude: 101m/332ft. Population: 35,700

Situation and Importance

Kiskunfélegyháza lies in the heart of the region between the Danube and Tisza rivers and is the historical centre of Little Cumania (see below). Having been laid waste by the Turks in the 16th c. it was 1774 before the town flourished once more; in that year it was granted its municipal charter and thenceforth developed into a thriving commercial town with increasing industry.

Little Cumania (Kiskunság)

This historical area of land between the Danube and the Tisza on the Hungarian Plain was named after the Turkish-speaking nomadic people, the Cumans, who originally came from the steppes of southern Russia.

Driven out by the Mongols in the early 13th c. Cuman tribes found their way on to the Hungarian Plain and, after being converted to Christianity, gradually became integrated with the Magyars. In the 19th c. Little Cumania became one of the major agricultural regions and earned the name of "The Fruit Garden of Hungary". Most of the people are still engaged in agriculture, although in the late 1960s oil and natural gas were discovered here and the chemical, plastic and textile industries became attracted to Little Cumania.

Sights

Few towns in Hungary can boast of a town hall as imposing and original as that in Kiskunfélegyháza. Designed by József Vass and built in 1911 in the centre of the town at Kossuth Lajos utca 1, it – together with the town hall in Kecskemét – can claim to be the most beautiful example of Hungarian art nouveau architecture.

*Town Hall

The rich floral ornamentation on the false gable-ends of the main façade is copied from the designs found in rural Hungarian folk-art, such as those seen on the embroidered cloaks and jackets worn by the shepherds. This ornamentation, together with the colourful majolica roof-tiles made in the Pécs Zsolnay factory, give the otherwise somewhat severe building a more cheerful note.

The ethnographic and local history collections of the Kiskun Múzeum are now on display in the Baroque building of 1753 at Vörös Hadsereg útja 9, formerly the headquarters of the military command of Little Cumania. In view of its earlier function as a gaol, the courtyard wing has been made into a prison museum. The exhibits on display here, such as instruments of torture, are a reminder of the time when bandits and robbers made the Great Hungarian Plain a dangerous place to live. Well worth seeing is the still functioning windmill dating from 1860 which now stands in the museum courtyard (open: daily except Mon. 10am–6pm).

Little Cumania Museum

The Baroque church of Our Lady on Béke tér, built in 1744–52, has Rococo side-altars and pulpit, as well as an 18th c. plait style font. The old tower collapsed and was replaced by a new one in 1770.

Church

Between 1820 and 1830 the father of the great Hungarian writer Sándor Petőfi (see Famous People) was the landlord of an inn in the Classical building at Szabadság tér No. 9. Today it is an arts centre. Although he spent his childhood here, Sandor Petőfi was in fact born in Kiskőrös, 30km/19 miles west of Kiskunfélegyháza.

"Swan House"

Surroundings

On the right bank of the Tisza, 24km/15 miles west of Kiskunfélegyháza on Road 451, lies the fishing village of Csongrád (pop. 23,000), a quiet little place reflecting some of the tranquillity of the region. Visitors may care to visit the little local history museum at Iskola utca 2 and the listed fishermen's huts at the mouth of the Körös. This backwater is now a nature reserve.

Csongrád

12km/7½ miles from Csongrád, along the left bank of the Tisza, lies Szentes (pop. 35,000). First documented in 1075, it developed after the Turkish period into an agricultural town and later the home of the food-industry. For a time it was the regional capital, as witnessed by the large town hall on Kossuth tér. It can lay claim to a long tradition of pottery and basket-weaving.

Szentes

St Anne's Church is the town's oldest building, dating from 1768; however, apart from the tower, it was rebuilt in the Classical style in 1847. On Kossuth tér stand the Neo-Baroque Town Hall (1912) and the Reformed Church,

Sights

built in Classical style between 1808 and 1825. The József Koszta Museum is housed in a Classical building in the little Széchenyi Forest on the River Kurca; as well as paintings by the landscape artist József Koszta (1864–1949) it also contains archaeological finds from the time of the great migration of the peoples as well as Szent pottery (open: Tue.–Sat. 2–6pm, Sun. 10am–6pm).

Kiskunhalas

50km/31 miles south-west of Kiskunfélegyháza, between the Danube and Tisza rivers, lies the little agricultural town of Kiskunhalas (alt. 113m/371ft, pop. 31,260), with a beautiful bathing lake on the edge of the town.

Lace Museum
(Csipkeház)

In 1903 the drawing teacher and local-art collector Árpád Dékáni founded a workshop to produce lace to his own designs, thereby pioneering the Kiskunhalas lace industry. The success of his enterprise was due in no small measure to the skills of one Mária Markovits who, assisted by a small work-force of lacemakers, translated his designs into high quality work which received international acclaim at the 1904 World Exhibition in St Louis. Mária Markovits also developed the normal Venetian technique of 10–12 stitches per cm into one of 40–50 per cm.

The former workshop at Kossuth utca 39 today houses the Lace Museum with some particularly beautiful examples of Kiskunhalas lace on display. In the garden there is a memorial and bronze bust of Mária Markovits (open: 9am–noon, 1–4pm).

János Thorma
Museum

The Local History Museum is housed in a late 19th c. building at Köztársaság utca 2. It also displays work by the naturalist painter János Thorma (1870–1937). Open: Tue.–Sun. 10am–5pm.

Windmill
(Szélmalom)

At one time there were a large number of windmills to be seen in the flat countryside of Little Cumania, but only a few have survived. On the northern edge of Kiskunhalas, at the corner of Kölcsey and Linhardt utca, a 19th c. windmill still stands.

Bugac (Puszta)   See entry

Kecskemét   See entry

Ópusztaszer   See Szeged, Surroundings

Handmade lace from Kiskunhalas

Kiskunság (National Park)

See Bugac (Puszta)

Kisvárda

See Nyíregyháza, Surroundings

Kőszeg (Güns)   B 2

Region: Vas
Altitude: 274m/900ft
Population: 13,600

Kőszeg is a pretty little town lying about 20km/12½ miles north of Szom-   Situation and
bathely on the Austrian border, on the southern slopes of the Güns Moun-   Importance
tains (Kőszegi hegység).
Although most of the buildings are 18th c. there are also some Renaissance
houses and a romantic castle – a popular destination for excursions.

After the founding of the state of Hungary the kings strengthened the town   History
as an important link in the chain of fortresses known as the *Őrség*, built to
defend the country against threats from the west. A stone castle was built in
the middle of the 12th c. (first documented in the second half of the 13th c.);
in 1532 Miklós Jurisics and a small number of men held out here for 25 days
against Sultan Suleiman II's army of 55,000 strong. The Turks finally withdrew before winter set in and a strong Austrian army arrived. During the
18th c. the town was of little strategic or economic importance. However, it
has a proud and strong cultural tradition, and there was a grammar school
here back in the 16th century.

Sights

To the south of the Old Town, on the main square (Fő tér; car parking)   Church of the
stands the Neo-Gothic Church of the Sacred Heart (Jézu Szive templom),   Sacred Heart
built in 1892–94, with a tower 57m/187ft high. The stained glass windows
portray SS Stephen, Ladislaus, Imre, Elisabeth and Margit; note also the
15th c. Gothic monstrance and a chasuble of turquoise satin bedecked with
pearls.

Heroes' Gate (Hősi kapu) at the end of Városház utca is the entrance to the   Heroes' Gate
historic centre of the town. The gate was built in 1932 on the site of the
14th c. Lower Gate Tower, to mark the 400th anniversary of the Turkish
siege. A relief reminds us of the brave defenders and of those who fell in the
First World War.

The heart of the Old Town is the well-proportioned Jurisics Square con-   *Jurisics tér
taining the Town Hall, two churches and some medieval town houses with
characteristic enclosed gables, although most are Baroque.

To the right behind Heroes' Gate, at Jurisics tér 2, lies "Arcade House", built   Arcade House
in 1774, with arcades in front of it at ground level; the town musician Josef
Bittner had it built as a tennis court. The most attractive part of the front of
the house is the architrave above the keystone, built in the 18th c. plait style
and adorned with rosettes and a garland.

The Tábornokház, a 17th c. Renaissance building at Jurisics tér 8 immedi-   General's House
ately to the left behind Heroes' Gate, was where the captain of the town's
cavalry forces had his quarters. A twin-arched loggia adorns the front. The

215

house is now the Jurisics Museum, displaying examples of local handicrafts (open: Tue.–Sun. 10am–6pm); from the museum tower there is a pleasant view of the square and the Old Town.

Town Hall

The Town Hall at Jurisics tér 8 (adjoining the museum) was built in several phases; the covered embrasures on the north side are 14th/15th c. Gothic; the Attic columns, covered by the twin pediments, are Renaissance, the inner doors Baroque, the main door Classical in style. The painted front is also Baroque (1712); on the outside the crest on the left is that of the Jurisics family, that in the centre that of old Hungary and that on the right shows the coat-of-arms of the town of Kőszeg. In between are paintings – probably late 19th c. – of the Virgin Mary, patron saint of Hungary, and of King Stephen.

Lady Column, Town Fountain

The convoluted Baroque Lady Column in the centre of Jurisics tér dates from 1739 and is the work of the Sopron stonemason Lorenz Eysenkölbl; he was paid by means of fines which the town imposed on Protestants who opposed Mariolatry. Eysenkölbl was also responsible for the Town Fountain; this eventually suffered from over-use and so in 1766 was enclosed within the 18th c. plait style pump room we see today.

Presbytery

This building at Jurisics tér 12 dates originally from the 14th/15th c., and is also known as "Lada House" after a former owner. It has been renovated on several occasions and now boasts a superbly stuccoed Baroque façade.

Ambrózy House

The last of the row of houses on the west side of Jurisics tér, No. 14, is a solid, almost fortress-like edifice with two fronts facing the street. It was built in Late Renaissance style *c.* 1560 by merging two or three existing houses into one; Baroque additions were made in the 18th c. The side looking onto the courtyard boasts a loggia with Tuscan pillars and graffito decoration.

Kőszeg: an inner courtyard   *Apothacary's Museum*

No. 5–7 on the east side of Jurisics tér, dating from the 16th c., is lavishly decorated by the graffito process, which involved scratching through the plaster to show the different-coloured under-surface. This process had then only recently been imported from Italy. Under the roof can be seen a Latin inscription which is a quotation from a Letter of St Paul the Apostle to the Romans, an indication that at one time the house was used as a presbytery.

Graffito House

The nearby 16th c. Renaissance house (No. 9a) was converted to Early Baroque two centuries later. The entrance door is arched and the double-doors are decorated with beautifully carved geometric patterns.

Batthyány House

A medieval town house at No. 11 was converted to a Jesuit monastery, and the monks ran it as a pharmacy. When the order of monks was dissolved in 1777 the chemist Mátyás Svalla bought the house together with the Baroque fittings and furnishings which had been installed c. 1740 by the Jesuit monks, and formed the town pharmacy known as "The Golden Unicorn". The museum also contains some turned wooden crucibles and lead-glazed earthenware vessels (open: Tue.–Sun. 10am–6pm).

Pharmaceutical Museum (Patikamúzeum)

Two churches stand one behind the other at the northern end of Jurisics tér. The newer one at the front is dedicated to St Imre and was built by the Protestants in 1615–18 over a medieval charnel-house. Its Gothic features suggest that the single-aisled building with its tall tower was modelled on the older Church of St James. In 1671, when the Catholics took over the church, a Baroque chapel and sacristy were added. There is a sculpture of St Imre above the main door. The reredos on the main altar is by Stephan Dorffmeister the Younger (1805) and shows St Imre taking his holy vows; Dorffmeister the Elder painted the picture of "The Visitation of Mary" on the right side-altar.

Church of St Imre

The second church on Jurisics tér, the most important historical building in Kőoszeg, was built in Late Gothic style in 1403–07, using the remains of a Romanesque Minorite church. In 1758 the front and furnishings were redesigned in Baroque fashion. In 1554 the church became Protestant, and from 1671 onwards it found itself in the possession of various Catholic orders, including Jesuits, Piarists and Benedictines, whose crests can be seen on the façade. The tower is 15th c., while the little Sanctus Tower above the choir was added in 1697. The interior of the triple-aisled edifice is Gothic; the keystone of the groin vault in front of the choir bears the arms of the founder, Miklós Garai. Along the south side of the choir are niche-seats with pointed arches, and above the tabernacle is a Gothic Madonna and Infant Jesus (c. 1500). Also Gothic are the wall-paintings on the end wall of the south side-aisle; these show the Magi, an outsize St Christopher, a protective Madonna, St Elisabeth of Thuringia, of Árpád lineage, and St Barbara.

* Church of St James

Chernel Street, which leads west from St James' Church and then turns south, is named after the historian Kálmán Chernel (1822–91) who worked in Kőszeg. Almost all the houses are late medieval, converted to Baroque. The most outstanding is the U-shaped Chernel House (No. 10). Above the door with its wickerwork arch, Rococo vase-shaped pillars support a convoluted architrave. The year 1766 is engraved in the keystone of the arch. Eugène de Beauharnais, Napoleon's stepson and viceroy, lived here in 1809.

Chernel utca

József Rájnis Street, leading northwards from the north-west corner of Jurisics tér, was named after the Jesuit monk and writer József Kőszegi Rájnis, who translated ancient Greek and Latin literature into Hungarian. Here, too, will be found some houses, originally medieval (built close together in step-like fashion for defensive reasons), later converted to Baroque or Classical. The best-known is No. 2 near St James' Church, built in 1677–80 to plans by the Italian architect Pietro Orsolini and which served

Rájnis József utca

first the Jesuits and later the Benedictines as a priory. It became a famous centre of learning, and numbered many major academics and artists among its students and tutors.

Jurisics Castle

Access to the castle at Rájnis József utca 9, on the north-western edge of the town centre, is through a gatehouse in front of it (with tourist accommodation). Matthias Corvinus conquered the medieval fortress in 1482 and added a Renaissance west wing, some windows of which have survived. After it had been destroyed by the Turks in 1532, Jurisics, to whom it had been gifted, rebuilt it. The conflagration of 1777 engulfed the castle; subsequently the south and west wings were rebuilt in Baroque fashion with two-storeyed arcades. Of the five towers only two were rebuilt to their original height. In the courtyard of the gatehouse, from which a brick-built bridge leads to the door of the castle itself, there stands a monument to Jurisics, designed by Sándor Mikus (1903–82); above the doorway can be seen the Eszterházy coat-of-arms and a painted Turkish tent, a favourite decoration on Hungarian castles. In the north wing stairs lead to the Miklós Jurisics Museum of Local History (open: Tue.–Sun. 10am–6pm). As well as its documents and books, particular mention must be made of the famous "Book of Viticulture", in which pictures of the new young vine shoots on St George's Day and notes on the grape harvest on St Ursula's Day have been entered ever since 1740 and right up to the present day. Theatrical performances are staged in summer in the inner courtyard of the castle.

Surroundings

Szabó Mountain

Szabó hegy (379m/1244ft) in the Kőszeg Mountains west of the town is a favourite spot for outings, and there is a scheduled bus service from Kőszeg. In the forest there is a playground and gymnasium as well as a ski-slope with a lift.

Cák

This village (pop. 300), 4km/2½ miles south-west of Kőszeg, is famous for its wine-cellars which lie above the town along a beautiful avenue lined with chestnut trees. The typical rural buildings are mainly thatched.

Velem

Velem (pop. 400), 9km/5½ miles south-west of Kőszeg, has the quintessential features of a typical village in this part of Hungary – old storehouses once lined both banks of a stream, and remains of these can still be seen. In the Bronze Age, c. 1000 b.c., there was a terraced settlement on the hillside with a fort on the top of Mount Vitus. Today the Baroque church of St Vitus stands there.
Courses in arts and crafts for the amateur are held in Velem every summer.

Bozsok

Bozsok (pop. 500), 9km/5½ miles south of Kőszeg, has some beautiful old buildings, such as the picturesquely situated Sibrik Palace (originally 15th c. with Late Renaissance extensions, a Baroque arcaded courtyard and façade), the Parish Church (mainly medieval, renovated in 1772) and St Joseph's Chapel (1775). The farmhouses with arbours are seldom encountered in rural architecture.

Bükfürdő

19km/12 miles east of Kőszeg lie the Bük baths, where a thermal stream was discovered when boring for oil in 1956; covering an area of 36ha/ 90 acres, this is one of the major bath establishments in western Hungary. The warm waters at Bük contain calcium, magnesium and hydrogen carbonate, with a comparatively high fluoride and carbonic acid content. They are used in the treatment of rheumatism, joint problems and accident injuries, and are drunk as an aid to digestive troubles and inhaled to ease chronic bronchial catarrh. However, situated as it is on a flat piece of land with no trees, the site is not particularly attractive, and the equipment is not in the best of condition.

Szapáry Palace, 5km/3 miles east of Bükfürdő and a beautiful and important example of the Baroque architecture of the Hungarian landed gentry, is now a hotel. When it was built *c.* 1696 master tradesmen from several areas of Hungary were involved; these included the architect Lorenz Eysenkölbl, the sculptor Johannes Unger and the stucco plasterer Pietro Antonio Conti. The banqueting hall with frescos by Luca Colombo from Lugano is particularly splendid.

Martonvásár

D 2

Region: Fejér
Altitude: 121m/397ft. Population: 4400

This little township lies 32km/20 miles west of Budapest in the lowlands between the Buda Mountains and the range of hills near Velence.

Situation

In well-tended parkland reminiscent of English landscaped gardens stands the palace which was built in 1775 for the Brunswick family and is now the home of an agricultural research institute. In 1875 it was renovated in English Neo-Gothic style. Countess Theresa Brunswick (1775–1861), who is buried in the crypt of the palace church, was an advocate of the teachings of Pestalozzi and in 1821 she founded the first Hungarian kindergarten school. However, Martonvásár became famous mainly through Ludwig van Beethoven, a friend of Count Franz Brunswick who often stayed at the palace. Josephine Brunswick, sister of Countess Theresa, was probably the "immortal beloved" to whom the composer wrote those enigmatic love-letters which he never posted. As the letters contained neither name nor date, historians can only speculate on the identity of the lady to whom they were addressed. It is thought that during one of his many visits to the palace Beethoven composed parts of the famous "Appassionata" piano sonata, which was dedicated to his host's family, and probably also the "Moonlight Sonata".

*Brunswick
Palace

Brunswick Castle in Martonvásár

Beethoven Museum	There is a small Beethoven Museum in the palace, and in summer concerts of his music are performed in the park.

Mátra Mountains (Mátra hegység)

See Gyöngyös, Surroundings

Mecsek Mountains (Mecsek hegysék)

See Pécs, Surroundings

Mezőkövesd

See Eger, Surroundings

Miskolc   F 1

Region: Borsod-Abaúj-Zemplén
Altitude: 130m/427ft. Population: 190,000

Situation and Importance	After Budapest, Miskolc is the major industrial centre and second largest town in Hungary. It lies in the eastern foothills of the Bükk Mountains, a region with charming countryside and ample tourist facilities, making it

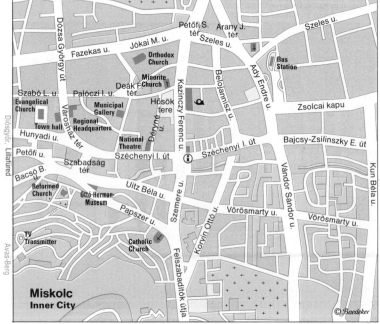

Miskolctapolca

one of Hungary's favourite holiday areas. The provincial town centre of Miskolc at the foot of Mount Avas is surrounded by rather mundane suburbs and industrial estates which sprang up in the post-war years. Miskolc's main attractions are Diósgyőr Castle in the district of the same name, and the holiday resorts of Miskolctapolca in the south and Lillafüred – the "Gateway to the Bükk Mountains" – in the east of the town.

Once just a trading town, Miskolc has developed since the 19th c., and in the post-war years in particular, into a major centre of heavy industry with giant steelworks, iron foundries and machine tool factories. A number of large electrical firms and paper factories have also set up here. The Technical University of Heavy Industry, which provides training for skilled and management staff, has been sited in Miskolc since 1949.

Economy

In the caves of the Bükk Mountains outside Miskolc skeletons of Ice Age man were found, some of the oldest of such remains to be found anywhere in Europe. Scythians also settled here some 2000–3000 years ago. A Magyar tribe known as the Bors (hence the regional name of Borsod) occupied the Miskolc region in the 9th c. Protected by Diósgyőr Castle the settlement developed during the Middle Ages into a small town, which was plundered by the Turks in 1544 and then burned to the ground. After capturing Eger Castle in 1596 the Turks occupied the town for almost one hundred years, until 1687. Like many another north Hungarian town, Miskolc supported the fight for liberation from the Habsburgs – Ferenc Rákóczi had his headquarters in Miskolc for part of the time – and paid for this in 1706 when Austrian troops burned it down once more, something from which it took years to recover.

History

From the late 18th c. the rich iron deposits in the Bükk Mountains were processed in the countryside around Miskolc, and by the end of the 19th c. there were already some industrial firms operating here. When the surrounding suburbs, Diósgyőr in particular, were incorporated into the town Miskolc became an industrial conurbation of some 130 concerns.

Sights

This busy shopping street, now pedestrianised, is the traditional centre of Miskolc. The street is dominated mainly by 19th c. buildings, interspersed with a number of pretty Baroque houses and quite a few attractive new buildings.

Széchenyi utca

The visitor's attention is drawn especially to the distinguished National Theatre building, the entrance to which is on the narrow side in Széchenyi utca, at the corner of Déryné utca. The country's first theatre once stood here, but it was burned down in 1843 and then replaced by the present Classical building.

National Theatre

Széchenyi utca enters Városház tér, where the carefully restored buildings bring an historical sparkle to this industrial town. Standing proudly on the right is the 1727 Regional Office, renovated in Classical style, a long building with two main storeys and a mezzanine floor. Horizontal mouldings serve to break it up horizontally and counteract the effect of the four Ionic columns above the entrance which unite the two upper floors.
The building of the Regional Office is rivalled by the two-storey Baroque Town Hall directly opposite. Other noteworthy buildings include Szeremley House (No. 5) and Almássy Palace (No. 13). The grape-pattern relief above the entrance to the house at No. 20 indicates that a Greek wine-merchant once lived here.

Városház tér

With the Kossuth Memorial in its centre and the inviting park benches, Szabadság tér is a particularly pretty square. The Ottó Herman Museum is housed in the Baroque buildings on the corner of Szabadság tér and Papszer utca (No. 1), on the banks of the Szinva. Ottó Herman, after whom the museum is named, was a native of Miskolc and was responsible for discovering the first prehistoric remains in the caves of the Bükk Moun-

*Szabadság tér
Ottó Herman
Museum*

Miskolc

Miskolc: Városház tér

Minorite church

tains. In addition to the local archaeological finds the museum's comprehensive exhibits include a collection of weapons, historical costumes, furniture and ceramics as well as items of folk-lore and local history (open: Tue.–Sun. 10am–6pm).

*Reformed Church

The walk to Mount Avas south-west of the town centre takes the visitor past the Reformed Church on the northern slopes of Kis Avas (Little Avas). Founded in the 13th c., it is the oldest building in Miskolc. Following renovation in 1470–90 it was given the form of a three-storeyed Gothic church with an ambulatory in the choir. Destroyed by fire, it was rebuilt between 1560 and 1569 as the Church of the Reformed Congregation; the Gothic columns were encased and the vaulted ceiling replaced by a wooden one. The Renaissance pews in the choir were probably brought here from the chapel of Diósgyőr Castle. A particular feature of the church is the separate bell-tower (1557) with its stocky, stone base, wooden gallery and pointed, shingle-covered helm roof.

Behind the church lies a pretty and picturesque cemetery with many old graves and weathered gravestones.

Mount Avas

There are large numbers of old wine-cellars going down 10–20m/33–66ft (in one case as deep as 100m/330ft) into Mount Avas, the local mountain, which stands 243m/800ft high. These wine-cellars are open to the public at week-ends during the summer months. A fine panoramic view can be enjoyed from the viewing tower on the mountain peak.

Minorite Church (Minorita templom)

By way of Széchenyi utca, past the National Theatre and then through Déryné utca, the visitor will come to the Baroque church on Hősök tér (Heroes' Square). It is the work of the Italian architect Giovanni Battista Carlone (1682–1747), whose studio was in Eger. The church was built between 1729 and 1734; two towers flank the gable end with a figure of the

Bell-tower of the Reformed Church   Diósgyőr Castle

Virgin Mary in the centre and statues of saints on either side. Frescos showing scenes from Mary's life adorn the interior.

Near the Minorite Church, on the corner of Deák tér, stands this beautiful church (Görögkeleti templom), built in the 18th c. plait style in 1785–88. It possesses a valuable 16m/52ft high iconostasis with a copy of the Black Madonna of Kashan in the centre, a gift from the Russian Czarina Catherine II.

Greek Orthodox Church

To the west of Miskolc town centre lies the district of Diósgyőr, the industrial quarter and site of the iron works, the giant machine tool factory and other large concerns. The state co-operative organisations such as the Cultural Centre and Uránia Observatory are also to be found here. However, the impressive castle ruins are Diósgyőr's main attraction.

Diósgyőr district

It was probably the invading Magyars who erected a fortress on the site of the present castle. This was destroyed by the Mongols in 1241. In 1271 Ban Ernye of Ákos had an oval-shaped stone castle built on this raised site. After it had passed into the possession of the throne in 1340, King Louis had the present castle built; modelled on those found in southern Italy, it is flanked by four towers and is protected by an outer ring of fortifications. After King Sigismund had given it to his queen to be used as a summer residence it became the practice for each successive queen to reside there. In the second half of the 15th c. Queen Beatrix of Aragon, wife of King Matthias, furnished it in luxurious Early Renaissance style. All that remains of these furnishings is the Diósgyőr Madonna, probably part of an altar from the castle chapel and the work of the Dalmatian artist Johannes Duknovich de Tragurio, who also carried out work in other royal palaces. In the 16th c. there were several changes of ownership, and additional fortifications were added, such as the round bastion in the north-east and the pentagonal one in the north-west. During the 16th c. the castle gradually fell into decay,

**Diósgyőr Castle

Diósgyőr
Castle

1 Double Gate Tower
2 Five-cornered Bastion
3 Kitchen with oven
 and well
4 Gaoler's House
5 Casemate
6 Grand Staircase, Ramp
7 Knights' Hall
8 Round Bastion
 (museum)
9 Pillared Bridge
10 Chapel

13th c.
14th–15th c.
16th–17th c.

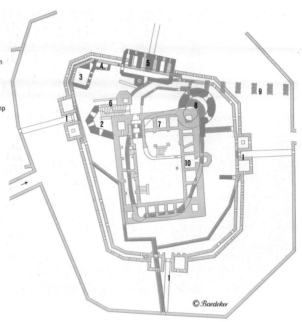

© Baedeker

and in 1678 it was blown up by Habsburg troops. During the 19th c. the debris was used as building rubble. Since 1968 the outer foundations have again been uncovered and parts of the inner fortifications reconstructed. As a result it is now possible to see the size of the great Knights' Hall in the north wing and the castle chapel in the east wing. Three of the four corner towers have been reconstructed, and in the south-west tower (where there is a viewing platform) the Late Gothic vaulting of the corner room has been rebuilt. Some of the stone-masonry and other castle finds are on display in the castle museum in the north-east bastion (open: Apr.–Oct. Tue.–Sun. 9am–6pm).

Open-air events are held in the castle courtyard during the summer months.

Surroundings

*Lillafüred

From Diósgyőr it is only a few miles through the valley of the little Szinva river to the health resort of Lillafüred in the Bükk Mountains. Although it is 12km/7½ miles from the centre of Miskolc it ranks as a suburb under the town's control.

In the deep cleft in the valley where the Szinva and Garadna rivulets meet the Hotel Palota towers up like a fairy-tale castle – a high-class hotel in the 1930s, it was converted into a workers' convalescent home during the Communist era, but has recently become a hotel once again. Behind the hotel the terraced garden with a small waterfall (which is often dry!) leads into a large woodland park which forms an enchanting backdrop, especially in autumn. Above the hotel lies the station for the old-fashioned narrow-gauge railway which plies between Miskolc and Garadna through a wild and romantic part of the Bükk Mountains. Not far from the hotel the Garadna flows into an artificial pond, the Hámori tó, where small boats can be hired.

Lillafüred is known in particular for its caves, all of which are to be found near the hotel. The entrance to the István Cave is on the Eger road, about 500m/550yd above the Hotel Palota. Some fantastic stalactite formations can be seen inside the cave, where the temperature remains constant at 10°C/50°F throughout the year. The Petőfi Cave (also known as Anne's Cave) with impressions of extinct plant species in the limestone walls lies only some 150m/165yd below the hotel. It is about one hour's walk from the hotel along a

An old-time narrow-gauge railway

Caves

gently ascending path to the Szeleta Cave, where evidence can be seen of the Ice Age "Szeleta culture". The items to be seen include some very skilfully made arrows and spears shaped like laurel leaves, which Ice Age man fashioned by splitting the quartz-like chalcedon stone.

See entry

Bükk Mountains

4km/2½ miles along the narrow road which leads past the Hámori tó pond into the Bükk Mountains, lies Újmassa, the "cradle" of the Hungarian iron and steel industry. Frigyes Fazola established Hungary's first iron foundry here in 1813. His father, Henrik Fazola, a skilled blacksmith who had moved to Eger from Würzburg in Germany, built a furnace to smelt iron-ore found in the Bükk Mountains. Frigyes moved production to Újmassa and built a new, larger foundry which is now an important item of industrial archaeology. A small museum provides information about the early days of iron smelting.

Újmassa

The bathing and health resort of Miskolctapolca lies 7km/4½ miles southwest of the centre of Miskolc in the midst of some superb woodland. The slightly radioactive thermal waters (30°C/86°F) have been renowned since medieval times for their value in the treatment of nerve and heart problems, hypertension and digestive disorders. The first pump-room was built in the 18th c.; the late 19th c. baths have remained in use right up to the present day, with only few alterations. They consist of two indoor baths, one open-air pool, and the very popular Cave Bath, in a natural cave (entrance via the thermal baths). A separate small pond, suitable for small boats, and a large open-air swimming pool complete the facilities.

Miskolctapolca

Mohács

D 4

Region: Baranya
Altitude: 91m/300ft. Population: 21,500

Mohács

Situated 40km/25 miles south-east of Pécs on the right bank of the Danube, Mohács became famous in sad circumstances as a result of the battle of 1526 in which the Hungarian troops suffered a devastating defeat at the hands of the superior Turkish army. For Hungary that meant the beginning of some 150 years of Turkish occupation and the end of the independent Magyar kingdom; for many years Mohács symbolised the threat which the Ottoman empire posed to western Europe.

History

Back in Roman times there was a camp on the banks of the Danube near Mohács; later the invading Magyars also settled here. After the Turkish wars the region went into decay until in the 18th c. the Habsburgs offered protection to Catholic immigrants from Germany who became known as the "Danubian Swabians"; Greek Orthodox Serbs also settled here in considerable numbers. From 1840 the border town had a harbour on the Danube. Traditional trades include fishing and silk-spinning.

Sights

The central square of Mohács is Széchenyi tér, with a votive church (Emlék-templom) on its south side and the Moorish Town Hall (1927) on the east, both designed by Aladár and Bertalan Árkány. As a symbolic gesture of national unity, soil taken from 3000 Hungarian towns and villages was used in the foundations of the votive church, which was consecrated in 1926 on the 400th anniversary of the battle of Mohács.

The Franciscan church (1740) in Kossuth Lajos utca has a tower and magnificent door on its narrow front façade and an altarpiece by Stefan Dorffmeister portraying St Stephen offering his crown to the Virgin Mary, patron saint of all Hungary. In the 18th c. the Serbs built their own church here, and its 45m/150ft tower is visible from afar. The former Episcopal Church and the Bishop's Palace in II Lajos utca were commissioned by Bishop Zsigmond Berényi of Pécs in 1742 and 1739 respectively.

The Dorottya Kanizsai Museum in Szerb utca contains documents relating to the battle of Mohács. At the point where the little Csele rivulet enters the

Mohács: modern carved figures on the former battlefield

Danube there is a memorial to King Louis II (1506–26) who drowned there when fleeing from the Turks.

An old tradition of the southern Slavs living in Mohács is the Shrovetide carnival, the *Busójárás*, which is held in February every year, starting from the Busó Column in Koló tér. Disguised figures wearing morbid masks and bells parade through the streets in an attempt to drive winter away. Folk-tradition has it that not only did the "Busó runners" drive winter away but they also forced the Turks to leave the country.

Shrovetide
Carnival

Before corrective measures were taken to prevent flooding the 380sq.km/150sq.mile area between the Danube and its branch near Baracska was the river's flood basin; today a number of villages stand on the island. In spite of the measures taken floods do still occur from time to time, the last occasion being in 1956 when almost all the houses were destroyed. A ferry connects the island with the town.

Mohács Island
(Mohácsi sziget)

In the quiet border country south of Mohács, not far from the town of Sátorhely, lies the 7ha/17½ acre National Park containing the Memorial to The Fallen in the Battle of 1526 (Mohácsi Történelmi Emlékhely). From Road 56 leading towards the border an avenue lined with chestnut trees goes off to the right and leads to the car park in front of the memorial. The park, which was opened on August 29th 1976, the 450th anniversary of the battle, is on the spot where archaeologists have discovered the graves of some 150,000 dead; the memorial site was designed by György Vadász. Visitors enter the park through a bronze gate, and the road then leads to an atrium-like building where information boards document the story of the battle.

Mohács
Historic
Memorial

The actual memorial site consists of a round area on the battlefield surrounded by trees. On the south-west side the line of trees is broken by a wedge of black Scots pine marking the place where the Turkish army are thought to have stood. The mass graves lie along pathways arranged in concentric circles. The 120 grave-stones in the form of ancient totem-poles were designed by well-known Hungarian artists. Some are abstract in form, such as the spears surrounding the bell-tower by Sándor Kiss which symbolise the independence and pride of Transylvania, while others are graphically expressionist, for example, the statue of the Sultan Suleiman with the heads of dead Hungarians in his rope basket.
The memorial park is open all the year round.

Mosonmagyaróvár

Region: Győr-Moson-Sopron
Altitude: 115m/377ft. Population: 29,900

For those tourists who come to Hungary from the direction of Vienna, Mosonmagyaróvár, 14km/9 miles beyond the Austro-Hungarian border crossing, is the first large town on Hungarian soil. Situated at the confluence of the Lajta and Mosoni Duna (Moson Danube) rivers, it is the site of a number of industries, such as agricultural machinery and food manufacturers, as well as of a branch of the Keszthely University of Agricultural Science.

Situation and
Importance

In the first century A. D. the Romans established the military camp of Arx Flexum here. King Stephen I built Moson Castle and in the 13th c. the rulers of Győr built the strategically important fortress at Magyaróvár, which was also an important centre in the cattle trade with Vienna. In 1529 and 1683 the Turks, in the course of their attempts to take Vienna, set fire to the castle. In the late 18th c. Magyaróvár castle was owned by the Governor of Hungary, Duke Albrecht of Sachsen-Teschen. The dual municipality of

History

Mosonmagyaróvár

Castle in Mosonmagyaróvár

Art nouveau house in Nagykanizsa

Mosonmagyaróvár came into being when the two towns (Moson and Magyaróvár) were merged in 1939.

Sights

Unfortunately the centre of the town of Mosonmagyaróvár has been somewhat spoiled by through traffic, but there are still some beautiful Baroque houses which are the subject of preservation orders.

Castle (Vár)

The asymmetrical 13th c. medieval Castle stands on an island in the River Lajta; today it forms part of the Keszthely Agricultural University. It has been subjected to a number of changes in its history; originally it had four towers, one at each corner, but the two northern ones were removed when renovations were done in the 19th c.

On the ground floor visitors can see the Lapidarium and a small exhibition of the castle's history. Beyond the castle park, on the far side of the River Lajta, lies a little wood with the modern university buildings.

Parish Church

The Baroque Parish Church on Szent László was built in 1777–87 on the site of a medieval church which was destroyed by the Turks. There is much of interest to be seen inside the church, including the frescos in the nave showing scenes from the life of St Paul, and the high altarpiece portraying King Stephen I kneeling before the Virgin Mary; both are the work of the Viennese artist Franz Schellmayer. The pulpit and font are also Baroque.

Lenau House

In 1822 and 1823 the poet Nikolaus Lenau (1802–50) lived in the house at Fő utca 139, on the road to Vienna.

Hanság Museum

The building at Fő utca 139 houses a collection of local history, archaeological and ethnographical items as well as some Baroque and Biedermeier furniture (open: Tue.–Sun. 10am–6pm).

Nagykanizsa

Region: Zala
Altitude: 168m/551ft
Population: 54,900

The busy industrial town of Nagykanizsa, the administrative centre of the Zala region, lies south-west of Lake Balaton and 25km/15½ miles from the border with Slovenia. The town was already inhabited when the Magyars invaded the country. The 13th c. castle became an critical defence position in 1566 when the Turks took Szigetvár, the most important bulwark in southern Transdanubia. However, it finally fell into Turkish hands c. 1600. In 1705 the Habsburgs razed the castle to the ground (to the south-east of the town; remains have been built over).

Situation and History

In the 16th c. Nagykanizsa became a major centre in the cattle trade with Italy and Styria in Austria. Its economic development was strengthened still further by the construction of the Budapest–Adriatic railway; at the end of the 19th c. food processing and furniture factories were built, to be followed after the Second World War by a lamp factory and oil exploration nearby.

Sights

According to tradition, this fountain on Szabadság tér once stood in the castle grounds. The water-spout is Baroque, the pillars above it are Classical in form.

Turkish Fountain

The György Thury Museum at the north end of Szabadság tér (open: Tue.–Sun. 10am–6pm) is housed in a Classical building of 1820 and is named after the castle governor György Thury, who was in command 1568–71, was killed in the battle of Orosztony not far from Nagykanizsa and is regarded as a legendary hero of the Turkish period. The older collections cover archaeology, the history of furniture-making and of folk-art, while a more recent collection provides information on life in the forests of the Zala region.

György Thury Museum

This Baroque building at Fő út 5–7, formerly part of the estate of the noble Batthány family, was built in 1705–12 using stones from the demolished castle. In front of the Gallery stands a monument to György Thury by Miklós Borsos, which was erected in 1971 on the occasion of the 400th anniversary of his death. In the Gallery (Thury György Múzeum Képtára, open: Tue.–Sun. 10am–6pm) are works by 20th c. Hungarian artists.

Art Gallery of the György Thury Museum

In the courtyard of the Classical house at Fő út No. 9 stands the simple Synagogue (Zsinagóga), built in Classical style in 1807–10 and renovated in 1890.

Synagogue

The Baroque church and priory in the south-west of the town (Zárda utca No, 9) were built in 1702–14 from stones taken from the demolished castle minaret and mosque; the tower on the left was not added until 1816. Items in the church include a particularly valuable 15th c. carved wooden figure of the Madonna. The font was made from the gravestone of Pasha Mustafa, the last Turkish commander of the castle. The altar-piece was painted c. 1770 by the Austrian Franz Kaspar Sambach (1715–95).

Catholic Church in the lower part of the town

Near the church stands the Baroque Franciscan priory, built in 1702–04, now a boys' college.

Nyíregyháza

Church in the upper part of the town	The Baroque church of St John of Nepomuk (1764) was given its Baroque tower with the pyramidal roof in the first half of the 19th c. Unfortunately, renovation work carried out in 1940 has detracted from its Baroque character.
Trinity Column	This richly decorated sculpture (1758) on Kossuth Lajos tér in the south-east of the town is surrounded by a decorative wrought-iron grille and is one of the most beautiful works of its kind anywhere in Hungary.
"Sándor Hevesi" Culture Centre	This imposing modern building on Eötvös tér bears the name of one of Nagykanizsa's most famous sons, the producer, writer and director of the Budapest National Theatre Sándor Hevesi (1873–1939).

Surroundings

Lazsnakpuszta	Leaving the town along Magyar utca to the north-west the visitor will come to the Inkey Mausoleum, a building with a central dome, four niches and an entrance guarded by four statues. In 1768 Boldizsár Inkey, a son of one of Nagykanizsa's most respected families, had it built for himself.
Szentgyörgyhegy	To the south-east of the town is the vine-growing upland of Saint George Mountain (Szentgyörgyhegy). The grape juice obtained here is some of the best in Hungary. The old half-timbered wine-press houses and cellars are fine examples of rustic architecture. The castle ruin is also worth a visit; it was built by the Bóth family in the 15th c. During the period of Turkish occupation it served as a summer retreat for the Turkish commander, a fact which was sufficient for it to earn the name of "Castle of Vice" (Romlott vár) among the citizens of Nagykanizsa.
Zalakaros	Zalakaros lies 18km/11 miles north-east of Nagykanizsa and 5km/3 miles from Zalakomár on the M 7. When oil-exploration operations were being carried out in the 1960s warm-water streams were discovered, and since then this little village (pop. 900) has became an internationally renowned spa, with comprehensive bathing and medicinal facilities. The water, which leaves the ground at a temperature of 92°C/198°F, contains alkaline chlorides, hydrogen carbonate and iodine, and is used to treat mobility problems, rheumatic and neurological afflictions as well as gynaecological disorders.

Nyíregyháza   G 1/2

Region: Szabolcs-Szatmár-Bereg
Altitude: 115m/377ft. Population: 114,000

Situation and Importance	Lying 245km/152 miles east of Budapest, the agricultural and industrial town of Nyíregyháza is the centre of the Nyírség district and the capital of the most easterly region of Hungary. It lies in the midst of one of the country's largest fruit-growing areas, famous for its "Jonathan" apples. Twenty percent of the population of this sprawling town live in detached farmsteads; widespread rural areas around the outside of the town contrast with the urban appearance of its centre. Nyíregyháza is also an educational and cultural centre with three colleges.
History	The first documentary record of a settlememt here is dated 1215; from the 14th to the 16th c. the town was owned by the influential Báthori family. In 1605 ownership passed to the Transylvanian Prince István Bocskai (1557–1606), who arranged for Haiduks to settle here as he did in the countryside around Debrecen. In the 18th c. Slovak families moved into the almost deserted town. The building of the rail link with Budapest in the second half of the 19th c. provided the impetus required to enable Nyíregyháza to develop into a major commercial centre.

The centre of Nyíregyháza lacks any buildings of outstanding historical merit and derives its character mainly from such edifices as the regional offices, the theatre and others all designed by the architect Ignác Aplár. Of interest to the visitor is the Jósa András Museum at Benczúr Gyula tér 21, with some absorbing finds from the time of the Magyar invasion, a department dealing with local history and ethnographic subjects, as well as a permanent exhibition of work by the Nyíregyháza artist Gyula Benczúr (1844–1920). On the square in front of the museum stands a monument to him as well as the sculpture "Birth of Venus" by Zsigmond Kisfaludy Stróbl.

Sights

The little resort of Sóstó lies only 6km/3¾ miles north of the town centre, by a salt-water lake which covers an area of 14ha/35 acres and is surrounded by reeds and sedge. This alkaline stretch of water consists of two linked ponds, one of which is excellent for bathing and the other for punts and pedal-boats. North of the lake will be found the excellently appointed Sóstófürdő thermal baths, with specialised pools for bathing of all descriptions. Along the promenade known as Blaha Lujza sétány, named after the famous actress who often holidayed here, lie a camp site and bungalows belonging to the holiday village of Igrice. There are rare species of plants to be seen in the carefully tended park.

Sóstó

Since 1979 Sóstó's Open-air Museum has been a further tourist attraction. On display to date are 45 typical farmhouses, churches and other public buildings such as a school and a fire-station from various parts of the region; there are plans to add further buildings. The thatched dwellings contain some original items of furniture. Open: Apr.–Oct. Tue.–Sun. 9am–4pm.

Open-air Museum (Múzeumfalu)

Surroundings

The region on the bend of the Tisza river north-east of the Great Hungarian Plain possesses a rich and fertile loamy soil and is an important fruit-growing area with giant apple orchards. The Nyírség is the home of the "Jonathan" apple, which is exported all over the world, and in addition maize, sunflower seed and tobacco are grown around Nyíregyháza. However, in spite of intensive fruit cultivation and the growth of the food processing industry, the Nyírség remains one of Hungary's poorest regions, the gipsy population of Sinti and Roma is disproportionately high and poverty and unemployment are the norm. As the land used to be very marshy it was more or less ignored by the Turks, so many old villages and medieval churches – including some particularly beautiful ones, such as the Reformed Church in Nyírbátor – have survived.

Nyírség (countryside)

When travelling from Nyíregyháza to Nyírbátor (see below) it is well worth stopping to view the wooden buildings on the edge of the wood near Nagykálló, which were designed by the young Hungarian architect Dezso Ekler.

Nagykálló

Nyírbátor

In the Middle Ages this rural town (pop. 14,000) 35km/22 miles south-east of Nyíregyháza belonged to the Báthori family, princes from Transylvania who become great feudal lords. Nyírbátor has them to thank for its two magnificent medieval churches, of which St George's Church, now the Reformed Church, is one of the major Late Gothic Hungarian edifices.

Having become rich during the Turkish wars, in 1484–88 István Báthori built on the castle mound a church dedicated to St George in which to house the family tomb. In the 16th c. the town was converted to the Calvinist faith, and members of the Reformed Church took over the now somewhat dilapi-

°Reformed Church

dated building and restored it. The Báthori coat-of-arms stands above the west door, with a projecting tower at the side; the main Renaissance-style door is on the south side. Remains of the walls of the old sacristy can still be seen on the north side. Inside the church, the visitor's eye will immediately be drawn to the filigree reticular vaulting in the roof of this single-aisled church with its large windows. The Renaissance influence which resulted from contacts made with the royal architects in Visegrád can be seen in the sculptural decoration in the sacramental niche, window and door-frames, the pew-niches in the choir and in various other details. The tomb in the choir is that of the writer István Báthori, who died in 1605; the founder of the church is interred under a marble gravestone in the crypt. The artistically decorated choir-stalls, which were carved in 1503–11 by a Florentine master craftsman, are kept in the Hungarian National Museum in Budapest. Near the church stands the shingle-clad bell-tower (1640) constructed of oak and representative of the type of tower found on many Reformed Churches in Hungary and Transylvania.

*Former
Minorite
Church

About 1480, at approximately the same time as he was building the family church, István Báthori donated a priory to the mendicant Minorite order of monks, and was buried in its church. About 1720 Count Károlyi had the priory and church converted to Baroque style, although the original plain front and long, multi-bay choir are still discernible. He gave the church a groin-vaulted roof by adapting the medieval vaulting, as well as a carved pulpit and several Baroque altars lavishly adorned with figures, turned pillars and gable fragments. The figures were carved by the Slovak sculptor Johannes Strecius. The 1731 Passion Altar on the north wall is deserving of special attention; this is also the work of a Slovak craftsman. The Stations of the Cross are depicted in Baroque settings with the use of realistic scenes similar to those found on medieval altars.

István Báthori
Museum

The István Báthori Museum in the priory near the church (1733–58) exhibits the ecclesiastical treasures, including the carved choir-stalls and valuable furnishings from the Renaissance Palace of the Báthori family in Transylvania. Open: Tue.–Sun. 9am–5pm.

Kisvárda

This agricultural town (pop. 19,000) with some small industrial concerns, situated 290km/180 miles north-east of Budapest and 45km/28 miles north-east of Nyíregyháza, is the centre of the Upper Tisza region in the extreme east of Hungary.

Sights

The town got its name ("Little Fortress") from the castle which was built c. 1400 and enlarged in the 16th and 17th c. into a fortified palace with four corner-towers and a covered walk on the side facing the courtyard. In the 18th c., when it no longer served its original purpose, the people of Kisvárda pulled it down and used the stone to build the new Catholic church and to rebuild fire-damaged houses, until the authorities put a stop to it in 1828. The castle was restored in 1957–61, and a lapidarium installed in the tower at the south-east corner (open: Apr.–Oct. Tue.–Sun. 9am–6pm).

Kisvárda's second place of historical interest is the Catholic Church of SS Peter and Paul, which according to local legend was built by King St Ladislaus (1040–95) in gratitude for his victory over the Cumans. The church was rebuilt in 1788–1805, but remains of the old walls and medieval corbels with human figures (12th c.) as well as Gothic details in the choir have survived. The town's collection of local history and folk-art items (Rétközi Museum) can be seen in the former synagogue (open: Apr.–Oct. Tue.–Sun. 9am–noon and 1–5pm).

Other places to visit in the vicinity

*Szatmár
(countryside)

The historical stretch of land known as the Szatmár lies between the Kraszna and Tisza rivers in the extreme east of Hungary, close to the

Nyírbátor: Reformed Church . . .

. . . the Passion Altar in the Minorite Church

The Reformed Church in Tákos

borders with the Ukraine and Romania. This region, thickly populated in comparison with the Great Plain and with a closely-knit network of country roads, is still relatively unspoiled by tourism and recommended for that reason. Anyone who refuses to be discouraged by the lack of modern facilities and the long journey (the best route to take is by way of Kisvárda or Nyírbátor) will be amply rewarded by discovering a rural Hungary which will be difficult to find elsewhere; sleepy villages with thatched houses and beautiful old churches with the characteristic bell-towers of the Reform period, horse-drawn carts on dusty country roads and an unspoiled landscape through which the Tisza river lazily flows.

Csaroda,
Tákos

Szatmárcseke

A visit to the villages of Csaroda and Tákos, lying some 40km/25 miles south-east of Kisvárda on Highway 41, should be high on the visitor's agenda. Csaroda still has its beautiful little 13th c. Romanesque village church with 14th c. Gothic frescos together with 17th c. paintings and wood-carvings. The little Reformed Church in Tákos is a beautiful example of the traditional method of construction using a framework of beams filled in with wattle and daub. Even further south-east lies Szatmárcseke, which is reached from Vásárosnamény by way of Jánd–Gulács–Tivadar–Kisar–Nagyvar, a total distance of about 30km/19 miles along country roads. In Szatmárcseke there is still an old cemetery with wooden gravestones the like of which cannot be seen anywhere else in Hungary. The cemetery is under a preservation order.

Ópusztaszer

Region: Csongrád
Altitude: 85m/280ft. Population: 2200

Situation and
Importance

In the region between the Danube and Tisza rivers, 28km/17 miles north of Szeged and 10km/6¼ miles east of the E5 Highway, lies the little town of Ópusztaszer. According to the ancient chronicles of Hungarian history written by the unnamed scribe "Anonymus", it was here that the seven tribal chiefs of the invading Magyars, headed by their army commander Prince Árpád, held their first legislative national assembly and divided the newly conquered country up into settlements. In 1945 a second meeting to apportion land was held in this spot, when a symbolic act removed large tracts of land from the great landowners, divided them up and parcelled them out among small farmers.

*National Historic Memorial Park (Nemzeti Történeti Emlékpark)

Access

In 1970–75 a National Historic Memorial Park was set up on the plot where the Magyars were said to have assembled in the year 896 to apportion their newly-acquired land. The park is open Apr.–Oct. Tue.–Sun. 9am–5pm. It lies outside the village of Ópusztaszer on the Csongrád–Szeged road; 1km/1100yd outside the town a narrow road leads off to the left and goes straight into the Memorial Park.

Entrance

Entrance to the park is through a richly decorated gateway, the work of the contemporary sculptor István Kiss. The bronze relief in the foyer, depicting Harvest Thanksgiving, is by the artist Veléria Tóth.

Árpád Memorial

From the entrance a path leads directly to the exit and the Árpád Memorial, a gift from the town of Szeged on the occasion of the millennium celebrations in 1896. The plans for this Classical temple-style edifice were by Gyula Berczik, and the figure of Prince Árpád on his throne is the work of Ede Kallós.

Garden of Ruins

Excavations near the Árpád Memorial revealed remains of the walls of a Romanesque Benedictine priory and of a triple-aisled church, as well as sculpture fragments.

Árpád Monument . . .   *. . . sculptures in the Memorial Park*

The Round Hall was built in 1987. The intention is that it should house the huge panoramic painting "Invasion of the Magyars" by Árpád Feszty (1856–1914), which measures some 120m/400ft long and 15m/50ft high. The picture was painted for the millennium celebrations in 1896 and was on display in a special pavilion in Budapest until it suffered serious damage during the siege of the capital in the Second World War. It is currently being restored and fixed to a woven backing.

Round Hall

This Open-air Museum which forms an integral part of the Memorial Park brings together into one collection a number of different types of building typically found in this region. These include small farms, a fisherman's hut, a blacksmith's forge, a harness-maker's and a cooper's workshop, a windmill, a railway station, a small general store, a bakery, church rooms, a post-office, a school and various dwellings.

Open-air Museum

Pannonhalma

C 2

Region: Győr-Moson-Sopron
Altitude: 128m/420ft
Population: 4000

Visitors come to Pannonhalma mainly in order to see the famous abbey of St Martin (Szent Márton hegy), the parent abbey and focal point of the Benedictine order in Hungary. Monks have lived here right up to the present day, apart from a short interruption between 1786 and 1802, when the building was secularised.

Situation and
*Importance

**Benedictine Abbey of St Martin

In 996 Grand Prince Géza invited monks to settle on his estate; in doing so he effectively sowed the seed of Christianity in what was mainly a heathen

History

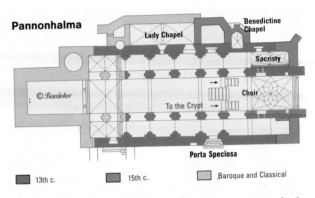

Pannonhalma

Benedictine Chapel

Lady Chapel

Sacristy

© Baedeker

Choir

To the Crypt →

Porta Speciosa

13th c.   15th c.   Baroque and Classical

Magyar kingdom. According to local tradition this spot was chosen for the abbey because St Martin, its patron saint, was born in the year 316 in the neighbouring Roman castle of Savaria Sicca (although some say that he was in fact born in the Roman town of Savaria, now Szombathely). In 1001 King Stephen officially founded the abbey and vested it with land and wide privileges equal to those enjoyed by the parent abbey of Montecassino in Italy. During the time when such spiritual bodies were secularised, especially in the 16th c., some prominent church politicians sat on the abbot's chair in the abbey, including even Cesare Borgia, a descendant of the famous Italian family of that name and the son of Pope Alexander VI. During the Turkish wars the abbey became part of the front line of defence in Győr, was besieged several times and finally burned down in 1575. It was rebuilt in 1699 after the Turks had withdrawn; the Classical additions and renovations which now characterise the building were carried out in the early 19th c.

Visits

Visitors may look round the abbey only as part of a guided tour. Open: Mon.–Sat. and state holidays 8.30am–4.30pm, and 1.30–4.30pm on religious holidays.

Tour

Like many Benedictine monasteries, the abbey stands proudly on the top of a mound, in this case St Martin's Mount. The entrance to the massive complex is in the south, between the grammar school and the residential quarters. After passing through a number of adjoining courtyards the visitor will arrive at the abbey forecourt, from where there is a magnificent view of the Bakony Forest and the Little Plain. The façade is dominated by the west tower, 55m/180ft high and built by János Packh c. 1830. The entrance to the three-storey church is through the door to the right of the tower.

Church

The present church stands on the site of two previous buildings. Of the first, founded in 1001, only the crypt foundations remain, while the red-marble fountain in the cloister is all that survives of the second building which was erected in 1137 after its predecessor had burned down. Under Abbot Urias a new Late Romanesque/Early Gothic edifice was built in the early 13th c. and consecrated in the presence of King Andreas II in 1224. The triple-aisled, groin-vaulted basilica betrays elements of Cistercian architecture – such as the flat end to the choir, for example – with which the architect had become familiar during his stays in Italy. The crypt below the choir, with its beautiful vaulted ceiling supported on round pillars, also dates from this period and is typical of such Benedictine places of worship. Tradition has it that the niche-seat in the west wall was used by St Stephen, but in fact it is of a later date. The Late Gothic vaulting in the choir and the north side-

Pannonhalma Benedictine Abbey

chapel are the result of renovations carried out by King Matthias in 1486. At the same time he had the cloister built which adjoins the church on the south and is very similar in style to the courtyard in the Royal Palace of Visegrád. The figures on the corbels of the cross-vaulted roof represent the human virtues and vices, such as Humility (head of a cow), Sensuality (a female face) or Vanity (a grinning caricature). Also worthy of note is the pillared door which was uncovered during restoration work to the south wing of the cloister, the entrance to the refectory (no admission). The monks entered the south side-aisle of the church through the "Porta Speciosa"; with its slender pairs of pillars in red marble and white limestone capitals. This is artistically the most important part of the cloister and one of the few Romanesque decorated doorways in Hungary which have survived the ravages of time. The scene portrayed in the tympanum shows St Martin sharing his cloak with a beggar (19th c.), recognised as the key to his way of life.

In the north wing of the convent lies the library and magnificent Library Hall, designed by Franz Engel and Johann Packh ca. 1830, when the west tower was built. The hall ceiling is enhanced by a fresco by the Viennese artist Josef Kleber which shows Minerva, the protectress of the Arts and Sciences. The library boasts a collection of some 330,000 books, manuscripts and incunabula, making it one of the largest religious libraries in Hungary. Of special importance are the documents kept in the archives relating to the history of the state of Hungary and the foundation charter in Latin of the Benedictine abbey in Tihany (see Lake Balaton) dated 1055, in which there appear for the very first time a considerable number of Hungarian words and suffixes. This makes it the oldest written example of the Hungarian language.

Library

Adjoining the library is an art gallery and a small museum with exhibits ranging from early history to the Middle Ages.

Region: Veszprém
Altitude: 154m/505ft
Population: 32,300

Situation and History

Pápa, once famous for its colleges, lies 45km/28 miles south-west of Győr where the Bakony Forest adjoins the Little Plain. This important medieval fort was first documented in 1051; in 1531 the famous Reformed Church was founded. In 1594 the Turks captured the town and it remained in their possession until 1683. At the end of the 17th c. Pápa was destroyed by fire and rebuilt in the 18th c. In the first half of the 19th c. a number of watermills were built to utilise the power provided by the little Tapolca river, and towards the end of the century the textile and tobacco industries became established here.

Sights

Townscape

Although the town has retained much of its medieval defensive structure, the buildings in the centre are mainly 18th c. Baroque. Those now to be described follow the route going from north to south along the main street of Fő utca to Fő tér.

Reformed College

The Reformed College, at the south end of Március 15. tér, was built in 1894–95. The college, founded in 1531, then moved to a new home from the Late Baroque house at Petőfi utca 13, where it had been since 1797; prior to 1797 it had been housed in the Arcade House (see below). The college has produced many of the great names in Hungarian history, including the poet laureate Sándor Petőfi (1823–49) and the Romantic novelist Mór Jókai

Pápa: the Great Church . . .

. . . and Eszterházy Castle

(1825–1904). The college still takes students as well as housing the library of the Reformed Church of Transdanubia (exhibition on the history of the college).

On Március 15. tér stands the new Reformed Church built in 1931–34.

In 1864 C. F. Kluge from Saxony in Germany founded a specialist blue dye-works in Pápa and in 1869 built himself a house at Március 15. tér. The latter is now a museum (Kékfestő múzeum) in which the visitor can see the old factory machinery, still complete and in working order, as well as some examples of blue printed material (open: daily 10am–4pm).

Museum of Textile Printing

The Baroque Church of Our Lady at No. 10 Fő utca was built in 1737–42 for the Pauline order and became the property of the Benedictines in 1805. Elliptical in shape, the single-aisled church contains some fine artistic Rococo furnishings (main altar, choir-stalls, pulpit) which the Paulines installed. The ceiling frescos date from 1868.

Benedictine Church

The Református Egyháztörténeti Múzeum is housed in the old Reformed Church (1783-84), a simple building in the 18th c. plait style in the courtyard of the Reformed Presbytery at Fo utca 6. The Edict of Tolerance issued by Emperor Joseph III allowed the building of Protestant churches only if they had no tower and were within an enclosed courtyard. Note the Rococo pulpit in the galleried interior.

Reformed Church Historical Museum

Dominating the main square (Fő tér) stands the Great Church, dedicated to St Stephen (the martyr, not St Stephen the King as is so often the case in Hungary). In the Late Baroque/Classical 18th c. plait style and very imposing for a parish church, it was built in 1774–86 first by Jakob Fellner (1722–80), the Eszterházy's own architect, and after his death by Josef Grossmann. The designs were drawn up by Franz Anton Pilgram. In the tympanum can be seen the coat-of-arms of the founder, Károly Eszterházy, and above the gable stands a statue of St Stephen by J. A. Messerschmidt of Bratislava, flanked by angels. The fine frescos in the Bohemian vaulted ceiling were painted by Franz Anton Maulbertsch and portray the life of St Stephen; the grey monochrome relief paintings in the spandrels are modelled on those in the church of San Stephano Rotondo in Rome. Maulbertsch was also responsible for the wall-paintings in the Chapel of Our Lady (to the left of the choir) and in the sacristy. The main altar-piece ("The Stoning of St Stephen", by the Viennese artist Hubert Maurer; 1785) is flanked by marble statues of the canonised Kings Stephen and Ladislaus by the Viennese sculptor Philipp Jakob Prokop. The cedarwood pulpit and pews are also very beautiful.

*Great Church

Of the many pretty town residences on Fő utca and Fő tér special mention must be made of the Baroque house at No. 12, built in the second half of the 18th c. The side facing the square has 19th c. Neo-Gothic features, while in front of the ground floor on Ruszek utca is an attractive row of arcades and shops.

Arcade House

In a park on the north side of Fő tér stands Eszterházy Palace, built in 1783–84 by Josef Grossmann (1747–85) using materials salvaged from a medieval castle. It was in this horseshoe-shaped building that Otto Nicolai, when a guest of the Eszterházys, composed parts of his opera "The Merry Wives of Windsor". At the end of the east wing lies the chapel, with a fresco by Maulbertsch. Some beautiful Baroque fireplaces and stoves have survived.

Today the palace is home to a cultural centre and the municipal museum and art gallery (open: daily 9am–6pm).

Eszterházy Palace

The Way of the Cross (Kálvária) along Győri út leading north from Fő tér existed as long ago as the end of the 17th c. and was given its present form – five Stations of the Cross with painted wooden figures and a hermitage – between 1740 and 1746.

Way of the Cross

Pécs

St John of
Nepomuk

The Nepomuk Statue (1753) on Győri út shows the saint in an unusual manner; a soldier in armour is raising his arm to strike down the kneeling form of St John, whereas according to tradition he died by falling from a bridge into the Vltava river. The Eszterházy coat-of-arms can be seen on the base of the statue.

Mills

Of the 22 watermills which were once driven by the Tapolca river only a few restored ones remain, as the river has dried up. In their day they provided power for paper-mills and various other factories (e.g. the blue dye-works mentioned above) as well as corn-mills.

Pécs   D 3

Region: Baranya
Altitude: 180m/590ft
Population: 170,000

Situation and
*Importance

The visitor will be attracted to Pécs both by the climate and by the charm of this town on the slopes of the Mecsek Mountains in southern Transdanubia. It also boasts a large number of first-rate historical buildings and works of art, ranging from Early Christian burial chambers to Turkish mosques, secular and religious buildings dating from medieval and later times and contemporary art exhibitions.

History

There are signs of human habitation in the Pécs region dating back to the Late Stone Age. On the site of a 5th c. B.C. Celtic village the Romans founded a settlement called Sopianae, and in the 3rd c. this was elevated to the status of administrative capital of the part of the province known as Pannonia Valeria. In the 9th c. the town already boasted five Christian churches, as indicated in its Latin name of Quinque Basilicae (Five Churches). In 1009 St Stephen founded the Pécs diocese. After being attacked by the Mongols in 1242–43 the town was rebuilt and soon blossomed both economically and culturally, and in 1367 it became the seat of the country's first university. The famous humanitarian, academic and writer Janus Pannonius (1434–72) was Bishop of Pécs 1459–72. During the 150 years or so of Turkish rule Pécs never lost its importance; on the contrary, as the headquarters of the military governor it became a lively town steeped in Turkish culture with large numbers of Moslem institutions and no less than ten mosques. After the Turks had been driven out the indigenous Hungarian population of Pécs was largely replaced by German settlers from Baden-Württemberg and Bavaria. In 1780 the good people of Pécs were released by the bishop from their feudal bonds. In the early 19th c. industrialisation and the discovery of coal in the Mecsek Mountains led to an economic boom, as witnessed by the many fine buildings of the period with their richly decorated frontages.

Culture

Education and culture have always played an important role in Pécs. The Pécs Theatre Ballet Company is internationally acclaimed as the forerunner of modern ballet. The University was re-established in the 20th c. and now offers courses in medicine, law, philology, technical and economic sciences and is one of the most renowned universities in Hungary. Pécs is also the cultural centre of the Germans, known as the "Danube Swabians", who have settled here since the 18th century.

Economy

Important industries in Pécs include uranium and coal-mining, tool-making, the leather industry and the manufacture of porcelain (Zsolnay Ceramics). Along the lower stretches of the Mecsek the mild climate aids the cultivation of excellent grapes.

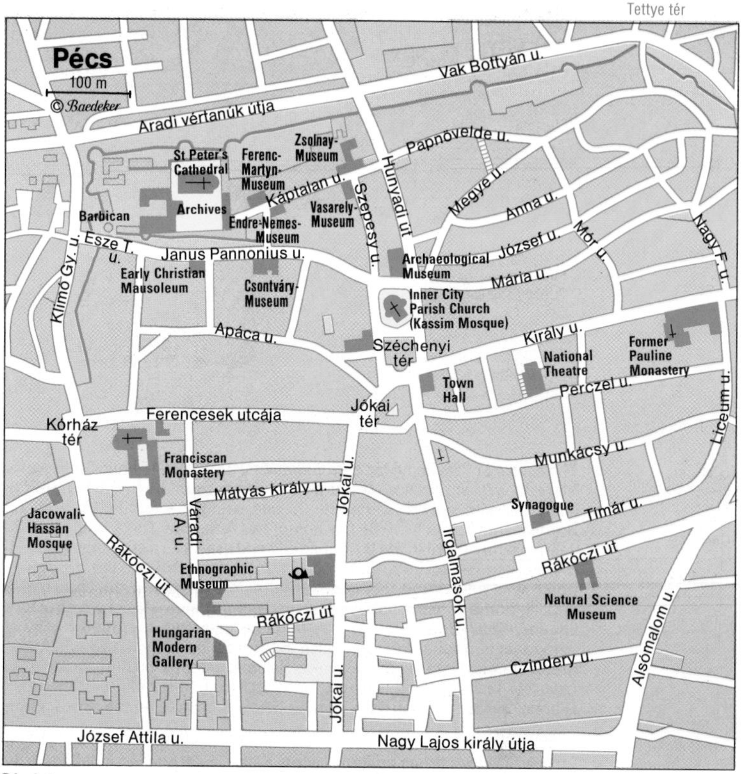

Pécs

100 m

© Baedeker

Idris-Baba-Turbe

Sights

Inner town centre

The medieval market place, the irregular shape and sloping situation of which make it particularly interesting and attractive, is today the bustling centre of Pécs. It is named after the Hungarian statesman and reforming politician István Széchenyi (1791–1860; see Famous People). — ****Széchenyi tér**

The Town Hall on the south side of the square (Széchenyi tér 1) will be recognised by its tall. slender tower. Originally built in 1710, it was converted to its present Baroque style in 1907. — **Town Hall**

Also on the narrow southern side of the square, in front of the Church of Mercy, stands this art nouveau fountain with its fluorescent eosin glaze. The water spurts out of the mouths of four animals around the sides. Erected in 1912, the fountain is in memory of Vilmos Zsolnay, the founder of the Zsolnay factory. — **Zsolnay Fountain**

On the east side of the square, at Széchenyi tér 11, towers the massive building (1720) with twelve rows of windows which was first a Jesuit and then a Cistercian priory. It is now a grammar school. — **Jesuit College**

Rich in tradition, the Hotel Nádor at Széchenyi tér 15 on the west side of the square was rebuilt in the early 20th century. — **Hotel Nádor**

Pécs

Inner City
Parish Church

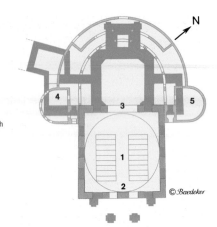

N

■ 1563

■ 17th–18th c.

□ 20th c.

1 Turkish part of the Church
2 Mihrab
3 Triumphal Arch
4 Sacristy
5 St Maur's Chapel

© Baedeker

**Central
Parish Church
(Dschami
of Pasha
Gasi Kassi**

The centre of Széchenyi tér is dominated by the Central Parish Church of St Mary; it was at one time the town's chief mosque, having been built by Pasha Kassim on the same site as and using the stones from an old Romanesque church of St Bartholomew. After the Turks withdrew the Jesuits renovated it in the Baroque style and used it as a church; in 1939–42 it was restored to its original condition and a semi-circular north-west porch was added and this is now the main entrance to the church. The Turkish dome construction is particularly impressive – the main structure, square in plan, is surmounted by a stalactite-vaulted roof followed by an octagonal tambour structure which in turn is topped by the 28m/92ft high green dome. Note also the typical Islamic feature of the prayer-niche (*mihrab*) facing Mecca, on the south wall near the main entrance. The Islamic crescent can be seen shining below the cross on the green dome.

Trinity Column

In the centre of the square near the church stands the Trinity Column or Plague Column; it was built by György Kiss in 1908 and is modelled on the original which was donated by the good people of Pécs after being saved from an epidemic of plague in 1710–14, but was later destroyed.

**Equestrian
statue of
János Hunyadi**

The large equestrian statue of János Hunyadi, conqueror of the Turks, was unveiled in 1956 on the 500th anniversary of his death. It is the work of the Hungarian sculptor Pál Pátzay (1896–1979).

**Jókai tér,
Ferencesek utca**

The small-town quarter between Széchenyi tér and Klimó Gyula (previously Landler Jenő utca) is charmingly picturesque. Jókai tér is a delightful little street on which will be found the "Moor" chemist's shop, named after the wooden statues of Moors outside. It is the oldest chemist's shop in Pécs, having been established in 1697. Inside can be seen the original fittings and utensils supplied by the Zsolnay factory in 1897. The neo-classical building opposite is the "White Elephant" inn, steeped in tradition and easily recognisable by its original sign hanging outside. The Late Baroque vaulted ceiling in the coffee-house of the restaurant is supported by a 13th c. cluster-column which was introduced at a later date.

At the western end of pretty Ferencesek utcája (formerly Sallai utca) lies the Franciscan priory, which was used as a mosque during the Turkish period. When the Turks left the Franciscan again took it over and in 1758 they built the Baroque church which still stands, although altered in the 19th century.

Király utca

Király utca, formerly Kossuth Lajos utca, enters Széchenyi tér. Now a pedestrian zone and a busy shopping street,, Király utca has retained most

Pécs: Inner City Parish Church in Széchenyi tér

of its original buildings. At the square end of the street the art nouveau building of the Hotel Palatinus (1916) will immediately catch the visitor's eye. Restored at great expense in 1989, this top-class hotel is magnificent both inside and out. After a few yards the street widens out into Színház tér. Here stands the Pécs National Theatre (theatre, opera, ballet). Built in 1893–95 in a mix of historical styles, it has recently been renovated. Its modern and distinctive productions have earned the ballet company an international reputation. At the eastern end of the pedestrian zone stands the Baroque church of St Pauline with its twin-towered front.

**Cathedral Precincts and Surroundings

In the north-west corner of the once fortified Old Town of Pécs lie the cathedral precincts with a number of important buildings and historical monuments. Below the cathedral square and in the courtyards of the houses at Apáca utca (formerly Geisler Eta utca) 8 and 14 will be found some graves dating from the 3rd and 4th c. A. D., and numbering among the most important surviving examples of Early Christian culture in Hungary. Dom tér (Cathedral Square) was laid out in the 19th c. It climbs up to the Cathedral in several steps and its beautiful trees, path-ways and park benches make it a popular rendezvous with both locals and tourists. On the highest point of the square towers the massive Neo-Romanesque Cathedral.

In the late Roman period there was probably a burial chapel on the site of the present Cathedral; some of the graves on the Early Christian cemetery have been uncovered and can be seen by visitors (see below). In 1064 a fire destroyed the first episcopal church and the adjoining bishop's palace belonging to the diocese which had been founded in 1009. Work on the new diocesan church, a triple-aisled columned basilica with apses on the east

*Cathedral
of St Peter
(Székesegyház)

Pécs

Pécs: St Peter's Cathedral

side, a raised choir and four corner towers, lasted until well into the 12th c. The building was clearly influenced by North Italian Baroque and the interior furnishings were the work of local sculptors and stone-masons in co-operation with master-builders from Dalmatia – which was then part of the Magyar empire – and Lombardy. In the 14th and 15th c., after having suffered severe damage in Mongol attacks, the church was given Gothic vaulted roofs in place of the original flat ones. During the Turkish occupation of Pécs it was used as a mosque and its crypt as an arms store. After the Turks withdrew there were plans to convert it in the Baroque style, but it was the mid-1700s before this came to fruition. By the early 19th c. the Cathedral was in extremely poor condition, and the measures carried out under the supervision of the Hungarian architect Mihály Pollack who added a second façade in 1805–30 in an attempt to prevent the outer walls from collapsing, did little to improve matters. Between 1882 and 1891 the church was completely rebuilt, to plans of the Viennese architect Friedrich Schmidt, and the result is what we see today. In accordance with contemporary ideas regarding the preservation of historical buildings, his brief was to reconstruct a supposedly Romanesque cathedral by retaining just the base structure and ground plan while in all other respects producing a completely new Neo-Romanesque edifice. The architect collected together all the existing architectural sculptures and stored them in the lapidarium (see below); they were used as models by György Zala when he designed the reliefs for the north and south passageways into the crypt. The high-altar is also a copy of the Romanesque original. Some well-known 19th c. Hungarian artists contributed to the interior furnishings; they included Károly Antal (the statues of the Apostles on the south front), György Kiss (relief in the tympanum above the south door showing Our Lady surrounded by Hungarian saints), Károly Lotz (frescoes in various chapels) and others. A particularly valuable 16th c. item of furnishing is the early 16th c. round-arched tabernacle of red marble in the Corpus Christi Chapel on the south-west side of the cathedral, which Bishop György Szathmáry of

Pécs later had converted to an altar. In that same chapel stands a brass font (1792) in Hungarian Baroque style. The beautiful alabaster epitaph in the Chapel of Our Lady in the north-west of the cathedral was made in Rome in the 17th century.

The original building sculptures, which were removed from the church during the renovation work carried out in 1881–92, are stored in the Lapidarium east of the Cathedral and can be seen by visitors. They include the west door, which was made from Roman gravestones, the reliefs from the crypt entrance and the 12th c. Altar of the Holy Cross.

Lapidarium

On the cathedral forecourt stand two imposing buildings. On the left is the Bishop's Palace, built in 19th c. Neo-Renaissance style, and on the right the Baroque cathedral archive (1780–83); when the latter was being built the graves of the first known Early Christian cemetery were unearthed (see below). Since 1972 a bronze statue of Janus Pannonius, carved by the Hungarian sculptor Miklós Borsos to mark the 500th anniversary of the great humanist's death, has stood in the former cathedral gardens to the south and west of the Bishop's Palace. The Barbican (round bastion) at the end of the road to the park was built at the end of the 15th c. and served to strengthen further the fortified "castle" precinct at the south-west entrance. At that time the south "castle" wall ran along the route of the present-day Janus Pannonius utca.

Bishop's Palace, Archive, Pannonius Statue, Barbican

In 1975–76, at the point where Janus Pannonius utca cuts through Dóm tér, archaeologists stumbled upon the foundations of a chapel and east apse, and under it a 4th c. Roman burial chamber. The walls of the chapel now stand above ground level, but the burial chamber remains below ground. The entrance to the latter by way of a covered staircase to the left of the chapel (open: Tue.–Sun. 10am–6pm) first leads into a small exhibition room documenting the archaeological dig. The burial chamber itself has a barrel-vaulted roof and three sarcophagi; its walls are decorated with naturalistic frescos in painted frames portraying Adam and Eve and Daniel in the Lion's Den; they date from the second half of the 4th c. and are very similar to those found in the catacombs of Rome.

**Early Christian Mausoleum (Öskeresztény Mauzóleum)

Early Christian Mausoleum

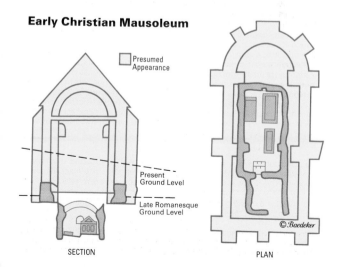

Presumed Appearance

Present Ground Level

Late Romanesque Ground Level

SECTION

PLAN

© Baedeker

Pécs

Other burial
chambers on
Dom tér

Some more underground burial chambers have been unearthed close to
the cathedral, but to date only that on the right-hand side of Dom tér (down
the slope on the south side of the archive building) is open to the public. Not
yet open to visitors are the Cella Trichora, a catacomb with three conches
(semi-circular vaulted roofs) and fragments of a mosaic floor on the west
side of the cathedral, Chambers 1 and 2 (also with wall-paintings) to the
south of the cathedral, and the most unusual catacomb below the archive
building, called Cella Septichora because of its seven apses.

Burial chambers
in Apáca utca
(formerly
Geisler Eta utca)

In the rear courtyards of the houses at Apáca utca 8 and 14 (open: Tue.–
Sun. 10am–4pm); can also be seen through the glass walls at other times)
archaeologists have uncovered parts of an Early Christian necropolis
around a chapel, consisting of three burial chambers and 110 Late Roman
graves. It is attractively and informatively presented with explanatory
boards (Apáca utca 4).

*Káptalan utca
(Oldest house
in Pécs)

Káptalan utca, to the east of the cathedral precincts, is a delightful street
lined with stately old buildings, once the residences of the cathedral can-
ons. No. 1 is the oldest house in the town; it is first mentioned in the town
records as having been the provost's house in 1324. It is likely that the
vaulted entrance and the first-floor window, both with Gothic niche-seats,
date from that time. The restored Renaissance windows on the first floor
are evidence of renovations carried out in the early 16th c.; the west
extension, originally an open loggia, was added in the 18th c. The Baroque
immaculata above the entrance is also from that period. The Zsolnay
Collection and a selection of works by the sculptor Amerigo Tot are tastefully displayed in its beautiful rooms (see Museums below).

Museums

Janus Pannonius
Museum

The various departments of the Janus Pannonius Municipal Museum are
distributed among a number of buildings in the town centre. The Archaeological Department is housed in an 18th c. plait style building behind the
former mosque at Széchenyi tér 12; it documents in an impressive manner
the long history of human settlement in the Baranya region. Among the
outstanding exhibits are the remains of a Early Stone Age settlement
(*c.* 60,000 B.C.), relics of a Late Stone Age culture found on Mount Mákar,
together with Celtic and Bronze Age finds from Mount Jakab (open: Tue.–
Sun. 10am–6pm). The Folk Art and Natural History Departments will be
found at Rákóczi utca 15 and 64 respectively. As already mentioned above,
the oldest house in Pécs at Káptalan utca 2 houses the Arts and Crafts

*Zsolnay Museum

collection. together with examples of the work of the Hungarian sculptor
Amerigo Tot on the ground floor; on the upper floor is the Zsolnay Museum
containing numerous pots and receptacles and other objects made in the
famous Pécs factory of that name. The varied and beautifully presented
exhibits provide a most impressive record of the firm's technical achievements. The various forms and types of pottery on display reflect the many
changes in style and taste which occurred within the framework of this
form of European art during the late 19th c. (open: Tue.–Sun. 10am–1pm
and 3–6pm).

*Vasarely
Museum

Káptalan utca 3 is a simple neo-classical dwelling situated diagonally
opposite the Zsolnay Museum; it was here that the artist Victor Vasarely
(actually Gyözö Vásárhelyi; see Famous People) was born in 1908. He spent
much of his life in France, but bequeathed to his home town some 150
paintings and drawings, which provide an interesting insight into the work
of this founder of the Op-Art school.

Csontváry
Museum

The large-scale paintings by Tivadar Csontváry Kosztka (1853–1919) are
now on permanent exhibition in a beautiful Neo-Renaissance corner-
house built in 1894 at Janus Pannonius utca 11. Csontváry, a chemist by

profession, did not begin to paint until he was 41 years of age. His pictures, full of gay colour and fabulous forms, show the influence of modern painting styles yet retain a clear individuality all of their own.

Next door, at Káptalan utca 5, the visitor can see a fine collection of works by Endre Nemes, who was born in Pécsvárad in 1909 and emigrated to France. His vast canvasses reflect the influence of Symbolism (open: Tue.–Sun. 10am–6pm).

Endre Nemes Museum

Ferenc Martyn (1899–1986) was an abstract painter. Some of his work is on display in his former house and studio at Káptalan utca 6 (open: Tue.–Sun. 10am–6pm).

Ferenc Martyn Museum

The comprehensive collections of the Modern Hungarian Gallery combine works of contemporary Hungarian artists with those of earlier 20th c. painters. The exhibition is housed partly in the Baroque house, formerly the cathedral canon's residence, at Káptalan utca 4, and partly in the exhibition rooms at Szabadság utca 2 (open: Tue.–Sun. noon–6pm).

Modern Hungarian Gallery

Two sections of Pécs' old system of underground workings are now used by the Mining Museum (Mária utca 9, formerly Déryné utca; open: Tue.–Sun. 9am–5pm) to demonstrate the technology of coal and uranium mining in the Mecsek Mountains.

Mining Museum

Exhibits displayed in the Municipal History Museum at Felsőmalom utca 9 (open: Tue.–Sun. 10am–6pm) provide information on the history of the town of Pécs from the end of the 17th c. to the Second World War, as well as on the development of the local leather industry.

Municipal History Museum

Other places of interest

This classical building on Szepesy utca (formerly Leonardo da Vinci utca 3) was designed by the Pécs architect József Piacsek in 1830. It has four Tuscan columns and a tympanum in the centre of the façade. The Library (Egyetemi könyvtár) houses large numbers of codices and incunabula.

University Library

It is just a short walk to the south-western corner of the town centre and to this Mosque, with its twelve-sided 23m/75ft high minaret at Rákóczi utca 2. Thanks to the excellent way in which it has been preserved it ranks among the major buildings of the Turkish period. The edifice is rectangular in plan with a massive square prayer-hall surmounted by a flat roof with an octagonal drum-dome. The outer walls are pierced by narrow pointed windows which provide some relief to the otherwise plain natural stone exterior. Apart from the restrained ornamentation and stalactite decoration the interior, too, is quite plain. The wall facing Mecca contains the obligatory *mihrab*, or prayer-niche. The little museum in the mosque is very informative.

*Mosque of Yakovali Hassan Pasha

In 1869 the Jewish community built their synagogue in the southern part of the town centre. It holds up to 1000 people, and is open to visitors except when services are being conducted.

Synagogue

In the garden of a children's hospital at Nyár utca 8 in the west of Pécs stands another Turkisk edifice, a small Mohammedan turban-stone chapel with an ogival doorway (Idrisz Baba türbéje), dating from 1591. It is in memory of Idris Baba ("Baba", roughly translated, means "father", and is an honorary title bestowed on older men) who is venerated as a saint because of his wisdom.

Idris baba Turban-stone

From Széchenyi tér it is a pleasant walk north-east to Tettye tér, a favourite excursion spot at the foot of the Mecsek Mountains with a beautiful view

Tettye tér

Zsolnay Fountain . . .   *. . . and Zsolnay Museum*

over the town. In a park can be seen the ruins of an early 16th c. Renaissance palace, which was inhabited by dervishes during the period of Turkish rule.

Surroundings

Mecsek Mountains (Mecsek hegység)

To the north of Pécs the Mecsek Mountains rise to a height of 680m/2232ft. The oldest traces of human settlement in Baranya (*c.* 60,000 B.C.) were found in caves in this central mountain range; these finds are now in the Janus Pannonius Museum in Pécs. The mild climate encourages the growing of grape-vines and even Mediterranean-type fruits on the southern slopes. The thick deciduous forests, criss-crossed with paths and well provided with resting-places and shelters, are very popular with hikers. From the terrace of the television tower on the Misina Peak (534m/1752ft) there are fine views of Pécs and of the Dráva beyond. On the way up to the peak there is a zoo and a leisure park.

Mánfa

10km/6 miles north of Pécs, on Road 66, lies the village of Mánfa, which dates back to the 12th c. Delightfully situated just outside the village stands its Romanesque church (The Visitation of Mary), construction of which was commenced in the 13th c. and completed in the Gothic manner in the 14th/15th c. Like many small churches of its type, it consists of a square nave with a rectangular east choir and a west tower. The stone-framed door has a Gothic pointed arch.

Sikonda

4km/2½ miles beyond Mánfa, in the midst of the hilly woodland countryside of the Mecsek Mountains, lies the holiday resort and spa town of Sikonda. When searching for coal in 1928 a thermal spring was discovered, and this pretty bathing resort has now grown up around it.

Komló

As well as being a holiday region the Mecsek Mountains are also a major iron-ore and coal mining centre, and unfortunately this is strikingly apparent when visiting Komló (250m/820ft; pop. 30,630). The coal required for the Dunaújváros steelworks has been mined here since 1950, with the result that a quiet lttle town of 6000 inhabitants has become a grey mining town with smoking chimneys and monotonous modern housing estates. In an old cemetery on a hill above the town's cultural centre lie the ruins of of a 15th c. Gothic church, of which only the font has survived.

An excursion to these two villages north-west of Pécs will be found rewarding. In Orfű the lakes will prove attractive to bathers and anglers, while in Abaliget there are guided tours of the 600m/660yd long dripstone cave.

Orfű,
Abaliget

Szigetvár

Szigetvár is a provincial town of 12,000 inhabitants, situated 34km/21 miles west of Pécs. The legendary defence of its castle against overwhelming Turkish odds has won this little town a permanent place in Hungarian history. In the summer of 1566 the 2400-strong garrison of this marshland town (Szigetvár means "island castle") held out for a whole month against a besieging force of 100,000 Turks before finally succumbing. In the course of the siege the Turkish army, led by Sultan Suleiman II, lost more than 20,000 men; the commander of the castle, Count Miklós Zrinyi (1508–66) and all his men were killed. A great-grandson of the Count, the poet and army commander Miklós Zrinyi the Younger (1620–64), who also fought against the Turks, composed a literary monument to this heroic deed in the form of his epic poem "The Siege of Sziget".

After finally storming the castle the Turks took possession of the "Szigetvár" and repaired the damage it had suffered. Surrounded by meadows and hedgerows, only a few sections of the castle have survived, but these are sufficient to show what the original structure must have looked like. The

Castle

Mosque of Jakovali-Hassan

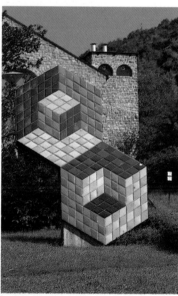

Sculpture by Vasarely

Ráckeve

8m/26ft high and 3–4m/10–13ft thick walls and the four massive defensive towers enclosed an area of 8·5ha/21¼ acres. Only the inner castle and a later Baroque tower have been able to withstand the ravages of time. A museum (open: Tue.–Sun. 10am–6pm) provides information about the time when it stood alone against the Turkish army.

Pécsvárad

In 1015 King Stephen I founded one of Hungary's first Benedictine abbeys at the foot of the 682m/2238ft high Mount Zengő, the highest peak in the Mecsek mountain range, about 20km/12½ miles north-west of Pécs. The abbey, which was rebuilt in the Baroque manner c. 1730, is now a hotel and museum. Of the Romanesque abbey church only the lower floor has survived. The "Maidens' Market", a traditional folk festival, takes place here in the month of October every other year.

Mecseknádasd

A further 10km/6¼ miles along Road 6 lies the village of Mecseknádasd, where in 1717 families from Hessen in Germany settled, to be followed later by more from Alsace-Lorraine and Styria (south-east Austria). There is a small local museum dedicated to the culture and traditional trades of these "Hungaro-Germans".

Ófalu

Beyond Mecseknádasd a narrow road on the right leads to Ófalu. Hidden among the hills, this village was founded by German settlers in the 18th c. Thanks to its secluded location (it was 1973 before it was linked to the outside world by a proper tarred road) their descendants have succeeded in retaining their original dialect and peasant culture. A small farm has been made into a local museum.

Siklós, Mohács, Harkány, Villány. See entries

Ráckeve

Region: Pest. Population: 8500

Situation and Importance

Founded in the 15th c. and formerly part of Serbia, this small town's attractions include one of the most beautiful Greek Orthodox churches in Hungary and the Baroque castle which belonged to Prince Eugen of Savoy, who defeated the Turks. Ráckeve is situated on Csepel (see Budapest, Surroundings), the 50km/31 mile-long island in the Danube, a popular resort for the citydwellers.

°Serbian church

About the mid-15th c. the Serbs, fleeing from the approaching Turks, settled on the island and built an Orthodox church which was consecrated in 1487. Structurally this well-preserved building has the appearance of a Christian Late Gothic church but with the division of the church into three being more in keeping with Orthodox liturgy (vestibule for the women, nave for the male congre-

Frescos in the Serbian Church

gation and the apse divided off by the iconostasis for the clergy). Particularly impressive are the apparently Byzantine frescos on the walls and vaulting (1765–71) by the artist Todor Gruntovics. Concealed beneath is a 15th c. painting which is currently being exposed. Beginning on the southern wall of the nave is the Life and Passions of Christ and on the west wall the Last Judgment. In the centre of the vaulting surrounded by angels is Christ the pancreator giving his blessing. The church decor also dates from the 18th c. with a valuable iconostasis from 1768.

Following his glorious campaigns Prince Eugen of Savoy, to whom the Habsburgs were indebted for the victory in 1697 over the Turks at Zenta, built a summer residence in Ráckeve (1700/02), in the centre of his estates. He engaged no less an architect than Johann Lukas von Hildebrandt (1668–1745), who ranks alongside Johann Bernhard Fischer von Erlach as the most important representative of Austrian High Baroque and went down in art history as the architect behind the Belvedere in Vienna. Ráckeve Palace was his first great commission, so to speak his début as a builder of magnificent mansions, from which he went on to command extensive knowledge. The palace (known as "House of Architecture" today) is situated in the Kossuth utca north of the Danube bridge and can only be visited from the grounds. The focal point of the three winged building around a courtyard (both the stable blocks down to the road are a later addition by Andreas Mayerhoffer) is the prominent central ressaut with the coat of arms of Prince Eugen in the tympanum. The balustrade is decorated with statues of Greek gods and heroes which reflect the virtues of the Prince. The octagonal tambour of the central ressaut was originally covered by an attic roof which was burnt down and replaced by the dome at the beginning of the 19th c. The central ressaut conceals the large hall which has two smaller adjoining rooms for functions. Behind is the open hall, known as the Sala Terrana, which leads to the gardens at the rear.

Savoy Palace

Surroundings

A visit to Ráckeve should include a short detour to Ócsa, which is situated about 35km/28 miles north of Ráckeve and only 5km/3 miles from the E5 Budapest–Kecskemét road and can be reached via Kiskunlacháza and Bugyi. Surrounded by small thatched farmhouses the Late Romanesque church from the first half of the 13th c. is a solid well-fortified building with two façaded towers and a prominent transept. It was built as the church of a Premonstratensian abbey and adopted by the reformed community in the middle of the 16th c. The late 13th c. frescos in the choir were exposed in the 19th c. (apostles, Saint Nicholas and Saint George, scenes from the life of the holy king Ladislaus and the Last Judgment).

Ócsa
Romanesque
church

Salgótarján

See Balassagyarmat, Surroundings

Sárospatak

G 1

Region: Borsod-Abaúj-Zemplén
Altitude: 96m/314ft. Population: 15,200

Sárospatak lies on the southern edge of the Zemplin range of hills, in the centre of the historic wine-growing area of Tokaj-Hegyalja. The main sight of this small town is the famous Renaissance castle above the Bodrog river, which has played an important part in Hungarian history. Since the founding of the Reformed College in the 16th c. Calvinist teaching has flourished.

Situation and
Importance

History

The area around Sárospatak was already populated at the time of the Magyar acquisition. Up until the end of the 14th c. the town belonged to the crown, then it was the property of the Pálóczi family and from 1526 Prince Péter Perényi. During the Thirties and Forties of the 16th c. he extended the castle, built a town wall and founded a school which was to become the Reformed College.

In 1616 the Rákóczi, a Transylvanian royal house, inherited Sárospatak as the dowry of Susanna Lórántffy, and became masters of the castle and town. The castle, which was extended in Renaissance style, became their favourite residence.

In the 17th and 18th c. resistance against the rule of the Habsburgs was continually flaring up in Sárospatak. Among those who met in the castle were supporters of the Wesselényi conspiracy. Ferenc II Rákóczi (see Famous People), the instigator of the Hungarian struggle for independence (known as the Kuruzzen uprising), made the town his headquarters and in 1708 made the castle into the state parliament. He fled abroad from here in 1710, a year before the end of the uprising.

Sárospatak went to the Habsburgs who installed various noble families as lords of the castle.

Sights

*Castle (Vár)

This imposing castle (Kádár Kata utca) lies to the south of the town centre; the castle grounds with its gardens and fortified walls stretch from the Kádár Kata utca to the bank of the Bodrog river. It is best to cross the Bodrog before visiting the castle (the castle entrance is on the west side) and look at the complex from the opposite side of the river.

The oldest part of the castle is the so-called Red Tower (Vöröstorony), a six-storied building with corner turrets. It was extended into a keep at the end of the 15th c. by the former owners, the Pálóczi family and around 1540 by Prince Péter Perényi into residential quarters in Renaissance style (currently under renovation). Rooms worth seeing in the Red Tower are the former chapel on the second floor and the so-called "Great Palace" on the floor above with fine Renaissance decoration. Perényi also built the two-storeyed wing with arcades on the ground floor, which today forms the east wing of the castle (also known as the Perényi wing).

Under Prince György Rákóczi I the castle was extended by the addition of

Sárospatak: the Castle, a fine Renaissance building

four wings around a courtyard. The east wing and the Red Tower are connected by the Lórántffy loggia (1645), named after the lady of the castle, which faces the west entrance to the courtyard, and is reached by a covered staircase. The elegant arcades of the loggia, which are continued into the narrow stairway, together with the richly decorated openings of the Perényi wing constitute a fine example of Renaissance architecture in Hungary. The present day appearance of the castle is the result of alterations by later owners, particularly the Bretzenheim family (early 19th c.).

The restored rooms of the castle house the so-called Rákóczi Museum (open: daily except Mon. 10am–6pm). The main focus of the exhibition is the documentation of the national struggle for independence and the history of the Rákóczi dynasty; other exhibits include furniture from the 16th–19th c., works from the glass foundries nearby, everyday objects from wine-growing and pressing in Hegyalja and some examples of the famous pottery from Sárospatak. The top floor of the east wing contains a particularly fine room of historic significance, the Sub Rosa Room, ornately decorated in stucco (17th c.), where the leaders of the anti-Habsburg Wesselényi conspiracy met.

Rákóczi Museum

The tree-lined Kádár Kata utca was once the main axis of the walled town joining the castle with the parish church. After leaving the castle the visitor should stop at the Trinity monastery on the left hand side of the road. A hotel (Borostyán) now stands behind its historic walls, which still retains much of the atmosphere of the monastery with its basic furnishings.

Kádár Kata utca

The parish church of the "Immaculate Conception", which originally joined directly on to the north town wall, at the northern end of the Kádár Kata utca, was built as a Gothic basilica and rebuilt at the close of the 15th c. as a triple-naved church. Of interest are the tombstones in the north nave and the Baroque high altar with the representation of the Immaculate Conception in the altarpiece. To the south of the church the foundations of a round chapel from the 11th c., possibly that of a royal residence, can be

Parish church

Sárospatak

seen. The modern bronze sculpture on the square in front of the parish church is the work of the Hungarian sculptor Imre Varga in memory of St Elisabeth (1207–31), later married to the Landgrave of Thuringia, daughter of the Árpád King Andreas II.

Reformed College

Outside of the medieval town, on the Rákóczi út, stands the building of the Reformed College (Református Kollégium) built between 1806–22, now a school. This 16th c. educational institution begun by Prince Péter Perényi developed in the 17th c. through the engagement of Zsuzsanna Lórántffy, wife of the Transylvanian Prince György Rákóczi, to become one of the leading Calvinist colleges in Hungary. From 1650 to 1654 the humanist and pedagogue Johann Amos Comenius from Moravia (1592 to 1670) was a profesor at the college. The jewel of the classical building is the two-storey library with a gallery designed by Mihály Pollack. The library contains over 2000 manuscripts and 200,000 books (guided tours only booked at the tourist office). A 7ha/42 acres park with beautiful old trees, assorted flora and sculptures by the patrons and famous scholars surrounds the college. The two-storey Late Baroque building in the courtyard (1771/72) houses a small museum which displays the scientific collection of the Reformed College and documents the life and works of Johann Amos Comenius, together with craft exhibits.

Modern architecture

As well as the historical buildings there are interesting examples of modern Hungarian architecture to be seen in this provincial town, such as the residential and commercial centre in the Rákóczi utca. This unconventional building, composed of individual cubes, with its unusual sloping windows and hood-like roofs, looks like a collection of goblins – a welcome contrast to the miserable prefabricated buildings left by socialism which fill in the gaps between historic buildings in many of Hungary's towns. The architect Ervin Nagy is a pupil of Imre Makovecz, who designed the neighbouring cultural centre (Muvelődési köspont) in the Eötvös utca.

Cultural centre

Makovecz belongs to the founders of a new "school of architecture" in Hungary for whom, with all their different representatives, the main con-

Sárospatak: modern architecture in the residential and shopping centre

cern is the human aspect of building and living. This is characterised in their preference for natural materials and organic shapes, which are partly reminiscent of anthroposophic architecture, and blend in with the surroundings. Traditional Hungarian styles and types of buildings which have long been forgotten provide the inspiration for these architects.

Surroundings

Karcsa is an idyllic little village about 20km/12 miles east of Sárospatak, near the Hungarian-Russian border. Unmetalled roads, traditional farmsteads mostly overgrown with vines and an atmosphere of rural isolation and tranquillity add to the charm of this village. It also makes an interesting diversion for the art lover as it possesses an unusual Romanesque church. Visible from the road, the rather unprepossessing church with a shingle hipped roof but without a tower was founded in the 11th c. for the nobility. It comprises a central round building of the Romanesque Palatinate or baptistry style which is now the choir. During the second half of the 12th c. the Knights of St John took over the church, built the nave and converted the round building into the choir apse. Further developments were discontinued as the Knights of St John withdrew from the area around Karcsa at the end of the 13th c. A notable Romanesque doorway can be found on the west side of the church which is a copy of the famous Porta speciosa in the royal palace of Esztergom. Inside the church a close examination of the capital of the south gallery pillar reveals an unusual motif – an argument between two men over a woman.

*Karcsa

Romanesque church

Sárvár

B 2

Region: Vas
Population: 16,000

This town at the confluence of the Rába and Güns is an economic and cultural centre in the west of Transdanubia, situated just 30km/19 miles east of Szombathely, and also has the tourist attraction of a well preserved castle.

An earth castle from the period of the Magyar conquest was the forerunner of the stone castle which was under royal ownership in the 12th c. The settlement at the foot of the fortification received its charter in the 14th c. In 1534 the castle and town became the property of the influential Nádasdy family. Under Tamás Nádasdy Sárvár was the focus of the reformist and humanist struggle in West Hungary; he made possible the publication of the first Hungarian translation of the bible

Situation and Importance

*Castle

Sárvár: Baroque wall-painting in the Castle

and a grammar in Hungarian by János Sylvester, a scholar of Erasmus. For the rebuilding of the castle he brought Italian experts in fortifications to Sárvár who designed the pentagonal Renaissance castle with its defensive ramparts. The famous Andrea Palladio is said to have been involved in the plans for the massive gate tower. Tamás's successor Ferenc Nádasdy, who completed the castle around 1650, was involved in the conspiracy of the Hungarian aristocracy against the Habsburgs ("Wesselényi conspiracy) and paid for it with his life; the Habsburgers took his art treasures with them to Vienna. It was the later owners who gave the building its Classical façade.

The Renaissance tower has been preserved in its original style of 1598. There is an impressive palatial room with stucco-framed frescos decorating its walls. The ceiling paintings, by an artist with the signature H.R.M., commissioned by Ferenc Nádasdy portray the Nádasdys as commanders in the Turkish wars; on the walls are scenes from the Old Testament by Stefan Dorffmeister (1769). The allegorical paintings in the tower room, are also his work, in which the role of the lord of the castle as patron of the arts and sciences is emphasised – a logical continuation of the frescos in the palatial room. Other rooms of the castle are also decorated with frescos and 18th c. furniture.

The Ferenc Nádasdy museum, housed in the castle, is devoted to the history of the family, regional folk art and the town's history.

Siklós   D 4

| Situation and Importance | This small town, situated about 30km/19 miles south of Pécs close to the border, is renowned for its famous castle, which is in a better state of preservation than most Hungarian fortifications. |

Sights | There are a few listed buildings in the town and a mosque on the Kossuth tér which was destroyed following the Turkish withdrawal and rebuilt in this century.

**Castle

History | A castle was built here during the 12th c. by the Siklósi family. After they died out it became the property of the Garai family. The defensive bastions were added by the next owner, the palatine (viceroy) Imre Perényi in the 16th c. as protection against the Turkish threat. From 1728 Siklós belonged to the counts of Batthyány who are responsible for the appearance of the castle today.

Tour | This impressive fortification stands on a plateau above the town. The enclosed four-winged castle is protected by an external fortified ring made of thick walls and ramparts, once circled by a wide moat.
The outside wall of the south wing is decorated by a reconstructed richly decorated Late Gothic oriel. Access to the castle is over a bridge on the south-west side and leads to the pinnacled round bastion (Barbakán) with the Batthyány coat of arms above the majestic doorway. There is a drawbridge in front of the doorway of the castle, laid out around a courtyard, which now accommodates a hotel and restaurant as well as display rooms and a museum.

*Castle chapel | The Late Gothic castle chapel built by the Garai family in the east wing is an architectonic jewel. The delicate fan ribbed vaulting in the choir (end of the

Siklós Castle

1 Barbican
2 Hotel, Inn
3 Castle Museum
4 Castle Chapel
5 Italian Bastion
6 Batthyány Fortifications

© Baedeker

15th c.) has often been compared with the vaulting in the Reformed Church in Nyírbátor (see Nyíregyháza, Surroundings). The frescos on the walls of the chapel date from the late 15th c. and were painted over at the beginning of the 16th c. They depict King Ladislaus, Louis of Toulouse, Christ the Man of Sorrows and the Lamb of God. The wall painting "Hiob and the Four Companions" was probably commissioned by the lord of the castle Hiob Garai.

Castle museum

The castle museum in the south wing is not so impressive. Thr rooms are from different historical periods from Romanesque to the Renaissance (torture chamber and dungeon, vaulted rooms, lapidarium).
There is a small but interesting collection of costumes and accessories from the 19th c. (on the ground floor near the entrance). Open: Apr.–Oct. daily 9am–6pm, other times 9am–4pm.

Bastions

The bastion named after the Batthyánys is a round tower near the Barbakán with a restaurant in Gothic style in the cellar. There are wonderful panoramic views from the roof terrace of the Spanish bastion. The extensive pentagonal Italian bastion surrounds the prominent oriel of the castle chapel.

Surroundings

Harkány

Travelling by car from Pécs to Siklós it is impossible to miss the small spa town of Harkány (alt. 101m/331ft; 3230 pop.) 5km/3 miles west of Siklós. As early as the 18th c. it was known for its sulphur springs which feed the thermal baths today which stand in a 12ha/30 acre park. The open air pool has five large hot water pools and a sports pool.

Ormánság

Harkány is the gateway to the Ormánság, a predominantly flat landscape north of the Dráva with about 30 to 40 small villages where the inhabitants

Siklós: entrance to Hungary's famous frontier fortress

Wine-cellar "cottages" in Villánykövesd

Sopron

have retained many idiosyncrasies. These include the special costumes and a particular style of building whereby the houses are built on girders as a defence against the threat of flooding from the Dráva.

On the road from Siklós to Villány there is an interesting detour to a bizarre sculpture park which is situated in a disused quarry away from the road (signposted). Sculptors are regularly invited here to partake, with costs paid, in working symposia as part of the state promotion of the arts. The result of their work can be seen at this "open-air" museum, which now contains over 100 exhibits (entrance fee).

Sculpture park

The two villages of Villány and Villánykövesd (10 and 14km/6 and 9 miles east of Siklós) are in the centre of the wine-growing region on the southern slopes of the Villány mountains. For the wine-lover or connoisseur a visit here is imperative, as wine can be bought directly from the producer at numerous, friendly little cellars. An interesting feature are the unusual wine cellar cottages which line the main streets, giving the villages their particular character.
Many German families are resident here as is evident from the bilingual town signs.

*Villány, Villánykövesd

See Mohács

Mohács

Sopron

B 2

Region: Győr-Moson-Sopron
Altitude: 212m/695ft
Population: 57,000

Sopron (German: Ödenburg), only about 65km/40 miles south of Vienna and 8km/5 miles from the Austrian border, between the eastern foothills of the Alps and Fertőtó (German: Neusiedler See), is a popular destination for excursions and recreation, not only because of its attractive situation and the famous Sopron "Blue Franconian" wine, but also because of its unusual townscape. Hardly any other Hungarian town has such well preserved medieval and Baroque buildings – there are 115 officially listed monuments and 240 protected buildings, in 1972 it was awarded the European prize for protection of historical monuments.

Situation and **Importance

Owing to its location on the Bernstein route, connecting the Baltic and Italy, Sopron was an important centre of trade before the Romans conquered

History

Sopron

Pannonia. In the 2nd c. b.c. the Roman settlement Scarbantia was an important town with a capitol, forum and town walls; it became the see of a bishop in the 4th c. The German name "Ödenburg" stems from the period of mass migration, when the Avars built fortifications on the ruins of the Roman town. A chronicle from the 12th c. bears the place name Suprun. The first German settlers arrived at this time and their descendants are well represented in Sopron today. In 1277 the town received the royal charter; between 1297–1339 the walls were built which survived the Turkish period and can still be seen in part today. Following the destruction caused by the fire in 1676 the town was rebuilt in Baroque style. After the Trianon peace treaty in 1921 the citizens of Sopron voted to remain in Hungary (as opposed to the Burgenland region which was part of Hungary). The Budapest Horthy government rewarded Sopron with the title "urbs fidelissima" ("most loyal town"). Sopron's industry dates back to the end of the 18th/ beginning of the 19th c. with a coal mine and sugar refinery; nowadays the main industries are light (carpet and clothing factories, wood processing).

Sights

**Townscape

All the buildings in the Old Town within the confines of the medieval town wall, built on the Roman ruins, are listed historical monuments. The majority are from the early Middle Ages but display features from other periods, such as Romanesque windows, Gothic niches, Renaissance loggias and Baroque or Classical decoration.

Mary Column

In front of the northern entrance to the Old Town the Mary Column commemorates the Church of Our Lady which was pulled down in 1632 (out of fear that the Turks could use it as a gun turret). Designed by Andreas Altomonte work on the column was carried out by the Viennese sculptor Jakob Christoph Schletterer in 1745.
The fire tower, the former defence tower, is visible above the stepped rows of houses.

Fire tower

The Fire Tower on the northern side of the Old Town is the emblem of Sopron. The foundations are Roman; the lower square base 14th c.; the cylindrical centre with the Tuscan arcade is Renaissance; the upper part – a clock tower with a multi-storeyed onion dome – was added from 1681–82 following the fire. The entrance to the 61m/222ft high tower, with magnificent views from its gallery over the town, is at Fő tér; it houses a local history collection (open: Tue.–Sun. 10am–5pm). To the south of the tower is the Loyalty Gate, presented to the town in 1921 by the government in Budapest following the referendum. The citizens of Sopron are depicted on the relief showing reverence to the crowned Hungaria.

Storno House

One of the finest palaces of the town stands next to the tower (Fő tér 8). It was built in the Middle Ages and King Matthias Corvinus lived here in 1482/83 during a campaign against Vienna. The Baroque exterior dates from the mid-18th c. István Széchenyi and Franz Liszt also resided here. In 1872 Franz Storno the Elder (1821–1907) bought the house; the name of this family of Italian and Swiss origin dates back generations in the town's history, its members were famous artists and art collectors. The collection housed here is quite diverse: old porcelain, furniture, paintings, guild shops, traditional wood carving, ceramics, etc. (open: Tue.–Sun. 10am–6pm). At the Korbbogentor are two lions and the Festetics coat of arms; the courtyard is formed from beautiful Renaissance arcades.

Apothecary museum (Patikaház)

The original medieval house on the other side of Főtér (No. 2) underwent much rebuilding until it acquired its present form in 1850. On the west side there is a Baroque oriel and on the south front three Gothic windows. The apothecary's shop, which is now a museum, was established in 1642 (open: Tue.–Sun. 10am–5pm).

The Town Tower, the landmark of Sopron

This fine Baroque column on Főtér (main square) was erected in 1695–1701 following the survival of the plague. The kneeling figures represent the patrons, Count Löwenburg and his wife; next to them are St Jacob, Johannes Nepomuk, Antonius and King Stephan as well as Barbara, Regina, Anna and Katharina.

Trinity column

The medieval General's House (Főtér 7, near the Storno House), was rebuilt in 1620 by the mayor Christoph Lackner. In the 18th and 19th c. the town commander lived here which explains the other name. The Classical balcony dates from 1830.

General's House or Lackner House

Behind the Baroque façade of the Fabricius House (Fő tér 6, near the General's House) is hidden a complex of houses from the 14/15th c., built on Roman foundations; part of the town wall is actually incorporated into the building. There is a striking oriel window two storeys high on the façade (18th c.); the courtyard has two-storey arcades and Tuscan columns (17th c.). The reverse side of the town wall dates from the first half of the 14th c., its stone façade (visible from the town wall) has two pointed and two straight Gothic windows with tracery.
The Gothic cellar houses a Roman lapidarium, the upper floor has finds from Illyrian, Celtic and Roman culture together with exhibits from the period of the Magyar conquest. The interior of the entrance to the municipal Franz Liszt Museum dates from the 17th and 18th c. The exhibitions, which have separate entrances, are open Tue.–Sun. 10am–6pm.
Adjacent to the Fabricius House is the Classical town hall built in 1830.

*Fabricius House

The southern end of Főtér is formed by the Goat's Church or Mary Church (Kecske templom). Legend tells of treasure which was scraped out of the ground by a goat and was buried when the church was built; however it was founded by the Geisel or Geisler family whose coat of arms is in evidence in the church. The 14th c. 48m/157ft high tower, octagonal at the

*Goat's Church

261

Apothecary's Museum (see p. 260)

top, was modelled on the west towers of the Stephan cathedral in Vienna and in its turn has inspired several church towers in the Sopron region. The triple-naved church was built between 1280 and 1491 for the Franciscans, the oldest part is the choir, which is as long as the square nave. There is well preserved Gothic decoration. The façade and interior are Late Baroque/Rococo: the wooden pulpit from 1754 bears the allegorical figures of Faith, Hope and Love; the high altar (with Mary's ascension) is the work of the carpenter Augustinus Löscher. The south organ gallery rests on consoles in the shape of goats. In 1456 the Franciscan monk Johannes von Capistran (1386–1456) recruited volunteers for the crusade led by János Hunyadi against the Turks from the stone pulpit in the south nave. During the 17th c. several parliamentary sittings took place in the church, as did the coronations of two queens and Emperor Ferdinand II was crowned King of Hungary in 1625. Following the dissolution of the Franciscan order in 1787 the church was used as a barn before it passed to the Benedictines; it was restored by Franz Storno from 1888–94.

Benedictine convent

In the former Benedictine convent (Templom utca 1, near the Goat Church), now a student residence, the chapterhouse of the Franciscan abbey, built around 1330, is one of the most significant examples of High Gothic in Hungary (restored about 1950). It stands in the north-east corner of the building and access is from the cloisters. The ribbed vaulting of the triple-naved building rests on two octagonal columns. Somewhat unusual is the decoration which reflects the function of the room as a place where the monks took confession communally; the figures on the consoles and capitals symbolise the Seven Deadly Sins, those on the keystones the Redemption. Another feature is a stone coat of arms with the goat of the Geisler family which used to be on the church tower.

Eszterházy Palace

The original Late Gothic house at Templom utca 2–4 was converted to a Baroque palace by Paul Eszterházy in 1752; Empress Maria Theresia stayed

Sopron: Trinity Column

A street with a view of the Town Tower

here in 1772 during her visit to Sopron. On either side of the splendid doorway (above which are the Eszterházy coat of arms and a copy of the Gracious Madonna from Mariazell) on the upper floor are wide enclosed oriel windows. The inner courtyard contains 17th c. arcades. The palace houses a museum on the history of coal-mining in Sopron and Hungary from 1245 (open: Tue.–Sun. 10am–6pm).

The Late Baroque church in the middle of Templom utca was built in 1782/83, the 52m/171ft high tower in 1862/63; originally it only had one roof turret as prescribed by the tolerance edict of 1781. Of particular interest in this triple-naved church with two-storeyed galleries is the high gilded altar dated 1730 decorated with statues, which was brought to Sopron from Kahlenberg near Vienna. The pulpit and pews are from 1780; the elaborately carved and decorated offertory box is from the 17th c. The melodic sound of the organ features regularly in concerts.

Evangelical church

Adjoining the church is the evangelical vicarage (Templom utca 12). The upper floor to this medieval palace and the façade were added around 1770. Ionic columns adorn the front of the house and an enclosed oriel window from the 17th c. projects over the entrance. The evangelical collection of the town of Sopron is housed in the palace (open: Mon., Thur., Sat. 10am–1pm).

Evangelical vicarage

On the north side of the Orsolya tér is the Arcaded House (Lábasház), built around 1750; the arcades are thought to have been walled in in the mid-19th c. and only came to light when the damage from the Second World War was cleared. Shops can be found on the ground floor and on the upper floor an exhibition on industrial history (open: Tue.–Sun. 10am–5pm).

Arcaded House

The lower part of the Új utca was the Jewish Street in the Middle Ages and separated from the northern part by a wall. In 1526 when the Jews were

Medieval synagogues

driven out of Sopron the wall was removed and the Új utca – the "new road" was formed. There are two synagogues here which are now museums.

Old synagogue

The Old Synagogue (No. 22–24) from 1300–20, one of the oldest in Europe, was the first house of prayer of the Jewish community in Sopron. The actual synagogue stands in the courtyard behind the two Baroque houses (façade from 1734) as non-Catholic churches were not allowed to be built on the streets; the front was used for shops and administration. Under a high pyramid roof the Old Synagogue consists of a large two-storeyed prayer hall, a prayer hall for women (joined to one other only by observation slits) and the ritual bath. Access to the main hall with its reconstructed wooden beams is via an Early Gothic doorway on the north side (open: Tue.–Sun. 10am–5pm).

The synagogue in the courtyard of the house at Új utca 11 was built in 1370 as the private prayer house of a Viennese Jew. It was converted into a residential house after 1526, as was the Old Synagogue; its original purpose was only discovered during restoration work folowing the Second World War.

Gothic House

The façade of the house opposite (No. 16), which is the Monument Office, is reminiscent of a Venetian palazzo. It represented the rear wing of a medieval palace on the Kolostor utca (No. 13; parts of the oldest secular building in Sopron are preserved). Restoration work at the beginning of the Fifties erased evidence of the 18th c. Baroque additions with the exposure of the Gothic windows and Renaissance arcades.

St George's Church

The single-naved cathedral church of St George's (Szent György utca), which is integrated into the row of houses, was built between 1380 and 1430 in Gothic style, restored following the fire of 1676 in Baroque style and side chapels were added in 1685. Restoration of the west façade revealed two tympanum reliefs above the portals; the northern one depicts St Margaret of Antioch, the southern one St George's fight with the dragon. The eclectic tower is from 1882. After the church had belonged to the Protestants from the end of the 16th c. (in 1631 the mayor and humanist Christoph Lackert was interred here) the Jesuits took it over in 1674, rebuilding the adjoining buildings (convent, college) to suit their own purposes.

Eggenberg Palace

The house at Szent György utca 12, built in the 15th c., after some rebuilding in 1674, came into the possession of Princess Eggenberg, who allowed Protestant services to be held here after St George's Church had fallen into the hands of the Jesuits. Sermons were held in the arcaded courtyard from the stone pulpit which bears the coat of arms of the Eggenbergs, a royal family of wine merchants from Radkersburg in Styria; above the main doorway is the Brandenburg coat of arms, to whom the Eggenbergs were related.

Caesar House

Situated opposite the Arcaded House is the magnificent palace at Hátsókapu utca 2 where the Bratislava parliament met in 1861; in reference to the building which is there it is also known as the "Green House". It was built in the second half of the 18th c. from medieval houses and part of the inner town wall. A giant Renaissance corner oriel window, flanked by Gothic windows, adorns the street side; on the courtyard side the wide Renaissance arcaded loggias are eye-catching. The name is attributed to the Caesar family who owned the palace from the end of the 19th c. to the middle of the 20th c.; in the Gothic cellar there is a wine cellar of the same name.

Town walls

The Várkerület, the ring road around the Old Town, follows the course of the oval, triple medieval town wall, which for the main part was con-

Sopron

structed on the Roman foundations. Between St George's Church and Caesar House are impressive parts of the Great Round Tower including the ruins of a Roman wall several metres thick. Further south both layers of the wall are exposed which together tower 8.5m/28ft high.

Outside the ringed wall to the south, on Széchenyi tér, stands the Baroque church dedicated to St Judas Thaddaeus, built in 1719–25 to a design by Lorenz Eysenkölbl. The façade is flanked by two towers completed in 1775 and decorated with figures of saints. The altar painting of St Dominicus is by the Sopron artist Stephan Schaller (1708–79).

Dominican church

On the site of a large bastion south-west of the Old Town (Május I tér) a historic villa was built in 1872, which has housed the municipal museum since 1913. Alongside local and ethnographical collections are paintings by important Baroque artists such as Maulbertsch, Troger and Altomonte (open: Tue.–Sun. 10am–6pm). Concerts and town events take place in the great hall. In the park of the so-called Baker's Cross from 1484 are 17th/18th c. tombstones from the evangelical cemetery and Baroque statues.

"Franz Liszt" museum and culture centre

North of the Old Town, on the road to Vienna, is the atmospheric Viennese suburb, the craftsmen's and wine-growers' quarter since the Middle Ages. Their houses line the narrow Ikvahíd utca, the bridge over the Ikva brook. The second (east) bridge is of medieval origin.

Viennese suburb

On the other side of the Ikva (corner Szentlélek/Dorffmeister utca) towers the 14th/15th c. Church of the Holy Ghost which in about 1780 received a Baroque façade and decor. The paintings in the main and side altar and the frescos were done by Stephan Dorffmeister the Elder in 1782.

Church of the Holy Ghost

The colourful private collection of Gusztáv Zettl at Balfi utca 9–11 (eastern continuation of the Szentélek) was assembled at the turn of the century and includes among its treasures weapons, finds from tombs, Roman containers, jewellery, porcelain, valuable paintings by Paolo Veronese and Dorffmeister as well as etchings by Dürer and Rembrandt (open: Tue.–Sun. 10am–6pm).

Zettl-Langer Museum

The Dorffmeister utca goes into Pozsonyi út (Bratislava Street). The house at No. 9 is a good example of early 18th c. rural Baroque; it gets its name from the two Moors which flank the doorway. They are the work, together with the figures and turned columns, of the builder Ignaz Leitner, a stonemason who based his work on old pattern books.

Két mór ház (House of the Two Moors)

Continuing along Pozsonyi út we come to the Romanesque-Gothic St Michael's Church (Szent Mihály templom), the town's first parish church. The Romanesque building from the 13th c. was extended to a triple-naved hall church by the 15th c. and altered again at a later date. In the course of time it was frequented by both Catholics and Protestants, the latter until 1674. Restoration work from 1859–66 by Franz Storno renewed the building to such an extent that it looks Neo-Gothic. The 48m/157ft high tower, more precisely its foundations and the octagonal second and third level, have retained their original appearance. Inside the church is a valuable Madonna figure from 1460, the high altarpiece is the work of Bartolomeo Altomonte (1739) and the other decor dates from the period of restoration.

St Michael's Church

The Szent Jakab kápolna near St Michael's Church, an Early Gothic 13th c. building, was a sepulchral chapel. It has an octagonal outline and three sides are enclosed by apses; above the doorway arch is a Romanesque relief (dragon with the tree of life). The interior wall paintings are by Franz Storno.

St Jacob's Chapel

To the south-west of the town is the residential and recreational area of the town reaching up the slopes of the Sopron mountains, known as the

Lővér Hills

Lővérek. There are numerous marked footpaths for walkers. From the Károly-magaslat, 398m/1306ft, a 23m/75ft high viewing tower provides a marvellous panorama of the surrounding area with Fertő tó (Neusiedler See) and the foothills of the Alps.

Surroundings

Fertőrákos
(Kroisbach)

The Ancient Romans established a quarry at Fertőrákos, 9km/6 miles north-east of Sopron town centre, which even supplied stone for building in Vienna. During the weeks of the Sopron festival in the summer, concerts and theatrical performances take place in the high "colonnaded halls" which resulted from the underground quarrying. It is open to visitors Nov.–Jan. 8am–4pm, Feb.–Apr. 8am–5pm, May–Sept. 8am–7pm, Oct. 8am–6pm. There is a fine view from the quarry hill over Fertő tó (Neusiedler See).

In the town the Bishop's Palace is interesting, a building of 16th c. origin which was decorated in Baroque style in 1745 under Bishop Franz Count Zichy. Also of interest are the 17th c. stocks and pillory, a water mill and the Catholic church, both also 17th century.

The border crossing to Mörbisch on the lake, 4km/2½ miles north is for pedestrians and cyclists.

Balf
(Wolfs)

Balf, a village with 640 inhabitants, is situated on Fertő tó 6km/4 miles south-east of Sopron. The Romans valued the healing properties of the sulphur waters which bring relief to rheumatic complaints. Nowadays the Late Baroque castle is a spa hotel. Close by on the main road is the Late Baroque spa chapel St Joseph's built in 1773; the frescos and altarpiece are by Stephan Dorffmeister the Elder (1725–97).

Nagycenk

In Nagycenk (14km/9 miles south-east of Sopron) is the ancestral home of the important Hungarian family of counts, the Széchenyi, whose name appears in many street names. The castle was built in 1750–58 and was rebuilt and extended around 1800 in Early Classical style; István Széchenyi (see Famous People) had the west wing added in 1834–40 with gas lighting and sanitary installations, an innovation for Hungary. The castle houses the István Széchenyi Museum (open: Tue.–Sun. 10am–6pm) and a hotel. In addition the Budapest Transport Museum has as part of an exhibition on Hungarian transport (on the upper floor) a display of old locomotives and carriages; a narrow gauge museum railway links the castle with Fertőboz. An avenue of lime trees 2.6km/1½ miles long planted in 1754 leads north from the castle to a monument. In the actual Széchenyi mausoleum in the village cemetery of Nagycenk lies the most famous son of the Counts, István Széchenyi (1791 to 1860), statesman during the Hungarian Reformed period and the struggle for independence against the House of Habsburg 1848/49; in 1860 he shot himself in a Viennese mental hospital. Széchenyi was responsible for such important initiatives as the building of the Budapest Chain Bridge and the regulation of the Danube and the Tisza rivers.

He commissioned the building of St Stephan's Church in the main square (Széchenyi tér) in 1861–64 by Miklós Ybi in Neo-Romanesque style; the tympanum of the former Romanesque building has been preserved (at the entrance to the tower). In front of the church is a monument to the Count by Alajos Stróbl (1897).

**Fertőd · Eszterháza Palace

History

27km/17 miles east of Sopron, in Fertőd, Eszterháza Palace is the largest and most beautiful mansion house in Hungary, the "Hungarian Versailles". The residence, in the typical "Habsburg ochre" and situated on the eastern side of the town, was built between 1760 and 1767 out of the small Süttör

Eszterháza Castle, showing the entrance portico and fine outside staircase

hunting lodge of 1720; the architect was Miklós, known as the shining one (Fényes) with whom the Eszterházy line reached its zenith. In only 150 years the Eszterházys went from being minor aristocracy to one of the richest royal families in Europe, with estates around the 100 mansions totalling about 5000sq.km/1930sq. miles and a corresponding lifestyle. This involved a permanent theatre ensemble, an orchestra and their own court director of music, Joseph Haydn, who was in Nikolaus's service from 1761–90 and who worked here from 1766. As supporters of the Habsburgs the Eszterházys were and still are quite unpopular in Hungary, unlike the Széchenyis, for example. After the death of Prince Nikolaus in 1790 the family moved to Eisenstadt, the Fertőd court was given up and the mansion fell into ruin until the main building was restored in 1958.

The main architects involved in this Rococo building, quite unique for Hungary, (as well as Nikolaus Jacoby and J. F. Mödlhammer) were the Tirolean Melchior Hefele, a pupil of Balthasar Neumann, and Johann Bernhard Fischer of Erlach. The magnificent wrought-iron gate through to the courtyard was also designed by Hefele. From the gate quadrant-shaped, single-storey passages lead to the two-storey side wings, which are linked to the main two-storey building dominated by the central tower (belvedere). In the courtyard is a fountain with dolphins.

House and grounds

Steps lead to a banqueting room with a fresco entitled "Apollo with a suncart" by Basilius Grundmann; the statues in the corners symbolise the seasons. Concerts are held here in the summer. The garden balcony enjoys a fine view over the part of the former 130ha/321 acre park which still remains. On the upper floor are the Chinese Salon, the Green Salon and the Maria Theresia Chamber; all are equipped with fine Rococo furniture and fireplaces (partly from other houses).

Below the banqueting hall, at ground level, is the Sala terrena, which opens out to the courtyard and garden (floor made of white Carrara marble,

Sopron

The elegant garden front

frescos by Joseph Ignaz Milldorfer (1766); on the ceiling, formed from garlands, are the letters FNE, the builder's monogram).

Within the grounds are the so-called grenadier houses (opposite the gate to the courtyard), accommodation for the guards and the musicians' house (Madách sétány 1, road to Fertőszéplak), where the court musicians lived, as did Joseph Haydn from 1766 to 1790.

Tours

There are guided tours for visitors around the house and Haydn Museum (open: Apr. 16th–Oct. 15th Tue.–Sun. 8am–noon, 1–5pm, otherwise until 4pm). The tourist office in Sopron has information on the programme and dates of the Haydn festivals (July/August), and also takes advance bookings.

There is also an unpretentious visitor's centre in the east wing, a school and an institute for plant research.

Fertőtó (German: Neusiedler See)

Situation and region

About 10km/6 miles east of Sopron is Fertő tó (Hungarian for "marshy lake"; Neusiedler See in German), the only steppe lake in Central Europe. In area it is 337sq.km/130 sq. miles (including the reed beds), of which 87sq.km/34 sq. miles are in Hungary. With a length of 35km/28 miles and a width of 5–15km/3–9 miles the lake is only 1–1.80m/3–6ft deep; this results in the slightly salty waters quickly heating up to over 25°C/77°F in the summer and freezing almost to the ground in winter. The water level varies in reponse to climatic changes; between 1866–69 the lake dried up completely.

The lake has few tributaries and no drainage and is almost completely surrounded by a 5km/3 miles wide belt of reeds; the south Hungarian part consists almost entirely of reed beds and is therefore unsuitable for water-sports (there is still boat mooring at Fertőrákos). Only on the Austrian east

268

bank near Podersdorf is the bank free from reeds (several beautiful bathing beaches).
Underneath the lake geologists have located a huge reservoir of mineral water.

Over 250 different species of birds live in the reed belt of Fertő tó and there are numerous rare plants found here. The water quality is under increasing threat of pollution: copper, lead, zinc and other harmful chemicals are getting into the water via the Wulka; the biological sewage plants of the Austrian communities use the reeds as part of the final purification process. Tighter regulations are being introduced to prevent further deterioration of the water quality. In the near future the entire area around the lake in both countries is to be declared a national park; most of the Hungarian part is already a protected area.

Conservation

From Sopron the Burgenland area of the lake with its pretty little towns, wine-growing villages and interesting salt steppes is a popular destination. Further information can be found in the Baedeker Guide to Austria.

Austrian part

Sümeg

C 3

Region: Veszprém
Altitude: 135m/443ft
Population: 7200

The picturesque little town of Sümeg, dominated by the castle on the hill, is about 20km/12 miles north of western Lake Balaton in the southern part of the Little Plain, in a basin bordered by the Keszthely Mountains and the western foothills of the Bakony Forest. It is best known for the frescos by Franz Anton Maulbertsch in the parish church, the first and most important work of this painter in Hungary.

Situation and Importance

Flints on the Mogyorós-domb provide evidence of a settlement here 6000 years ago; the foundations of an early Christian basilica date from the late Roman period. A castle was built in the second half of the 13th c. and in 1301 Sümeg was officially documented. When Veszprém was taken by the Turks in 1552 the diocesan seat moved from there to Sümeg for 200 years creating in the small town the atmosphere of a royal residence which can still be noticed today; particularly attractive are the groups of houses in Kossuth utca, on Szent István tér and Udvarbíró tér.

History

Sights

This beautiful bishop's palace (Szent István tér 10) was rebuilt from a Renaissance house in 1748–55 by Bishop Marton Padányi Bíró. Its front has a balcony over the doorway supported by Atlantis and decorated with garlands, over the balcony is the bishop's coat of arms on the central ressaut. To the right of the door is the chapel with decoration by Antonio Orsatti and frescos by Gregor Vogl (about 1750).

Bishop's Palace (Püspöki palota)

The Baroque buildings of the Ferences kolostor (Franciscan convent) on Szent István tér were built between 1652 and 1657 on the initiative of the Bishop of Veszprém György Széchenyi; they were inspired by the discovery of a wooden relief of the Pietà in the ruins of a castle church, which the bishop had copied and today stands above the altar. Martin Athanasius Witwer, a Carmelite monk, led the restoration of the church in 1720 (passion chapel near the tower with splendid wrought-iron gates). The impressive altar (1743) was designed by Witwer and made by Franz Richter (see also Győr, Carmelite church).

Franciscan church and convent

Sümeg

The 17th c. convent adjoins the church.

Kisfaludy
Museum

Lake Balaton was the main theme of the lyric poet Sándor Kisfaludy (1772–1844). The house on Kisfaludy Sándor tér (a few yards from the Franciscan church), where he lived and worked, is a museum dedicated to his memory (open: Tue.–Sun. 10am–6pm).

**Parish church
of the Ascension

The interior decoration of the outwardly insignificant Church of the Ascension in Deák Ferenc utca dar is a unique work of art. The entire single-naved interior of this building (1756–57) was designed by Bishop Márton Bíró and carried out by Franz Anton Maulbertsch between 1757 and 1758, probably the most important representative of Austrian Late Baroque painting. Born in 1724 in Langenargen on Lake Constance he moved in 1739 to Vienna where he painted the dome of the piarist church in 1752/53 and was professor of the art academy from 1770. The frescos in Sümeg were protoypes for the first main period of his art, which is characterised by bright colours, active composition and expressive gestures of the usually (as with Goya) rounded figures.

The paintings are in order of the gospel story: below the organ gallery are the Old Testament figures of Adam and Eve, Moses, Noah, and the prophets awaiting salvation in limbo (in the side chapel the sacrifice of Abraham; above the gallery a picture of Bishop Bíró). 1st truss: the Annunciation, right side altar the Adoration of the Shepherds (self portrait of the artist as a shepherd presenting cheese and bread) left side altar the Circumcision of Jesus. 2nd truss: Star of Bethlehem, which corresponds with the Adoration of the Three Kings in the right side altar (in the background the murder of the innocents in Bethlehem), while the solar and lunar eclipse on the left lead to the Crucifixion on the left side altar. 3rd truss, beginning on the right: the right side altar the Resurrection, in the dome the risen Christ with the disciples, night sky with angels, the outpourings of the Holy Spirit, left side altar St Peter's first sermon. The

Sümeg: "The Adoration of the Magi", a Baroque painting in the parish church

grisailles of the choir depict the four church fathers, the vaulting the transfiguration of Christ. In the triptych of the high altar in the centre is the Ascension with symbols of faith, hope and love; on the left the triumphant church (Mary with saints, popes), on the right the fighting and suffering church (Maulbertsch's signature bottom right). It is noteworthy how the architectural framework is incorporated into the composition – a stylistic device which features often in Late Baroque/Rococo with the effect of increasing the impression of space.

The frescos were first restored in 1938 and again in 1966–69 to rectify war damage. In the porch there is a machine to illuminate the frescos.

Below the castle (Váralja utca) in the former bishop's stables from the mid-18th c. is a museum illustrating the development of saddles and bridles (Lószerszám múzeum; open 7.30am–4.30pm, conducted tours). Breeding stallions are also kept here; behind the museum is a riding arena and horse-drawn coach trips are also available.

Horse harness museum

A paved path leads from the Franciscan church to an imposing, extensive ruined castle on the 260m/853ft high hill above Sümeg. In the 16th c. the castle was the property of the bishops of Veszprém, who extended it in 1552 with Renaissance Italian-style bastions against the Turks, who were unable to take it. At the beginning of the 18th c. it was an important military base of the Rákóczi rebels resulting in its being set on fire and blown up by the imperial troops in 1713. Some parts were reconstructed after 1959 including a residential tower in the south of the courtyard (castle museum). Above the inner castle entrance is the coat of arms of the Veszprém Bishop Vetési (2nd half 15th c.). From the castle hill there are wonderful views of the surrounding area. Open April–May, Sept.–Oct. daily 8am–5pm, June–Aug. 8am–7pm.

Castle

Ruined castle above Sümeg

Region: Békés
Altitude: 85m/279ft. Population: 20,000

Situation and Importance

Situated in the southern part of the Great Plain, on Road 44 from Kecskemét to Békéscsaba, Szargas is best known for its arboretum. This once prosperous market town was destroyed during the Turkish wars and remained uninhabited until it was populated by Slovakian families in the 18th c. It owes its economic and cultural revival to the evangelical priest Sámuel Tessedik (1742–1820), who built the evangelical church, pushed forward plans to develop the town and in 1790 founded the Practicum Economicum Institutum, one of the first agricultural schools in Europe, now a university.

Arboretum

In the north of the town is the famous arboretum, also known as Pepi-kert (Pepi Garden) after the pet name of its founder. When József Count Bolza, the Guards officer of the imperial army, took leave of the town around 1830 he had a 5ha/12 acre botanical garden laid out on his land in Szarvas, modelled on the gardens at Schönbrunn. His grandson Pál Bolza had the gardens moved from the Anna Woods to their present site because of river control of the Körös. Following his death the arboretum which had expanded to 42ha/210 acres passed into state ownership. Today there are 1660 species of tree from all over the world on 84ha/420 acres, including such rare examples as the gingko, the sacred tree of the Japanese, and the Californian giant redwood. The yellow-brown leaves of the Japanese maple are especially beautiful in autumn. Open April 15th–November 1st, daily 9am–6pm.

Sámuel Tessedik Museum

The school of economics founded by Pastor Tessedik is housed in the Late Baroque building at Vajda Péter utca 1 built in 1790. Archaeological finds, regional folk art and documents on the economic history of the region are displayed (open: Tue.–Sun. 10am–4pm).

Evangelical church

In the same street Sámuel Tessedik built the evangelical church (1786/88) for his congregation. The neo-classical interior decor dates from around 1800.

Drying mill (Szárazmalom)

Built in 1836 the mill driven by horse power at Ady Endre utca 1 is an interesting monument of agricultural history (open: daily 1–4pm).

Traditional Slovakian house

In the Szlovák tájház a long farmhouse with a reed roof and pergola at Hoffmann utca 1 dated 1885 houses an exhibition on the lifestyle and culture of the Slovaks who lived in Szarvas.

Elisabeth Wood

By the Dead Körös the 13ha/65 acre park, over 100 years old, is named after the popular Hungarian queen and Austrian empress Elisabeth. The former residence of the local artist György Ruzicskay (1896–1989) contains a permanent exhibition of his paintings.

Szécsény

See Balassagyarmat, Surroundings

Szeged

F 3

Region: Csongrád
Altitude: 84m/276ft. Population: 177,000

Situation and Importance

Szeged is the lively economic and cultural centre of the southern lowland plain, capital of the Csongrád region and with around 180,000 inhabitants the fourth largest town in the country. Important food and textile industries have been established here. Both the Biological Research Institute in Újszeged and the university enjoy international recognition. The biochemist and Nobel prize winner Albert von Szent-Györgyi who succeeded in isolating ascorbic acid (vitamin C) in 1928 taught here for a while.

Settlement in the Szeged region dates back to the Stone Age. Since the time of the Romans a trading centre has existed here for the salt deliveries from Transylvania. First officially documented in 1138 when it was already an important trading centre it was fortified with a castle in 1241 by King Béla IV after the devastating Mongol attack. Following the conquest by the Turks (1543) Szeged enjoyed the status of a Khas town, directly under the command of the sultan. On the extensive grazing land around the town, cattle rearing became another important branch of the economy. Owing to its involvement in the Rákóczi uprising the town was plundered and destroyed at the beginning of the 18th c. by the Habsburg troops. By 1787 the number of citizens in Szeged had reached 21,519. The economic upturn brought about by industrialisation did not take off until the beginning of the

History

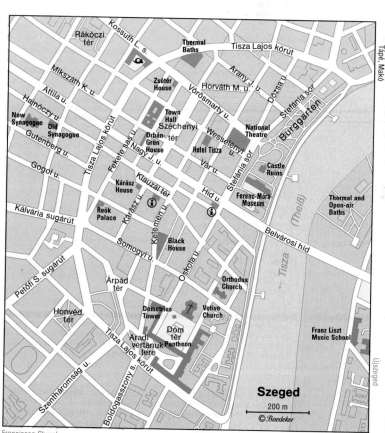

Szeged

200 m

© Baedeker

Franciscan Church

273

next century. Large parts of the town were destroyed by devastating floods in 1879, about 5500 houses collapsed and 60,000 people were made homeless. When the waters of the Tisza retreated, only 256 houses were left standing. Reconstruction of the city, which was planned and carried out within a few years, was made possible by the generous financial support of various European countries; Szeged's middle ring road is named after the capitals of these countries in recognition of their help – Bécs (Vienna), London, Párisz (Paris), Brüsszel (Brussels), Moszkvai (Moscow) and Róma (Rome). Trade and transport no longer play a key role in Szeged; in the 20th c. it has developed into an important industrial centre for food production (Szeged salami) and into an administrative centre and university town.

Sights

Townscape

Following the flood damage of 1879 the centre of Szeged was rebuilt on the model of large European cities: extensive green areas, wide arterial roads together with an inner and outer ring road make up the structure of the inner city. The provincial development gave way to high elegant houses or whole complexes built in the historicist style or the latest art nouveau, of which numerous fine examples have been preserved.

Around the Széchenyi tér

Széchenyi tér

After the flooding the old marketplace was replaced by the wide Széchenyi tér edged with plane trees. Statues of the nation's heroes and important citizens of the town line the paths of the park-like square. To the south of the square a monument commemorates the great reformist István Széchenyi. The allegorical figures around the pond in the middle of the square symbolise both the life-giving and destructive properties of the River Tisza.

Town hall

On the north-west side of the Széchenyi tér is the yellow painted Town Hall crowned with a central tower. It was built in 1883 to plans by Ödön Lechner and Gyula Pártos. The founder of Hungarian art nouveau made use of Neo-Baroque forms in which the two-dimensional rather than three-dimensional conception of the façade was suggestive of the new architectural style. A narrow thoroughfare on the first floor similar to the Bridge of Sighs in Venice links the town hall with the neighbouring buildings.

Hotel Tisza

The renowned Tisza Szálló on the opposite side of Széchenyi tér (corner of Wesselényi utca) has always been the focal point of the city's social life. Szeged society attended concerts and other cultural events in the great hall of this prestigious hotel built in 1866.

Orbán Grün House

This classical house at Széchenyi tér 13 was built in 1901 by a book printer. Stone consoles support an oriel window with wrought-iron grilles and the figure of a Roman legionary in cast-iron.

Zsóter House

One of the buildings which withstood the floodwaters is the house at Széchenyi tér 9, built in 1844 in Late Classical style for the wealthy shipping merchant and corn handler János Zsóter.

Klauzál tér, Kárász utca

South of the Széchenyi tér is the charming Klauzál tér, an intimate square by Szeged standards, with one of the best cafés (Café Virág) far and wide. Together with the Kárász utca it is a popular pedestrian quarter and commercial centre of the town. The balcony of the so-called Kárász House (Klauzál tér 5) is of particular significance to the people of Szeged. Lajos Kossuth gave his final speech in Hungary from here before going into exile.

Dom tér and surroundings

Dom tér

A unique example of the Expressionist town architecture of the early 20th c. is the complex situated around the cathedral square in the south of the inner town. The starting point is the votive church (cathedral) on the north side of the square, built 1913–29, followed by the development of the Dom

Szeged: Town Hall   *Ferenc Móra Museum*

tér to plans by Béla Rerrich (1881–1932). The horseshoe-shaped complex of buildings with a façade of fired and glazed clinker brick consists of the administrative offices of the university and the theological college in the west wing, the bishop's palace in the south-west and the science and medical institutes in the south and east. On the ground floor the round arched arcades of the three-storeyed wings open out onto the Dom tér. The severe, almost oppressive, monumentality of the 300m/984ft-long row of arcades is only mitigated by the different shaped columns (the Baroque style columns are especially beautiful). Below the arcades is the so-called "Szeged Pantheon", a collection of 89 busts and reliefs of important personalities from Hungarian history, art, literature and science. The eminent Hungarian sculptor Alajos Stróbl laid the foundations for this "gallery of fame" with his portraits. Since the completion of the cathedral square, the Szeged open air games, at which over 6000 people can take part in each event, have been held annually against the imposing background of the Votive Church (the steps to the main doorway serve as a stage).

Arcades

"Szeged Pantheon"

The town owes its splendid cathedral, which adjoins the north side of the Dom tér, to a vow by the citizens of Szeged during the floods. The plans for the church, built in 1913–30, were by Ernő Foerk and Frigyes Schulek, whose design for the façade was inspired by the Italian Romanesque cathedrals. Above the main doorway is the 3m/10ft-high statue of the Madonna, the patron of the church and protector of Hungary (Patrona Hungariae). To the left and right of the Madonna are the twelve apostles in the form of mosaic pictures. An interesting representation of the Madonna can be found inside the cathedral in the mosaic by Ferenc Márton over the baldachin of the high altar. It is also known as the "Madonna in a fur coat", as she is depicted wearing a richly decorated fur coat, typical of the Great Plain region, as well as red slippers typical of Szeged. There is a notable crucifix by János Fadrusz on a side altar.

Votive Church (Fogadalmi templom)

Szeged

Szeged: Votive Church

"Szeged Pantheon"

Demetrius tower
(Dömötör-torony)

This tower is of particular significance because it was the only medieval historical monument to survive the catastrophic floods of 1879. The lower, square part of the tower originates from the period when the first Demetrius church was built in the 12th c., the octagonal part of the tower was a 13th c. addition. The tower, incorporated into a new building, only came to light in the 18th c. with the redesigning of the cathedral square when the ruins of the Baroque cathedral were cleared. It was restored and rebuilt as a baptistry to a design by Béla Rerrich. In the tympanum of the porch a Romanesque relief (12th c.) of the Agnus Dei was transferred from a church in the neighbouring village of Kiskundorozsma, now incorporated into Szeged. The interior of the chapel is decorated with paintings with historical themes by Vilmos Aba-Novák (1894–1941).

Musical clock

In 1935 the Szeged watchmaker Ferenc Csúri completed the clock for the cathedral square. On the hour figures of well known statesmen, writers, former rectors and deacons of the university appear to the sounds of a tuneful melody.

Greek Orthodox
Church

North-east of the Votive Church is the Greek Orthodox church of St Nicholas (Görögkeleti Szerb templom) built in 1773–78 by the new Serbian citizens in Baroque style. It has a fine iconostasis made up of 80 icons in a pearwood frame.

Other sights

Cultural palace
Ferenc Móra
Museum

During the reconstruction of Szeged the library at Roosevelt tér was built in Classical style with an ancient triangular gable on the main façade in keeping with its function as a place of education and science. Known as the cultural palace this building houses not only the municipal library but also the Ferenc Móra Museum, named after the popular writer and researcher of ancient history Ferenc Móra (1879–1934). He laid the foundations for the museum with his private collection of regional early and prehistory. In front of the building are statues of both the first directors of the museum, Ferenc Móra and István Tömörkény.

North of Roosevelt tér by the Tisza the castle garden (Várkert) stands on the site of the castle built in 1246. After the floods the remaining walls of the castle were dismantled because they did not fit in with the new concept of the town. Only a square bastion remains. Since the restoration a museum and a lapidarium have been built using building material from the earlier castle. In the south-east corner of the castle garden there is a monument to Elisabeth ("Sissy"), Empress of Austria and Queen of Hungary, hewn from Carrara marble.

Castle garden, castle museum, lapidarium

The famous Viennese architects Fellner and Helmer were commissioned to build the new theatre in 1883, a magnificent building with a Neo-Baroque façade. The semi-circular entrance side is on Dócza utca.

National theatre

The finest art nouveau building in the town is the Palais Reök in Tisza Lajos utca, built by the local Szeged architect Ede Magyar in 1906/07 for the water engineer Reök. This recently renovated building combines the superior elements of French and Hungarian art nouveau and its serene elegance is captivating. There are other fine examples of art nouveau houses (mostly residential and commercial properties) from around 1900 in the vicinity of the Palais Reök.

*Palais Reök

In Hajnóczy utca (No. 12) stands the Jewish synagogue, built in neo-classical style in 1843. An inscription on the outer wall in Hungarian and Jewish indicates the level of the floodwater in 1879.

Old synagogue

National Theatre by Fellner and Helmer

277

Szeged

New synagogue

The new synagogue between Hajnóczy utca and Gutenberg utca , a Secessionist building from 1900–03, was the largest church in Szeged until the Votive Church was built. The domed interior is superbly decorated: the 24 tambour pillars symbolise the hours in the day, the blossom of the hawthorn, faith and the stars of the universe. The dome is crowned by a star of David circled by rays of light.

Former
Franciscan
church

An important medieval edifice has been preserved south of the town centre on Mátyás tér in the lower town (Alsóváros). The Franciscans, who had lived in Szeged since 1444, built a church in 1490 on the foundations of a Romanesque church. It is thought to have been completed in 1503. The nave of this hall church is spanned by magnificent fan vaulting or star vaulting (choir), comparable with the Reformed Church in Nyírbátor. Further remains of this Late Gothic building are the pointed arch windows between the delicate buttresses.

After the Turks had left the town again, the interior of the church was decorated in Baroque style (around 1720) and a Baroque tower was added. The pulpit and the ornately carved high altar with figures in the choir, by the Franciscan monk Antal Graff, originate from this period.

Újszeged

The Belvárosi híd (Old Bridge) in the extension of the Híd utca leads to the Újszeged district on the left bank of the Tisza. North of the bridge on the flood plain is the swimming pool (Partfürdő) with a thermal water pool and sports pool.

Botanical
gardens

In the Füvészkert district on the left bank of the Tisza (Lövölde utca 22) the Szeged Botanical Gardens (Füvéskert), laid down in 1922, cover an area of 17ha/42 acres. Alongside various species of deciduous trees, shrubs and about 70 types of pine tree, there are 1500 species of tropical plants and numerous types of roses. In the ponds white waterlilies and Indian lotus flowers blossom.

Surroundings

Fehér-tó

5km/3 miles north of Szeged on the E75 towards Kecskemét is the Fehér-tó nature reserve, a wetlands habitat where rare species of birds nest.

Kiskundorozsma

8km/5 miles north-west, on the road to Kiskunhalas, is the old village (today incorporated into the new), first mentioned in 1138, with a windmill dated 1821 (Szélmalom utca). In 1905 there were still 23 windmills in Dorozsma. Beautifully situated among poplar and pine woods on the outskirts of the town is a bathing lake (Sziksósfürdő). Its warm waters at a temperature of 30°C/86°F containing soda are very inviting. At weekends the campsite is very popular.

Szentmihálytelek

Situated 7km/4 miles south-west of Szeged this is the centre of the paprika-growing area. The small paprika museum (Vöröshadsereg útja 50) illustrates the traditional methods of growing, drying and milling.

Opusztaszer

See Opusztaszer

Tápé

In the small fishing village 3km/2 miles east of Szeged (on the main road to Makó) the customs and culture of the Lower Plains are still maintained. The remains of Gothic frescos have been preserved in the choir of St Michael's Church in Honfoglalás utca (around 1300). The Baroque transept together with the tower were built in 1770, the main nave in 1941. A private collection of ethnology and local history belonging to József Lele is open to visitors in his own house in the Vártó utca 4 (open daily except Tue. and Fri. 1–6pm).

4km/2½ miles before Makó (branch off Road 43) is the village of Kiszombor with its interesting Romanesque church (11th c.). The small round building was probably built in the 11th c. for the nobles and later integrated into a larger church. During restoration work (1981) frescos from the 14th c. were exposed.

Kiszombor

Makó

Joseph Pulitzer, the famous American newspaper publisher and the founder of the prizes for journalism, literature and music named after him, was born in 1847 in this market town on the Hungarian-Romanian border. Since then Makó, situated on the banks of the Maros, about 30km/19 miles east of Szeged, has developed into an industrial city with a population of about 30,000. For years the most important product of Makó has been onions, which are traditionally grown here. Their outstanding quality is a result of the special methods of cultivation, the clayey soils and the long hours of sunshine. The town is named after a heroic follower of the king, a ban (commander in the Hungarian border guard) who governed the region in the 13th c. and was awarded the settlement as a fief. During the Turkish period Makó shared the fate of many of the towns of the Great Plains, that of devastation and migration of peoples. In 1821 the Maros burst its banks and almost destroyed the entire town, which, like Szeged, was completely rebuilt afterwards.

The Hungarian poet Attila József (1905 to 1937) lived at Kazinczy utca 6 for more than a decade. The local history museum is named after him at Felszabadulás útja 4. Built in 1981 to a design by Mihály Vincz it has a wooden sculpture by Imre Varga. The life of Joseph Pulitzer (1847–1911), who was born in Makó, together with the history of the town are documented here. In the museum courtyard there is a house from the beginning of the century with original features, a forge and a cooper's workshop, granary and a cottage (open: Tue.–Sun. 10am–6pm).

Attila József Museum

The Baroque Reformed Church on the Kálvin tér was rebuilt and expanded in 1722–78 in Classical style following the floods of 1828. The interior is also of this period and is the work of a carpenter from Makó. The Baroque parish church of St Stephan on the Szent István tér from 1765/1772 has a Rococo pulpit and a Classical font. A trinity column has stood in the church square since 1888.

Churches

This Classical building (Fő tér) has stood on the site of its Baroque predecessor since 1839, which was the administrative centre of the Csongrád region until 1850.

Town hall

Hódmezővásárhely

Hódmezővásárhely (83m/272ft a.s.l.; pop. 54,000), situated 25km/16 miles north-east of Szeged, is an agricultural town typical of the Hungarian Lower Plain. The actual centre is surrounded by a broad belt of village settlements, interspersed with individual farmhouses. The transition from country to town is almost imperceptible and the expanse of individual plots which still fall within the town's boundaries makes a considerable impression. Hódmezővásárhely's development into an industrial town has not altered the rural landscape. Like Szeged, the town's history goes back a long way with a long tradition as a trading and market centre. The large proportion of agricultural workers and small farmers resulted in the town becoming the centre of the agricultural socialist movement at the turn of the century. Some traditional arts and crafts have been preserved and even reactivated, such as the manufacture of majolica and porcelain. Knitwear, hosiery and furniture from Hódmezővásárhely are of good quality.

Situation and Importance

Szeged

János-Tornyai Museum in Hódmezővásárhely

Reformed Church and granary

The Baroque church built in 1713/22 on the central Kossuth tér had a sumptuously decorated gallery, which was transferred in 1892 to the Arts and Craft Museum in Budapest. In the neighbouring house, which is in the rural Baroque style, the church stored natural goods.

Kossuth tér

The central square of Hódmezővásárhely is Kossuth tér with the historic town hall (1893) offering fine views from its 57m/187ft high tower. The 20 hundredweight bell from the town hall tower was found a new location in a nearby park following a fire of 1970. The hotel "Fekete Sas" ("Black Eagle") on the west side of the square was designed by Gyula Pártos, whose best known work is the art museum in Budapest which he designed with Ödön Lechner. The leader of the agrarian revolt, János Szántó Kovács (1852–1908), is commemorated by the town with a statue by József Somogyi (1965). Together with 123 other rebels Kovács was sentenced in the great town hall of Hódmezővásárhely in 1895.

Greek Orthodox Church

The resident Greek and Serbian merchants built a church at Szántó János utca No. 9 in 1786–1807. Several tombstones can be seen on the outer wall of this Late Baroque church, inside is a fine iconostasis with the icon of St Naum and a 18th c. Greek cross from Mount Athos.

János Tornyai Museum

The municipal museum which was established in 1904 in the buildings opposite the church (No. 16–18) is well worth a visit. It houses a collection of paintings by János Tornyai (1896–1936), the "painter of the Lower Plain" and founder of the artist colony in Hódmezővásárhely, which developed in the first decades of this century. The local history department of the museum has examples of furniture and fine specimens of local pottery. The prize exhibit is the early Stone Age Venus statuette, called "Venus from Kökény domb", a fertility symbol, uncovered during excavations.

Székesfehérvár

Region: Fejér
Altitude: 111m/364ft
Population: 110,000

Hardly any other town is so closely linked with the beginnings of the Hungarian monarchy as Székesfehérvár. It can claim to be the oldest seat of the monarchy and also possesses (still present as ruins) the former sepulchral and coronation church of the Hungarian kings. This town, situated between the foothills of the Bakony Forest and the Velencei Mountains, has a well preserved inner town, which is almost provincial Baroque in appearance with numerous places of interest. Székesfehérvár is the regional capital and important industrial centre (aluminium, electronics, automobile manufacture).

Situation and **Importance

The Magyars are said to have already settled in the region around Székesfehérvár at the time of the conquest. Prince Géza, the father of King Stephan I, erected a castle in 972 on a hill surrounded by marshes, where he

History

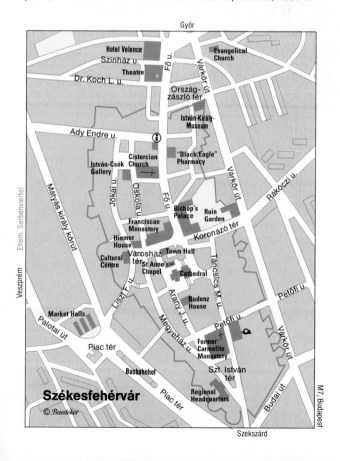

Székesfehérvár

© Baedeker

was interred in 997. The town, which, under Stephan I, rose to be the second most important town after Esztergom, was first recorded as "Alba regia" (Latin: "white chair") in 1002. Around 1000 Stephan I commissioned the building of a Romanesque church in which Hungarian kings were crowned and interred until the 16th c. The town was spared the ravages of the Mongol attacks in the 13th c. but not its capture by the Turks in 1543, who remained in Székesfehérvár almost 150 years (until 1688). At a time in which the Habsburgs and Ottomans were dividing up the empire between them and the seat of parliament had been moved to Bratislava the old royal town was compelled to forfeit its importance. Following its elevation to the seat of a bishop in 1777 it had expanded into a Baroque town by the end of the century with 12,000 inhabitants. In the 19th c. the citizens drained the marshes and dismantled the town walls in order to extend the town outwards. Not until after the Second World War did the regional capital of Féjer develop into an important industrial centre.

Sights

Note

The narrow alleys of the historic town centre are closed to traffic; sights are easily accessible on foot.

*Ruined garden (Középkori romkert), Royal basilica

On Koronázó tér, hidden behind the bishop's palace, is the archaeological site of the Romanesque royal basilica with its foundations which have been exposed in several excavations since 1936 (open: Tue.–Sun. 10am–6pm). The church, a triple-naved basilica with semi-circular apse in the east was founded by King Stephan prior to the year 1000 and rebuilt several times until the 15th c. with the addition of a sepulchral chapel. It was of outstanding importance in the Middle Ages as the coronation church and place of interment of the Hungarian kings (altogether 11 kings are interred

Royal Basilica

- 11th–12th c.
- 14th–15th c.
- 18th–20th c.

1 Funeral Chapel
  of King Matthias
2 Courtyard (11th c.)
3 Sacristy and Treasury
4 Choir with St Mary's Altar
5 Funeral Chapels
6 Bell Tower
7 Choir
8 Tombs

9 Podium
10 Pulpit
11 Tomb of King Stephen
12 Gate
13 Funeral Chapel of St Catherine
14 St Anne's Chapel
15 Tower
16 Domicile
17 Bishop's Palace

here). The Turks plundered the kings' tombs, used the basilica as a mosque and later as a munitions store. The ruins of the church which was badly damaged by an explosion in 1601 had to give way to the new bishop's palace in 1789. Triggered by the sensational discovery of the two intact sarcophagi of King Béla III and his wife Anna of Châtillon, which were transferred to the cathedral crypt (the relics rest in St Matthew's church in Budapest, the burial objects are preserved in the National Museum) work began in the middle of the 19th c. on the systematic excavation of the area. Relics from the Romanesque church, especially building sculpture, tombstones, as well as a part of the red marble sarcophagus of King Louis I, are on show in the round arched hall in the east of the exhibition site (1936/38). Also to be found here is the notable marble sarcophagus, which was long thought to contain the remains of St Stephan or his father Géza. Recent research suggests that it is the coffin of Prince Imre, son of Stephan I, who died prematurely. This Roman coffin, with ornamental figures and reliefs was carved in the first half of the 11th c. by a Venetian stonemason. At one end is an angel figure holding a babe-in-arms which symbolises the soul of the deceased.

*Marble sarcophagus

The Baroque buildings around the Városház tér create a fine picture. The dominant building on the square is the Bishop's Palace, built 1790–1801 from the stones of the medieval basilica. The single storey palace was designed by the architect Jakob Rieder in 18th c. plait style.

*Városhaz tér, Bishop's Palace, Town Hall

The south side incorporates the town hall which consists of two buildings. The older, somewhat lower Baroque palace (1690), is decorated by an arched gateway made of interwoven columns showing personifications of intelligence and justice, by the Eisenstadt sculptor Thomas Walch (1717). The modern sculpture symbolising an imperial orb (reference to the historical importance of the town) is by Béla Ohmann (1890–1968). The equestrian figure of Pál Pátzay (1936) commemmorates Székesfehérvár's famous regiment of hussars. Diagonally opposite the town hall, on the corner of

Székesfehérvár: Bishop's Palace

Fő utca

283

Székesfehérvár

⃰Hiemer House

Városház tér and Jókai utca, is Hiemer House (around 1770). Despite its poor condition it is one of the most impressive Baroque buildings in the town. Fine details of the façade include the stucco decoration of the corner oriel window on mask-bearing consoles and a niche statue of St Sebastian. From Jókai utca the visitor can glimpse the arcaded courtyard which it is hoped will soon be restored to its former glory.

Jókai utca, Oskola utca

The narrow streets of the Old Town with their predominantly Baroque two-storey patrician houses lead into Városház tér. One of the oldest houses in the town is in Oskola utca. On removal of the Baroque façade a gabled building of undressed stone was exposed with small, deeply set round-arched windows on the entrance side.

Fő utca, former Cistercian monastery

The Fő utca forms the main axis of the north Old Town. The Cistercian church and house was built 1745–51 by the Jesuits, later used by the Paulines and finally the Cistercians. Nowadays the house contains a branch of the István Király Museum (see below). Behind the twin tower façade of the church the interior is less impressive but contains a few notable pieces, namely, the ceiling frescos by the Viennese Baroque artist Caspar Franz Sambach (1715–95) and the pulpit by Carlo Bebo from Óbuda. The artistic carpentery (pews, picture frames, etc.) are the work of the Jesuits, whereas the magnificent Rococo decor of the sacristy (entrance János köz) is by Pauline monks.

⃰Fekete Sas

The inconspicuous two-storey building diagonally opposite (Fő utca 9) with the inscription "Fekete Sas" over the entrance is the "Black Eagle" pharmacy. It houses the superbly crafted interior of the former Jesuit pharmacy which was completed in the order's workshop in 1758 and transferred to this building following their dissolution in 1776 (open: Tue.–Sun. 10am–6pm).

Hotel Velence, Theatre

The Hotel Velence, designed by M. Pollack about 1830, on the Fő tér near the theatre is a fine example of Hungarian Classicism.

István Király Museum

In the north-east corner of the Old Town, Országzászló tér 3 a narrow building houses the extensive collections of the István Király Museum with numerous exhibits on the history and culture of the town and region. The Roman finds are particularly interesting, together with those from the Magyar empire and stonemasonry from the Royal Basilica (open: Tue.–Sun. daily 10am–6pm)

Southern Old Town, St Peter and St Paul Cathedral

The best place to begin the tour through the southern part of the Old Town is at the Városház tér. From here the Arany János utca turns off south and on the left hand side and at the highest point in the town on the site of the former castle of the Árpáds rises the Cathedral of St Peter and St Paul. Great Prince Géza, who instigated the affiliation of the Magyars to the Roman Catholic church, built a small church here (see markings on the pavement), in which he was interred. In 1235 it became a Gothic parish church which in turn gave way to the new cathedral when Székesfehérvár was elevated to a diocesan town (1759–78). The architect Martin Grabner retained the Gothic windows of the earlier church in the west towers of this mighty rather overpowering Late Baroque edifice. The interior frescos depicting scenes from the life of King Stephan (the Saint) and the paintings of the side altars are by Johann Cymbal from Vienna (1768). The choir and the high altar (1775) were the work of the Viennese architect Franz Anton Hillebrand; the altarpiece (King Stephan kneeling before the Mother of God) is by Vinzenz Fischer.

St Anna's Chapel

Szent Anna kápolna to the left of the cathedral is the only completely intact medieval building in the town. Built in 1478 as a cemetery chapel and used as a mosque during the Turkish period this small church was again Christian in the early 18th c. and furnished with a Baroque altar; the roof ridge is

St Anna Chapel

Serbian church

a 19th c. addition. A window rose crowns the narrow portal; the three narrow-arched windows display High Gothic tracery (foils).

József Budenz (1836–92), who developed comparative Finno-Ugrian linguistics, was born in the charming Rococo building (1781) at Arany János utca 12. Nowadays it accommodates the Ybl Museum which has the art collection of Ervin Ybl and documents and personal items belonging to the architect Miklós Ybl (open: Tue.–Sun. 10am–6pm). Ybl is the most significant representative of historical architecture in Hungary.

Budenz House

Arany János utca comes to a point at Szent István tér with the regional town hall (1807–12) by Mihály Pollack and Johann Tegl on the long right side. In the middle of the square is the equestrian statue of King Stephan by Ferenc Sidló in 1938.

Szent István tér

The inconspicuous exterior of the church on the corner of Kossuth/Petőfi utca (entrance through the former house, now a priests' home, in the Petőfi utca) bears no indication of the exceptionally impressive interior concealed behind it. The most important art treasure of this Rococo style church built in 1745–48 are the ceiling frescos (1768/69) by the Baroque artist Franz Anton Maulbertsch from Upper Swabia depicting scenes from the life of Mary: in the first bay "The birth of Mary" (with Abraham, Isaac, Jacob and David in the spandrels), in the second bay "Mary's Ascension" and in the choir the "Immaculate Conception". The paintings in the side altars (death of St Joseph and St Anna) are by the same artist. On the ground floor of the monastery there is a small museum of church art.

*Former Carmelite monastery and church

No. 15 Kossuth utca was formerly the Pelican Inn where, in the 19th c., the town's actors used to meet and perform. A few yards on the road opens out (at the point where Táncsics utca joins) to a small square with a striking art nouveau house, almost oriental in appearance, and adjoining domed baths.

Kossuth utca

Székesfehérvár

Former Serbian
quarter,
Serbian church

The old Serbian quarter lies in the west of the Old Town in the Rác utca. Some houses have been converted to an open-air museum, documenting the art and lifestyle of the Serbs. The Greek Orthodox church is a narrow Baroque building from the first half of the 18th c. It has a fine iconostasis and a 15th c. Madonna icon.

Surroundings

Várpalota

Situated on the edge of the Bakony Forest, 23km/14 miles west of Székesfehérvár, Várpalota is an important industrial centre, which was formed at the end of the Sixties by the amalgamation of three districts: Várpalota with its large lignite works, Inota with a power station and aluminium foundry and Pétfürdő with the largest Hungarian artificial fertiliser plant and chemical works. Inota was an important settlement on the military road which passed by here at the time of the Romans. Near Pétfürdő, which was famous for its spa baths, there is still a 1800 year old Roman dam, 300m/984ft long and in places as high as a house, built from massive blocks.

Castle

There has been a castle in Várpalota (= castle) since the 14th c., which was extended from 1439 to 1445 and rebuilt in the early 16th c., incorporating the latest defensive architecture to repel the approaching Turkish armies. It is a square site with four bastions let into the walls and moats. It changed hands often during the Turkish period. When the Zichy counts took over the building in the 17th c. they turned it into a residential castle in 1699/1702. In the 19th c. the north corner tower was demolished and the building left to decay. Restored in the Seventies the castle today contains a collection of local history and the Hungarian Museum of Chemical Industries (open: April–September Tue.–Sun. 11am–5pm).

Zichy Castle

Built in 1725 the castle was converted in a romantic historicist style by Miklós Ybl in 1863. Nowadays it houses an artillery museum (open: Tue.–Sun. 10am–6pm).

**Roman Settlement Tác Gorsium Herculia

Situation and
Importance

One of the largest and most impressive Roman excavation sites in Hungary is about 16km/10 miles south of Székesfehérvár near the small town of Tác (signposted from here).

History

On the site of a former Celtic settlement, at the crossroads of strategically important long distance routes, the Romans established a military camp in the 1st c. which was awarded its town charter by Emperor Hadrian in the 2nd c. and raised to the status of provincial parliament for Lower Pannonia. The annual provincial gatherings in May/June were accompanied by cult celebrations in honour of the emperor requiring the appropriate official buildings, places of worship, public squares and other institutions. In the 2nd and 3rd c., devastated by the Sarmatians, the town was rebuilt at the end of the 3rd c. and named Herculia, after Maximianus Herculius, the co-ruler of Emperor Diocletian. At its peak about 7000–8000 people lived in Gorsium Herculia.

The town's final heyday lasted until the middle of the 5th c. when it gradually depopulated and disappeared off the map.

Tour

The main part of the excavations is to the north of the ticket office on the car park. The former north-south road (Cardo maximus) with attractively

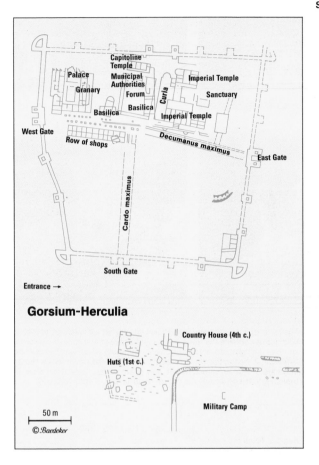

Gorsium-Herculia

Capitoline Temple
Palace
Municipal Authorities
Imperial Temple
Granary
Forum
Curia
Sanctuary
Basilica
Basilica
Imperial Temple
West Gate
Row of shops
Decumanus maximus
East Gate
Cardo maximus
South Gate
Entrance →

Country House (4th c.)
Huts (1st c.)
Military Camp
50 m
© Baedeker

carved stone reliefs and tombstones (copies and originals) leads to the town centre of Gorsium Herculia. A main road (Decumanus maximus) ran in an east-west direction through the town; on its south side a business quarter with shops and workshops has been excavated. On the other side of the main road were the public buildings and squares. Over to the west (standing to the left in front) are the foundations of a large palace which had a bath consisting of four rooms that could be heated, several halls on the north side and a granary in the east. The former Christian basilica to the right towered over a residential house where the wall paintings and floor mosaics have been restored. The east side of the basilica adjoins the forum with its public facilities and the Capitoline temple. Adjoining it is the holy area (area sacra) with the official buildings of the provincial congress, several places of worship (imperial temples) and the cellar of a building extensively decorated with frescos. The holy area was closed off down to the main road by a wall into which two beautiful (restored) fountains were built.

Gorsium-Herculia: stone statue . . .   *. . . and remains of walls*

The ruins of a residential house (Villa Leporis), which was part of a 4th c. villa quarter outside the town walls, were exposed in a small shady wood south of the ticket office, together with a cemetery which was laid out later (4/5th c.). A visit to the small museum is highly recommended to see the originals of the stone sculptures and grave stelae as well as other interesting finds, especially the charming bronze statuettes of Venus.

Museum

Szekszárd

D 3

Region: Tolna
Altitude: 110m/360ft
Population: 37,500

Situation and Importance

This pretty little town, surrounded by hills, 145km/90 miles south from Budapest, provincial centre of Tolna, is famous as the main town in an important wine-growing region. Grape varieties grown include Kadarka and Bull's Blood, both hearty, strong red wines, Blue Franconian, Cabernet and Riesling. The surrounding area is agricultural (cereal-growing); alongside the traditional furniture industry and a dairy, there is an important chemical industry. Szekszárd is situated in Sárköz country where folk art still thrives.

History

The Romans, who settled in the Celtic settlement which existed here, called it Alisca. The Benedictines built a monastery in 1061. In the 18th c. Germans settled in this region which was heavily depopulated after the Turkish rule. Wine-growing dates back to the time of the Romans; in the 14th c. it was the Hungarian and Turkish wine-growers, later the German settlers, who were responsible for the respected reputation of Szekszárd wine at home and abroad. Szekszárd was the home town of the "Hungarian Münchhausen"

János Háry, whose glorious deeds were described by the writer, born in Szekszárd, János Garay: Zoltán Kodály wrote a lyrical drama on the story, the music of which has become famous as the "Háry János Suite".

Sights

Ádám Béri Balogh, a general under Prince Rákóczi in the liberation struggle, was born in Szekszárd. The museum (Mártírok tere 26, open: Tue.–Sun. 10am–6pm), a neo-classical building from 1895, contains a good archaeological collection from local excavations; there is a fine specimen of a bronze statue of Pallas Athene. The ethnographic collection consists chiefly of folk art from Sárköz.

Ádám Béri
Balogh Museum

The Babits Mihály Művelődési Központ (Mártírok tere 10) is a modern building by András Máté and Ernő Tillai. Mihály Babits (1883–1941), a great Hungarian poet of the 20th c., came from Szekszárd; the house contains memorabilia and manuscripts with a monument to him in front of the entrance.

"Mihály Babits"
House

The residence of Baron Antal Augusz (Széchenyi utca 36–40), built in 1820, is a very colourful sight: the white central part is Classical, the pink-coloured right wing resembles the Castello Miramare in Trieste, the grey left wing is German Baroque. Franz Liszt was often a guest here giving concerts. At the baron's request Liszt composed a mass for the consecration of the church in the new town; however, this "Szekszárd Mass" was not performed until later. Nowadays the building is used as a music school, tourist office and a Liszt museum. In the garden behind the house is a bust of Liszt by Borsos.
The Hotel Garay opposite Augusz House is the former Grand Hotel, built around the turn of the century (wine bar in the cellar).

Augusz House

The design for this beautiful classical building with Doric columns and a central ressaut (1828–33) on Béla ter is by Mihály Pollack (1773–1855). In the courtyard the ruins of a Romanesque Benedictine monastery church, built by King Béla I in 1061, were discovered in the Seventies. Numerous medieval documents together with letters from Liszt are stored in the archives.

Regional House
(Megyeháza)

The church on Béla tér, one of the largest single-naved churches in Hungary, was built by Johann Joseph Thalherr (architect of the Eszterházy Palace in Bratislava), in 1802–05 in Rococo style. The ceiling paintings are by G. Darlach.

Catholic
parish church

The neo-classical Romantic town hall (Béla tér 8) dates from the middle of the last century; during renovation work in 1904 art nouveau elements were added.

Town hall

This house in 18th c. plait style dating from 1780 (Babits Mihály utca 13) is dedicated to the poet (open: Tue.–Sun. 9am–5pm).

Birthplace of
Mihály Babits

Muhme Cenci was the grandmother of Mihály Babits, one of whose novels was a tribute to her. The courtyard on Bartina Hill above the town, 25 minutes' walk from Kadarka utca (north of Babits' birthplace), was built in 1826 and belonged to the Babits family; old pressing equipment is on display in the wine cellars. There is a fine view over the Sárköz countryside down to the Danube. The Baroque crucifix above the farmhouse was erected in 1827.

Muhme Cenci
courtyard
(Cenci néni
majorja)

Surroundings

Decs (9km/6 miles south-east of Szekszárd) with 4300 inhabitants is the largest district in the Sárköz and a centre of folk art. The "Folk Craft Museum of the Sárköz Region" contains displays of costumes, furniture

Decs

Szekszárd: Town Hall

and other craft products. Every two years in Decs the "Sárköz Wedding" is celebrated when the wedding couple and all the guests wear traditional 19th c. costumes. The Gothic reformed church (15th c.) underwent Baroque decoration in the 18th c.

Gemenc Forest

About 12km/7 miles east of Szekszárd the Gemenc Forest, 500 sq.km/193sq. miles of protected countryside, stretches along the right bank of the Danube. The unspoilt meadowland with dead river tributaries provides a habitat for many rare species such as the river eagle and the black stork. The reserve is only accessible from Gemenc (bus to Szekszárd) by narrow gauge railway or boat. Trips are organised by Tolna Tourist (Szekszárd, Széchenyi utca 38). The train runs all year round, the boats only operate May–October.

Szentendre

E 2

Region: Pest
Altitude: 101m/331ft
Population: 18,300

Situation and
**Importance

This small town on the hilly right bank of the Danube about 20km/12 miles north of Budapest is one of the most popular destinations for people from the capital. The individual character of this lovingly restored Old Town with its narrow streets and picturesque views of the Danube was shaped in the 18th c. by the immigrant Serbs whose culture, religion, traditions and above all building methods left their mark on the town. At the beginning of the 20th c. numerous artists were attracted to this charming little town by the river and many still are today. Small museums and galleries invite the visitor to inspect their work and there is no shortage of souvenir shops

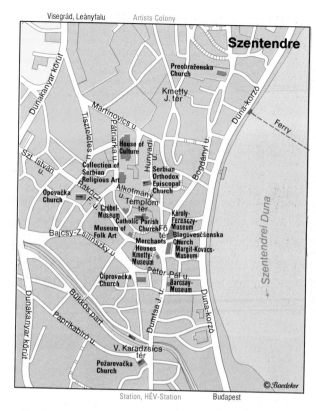

selling folk art. During the summer months the town is full of countless tourists.

Szentendre is linked to Budapest by the suburban train HÉV. In summer boats operate between the Budapest mooring post Vigadó tér and Szentendre. The centre of the town is closed to traffic and the sights can easily be reached on foot.

Transport

The origins of this settlement go back to the 4th c. when the Celts were present here. The Romans established a military camp on the banks of the Bükkös stream in the 1st c. and called it Ulcisia Castra (Wolfsburg). The conquering Magyars were also taken with the location and settled here. The settlement was first officially documented as "Sanctus Andreas" in 1146 under possession of the bishop of Veszprém. From the 14th c. several waves of Greek Orthodox Serbs came to Szentendre, fleeing to escape the Turks. For Szentendre Turkish rule was also synonomous with population losses, migration and devastation. As the Turks had withdrawn from Hungary, but not from the Balkans, at the end of the 17th c. many Serbs, who had fought on the side of the Habsburgs, fled to the Hungarian lands. In Szentendre 6000 refugees alone settled, most of them craftsmen and merchants. Through their busy trade the town flourished in the 18th c. Outward signs of this prosperity are the Baroque churches (seven in total), instead of

History

291

wooden ones, dominating the skyline with their silhouettes. The town became the religious and cultural centre of the Hungarian Serbs and seat of the Greek Orthodox bishopric. Epidemics, including the devastating vine pest in 1880, and floods retarded the development of Szentendre in the 19th c. At the beginning of the 20th c. painters, sculptors and designers discovered this small town, untouched by industrialisation, thereby encouraging tourist development in Szentendre.

Sights

Opening times

The museums and galleries in Szentendre are open Apr.–Oct. Tue.–Sun. 10am–6pm, unless stated otherwise; on Wednesday there is no entrance fee. With the exception of the Blagoveščenska Church and the Catholic parish church on Templom tér the Baroque churches are usually only open at the weekend.

*Fő tér

Lined with attractive merchants' houses in Baroque and 18th c. plait style, the triangular Fő tér, the main square in Szentendre, is under historical protection. In the middle of the square stands the "Merchants' Cross", a wrought-iron cross on a stone pedestal decorated with icons, erected by the "Privileged Serbian Business Community" in 1763 following a plague epidemic.

*Blagoveščenska Church

On the Danube side of Fő tér (corner of Görög utca) towers the beautiful Serbian Orthodox Blagoveščenska church which was built in 1752/54 according to plans by Andreas Mayerhoffer (1690–1771) and is dedicated to the Annunciation.
The façade of the church is formed by lisières which lead along the narrow entrance hall out over the main ledge to the helm roof of the integrated façade tower. Focal point of the simple entrance side is the doorway with a

Szentendre: Blagoveščenska Church

"Belgrade" Church

Margit-Kovács Museum

Serbian Orthodox Church ecclesiastical art

Baroque curved balcony above it. On the fresco above the side entrance is the expansive representation of Emperor Constantine and his mother Helena with the cross of Christ. The iconostasis within the church is the work of the Serbian artist Michael Živkovič.
Open Tue.–Sun. 10am–5pm.

The 18th c. plait style building from 1797, situated to the left of the Blagoveščenska church (Fő tér 6) contains the art treasures of the Ferenczy family, particularly the works of Károly Ferenczy (1862–1917), the famous Impressionist painter, born in Szentendre. Other artists represented include his wife Olga Fialka and their children, the painter and designer Valér Ferenczy (1885–1954), the renowned tapestry weaver Noémi Ferenczy (1890–1957) and her twin brother Béni Ferenczy (1890–1967), famous representative of modern Hungarian sculpture. Open: Tue.–Sun. 10am–5.30pm.

Károly Ferenczy Museum

These six narrow houses and shops (Fő tér 2–5) all under one roof, which originally were the homes of six merchants' families, make an interesting architectural ensemble. The shops were on the ground floor of each building with the living accommodation above; the roof was used as a warehouse. Nowadays the ground floor of the complex is a gallery which shows paintings by local artists.

Merchants' houses, Art gallery

On the opposite side of the square a permanent exhibition in the Baroque house at No. 21 shows the work of the Cubist painter János Kmetty (1889–1975). Notable is the so-called Dalmatian shop window, where during business hours the wooden shutters were taken down and used as a counter.

Kmetty Museum

The picturesque Görög utca, where predominantly Greek families built their homes and trading houses in the 18th c. (görög=Greek), leads down from the Fő tér to the banks of the Danube. The Baroque house on the

Görög utca, Margit Kovács Museum

293

corner of Görög utca and Vastagh György utca was used as a salt house in the 18th c. Its small front windows with grilles and its magnificently ornate arched gateway make it one of the finest Baroque buildings in the town. In ten rooms of the building are works by the renowned sculptress and ceramics artist Margit Kovács (1902–77), who combined modern and traditional elements in her work. The ceramics collection is one of the most popular in the country. In the basement and in a wing opened later her religious inspired works are on show. Open: Tue. to Sun. 10am–6pm.

Barcsay Museum

The southern extension of Fő tér is formed by Dumtsa Jenő utca. At No. 10 several hundred works by the painter and mosaic artist Jenő Barcsay (1900–87) are exhibited. Open: Tue.–Sun. 10am–6pm.

Čiprovačka Church

To the south of Fő tér in Péter Pál utca, on the site of a wooden church from 1708, stands the Serbian Orthodox Čiprovačka church, known as the Peter and Paul Church since 1857. Burnt down in 1800, it was rebuilt in the second half of the century and today serves the Catholic community.

Opovačka Church

The Opovačka Church in Rákóczi Ferenc utca now belongs to the Reformed community of Szentendre.

Požarevačka Church

The Greek Orthodox church on the Vuk Karadzcics tér was built by immigrants from the region around Požarevac (south-east of Belgrade) on the site of a wooden church from 1690. According to the Orthodox faith the choir had to face east which is why the rear of the church faces the street. The iconostasis was probably brought by the refugees from their homeland. The central part has a double winged entrance known as the Tsars' Gate which is very beautiful.

Rákóczi utca, Folk art museum

Returning to Fo tér a short walk through Rákóczi utca is recommended. On the right side facing the castle hill the old building of the Museum of Folk Art still provides a reminder of traditional building methods. The cellar (still in use) was at street level, a steep covered stairway leads up to the entrance of the house. The exhibition only consists of two rooms of ethnographical collections and curiosities of folk art, so after a short look the visitor can proceed up to the castle hill, on which lies Templom tér (church square).

Templom tér

*View

The walled Templom tér on the top of the castle hill was the focal point of the settlement in the Middle Ages. In the 18th c. Catholic Croats from Dalmatia settled here around the church. Nowadays it is chiefly tourists who come to enjoy the splendid view over the rooftops. In summer the church square is bustling with market stalls offering a wide choice of souvenirs.

Catholic parish church

This church dedicated to John the Baptist on Templom tér is thought to originate from the beginning of the 14th c., with 15th c. additions, and to be built on the site of an older small church. The Gothic period resulted in a Romanesque and a Gothic tower window and a sun dial on the south-west buttress. In the 18th c. Catholic immigrants from Dalmatia took over the church which had been abandoned and damaged by the Turks, restoring it in 1710 and again in 1780 in Baroque style. Modern frescos can be found inside the church.

Czóbel Museum

In the house opposite the church (Templom tér 1) the artistic heritage of the Hungarian painter Béla Czóbel (1883–1976) is on show.

Serbian Orthodox Episcopal Church ("Belgrade" Church)

The most elegant of the seven Baroque churches in Szentendre is the one north of the castle hill in Alkotmány utca, the Episcopal Church consecrated in 1764 (Görög-keleti székesegyház; known as the "Belgrade" church), recognisable by its red and yellow façade. A wrought-iron gate (1771/72) from the workshop of the local artistic locksmith Márton Ginesser leads

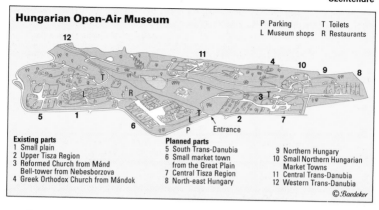

Hungarian Open-Air Museum

P Parking   T Toilets
L Museum shops   R Restaurants

© *Baedeker*

Existing parts
1 Small plain
2 Upper Tisza Region
3 Reformed Church from Mánd
  Bell-tower from Nebesborzova
4 Greek Orthodox Church from Mándok

Planned parts
5 South Trans-Danubia
6 Small market town
  from the Great Plain
7 Central Tisza Region
8 North-east Hungary

9 Northern Hungary
10 Small Northern Hungarian
   Market Towns
11 Central Trans-Danubia
12 Western Trans-Danubia

into the church garden. As with the Blagoveščenska church on Fő tér the nave wall on the entrance side merges with the soaring tower to make it vertically dynamic. The most imposing part is the gilded iconostasis carved from limewood.

Diagonally opposite the Episcopal Church in the former Bishop's Palace the Serbian Collection of Church Art comprises valuable sacral objects belonging to the Orthodox church. Together with other older works of art brought by the Serbs from their homeland the collection contains liturgical requi-

Serbian Church Art Collection

Hungarian open-air museum . . .   *. . . near Szentendre*

sites, chasubles, icons, etc. from the 17th–19th c. Open: Wed.–Sun. 10am–4pm

Other museums
The museum at Hunyadi utca 1 is dedicated to the picturesque work of the Surrealist Lajos Vajda (1908–41). The artist couple Imre (1907–44) and Anna Margit (1913–91) Amos are commemorated in the single-storey Baroque house at Bogdányi út 10. Imre Amos was a victim of the holocaust. A small glass pavilion at Ady Endre utca 5 houses sculpture and small models by Jenő Kerényi (1908–75).

Preobraženska Church
The Greek Orthodox church in the Bogdányi út 40 at the foot of the Szatmár hill, one of the finest Pravoslavic churches in Szentendre, was built by tobacco farmers and tanners in Baroque style. Women were only allowed to enter the rear of the church. Focal point of the interior is the dark green iconostasis with five overlapping rows of pictures and gilded Corinthian columns. Particularly beautiful is the gilded wood carving of the Tsar's Gate in the centre and the eight icons which surround it.

Artists' colony
Further north of the church, at Vörös Hadsberg útja 51, is the artists' colony founded in 1928 with several artists still working there. Exhibitions are held in the gallery.

Szentendre Island
Opposite the town there is an island in the Danube, 31km/19 miles long and 2.3km/1½ miles wide, which stretches as far as the city of Budapest. A bridge at the village of Tahitótfalu, 10km/6 miles away, connects the island, which consists mainly of arable land, vegetable fields and allotments, to the mainland. Horány and Surány are holiday resorts.

Leányfalu
2km/1 mile north of Szentendre is the resort of Leányfalu with holiday homes, a swimming pool and a campsite by the Danube.

Surroundings

**Ethnographical open air museum
An excursion to the open air museum about 3km/2 miles north-west of Szentendre on the road to Visegrád is highly recommended. It was opened in 1974 and when all the buildings and settlements have been moved from their original sites and rebuilt it should be the largest of its kind in Hungary. The plan is to recreate the rural architecture and lifestyle of ten different settlements with buildings typical of the region, predominantly from the 18th and 19th c. Scattered about the gently rolling landscape the individual "villages" are linked by pathways. Some buildings from West Transdanubia have already been reconstructed as well as a settlement from Upper Tisza region and the Little Hungarian Plain. Together with the houses, which have been reproduced in great detail, the various working quarters, mills, stables, barns, a forge, a weaver's workshop and a village church provide an insight into the everyday life of the rural population. The main attraction of the settlement from the Upper Tisza region, the wooded area on the eastern border of present-day Hungary, is the Reformed Church from the village of Mánd, built in 1787/90. The free-standing clinker-covered 17th c. bell tower once belonged to the daughter church in Nebesborzova. On the hill above this settlement is the log-cabin style Greek Orthodox church from the little village of Mándok, which is representative of the basic type of Orthodox church in the North and South Carpathians. The interior of this 18th and 19th c. church meets the liturgical requirements of both the Greek Orthodox and Roman Catholic churches.

Pilis Hills
See Esztergom, Surroundings

Szolnok

Region: Jász Nagykun Szolnok
Altitude: 89m/292ft
Population: 78,600

Szolnok, 100km/62 miles south-east from Budapest on the confluence of the Zagyva and the Tisza, is the most important centre for transport and communication in the Great Plain (with a river port). The frequent devastation of the town means that little of historical interest remains, except for handsome 19th c. streets in the inner town. The town is mainly industrial (railway carriages, sugar, paper and shoe factories, chemicals). Szolnok is also a spa town.

Situation and Importance

The history of the town has for centuries been determined by its situation at a strategic crossing point on the Tisza – altogether it has been destroyed 17 times. King Stephan built a castle here in 1075. In 1552 the Turks conquered the castle; for 130 years Szolnok was a "Sandschak", a Turkish administrative and military centre. The first pile bridge was built over the Tisza in 1562. From 1706 the castle was the headquarters of the freedom fighter, Rákóczi (see Famous People), in 1709, along with so many others, it was taken by Imperial troops and blown up. In 1847 the economy was considerably boosted by the opening of the Pest–Szolnok railway and the regulation of the Tisza. As it was still of strategic importance 35% of all houses, half of the industrial sites and numerous bridges were destroyed in the Second World War. Since the end of the war industry has undergone recovery and expansion.

History

Sights

To commemmorate the 900th anniversary of the town in 1975 the New Station (Új pályaudvar) was opened and the Jubilee Monument unveiled. The reliefs by the sculptor Ferenc Gyurcsek and the architect Miklós Kempis depict the most important events in the town's history.

New station
Jubilee monument

On Kossuth tér (No. 4), the old main square of Szolnok, stands the Late Classical former Hotel Magyar Király Szálloda, today the Damjanich Museum with an extensive archaeological department and an interesting art collection (open: Tue.–Sun. 10am–6pm). Janos Damjanich (1804–49) was a leader of the Independence struggle and was executed following its defeat. Ferenc Verseghy (1757–1822) was a writer and linguist of the Enlightenment.

Damjanich Museum, Verseghy Library

The historic complex of the regional town hall (Kossuth utca, east of the Kossuth tér) dates from 1878. The revolutionary government of Imre Nagy was proclaimed here in November 1956.

Town hall

In the district of Tábán north of Szabadság tér (Tábán utca 7, 8, 19, 51 and 63) there are interesting old farmhouses on the west bank of the Zagyva with wooden gables.

Tábán district, farmhouses

On the site beyond the bridge over the Zagyva stood the castle, but there is nothing left to be seen today (monotonous modern residential area). The castle church on the Tisza was built in 1824 using material from a demolished Turkish mosque. Behind it is a classical statue of St Johann Nepomuk from 1804.
On the left hand side behind Gutenberg tér are the houses of Sándor Bikari and Adolf Fényes which formed the artists' colony in 1902. Many significant Hungarian sculptors and painters have worked here since then (e.g. Ferenc Chiovini).

Old castle
Gutenberg tér

Szolnok
Artist colony

Crossing the Tisza bridge – the first steel bridge was built in 1911, the present one dates from 1945 – leads to a wood surrounded by a dam on the left bank with a sports hall, bathing beach, thermal baths and campsite.

Tisza woods

From the Tisza bridge along the right bank an attractive park stretches downstream ending at a complex which comprises the Hotel Tisza and

Thermal baths

thermal baths. The waters are 56°C/133°F and are used in the treatment of rheumatism, arthritis and gynaecological disorders.
Opposite the hotel is the Szigligeti Theatre opened in 1912.

Szolnok Art Gallery	The former synagogue (Koltói Anna utca 2, west of the thermal baths), built in 1899 by Leopold Baumhorn, houses the picture gallery of the Damjanich Museum. It shows works from the Szolnok artists' colony since its earliest beginnings (open: Tue.–Sun. 10am–6pm).
Franciscan church and convent	The Baroque Franciscan church not far from the gallery (Koltói Anna utca 8) was built in 1724–57 and is the most important historical monument in Szolnok; the architect was the Italian Carlone, who designed other buildings in Eger. In the main altarpiece the disciples are wearing 18th c. Hungarian costume. Unfortunately the church is only open during services. The convent (1723–51) and the church form a closed square.

Surroundings

Cegléd	Cegléd, with 42,000 inhabitants the largest town in the region of Pest, is situated 30km/19 miles west of Szolnok in the north of a large fruit and vegetable growing region. It played an important role in the 1848 freedom struggle; Lajos Kossuth began his tour here on September 24th 1848 with a fiery speech recruiting volunteers for the revolutionary army. The Baroque Trinity Column has stood on this historical site on Kossuth tér since 1896. The Classical Reformed Church (Szabadság tér) with over 2000 seats, 40m/131ft towers and a 60m/197ft high dome was built by József Hild, the superb Hungarian Classicist, in 1835 (e.g. cathedrals in Eger and Esztergom); the interior is plain (only open for services). The relief with the picture of Szegedi Kis, the reformer about 1545, was by Miklós Borsos. The Kossuth Museum, housed in an art nouveau building (Múzeum utca 5), illustrates the independence struggle of 1848 and the exile in Turin of Kossuth (1861–94) and contains a collection of local crafts and history (open: Tue.–Sun. 10am–6pm).

Szombathely B 2

Region: Vas
Altitude: 216m/707ft
Population: 86,300

Situation and Importance	Szombathely, about 50km/31 miles as the crow flies south of Sopron on the eastern edge of the Alps, is the second largest economic and cultural centre in West Transdanubia. This busy industrial town (agricultural machinery, precision engineering, shoes, textiles) is the administrative seat of the Vas region with a teacher training college and a renowned art gallery; the Savaria festivals take place in summer. Only a few buildings remain of the Late Baroque town, as much of Szombathely was destroyed in the Second World War.
History	Since the Stone Age the town was situated on important trade routes; the Bernstein road linking Italy with the Baltic ran past here. The Romans founded the "Colonia Claudia Savaria" in 43 B.C., in 107 it was the capital of the province of Pannonia Superior; in 193 L. Septimius Severus was elected emperor. No less a person than St Martin was born in Savaria in 316. By the 5th c. the population of the town had grown to 30,000, but in 455 an earthquake had such devastating consequences that the name of Savaria did not appear again for centuries. Under Charles the Great the town came under Frankish rule; its German name Steinamanger stems from this time, which probably referred to its abandoned state. From the 13th c. Szombathely belonged to the bishops of Győr. In 1777 Maria Theresia was

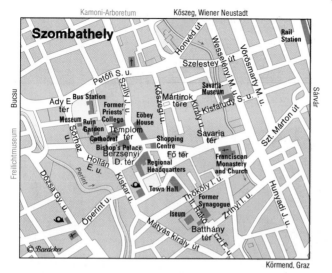

Körmend, Graz

responsible for the town becoming the seat of a bishop and undergoing an economic and cultural revival. The first bishop of Szombathely, János Szily, had Szombathely rebuilt and expanded into a residential town. Following the Second World War the town recovered quickly.

Sights

Berzsenyi Daniel tér is the centre of Szombathely as it was in Roman times. The forum of Savaria probably stood where the cathedral now stands. The cathedral, bishop's palace, former priests' seminary and Eölbey House – all works by Melchior Hefele – together with the square form an ensemble where the influence of Bishop Szily is still apparent (his monument stands in front of the cathedral). The rather uninspiring façade of the cathedral, which Hefele worked on from 1791 until his death in 1797 dominates the square; the building was completed in 1814. The tower roofs were later additions. Unlike the façade, a cross between Late Baroque and Classicism, the interior (including frescos by Maulbertsch), which was destroyed in the last war, was ornate Baroque. The altars were either reconstructed or restored; a picture by István Takács (1951) replaces the Maulbertsch painting in the high altar. The statues at the main altar and those of the façade (Moses, John the Baptist; the apostles Peter and Paul and allegorical figures) are by Philipp Prokop. The pulpit, still intact, was completed by Martin Rumpelmayer to a design by Hefele.

Cathedral

Opposite the cathedral is Eölbey House, built in 1796, which accommodates the Revolution Museum of the Vas region (open: Tue.–Sun. 9am–6pm).

Eölbey House

The Late Baroque group of buildings (1778–83) which occupies the south of the square (Berzsenyi tér 3) is entirely in the Hungarian 18th c. plait style. The attic, which adjoins the central ressaut, has allegorical figures of the virtues and the coat of arms of Bishop Szily. The palace is open to visitors by prior arrangement (tel. 1 32 42). On the right of the ground floor is the Sala terrena with a wall painting by Stephan Dorffmeister (1784); the

Bishop's Palace

Szombathely

Szombathely: Baroque hall

banqueting hall on the upper floor, one of the finest Hungarian Baroque halls and Hefele's most successful creation, boasts frescos by Maulbertsch.

Regional town hall

The present form of the town hall, built in 1775–79 next to the Bishop's Palace (Berzsenyi tér 1), seat of the regional council, dates from 1880 and is the work of Alajos Hausmann (1847–1926), who also planned the conversion of the Buda castle mansion. It is adjoined on the east side by the neo-classical so-called Little Town hall from 1848.

Former priests' seminary

The former priests' seminary to the right (north) of the cathedral, built in 1777–79, houses a girls' school and the cathedral library with 60,000 volumes, valuable incunabula and manuscripts. The ceiling paintings in the library are by Stephan Dorffmeister (1791).

Ancient ruins

The "Járdányi Paulovits István Romkert" ruins behind the cathedral (open April–Oct. Tue.–Sun. 10am–3pm; entrance between the cathedral and priests' seminary), discovered during building work in 1938, are the heart of old Savaria. A semi-circular apse and a 25m/82ft long mosaic (acanthus ornaments, Christian symbols) by a master from Aquileia have been preserved from the St Quirinus basilica (4th c.) which was rebuilt from parts of the former governor's palace. Quirinus, bishop of Siscia (Sisak in Croatia) is said to have been drowned in 303 in Savaria. On the west part of the site a section of the Roman road paved with rough basalt blocks can be seen as can the foundations of houses in the herringbone stonework, and near the apse of the cathedral are remains of the medieval round castle which belonged to the bishops of Győr, which is said to have once measured 40m/131ft in diameter.

Köztársaság tér

Going east from Berszenyi square, the "Republic Square", Szombathely's shopping centre (pedestrianised) is reached. Alongside the modern façades in the medieval market place are Baroque, historicist and art nouveau styles. The Centrum department store in the north on Széchenyi utca is an art nouveau building with an interesting glass roof.

East of Köztársaság tér on Savaria tér stands the Franciscan church and adjoining monastery. The Baroque church was built in the 17th c. from a 14th c. Gothic building; a Renaissance doorway (statue of St Elizabeth above it) upgrades the simple front face. Within the Baroque interior of this triple-naved church the picture of St Florian in the left side altar (Dorff-meister 1749), with the town of Szombathely in the background, stands out. Melchior Hefele is interred in the church.

Franciscan church and monastery

The Savaria Museum, housed in a historic building from 1905–08 (Kis-faludy Sándor utca 9, open: Tue.–Sun. 10am–6pm), has an outstanding collection of Roman antiquities. The lapidarium in the basement contains statues and mosaics, etc. from Savaria as well as ornaments from the church in Ják; on the upper floor are extensive exhibitions of archaeology and natural history of the Szombathely region.

*Savaria Museum

In the 1st–2nd centuries A.D. the worship of oriental deities spread through the Roman empire; the Egyptian Isis cult was especially popular. The Isis temple in Savaria (Rákóczi Ferenc utca 2, south of the Köztársaság tér) was founded in 188, extended in the 3rd c. and destroyed by an earthquake in 455; it was excavated in 1958–59 and prepared in 1961–63. The site consisted of several interconnected colonnades with the altar in the centre (indicated by a pedestal in the lower lying area). Behind it lay the inner sanctum, its portico has been restored; the timbers contain remains of reliefs from the 2nd c. (Isis riding on her dog Sothis, with a sistrum in her hand; Victoria with the inscription "The exalted holy Isis"; Fortuna, Mars, Hercules among others). The temple is open: April–October Tue.–Sun. 10am–6pm.

Iseum

On the north corner of Batthyány tér, surrounded by 19th c. town houses, stands the splendid synagogue, built in 1881 in Moorish style. There used

Former synagogue

In the Savaria Museum

to be a sizeable Jewish community in Szombathely which made a considerable economic and cultural contribution to the town. Since 1975 the synagogue has been used as a concert hall.

Municipal art gallery	The Szombathelyi Képtár (Rákóczi Ferenc utca 4) was built in 1885 by Lajos Mátis and Miklós Sólyom using donations from citizens of the town. The gallery specialises in 20th c. Hungarian works and includes paintings by Gyula Derkovits (1894–1934) and István Dési Huber (1895–1944; open: Tue.–Sun. 10am–6pm).

Kámoni Arboretum

The botanical gardens on the northern edge of the town (Szent Imre herceg útja 108) were laid out at the end of the 19th c.; today 3000 species of trees, 260 alone of which are conifers, grow on 25ha/68 acres. There are also beautiful rose and cactus gardens. The park, open from 8am until dusk, can be reached by bus No. 2 or by car heading for Gencsapáti.

Open-air museum of the Vas region

The Vasi Múzeumfalu on the western edge of the town (Árpád utca 30) presents over 6ha/15 acres of varied rural architecture of the Vas region, which has been home to Slovenians since the 9th c. Visitors can see the furnished thatched farmhouses, a mill and even a fishing pond. The museum is open May–Oct. Tue.–Sun. 10am–6pm, otherwise until 4pm; it is signposted from the Hotel Claudius with the word "Múzeumfalu".

Excursion to Csempeszkópács

22km/14 miles south of Szombathely (Road 87) is Csempeszkópács with a particulary attractive Romanesque village church (mid. 13th c.). The southern doorway with Norman serrated decor is stylistically similar to Ják (see entry). The church interior contains remains of medieval and Baroque frescoes. The high altar is by Stefan Dorffmeister.

Tata   D 2

Region: Komárom-Esztergom
Altitude: 160m/525ft
Population: 25,700

Situation and Importance

Situated 70km/43 miles west of Budapest on the slopes of the Gerecse Hills and on the banks of the Old Lake (Öreg tó), Tata is an important communication centre and a popular recreational resort.

History

The lakes interconnected by channels which surround Tata were formed in the 18th c. with the draining of the marshes; Tata therefore became known as the "town of lakes". It was inhabited as far back as the Roman period; the first official documents date from 1221. In the 13th and 14th c. the town belonged to the crown; in the 16th c. it was enlarged and fortified against the Turks and taken and stormed by both sides on several occasions. From 1727 Tata belonged to the Counts of Esterházy under whom it developed into an attractive residential town. Many of the 18th c. Baroque buildings are the work of Jakob Fellner, the architect of the Esterházys.

Sights

Clock tower

The original clock tower (Óratorony) in the centre of modern Tata, on the Ország-gyülés tér, was built by a local carpenter in 1763 to plans by Jakob Fellner. The wooden bell cage with four clocks and sound openings sits on a brick octagonal base.

Capucin church

From 1734–46 the young Jakob Fellner worked alongside the master builder József Kuttner from Komárom on the Capucin church in Bartók Béla út, which leads from the main square in a south-west direction. The interior of the triple-naved church is also of 18th c. origin.

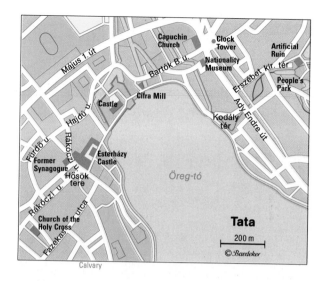

Calvary

The oldest building in Tata at Bartók Béla út 3 can be demonstrated to date from 1587. During the period of Turkish occupation it is said that the miller milled corn for the foreign rulers on even days and for Hungary on odd days. The windows of the single storeyed building are carved from red marble. The ceiling of the large hall on the ground floor is held up by voluted wooden Baroque columns. In 1755 Jakob Fellner undertook some alteration work to the water mill.

Cifra Mill
(Cifra-malom)

On the banks of the Old Lake (Öreg tó), which is very popular with water sport enthusiasts, stands the castle which was built in the second half of the 14th c. and reinforced with four corner towers around 1400. In the 15th c. it was owned by the Hungarian kings who often stayed here. Under King Matthias it was extended to form a border fort against the Turks, by whom it was conquered more than once. In 1727 Count Eszterházy acquired the ruins and commissioned Jakob Fellner with its reconstruction, but only the bridge was built. During its rebuilding in Neo-Gothic style in 1893 it was attempted to restore it to its supposed original appearance – a move which was extensively undone in 1980.

Castle

Only the five-storey tower and the southern wing remain of the once mighty castle which today houses the Domonkos-Kuny Museum with documents relating to local history, Roman and medieval decor and examples of the local faïence industry (open: Tue.–Sun. 10am–6pm).

This complex of buildings on the west bank of the lake was built by Jakob Fellner for the Eszterházy family in the second half of the 18th c. There is a two-storey main building completed in 1777 with an attic roof and two corner towers (now a hospital), the Small House built in 1751 for administrative purposes, the magnificent stables divided by red marble towers and the Turkish bath which existed in the Middle Ages and was renovated in simple Baroque style in 1733–38. – Emperor Franz I of Austria, fleeing from Napoleon, signed the peace treaty of Schönbrunn here at Tata and Emperor Charles I made a final attempt here to restore the Hungarian royalty to Habsburg rule.

Eszterházy House

On the Hősök tere, opposite Eszterházy House, replicas of ancient sculpture can be seen in the former synagogue (Görög-római Másolatmúzeum).

Former synagogue

Tata Castle, once an important frontier fortress

Church of the Holy Cross	Franz Anton Pilgram designed the Late Baroque church (Szent Kereszt-plébániatemplom) on the Kossuth tér, and the work was carried out by Jakob Fellner and after his death in 1780 his scholar Jószef Grossmann. The common model of the Baroque twin-towered façade with a false gable, under the influence of 18th c. plait style, creates a rather austere and plain effect here. The interior of this single-naved church is of 18th c. origin with a particularly attractive high altar by Grossmann with four columns and figures by Anton Schwaiger (1786).
Municipal park (Nép kert)	To the east of the lake is the 46ha/114 acre park laid out in the second half of the 18th c. around the Cseke lake (Cseke-tó). On the north bank of the lake are the artificial ruins of a medieval church (designed by Charles-Pierre de Moreau), which was built in 1801 from stones from the Benedictine church in Vértesszentkereszt and Roman tomb stones.
Calvary Hill (Kálvária domb)	There are fine views over the town from Calvary Hill in the south-west of Tata with the Calvary chapel, built by Jakob Fellner in 1755 incorporating the choir of the medieval church of St Johannes. The crucifix in front of the church is by Anton Schwaiger, who lived in Tata from 1768 until his death and also made the figures for the high altar of the Church of the Holy Cross.

Surroundings

Komárom	This border town (pop. 20,000) about 25km/16 miles north-west of Tata on the motorway to Vienna on the right bank of the Danube, is linked to the Slovakian town of Komárno by a railway bridge. For almost a century the Hungarian town and the Slovakian town were one settlement and capital of the former Komárom district only being divided into two by the peace treaty of Versailles-Trianon in 1920. The Hungarian part was originally a suburb of the present Slovakian half and has since fused with Szőny, which was an important Roman camp in the province of Pannonia.

The castle at Komárom was laid siege to by the Turks several times but never conquered. During the Napoleonic wars the Austrian imperial court took refuge here. The former Igmánd castle houses the György Klapka Museum which contains interesting finds from the Roman military camp Brigetio (open: Tue.–Sun. 10am–6pm).

Castle

On the road to Tatabány, 5km/3 miles south of Tata on road 100, evidence of primitive man, who lived here about 500,000 years ago, was discovered in the 1960s. In the open-air museum bones and everyday objects of this culture are on display.

Vértesszőlős

5km/3 miles further on is Tatabánya (pop. 77,000), regional seat of the district and a mining town which has developed into a centre of heavy industry. On the heights above the town towers the Turul monument (emlékmű), erected in 1896 to celebrate the thousandth anniversary of Hungary's existence. A giant eagle-like bird from Hungarian mythology is linked with the legendary origin of the Árpads, the first kings of Hungary. According to legend the bird appeared in a dream to the ancestress of the kings, Emese, and predicted that she would be the progenitrix of glorious rulers.

Tatabánya

A short detour from Tatabánya into the Vértes Hills is recommended. From Oroszlány, about 15km/9 miles south-west of Tatabánya, the road leads to Csákvar (former castle of the Eszterházys from 1823; today a sanatorium) through wooded hills.

Excursion to Vértes Hills

After 2km/1 mile is the turning for Majk Puszta where in the 18th c. Kamadulens monks retreated to a hermit-like existence. A Baroque monastery was built and renowned architects such as Franz Anton Pilgram and Jakob Fellner were engaged in its construction and furnishing. The monastery consists of a main building (now a conference centre) and 17 hermits' cells. Only the tower (end of 18th c.) remains of the church.

Majk Puszta

Ruins of the Romanesque "family" church in Zsámbék

Tihany

*Zsámbék,
Dynastic
church

An extremely interesting historical monument stands on the M1 motorway to Budapest, 7km/4 miles north of the exit for Herceghalom. Above the village of Zsámbék tower the ruins of a large Romanesque church, which together with the church in Ják (see entry) ranks as one of the most outstanding examples of this type of church. The triple-naved basilica was begun in 1220 and after the Mongol invasion around the middle of the century was probably finished by a French churchmasons' guild. An earthquake in the 1860s caused the collapse of this huge church; the west façade with the two towers and remains of the nave have been preserved thanks to conservation measures in the 19th c. and convey an impression of the former greatness of this building at the transition from Romanesque to Gothic.

Tihany

See Balaton, North Shore

Tisza   F 3–H 1

Course of
the river

For Hungarian writers, especially the Romantics, it was the Tisza – and not the Danube – which epitomised the Hungarian river. If national pride seems a litle exaggerated it should be pointed out that the main part of the course of this river lies in Hungary and that it has fundamentally shaped the landscape of the Great Plain.

The Tisza is a left-hand tributary of the Danube; it is 977km/607 miles long, 597km/370 miles of which flow through Hungary. Its catchment area is 157,186 sq.km/60,690sq.miles, 47,000 sq.km/18,147sq.miles of which are in

A former arm of the Tisza

Hungary. The river rises from two sources in the Ukrainian Forest Carpathians, flows through the Marmarosch basin, breaks through the Carpathians and reaches Hungarian territory at Tiszabecs. South of Szeged the Tisza leaves Hungarian soil and joins the Danube at Titel in Serbia.

As the river regularly used to flood the land causing serious damage its regulation was of utmost importance and was undertaken in the second half of the 19th c. Gradually the course of the river was straightened and as a consequence the river decreased in length from 1420km/882 miles to 977km/607 miles. The results of the regulation are 3500km/2175 miles of embankments, 2.8 mill.ha/6.9 mill. acres of land protected from flooding and 461km/286 miles of navigable river. In the 1950s a hydro-electric power station was built at Tiszalök together with the main channel to the east for irrigation purposes. A reservoir dam and power station at Kisköre followed, giving rise to the reservoir Tisza tó.

With 80km/50 miles of banks and a surface area of 127sq.km/49sq.miles Tisza tó is the second largest lake in Hungary. It has an average depth of 2m/6½ft and in summer the water temperature reaches 22–26°C/72–79°F. The lake and surrounding area quickly became a recreational area attracting increasing numbers of foreign tourists. From Budapest the M3 motorway via Gyöngyös and Füzesabony leads to Tisza tó and the resort of Tiszafüred on its north bank.

Tisza tó reservoir

Tokaj (Tokay)

Region: Borsod-Abaúj-Zemplén
Altitude: 94m/308ft (town), 512m/1679ft (Tokaji-hegy)
Population: 5700

This traditional wine-producing town, centre of the famous vine-growing region in the north-east of Hungary, lies at the foot of the Tokaj Hills (Tokaj-hegyalja), where the Bodrog and the Tisza meet.
Numerous anecdotes and quotations sing the praises of the world famous Tokay wine (see Baedeker Special). The grapes for this noble drink grow on loess soils of volcanic origin on sheltered slopes and remain on the vine until late autumn.

Situation and Importance

Soon after the national conquest in the 10th c. the Magyars settled in the area around Tokaj; one of their leaders built a moated castle here. The resulting pentagonal castle, important to the transportation of salt on the Tisza, fell into Turkish hands in 1576. It was almost completely destroyed in 1604 by the Habsburgs. Four earth bastions and some ruins of the walls are all that remain of this fortification. The town which received its official charter in 1478, developed into an important trading centre, which was helped to recovery by the Greeks fleeing from the Turks in the 17th and 18th c. Vine-growing and the wine trade were the dominant economic activities of the town then as now. The inhabitants of the villages in the area around Tokaj also depend on vine-growing for their living.

History

Sights

The house at Bethlen Gábor utca 7 was built around 1790 by a Greek merchant in 18th c. plait style. The ground floor is reserved for an exhibition of sacral art, while on the upper floor the history of the settlements of Hegyalja from the 16th to the 20th c. is documented and the visitor is given an insight into the lifestyle of the region. The exhibitions in the attic and in the vaulted cellar are devoted to vine-growing. Open daily except Mon. 10am–5pm.

Tokaj Museum

The historic wine cellar has 24 underground passageways and is 1.5km/1 mile long. It can only be visited in conjunction with a wine tasting (usually about 11am and 2pm).

*Rákóczi cellar (Rákóczi pince)

Tokay wine

"**V**inum regum, rex vinorum" – the Sun King Louis XIV (1710–74) testified that this amber liquid was the "wine of kings and king of wines". He was referring to Tokay, a wine about which stories are told. In earlier centuries it was even used for medicinal purposes. The French empress Eugénie, consort of Napoleon III renowned for her beauty, attributed her constantly youthful appearance and her good health to a daily ration of two glasses of Tokay wine – when she died in 1920 she had reached the ripe old age, for those days, of 94.

The Furmint variety, which is what Tokay primarily consists of (together with lime leaf or Hárslevelü and some Muscatel-Lunel or Sargamuskotaly), used to be taken for anaemia and loss of appetite. Available in chemists it is alleged to be a passable aphrodisiac. Not surprising that many princes of past ages paid homage to this wine. No less a poet than Heinrich Heine wrote, "noble gentlemen with good taste partake of Tokay every day" and in Goethe's Faust Mephisto declared "may Tokay flow for you at once". Thus the prince of darkness complied with the request for a "glass of real sweet wine", the classical variety of Tokay, famous throughout the world, which was first produced in the first half of the 17th c. around 1631.

The preacher Máté Szepsi Laczkó is regarded as creator of the first aszú. This expression refers to grapes which are affected by noble rot (botrytis cinerea). During harvesting these grapes are hand picked from the vine, a tedious task, carried out by several thousand workers on the 6000ha/2428 acres of vineyards. The shrivelled grapes with concentrated sweetness are collected in small 25kg vats (puttony) and gently squashed to a mushy pulp or "must". It is then "married" with normal young wine in small barrels (136 litre). Depending on the vintage three, four or five vats of aszú must are added to the wine. The juice is stirred for a few days so that the natural sugars and flavour are brought out. Then the mixture is separated and the wine begins to slowly ferment in small Gönc barrels.

It takes years before the wine is ready for bottling. Hungarian wine laws require the wine to be stored in the barrel for two years and then as many years more as the number of vats that were added. So an aszú of four vats will have fermented for six years. The barrels (stored in historic cellars below the vineyards) are only filled up to three-quarters full for a few months as oxidisation, in the same way as with sherry, has to take place. A particular speciality are the aszú eszencia with natural sugars and extracts in addition to the already rare six-vat aszú, as well as the eszencia. Grapes with noble rot are collected in special tubs with double mesh bottoms. Without any pressing, just the weight of the grapes themselves (!) is enough for some juice to be extracted which goes to make a delicious nectar. Aszú wines make up to ten per cent of the production. The others are called Szamorodoni ("as grown"). In this way the harvest is not selected. The more noble rot grapes it contains the sweeter (édes) the wine. In less good years it turns out dry (száraz).

The Tokay tradition in Hungary was neglected for a long time. Most of the wines were cheaply marketed in the east; it was almost exclusively consumer goods which reached the west. After the fall of the Iron Curtain major wine producers from France, Italy, Spain, Japan and Germany invested in Tokaj-hegyalja, so that now a Renaissance of the "king of wines" is under way.

In the centre of Tokaj there are some other fine buildings from the 17th/   Other
18th c. such as the 18th c. plait style town hall (Városháza) at Rákóczi utca 54   interesting
(around 1790) and the János Szapolyai Palais (Szapolyai János-palota) at   buildings
Bem József utca 2, which the Russian tsar Peter the Great procured as
quarters for the Cossacks who were guarding his wine cellar in Tokaj. The
most handsome building in the town is the Rákóczi Dessewffy Castle
(Rákóczi Dessewffy kastély) at Bajcsy Zsilinszky út 15–17, a two-storey
Baroque building from around 1700. The Late Baroque Greek Orthodox
church (Görögkeletei templom) in the Bethlen Gábor utca 14 dates from
1770 and has a tower and six pillars on the front face which support a ledge
with a tympanum. Today it houses an exhibition of local history.

Surroundings

The wine-growing town 8km/5 miles west of Tokaj also has a Rákóczi cellar   Tarcal
with a wine museum. A road leads from Tarcal to the 512m/1679ft high
Tokaji-hegy (footpath begins in Tokaj).

A further 9km/6 miles north-west is the town of Mád, also renowned for its   Mád
good quality wines. Of interest are the Catholic church and the 18th c. plait
style synagogue from 1771 (today a library).

9km/6 miles behind Mád and 26km/16 miles north-west of Tokaj is the   Tállya
vine-growing town of Tállya (pop. 2600). The interior of the parish church of
St Ladislaus (Szent László) is a wonderful example of Baroque art. The
painting on the left-hand altar with a representation of St Wendelin, the
patron saint of shepherds, is by Franz Anton Maulbertsch. In 1802 Lajos
Kossuth was baptized in the font of this Late Baroque evangelical church,
8km/5 miles away from his birthplace in the village of Monok (commemorative museum in the house where he was born).

Vineyards and . . .   *. . . wine cellars of Tokaj-hegyalja*

Tolcsva

The wines from Tolcsva, 25km/16 miles north-east of Tokaj, are very popular with the Hungarians. The town has a 15th c. Gothic church and a museum on viniculture can be found in an Early Baroque house.

Zemplin
Mountains
(Zempléni-
hegység)

The Zemplin Mountains between the Hernád and Bodrog rivers form the north-eastern edge of the North Hungarian Central Uplands. They are of volcanic origin; the highest of them, Nagy-Milic (896m/2940ft), lies right on the border with the Slovak republic. Numerous fruit plantations and several vine-growing areas are found among the stepped uplands. The best known is Hegyalja where the grapes ripen for the Tokay wines. The dense woods consist of oak, beech and spruce. The volcanic activity resulted in mineral veins (precious metals), kaolin and betonite. Andesite and perlite are also mined.

Vác   E 2

Region: Pest
Altitude: 100m/328ft
Population: 35,700

Situation and
Importance

Vác, situated on the left bank of the Danube Bend (see Danube Bend) 34km/21 miles north of Budapest, has retained the charm of an attractive small Baroque town despite the industrial development on the outskirts. The best view of the town's silhouette with its characteristic church towers is from the Danube Island which is accesible from Vác by car ferry.

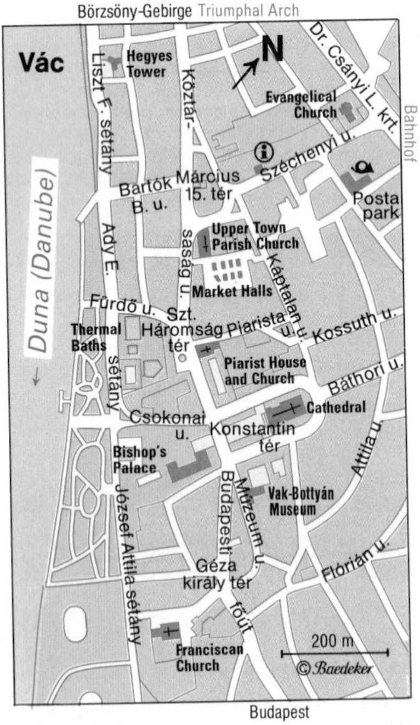

Börzsöny-Gebirge Triumphal Arch

Vác

History

There were already settlements here dating back to prehistoric and Roman times. At the beginning of the 11th c. St Stephan founded a bishopric here and it was offically documented for the first time in 1075. Favourably situated at a crossing point on the Danube, the town was a regional trading centre in the High Middle Ages under the protection of a royal castle.

Around the middle of the 13th c. on the site of the present day town centre stood the walled German town. The Turkish wars in the 16th and 17th c, brought devastation to the town and the population migrated elsewhere. Not until the end of the 17th c. when the bishops settled back in Vác, was the Baroque town established north of the medieval castle, undergoing economic revival in the 18th c. This development continued into the 19th c.

with the first Hungarian railway line being opened from Pest to Vác in 1846. After the Second World War various industries were established on the periphery of the town (chemicals, chalk and cement works, docks, etc.).

Sights

The historic centre of Vác stretches primarily between the eastern bank of the Danube between Konstantin tér, dominated by the cathedral, and Március 15 tér (March 15th Square) to the north, lined by fine patricians' houses. The road approaching the town from Budapest crosses the twin-arched bridge from 1757 with its statues which spans the Gombás river. Following Mártirok útja the visitor will reach Géza király tér (King Géza Square) with its Franciscan church.

Townscape

On the south-west side of the King Géza Square stands the Baroque triple-naved Franciscan church built in 1721–66 using stone from the medieval cathedral. The gable wall is decorated by a sculpture of the order's founder and Franciscan emblems. Also on Géza király tér, in the grounds of a new school, are a few ruins of the walls of the former royal castle. Only a stump remains of the ten-sided gate tower. Among the ruins is the figure of the "Happy settler of Vácz", from where, according to legend, the town takes its name.

Géza király tér

Only a short distance from Géza király tér, in the Vak Bottyán Museum at Múzeum utca 4, the sculpture from the old episcopal church has been preserved and the town's history is documented. The municipal museum is named after the one-eyed general who campaigned against the Habsburgs in the Independence War under Prince Rákóczi.

Vak Bottyán Museum

On the spacious Konstantin tér towers this imposing church (Székesegyház) which, with its Classical lines and massive proportions, seems a little out of place in the small Baroque town. It was the first time that this post-Baroque style, developed in France, was applied to an episcopal church in Hungary and it was destined to be the forerunner of later cathedrals in Eger, Esztergom and elsewhere. Bishop Károly Eszterházy, who had commissioned Franz Anton Pilgram to produce the design of the new church in 1760, transferred shortly afterwards to Eger. His successor, the miserly young Christoph Migazzi, awarded the project to the Viennese court architect Isidore Canevale, who was already familiar with Classical forms. This is most apparent from the ancient-style colonnaded porch on the west façade which is crowned by six statues by the stonemason Josef Bechert. The interior with the massive domed roof has both elements of 18th c. plait style and Classicism. The fresco in the dome ("Triumph of the Holy Trinity") from 1771 and the "Visitation of Maria" behind the altar are by Franz Anton Maulbertsch, the prolific Baroque artist. On the wishes of

*Cathedral of Mary's Ascension and St Michael

Panorama from the Danube island of the Baroque town of Vác

Vác

Vác Cathedral, an early example of Classicism in Hungary

Bishop Migazzi this fresco was concealed behind a wall and replaced by a painting by Martin Johann Schmidt (1718–1801), known as Kremser-Schmidt, until its rediscovery in 1944. The altarpieces on both side altars at the entrance to the church are also by Schmidt.

The pillars of the rood screens are relics of the medieval cathedral; remains of pillars from the earlier building can be seen in the crypt.

Standing in front of the east side of the cathedral it is only a few yards to the music school established in 1972 by Béla Bártók on Kossuth tér which blends harmoniously into the Baroque surroundings.

Bishops' Palace

While the cathedral was still under construction Bishop Magazzi commissioned a two-storey palace with a central ressaut on the opposite side of Konstantin tér from the Viennese architect Josef Meissl (1768–75). West of the building the rather overgrown palace gardens run down to the banks of the Danube.

Piarist Church (Piarista templom)

The dominant building on Szentháromság tér (Holy Trinity Square) is the former piarist church of St Anna (completed in 1745 after 20 years), recognisable by its narrow towers with pointed spires. The Piarist order house adjoins the church. The Baroque Trinity Column (1755) in the centre of the square is a prime example of this type of sculpture, which is prevalent in Hungary.

Thermal baths

Opposite the piarist church is one of the entrances to the thermal baths in Vác (the other entrance is at Ady Endre sétány 11). There is a park between the baths and the banks of the Danube with an avenue of planes fenced off by a wrought-iron railings by the Hungarian architect and craftsman Frigyes Feszi (1821–84).

312

The triangular "March 15th Square" (outbreak of the Hungarian revolution in 1848) was the centre of the Baroque town and site of the market until it was redesigned in 1951. The surrounding Baroque and 18th c. plait style houses create an idyllic ensemble. The square itself is somewhat sunken with ornamental paving stones, four Baroque sculptures and a fountain.

*Március 15 tér

The town hall (No. 11), a Baroque building, was built in 1735–69 on the site of a Turkish bath. Above the handsomely shaped entrance is a pleasing wrought-iron grille and a group of figures. In the 18th c. two medieval houses were joined together and underwent alteration to become the first bishop's palace (No. 6), which was converted into a monastery after the construction of the new bishop's residence and has accommodated an institute for deaf mutes since 1802, one of the oldest institutions of its kind. On both sides of the two-storey building is a magnificent Baroque doorway. On the south side the Március 15 tér is framed by the simple but not unpretentious façade of the former Dominican church, now the parish church of the upper town. The fine Rococo interior of the church built between 1699 and 1745 takes the visitor by surprise.

Town hall

North-west of Március tér on the river bank is the so-called Hegyes tower (Liszt Ferenc sétány 12), the last remains of the old town wall. A modern house adjoins the single-storey round edifice. The promenade continues along the river bank with moorings for boats and ferries to one side.

Hegyes tower

A few roads north of Március tér, on the earlier edge of the town, the Classical triumphal arch rises majestically in Köztársaság út. This imposing monument was erected in 1764 when Empress Maria honoured Vác with a visit. Bishop Magazzi again commissioned the court architect Isodore Canevale who was already engaged with planning the cathedral. Canevale created a triumphal arch on ancient Classical lines with relief medallions

Triumphal arch

on the attica. They depict the portraits of the imperial couple, the archdukes Joseph and Leopold together with both the Habsburg emperors Ferdinand and Maximilian, predecessors of Maria Theresia.

Surroundings

Vácrátót, situated about 10km south-east of Vác, has one of the most beautiful botanical gardens in Hungary, laid out by Count Sándor Vigyázó in 1872 in the style of an English country garden. Laid out with rocks, a waterfall, artificial ruins and other romantic details the gardens are looked after by the Academy of Science which also tends the arboretum with its 15,000 varieties of plants. Some of the best features of the botanical garden are the bushes and deciduous cypresses growing around the man-made

Vácrátót

pond. On the estate is a country house with a park where concerts of Mozart's works are held throughout the year.

Börzsöny
Mountains

For nature lovers a trip into the unspoilt countryside of the Börzsöny Mountains is recommended, of which the on average 300–400m/984–1312ft-high volcanic peaks form the western foothills of the North Hungarian Central Uplands. In the south, west and north they extend as far as the Danube and Ipoly, in the east they descend into the Nógrád Basin. Around the Csóványos, the highest peak at 938m/3077ft, lies the 18,000ha/44,478 acre conservation area of Magas-Börzsöny. The varied landscape is characterised by wooded slopes, deeply incised valleys with numerous springs and river courses. In the lower regions the vegetation is mainly oak woods, with beech woods on the higher slopes. On a walk through this untouched, restful countryside it is quite possible to encounter stags, wild boar and moufflon.

Nógrád or Diósjeno (about 20km/12 miles north of Vác) are ideal starting points for walks of one day or more. For the less energetic there is the narrow gauge railway which crosses the Börszöny Mountains from Veröce (5km/3 miles west of Vác).

Cserhát (upland)

See Balassagyarmat, Surroundings

Várpalota

See Székesfehérvár, Surroundings

Velencei tó (Lake Velence)   D 2

The warmest lake in Europe is about 45km/28 miles south-west of Budapest and 15km/9 miles east of Székesfehérvár at the foot of the high Velence range. It is 10km/6 miles long and on average only 2.5km/1½ miles wide and covers an area of 26 sq.km/10 sq.miles. Its depth is between 120–160cm/47–64in.; it warms up quickly in summer to 22–26°C/72–79°F. The 400ha/9884 acre reed-covered area around the lake is an ideal nesting place for different species of birds. A bird reserve has been established on the north-west side of the lake where silver heron, thrush reed warblers or black-headed gulls have made a home. Swimming, sailing and boating is possible from the flatter, less scenic south bank where the resorts of Velence, Gárdony and Agárd are situated. On account of its proximity to Budapest and Székesfehérvár Lake Velence is second in popularity to Lake Balaton with holidaymakers who enjoy being by the water. The tourist

Velence

infrastructure is being developed especially along the south bank. In Velence there is a watersports school and a 2300m/7546ft long stretch for kayak, canoe and sailing regattas which meets international competition standards.

Gárdony,
Agárd

Gárdony has existed since the 13th c. Nowadays the resort, which has almost completely joined up with Agárd, has a population of 7800 who depend chiefly on tourism for their livelihood. Agárd is the largest resort on the lake, with moorings for the scheduled boat services and also the largest sailing harbour. There are also modern thermal baths for visitors.

Excursions
in the
surrounding area

Around the lake there are several interesting places to visit, above all, of course, the old town of Székesfehérvár (see entry), the impressive Roman settlement Tác Gorsium Heculia and Martonvásár (see entry) with Brunswick Castle. In the village of Nadap on the north bank riding demonstrations and coach trips into the delightful upland countryside of the Velence hills are on offer. From the commune of Sukoró the path leads to the highest point of this range, the 352m/1155ft high Meleg hegy (Mount Meleg) where the view extends over the lake beyond Székesfehérvár to the foothills of the Bakony forest. Pákozd, also reached by boat, has found a place in the annals of Hungarian history: the first battle of the Independence Wars was fought here on September 29th 1848. The soldiers, members of the national guard and rebels from the common people who made up the troops forced the Habsburg army to retreat. A monument on Mészeg-hegy above the battlefield commemorates the glorious day.

Veszprém (Veszprim)

C 2

Region: Veszprém
Altitude: 260m/853ft
Population: 61,900

The "town of queens" lies on the south-eastern foothills of the Bakony Forest, about 15km/9 miles distant from the north-east bank of Lake Balaton. The main sight in Veszprém is visible from afar, the old diocesan town on the narrow rocky spur of the castle hill, which is one of the most beautiful collections of buildings in Hungary. Its proximity to Lake Balaton and the charming Bakony Forest are also favourable factors in its development into a popular tourist centre. As regional capital and university town with famous scientific and cultural institutions it also fulfils educational and administrative functions.

Situation and *Importance

Settlement at Veszprém dates back to the Bronze Age. The Romans did not settle here – probably on account of the exposed position – but later the

History

Avars and Slavs occupied the land around Lake Balaton before the arrival of the Magyars. Christianity was spread from Salzburg and as early as the middle of the 9th c. Veszprém had a church dedicated to St Michael. In the 10th c. Veszprém was in the possession of the Arpads. Shortly after 1000 King Stephen I raised the town to the seat of a bishop and the church to a cathedral. The town owes its name to his nephew Besprem, whom he installed as administrator. The palace built by Stephen was primarily the residence of his wife Gisela and after her a succession of later queens who were crowned by the bishop of Veszprém (thus the epithet "town of queens").

During the Renaissance the town experienced its heyday, which was brought to an end by the Turkish wars. After the Habsburgs had reconquered the town they blew up the castle to crush the Independence struggle in Hungary. In the 18th c. the town was rebuilt in Hungarian Rococo-Baroque style. Veszprém was heavily damaged in the Second World War.

Sights

**Castle quarter (Várnegyed)

The walled castle quarter built on a narrow dolomite rock is an impressive work of art which through continual renovation of the individual buildings has retained its splendour. At the point where the slope becomes less steep stands the gate which is the entrance to the bishop's castle from the town. The medieval structure with only one road (Vár utca) in the middle of the castle hill still stands, the buildings themselves are from the 18th and 19th c.

Veszprém: Castle Hill dominates the town

On the site of the old castle gate the Neo-Romanesque Heroes' Gate (Hoőosök kapuja) was erected in 1936. A small museum above the gateway chronicles the history of the castle quarter (open May–Oct. Tue.–Sun. 10am–6pm).

Heroes' gate

Just a few yards further on is the large group of buildings which used to be the Piarist grammar school on the east side of the road. Painted niches in the wall decorate the façade. The church built between 1828–36 in Classical style adjoins the grammar school which was built in the second half of the 18th c.

Former Piarist grammar school and church

The canon's house built in 1751 at Vár utca 9 is particularly charming. A basket arch spans the entrance to the house above which is a triangular gable with two angels. The rear of the house nestles against the castle wall where the only medieval round tower stands.

Dubniczay House

At the point where the narrow Vár utca opens out into a square the Bishops' Palace (1765/76) stands on the site of the medieval queens' palace, designed by the prolific architect Jakob Fellner. In keeping with the design of Baroque palaces it is U-shaped with two side wings embracing a courtyard with a drive leading up to the entrance gate. The façade facing the valley has a protruding central ressaut and loggia on the ground floor which give it the appearance of being the front face.

°Bishop's Palace

Somewhat hidden between the Bishop's palace and the provost's palace is the most important historical monument in Veszprém, the Gisela Chapel. It was built in 1230 and served as a private chapel to the bishop as well as the queens who resided here (not, however, Queen Gisela, whom it is named after). The upper floor of the church was dismantled during the building of the bishop's palace and the ground floor disguised with Baroque features.

°°Gisela Chapel

Bishop's palace

Cathedral

The small harmonious interior contains fine cross-ribbed vaulting with the original paintings and notable keystones. On the north wall frescos from the time the church was built were exposed during its sensitive restoration. They depict six apostles arranged in pairs, incorporeal floating figures, which suggest Byzantine influence (open: May–Oct. Tue.–Sun. 10am–6pm).

Provost's
Palace

Connected to the bishop's palace by the Gisela Chapel is the Provost's Palace, also designed by Fellner, which has been recently restored to preserve the beautiful 18th c. plait style façade.

Franciscan
church

On the west side of the square stands the Franciscan church (Ferences templom). This church from around 1730 burnt down in 1909 and was replaced by a new building, its Neo-Romanesque façade reflects the style of the cathedral opposite. The adjacent order house of 1776 extends to the west wall of the castle hill. It houses the museum of the church art treasures belonging to the bishopric of Veszprém. There is fine carving and stucco in the refectory.

St Michael's
Cathedral

To the north of the square is the cathedral. It stands on the foundations of a bishop's church founded by King Stephen, first documented in 1001, which was often destroyed and rebuilt (for example, 1723 in Baroque style). During the last rebuilding in 1907/10 it was redesigned in Neo-Romanesque style. Some evidence of earlier styles remains, such as the Late Gothic choir from 1380/1400, the Gothic vaulting in the crypt and the tombstones of the bishops and queens interred here.

Trinity
column

A stone balustrade surrounds the Baroque trinity column (1749/51) on the square in front of the cathedral.

Ruins of
St George's
Chapel

To the north of the cathedral the remains of the walls of St George's Chapel, discovered in 1957/1959, can be seen (Szent György-kápolna romjai; open May–Oct. Tue.–Sun. 10am–6pm). Above a round chapel from the early 11th c. an octagonal chapel was built in the second half of the 13th c., which was converted by Bishop Albert Vetési around 1450 into his tomb.

Viewing
platform

At the end of Vár utca there is a good view over Veszprém and its surroundings from the viewing platform (Kilátóbástya) with both the larger than lifesize figures of St Stephen and his consort Gisela on the balustrade (1938).

Other sights

Óváros tér

Directly below the castle is the square surrounded by attractive patricians' houses. Of interest are the so-called Pósa House (No. 3), from 1793, in 18th c. plait style and some art nouveau houses with unusually fine traditional decor. At the beginning of Vár tér, which leads to the castle, is the 48m/157ft high fire tower (upper part 19th c.)

Municipal
theatre

The municipal theatre stands on one of the main arteries into the town, an unusual art nouveau building. It was built in 1908 by István Medgyaszay, a student of the Viennese art noueau architect Otto Wagner.

Bakony
Museum

The Bakony Museum near Megyeház tér chronicles the history of the region. Directly next to the museum is a small farmhouse with a typical pergola and original features.

Szent István
Bridge

The 50m/164ft high viaduct over the Séd valley was constructed in 1938 to a design by Róbert Folly and is regarded as an important technical achievement. The view encompasses the castle in the east, the Betekints valley in the west and the peaks of the Bakony in the north.

Below the viaduct in a side corridor of the Betekints valley there is the 100ha/247 acre Veszprém wildlife park. One of its attractions is the large aviary where the birds are free to fly among the visitors (open daily from 9am until dusk).

Zoo
(Allatkert)

Surroundings

The most important part of the Transdanubian Central Range is the Bakony, also called Bakony Forest. It extends north of Lake Balaton to the Little Plain (Kisaföld) and as far as the Vértes Hills, from which it is separated by the Mórer Valley. Both the Balaton Uplands running parallel to the north bank of Lake Balaton and the adjoining Keszthely Hills are part of the Bakony. The highest point of this wooded area of 4000sq.km/1544sq.miles is Koris, 704m/2309ft high, close to the town of Zirc. The most valuable mineral in the Bakony Forest is bauxite. Mountains, woods and valleys add to the charm of the region as do numerous historical monuments in both the smaller and larger towns. The Bakony consists of two parts: the southern part with the largest town of the Central Range, the regional capital Veszprém, together with the towns of Várpalota (see Székesfehérvár, Surroundings) and Sümeg (see entry) and the northern part also called Upper or Old Bakony. There are unspoilt romantic places here for walking and excursions. The best known town in this region is Zirc (see entry). The chain of hills of the Bakony Lowland on the west edge of the range is also part of the Bakony Forest linking it to the Kisaföld. Papa (see entry) is the largest town here.

Bakony

This small town (310m/1017ft a.sl.; pop. 2920) in the Bakony, about 15km/ 9 miles north-west of Veszprém, is famous for its porcelain of the same name. The firm was established in 1826 and taken over by Mór Fischer in 1839 who made its products famous throughout the world within a few decades. In 1851 he took his porcelain to the World Exhibition where it attracted a lot of attention. Queen Victoria ordered a Herend dinner service decorated with butterflies and flowers, inspired by Chinese porcelain painting. This pattern has since carried the name Victoria. Hand-decorated porcelain is still produced in Herend (factory visits by arrangement with the tourist office at Veszprém). A visit to the museum in the old main factory building is recommended. Selected pieces illustrate the 150-year-old history of the firm and the changing shapes of its products.

Herend

Nagyvázsony

This tranquil village on the southern foothills of the Bakony Forest and at the foot of Mount Kab (599m/1965ft) is a popular place to visit in the hinterland of Lake Balaton, not far from either Veszprém (21km/13 miles in a south-west direction) or Balatonfüred (20km/12 miles north-west).

*Townscape

In Nagyvázsony the fortification is relatively well preserved, having been converted in the early 15th c. into a residential castle. In 1472 King Matthias I presented the castle together with the surrounding estates to Pál Kinizsi, a former miller's boy, born in Nagyvázsony. Kinizsi had won the king's favour through his victorious leadership of the royal army, the so-called "Black Troops". Kinizsi had the castle extended to its present form. During the wars of the following centuries it withstood numerous attacks; in the middle of the 17th c. both castle and village became the property of the counts of Zichy. The Zichys' loyalty to the emperor prevented the castle from being destroyed by Habsburg troops at the beginning of the 18th c. Access to the inside of the castle is through the outer round gatetower and a bridge over the moat. Here the 28m/99ft-high Gothic residential tower has dungeons in the lower part. The upper floors with rooms for the servants, banquet hall and living quarters for the lady of the castle have been

*Kinizsi
Castle

Kinizsi Castle in Nagyvázsony

restored in their original style and fitted with Renaissance furniture (castle museum). In the castle chapel in the north-west the first lord of the castle Pál Kinizsi lies below a red marble memorial slab. His grave was originally in the Paulinist monastery, which he founded, remains of which can be seen on the northern edge of the town. Below the vaulting in the castle chapel there is a lapidarium (open daily 8am–6pm during the summer months, otherwise 8am–2pm).

Open-air museum (Néprajzi múzeum)

At Vár utca 1 is a pretty house with a typical pergola from 1825. Furniture, household objects and exhibits of local history are collected and displayed here. There are also stables, a cellar and a barn (open Tue.–Sun. 9am–5pm).

Postal museum

The horses of the post coaches on their way from Buda via Fehérvár and Veszprém to Tapoica used to be changed in front of the building opposite. Today it is a small but not uninteresting postal museum (Postamúzeum; open Tue.–Sun. 10am–6pm).

St Stephen's Church

The Catholic church of this medieval settlement built around 1400, was rebuilt in Gothic style by Pál Kinizsi around 1480. The polygonal choir, the cross-vaulting in the sacristy and the fan vaulting in the nave date from this period. The church was rebuilt in Baroque style about 1740 when the counts of Zichy had the church rebuilt after it was badly damaged by the Turks.

Zichy House

The 18th c. Baroque palace on the main thoroughfare, nowadays a riding school, displays Classical features. The middle of the front façade has a tympanium supported by four Ionian columns. In the surrounding park and castle, riding displays take place annually in summer.

Visegrád   D 2

Region: Pest
Altitude: 106m/347ft
Population: 2100

Visegrád is picturesquely situated at the exit of a loop in the Danube in the
Danube Bend (see Danube Bend) about 40km/25 miles north of Budapest.
This historical town is a popular destination for excursions because of the
ruins of the royal palace and the views from the citadel.

Situation and
**Importance

The Romans took advantage of the strategic location above the Danube
founding a military camp on the Sibrik Hills in the 4th c. (reconstruction of a
watch tower near Fő utca). In the 9th c. Slavs settled in the ruins of the
Roman fort and named the settlement Višegrad (Slavic: high castle); later
the conquering Magyars took over the castle. After the invasion of the
Mongols in 1241, to which Visegrád also fell victim, King Béla IV built
castles to defend the land. In Visegrád a lower castle was built with a
defended residential tower in the centre (the Solomon tower) which was
connected by a wall with the massive citadel on the hill (upper castle).
During the regency of Charles I of Anjou, who transferred his residence
here in 1316, Visegrád developed into a flourishing political and cultural
town. Charles kept the Hungarian coronation insignia, and following the
coronation of his son Louis as the king of Poland (1370), the Polish crown
jewels in a purpose-built tower inside the citadel. A new royal palace was
built on the slope of the castle mound in 1330 which was the summer house
of his son Louis, who moved his residence back to Buda. Visegrád experienced a final if brief climax in the second half of the 15th c. when King
Matthias I had the royal palace rebuilt in Early Italian Renaissance style. On
Matthias's death the town began to decline. The upper castle was laid siege
to several times during the Turkish wars, taken by various parties and
destroyed; the towers which were left standing were blown up by the
Austrian Emperor Leopold in 1702. In the 18th c. German settlers lived in
Visegrád who built their houses from the stones of the ruined palace. A
landslip buried the rest of the palace; the only evidence of its former glory
until its discovery in 1934 being the comtemporary written sources.

History

Sights

As part of the lower castle the Vizibástya on the banks of the Danube was
connected to the Solomon tower by a wall and served as a watch tower for
the waterway and the palace's water supply. The multi-storeyed Romanesque construction was an obstacle to laying a road and so was torn down.
The reconstruction was built on the same site in 1937.

Water bastion

The hexagonal originally 311m/102ft high Salomon torony (walls up to
8m/26ft thick!) is an impressive relic of the Visegrád lower castle. The road
along the river bank was surveyed from here. A popular explanation of its
name is that in the 11th c. King Solomon, who was under the protection of
Emperor Henry IV was kept prisoner here by the Hungarian aristocracy.
However, this cannot apply to the present tower as it was not built until the
13th c.

*Solomon tower,
museum

The tower, which suffered damage during the Turkish wars, has been
successfully restored and houses a museum with finds from the former
splendid palace (open May to October, Tue.–Sun. 9am–5pm).

In the Anjou room on the ground floor is the superbly crafted Anjou
fountain from the second half of the 13th c., a major work of medieval
Hungarian stonemasonry, which in its present form is the result of exem-

plary reconstruction out of numerous minute original pieces. King Matthias removed it from the courtyard of the royal palace in the 15th c. and replaced it with a "modern" Renaissance style Hercules fountain which is in the adjoining Matthias room. This valuable red marble fountain is thought to be the work of an Italian sculptor from the circle of the Florentine artist Desiderio da Settignano. He is also thought to have sculpted various other works in the royal palace which are kept in the Solomon tower, including the red marble Madonna relief from the high altar of the palace chapel, which earned him the name "master of the marble madonnas". Remnants of the lion fountain which stood in the royal private garden of the palace, can also be seen in the Matthias room. On the top floor of the Solomon tower the medieval vaulting has been reconstructed by means of metal netting. There is a marvellous view over the Danube and the Visegrád Hills from the roof terrace.

Royal palace
(Királyi palota)

The first royal palace was built under Charles I after he and his court moved to Visegrád in 1316. More than one hundred years later King Matthias had the residence extended and rebuilt for himself and his Aragonese wife Beatrix and summoned Italian, or artists trained in Italy, to Visegrád, which thereby became an artistic and cultural centre of the Early Renaissance in Hungary. The praise heaped upon it by contemporaries gives an indication of the former splendour of the palace; the Italian humanist Antonio Bonfini (1427–1503): "The magnificent dining rooms have splendid coffered ceilings. There are also halls with gilded columns and homely rooms, exquisite marble fountains, impressive window grilles, delightful ballrooms, fortified treasure rooms and splendid courtyards with tall marble fountains. There is no lack of gardens, below open colonnades the scent of stocks waft, all kinds of boxwood trees line beautiful promenades (...) Among the wide clearings in the gardens there would be enough space for council chambers. No less attractive to the visitor are the shimmering green canals, the fish ponds, the showjumping ground and the extensive horse racing track along the banks of the Danube" (quoted from: Janus Pannonius,

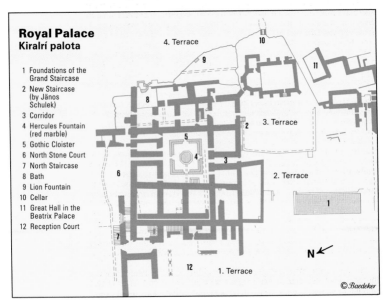

Royal Palace
Kiralrí palota

1 Foundations of the Grand Staircase
2 New Staircase (by János Schulek)
3 Corridor
4 Hercules Fountain (red marble)
5 Gothic Cloister
6 North Stone Court
7 North Staircase
8 Bath
9 Lion Fountain
10 Cellar
11 Great Hall in the Beatrix Palace
12 Reception Court

4. Terrace

3. Terrace

2. Terrace

1. Terrace

N

© Baedeker

Visegrád: Court of Honour of the royal palace of Mathias I

Humanists in Hungary). During the Turkish wars the complex fell into decay and later into oblivion; what was not buried by the sliding masses of earth was used as a quarry. The discovery of the legendary palace is credited to János Schulek, son of the famous architect Frigyes Schulek, who led the excavations of the site in 1934.

Tour

The site of the ruins is situated in Fő utca (entrance at house no. 27) which runs parallel to the banks of the Danube. The northern part of the palace, the king's residence, has long been opened up whereas the main part of the Beatrix palace is still below ground.

Access to the site is by the lowest of the four terraces that rise up the slope, which was originally at ground level. This was the reception surrounded by colonnades with steps at the rear leading up to the second terrace. A narrow corridor with narrow niches for servants to sit in let into the wall leads to the courtyard, centre of the former residential palace of the king. A cloister-like arcaded walk leads around the courtyard. Its east wing has been preserved with magnificent Late Gothic fan vaulting, evidence of a highly developed medieval vaulting technique. In the middle of the courtyard was the Hercules fountain. A marble slab of the fountain basin remains in front of the town while the other parts are kept in the Solomon tower. The Renaissance balustrade above the courtyard belongs to a loggia on the third terrace with majolica patterned floors. Other rooms from the royal palace are in rows behind the loggia. Between this and the Beatrix palace was the 14th c. castle chapel. King Matthias had a golden wooden ceiling installed in the relatively large chapel and a marble altar with a madonna relief which can be seen in the museum of the Solomon tower. One terrace higher in the northernmost part of the palace site are the remains of a bath with a steam room and a coldwater basin and to the south the former private royal garden with a copy of the red marble lion fountain which illustrates the transition from Late Gothic to Renaissance.

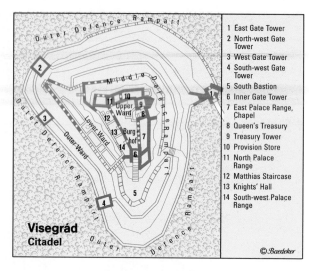

1 East Gate Tower
2 North-west Gate Tower
3 West Gate Tower
4 South-west Gate Tower
5 South Bastion
6 Inner Gate Tower
7 East Palace Range, Chapel
8 Queen's Treasury
9 Treasury Tower
10 Provision Store
11 North Palace Range
12 Matthias Staircase
13 Knights' Hall
14 South-west Palace Range

Visegrád Citadel

© *Baedeker*

*Citadel (Fellegvár)

A signposted road in the middle of the town leads up to the 315m/1033ft-high upper castle, which is still a majestic sight today, even from a distance. In 1250 King Béla IV founded the fortification which was further expanded by his successors up to Matthias and was of great political importance as the place where the royal insignia were kept for a while. Despite repeated sieges and conquests the castle survived the Turkish wars but not the punitive expedition of the Habsburgs against the Rákóczi uprising in 1702. Since then it has remained in ruins and is open to visitors. The middle of the castle, which is surrounded by several protective walls and fortified with a system of gates, narrow passages and drawbridges, consists of three wings around an enclosed courtyard (upper castle yard) which form an irregular triangle. In the east wing is the treasury tower, the former hoard of royal insignia.

*View

A steep staircase leads up to the reconstructed Inner Tower in the east (open: daily 9am–5pm) which has the best views over the countryside of the Danube Bend (see Danube Bend).

Surroundings

Nagyvillám

From the castle a signposted path leads to the Nagyvillám Hill (378m/1240ft). From the viewing tower the Börzsöny and Cserhát Hills are visible.

Pilis forest park

Visegrád lies in the middle of the 35,000ha/86,485 acres of Pilis forest park. In the Gisella dairy on the river bank there is a riding school where horses are available for hire for riding in the forest.

Lepence forest spa

1.5km/1 mile from Visegrád a scenic road with picturesque viewpoints leads to the forest spa.

Nagymaros

On the left bank of the Danube, opposite Visegrád, at the foot of the Börzsöny Hills (see Vác, Surroundings) lies the small town of Nagymaros (pop. 5000) which is becoming increasingly popular as a recreational area. Many artists are attracted by the lovely countryside (artists' colony). The history of Nagymaros is closely linked with that of Visegrád, which was the summer residence of the kings in the 13th and 14th c. Many servants at the court lived on the other side, in Nagymaros. During the Turkish period the town was devastated and depopulated, in the 19th c. fruit orchards were planted here. The appearance of the town suffered during the Eighties with the construction work for the Danube power station Gabčíkovo-Nagymaros (see Facts and Figures, Rivers and Lakes) jointly planned with what was Czechoslovakia. In response to nationwide protests construction was halted in 1989.

The Catholic church with its octagonal tower was built in the 14th c. in Gothic style (pointed arch door and window frames) and later altered in Baroque style. In Váci utca (no. 21) there is a local history exhibition and works by the sculptor Jenő Gratner (b. 1907) (open: mid-May–Sept. Sat. and Sun. 10am–6pm).

Sights in
Nagymaros

Zebegény lies 8km/5 miles east of Nagymaros, also on the left bank of the Danube, where the river first flows south and then makes a bend in a north-east direction. This village has also been discovered by artists. On the hillside, at Bartóky utca 7, István Szöny (1894–1960), an important representative of modern Hungarian painting, lived. In his house a museum is dedicated to his life and works (open: Tue.–Sun. 9am–5pm).

Zebegény

See Esztergom, Surroundings

Pilis Hills

Zalaegerszeg

B 3

Region: Zala
Altitude: 156m/512ft
Population: 59,800

Zalaegerszeg lies about 50km/31 miles south-east of Szombathely in the south-western part of Transdanubia. This charming hilly area, called "Göc-sej", is famous for its rich folk culture. After the war the capital of the Zala region rapidly developed into a modern industrial city on account of oil extraction in the surrounding area; the pretty town centre still has numerous interesting Late Baroque buildings.

Situation and
Importance

Zalaegerszeg was first mentioned in 1247. In the 16th and 17th c. it was the military centre of the surrounding fortifications in the war against the Turks. After the end of the Turkish rule the town decreased in importance and the economic revival in the 19th c. failed to materialise as the town was only connected to the railway network about 1885. Not until 1930 did its fortunes begin to improve with the discovery of oil reserves in the area. After the Second World War many industrial concerns settled here, including, besides an oil refinery, food, clothing, furniture and electronics.

History

Sights

The centre of the town has always been Széchenyi ter; it is surrounded by Baroque palaces, patricians' houses with vaulted arches and several official buildings. The Baroque parish church of Maria Magdalena was built between 1750 and 1760; following a fire in 1826 it was rebuilt. Noteworthy are the painting "Maria Magdalena", the frescos by Johann Cymbal and an 18th c. pietà. The trinity column near the church dates from 1790.

Catholic
parish church

The historic building of the Golden Lamb Hotel (Széchenyi tér 1) was built in 1893 by János Brenner.

Hotel
Arany Bárány

Zalaegerszeg

Archives	The building at Széchenyi tér 3 was completed in 1891 in Neo-Renaissance style. The regional coat of arms is located above the entrance.
District office	The Járási hivatal (Széchenyi tér 5) bears the characteristics of several styles; built around 1765 a Classical room was added to the north side of this Baroque building in 1891, a year later another floor was added. The Neo-Baroque façade is also from this period.
Regional court	The beautiful Baroque palace on Szabadság tér (no. 7) west of the parish church was built in 1730–32 to plans by the Viennese master builder Franz Allio; a side wing was added in the 19th c.
Modern buildings	The new residential and commercial buildings in the town centre were built between 1977 and 1980 to plans by György Vadász, a renowned Hungarian architect, whose style heralds the "postmodernist" fluidity of structure.
Göcsej Museum	The Göcsej Museum (north of the parish church, Batthyányi utca 2; open: Tue.–Sun. 10am–5pm) is housed in a horseshoe shaped art nouveau building. Its comprehensive collection comprises chiefly everyday objects and folklore from the Göcsej area, which consists of 70 districts from the Zala region. Works by the Zalaegerszeg-born sculptor Zsigmond Kisfaludy Stróbl (1884–1975) are also on show.
Göcsej village museum	The Göcsej Falumúzeum, a very interesting open air museum on a dead arm of the Zala, informs the visitor about rural life 150–200 years ago in Göcsej. About 50 original buildings were erected here: farmhouses, wine cellars, barns, forges, granaries, a schnaps distillery and a bell cage. All the buildings, fitted with furniture or equipment and tools, are made of wood and have a thatched reed or straw roof. On Sundays and public holidays everyday goods are made in the traditional way and can be bought. The museum is open from April to October Tue.–Sun. 10am–5pm; it is situated on the west side of the town (signposted on the road from Körmend). As well as the village museum there is a museum of Hungarian oil industry (Magyar Olajipari Múzeum) with drilling towers, pumps and other equipment.

Surroundings

Egervár	In Egervár 10km/6 miles north of Zalaegerszeg there is an impressive mansion house which originates from the Renaissance. This four-winged house was built by the Nádasdy counts from 1540–69 and converted in Baroque style in 1712 by Count Széchenyi. Nowadays it is a tourist hotel. The remains of a Gothic Franciscan church can be seen in the Baroque parish church.
Körmend	This small town with a population of 12,000 is situated 27km/16 miles north-west of Zalaegerszeg. The area was inhabited shortly after the Magyar conquest; the settlement which grew up on the crossing of important trade routes was elevated to the status of a town in 1244. At the beginning of the 17th c. the Batthyányi family of counts built their residence in the middle of their estates, helping to bring a revival to the town.
Körmend, Mansion house	The mansion house (Liszt Ferenc utca) was preceded by a 13th/14th c. castle. In the 17th c. the Batthyányis expanded the castle and converted it into a Baroque house. A Baroque façade with Classical overtones together with another floor were added in the 18th c. Part of the house is open to visitors and houses a museum with exhibits of local history and pieces from the Batthyányi family collection (open: Tue.–Sun. 10am–6pm). The 49ha/121 acre park was laid out in the 18th c. based on French designs.

Szentgoyyhárd: frescoes in the parish church

Just 30km/19 miles west of Körmend is the border town of Szentgotthárd with an interesting parish church, built as a Cistercian monastery church in 1748/64 to plans by Franz Anton Pilgram. The single-towered façade is impressive with the clarity of its large shapes and the sweep of its gently concave lines; the interior is also characterised by its monumental uniformity. The most notable of the frescos in the vaulting is that in the first bay by Stephan Dorffmeister (1784). It portrays the battle near Szentgotthárd (1664) in which the Habsburg troops achieved a decisive victory over a mighty Turkish army. The altar paintings and the ceiling fresco in the second bay are by the Cistercian monk Matthias Gusner.

Szentgotthárd (St Gotthard), *parish church

The varied, hilly wooded countryside in the triangle between Körmend in the north, Zalaegerszeg in the east and the Hungarian-Austrian border in the west has an interesting ethnographic and cultural history. Part of this region, the so-called Upper Wart, fell to Austria after the treaty of Versailles in 1920; on the Hungarian side the population of this border region carried out watch duties for the Hungarian rulers as far back as the 10th and 11th c., from where the name "Wart" (= watch) is probably derived. They were rewarded for these voluntary duties with privileges and greater autonomy. Typical of the Wart are tiny settlements or hamlets, known as "szer" in Hungarian, which form a chain of border posts.

Őrség (German: Wart)

The houses, mainly of wood with wide overhanging roofs, are grouped with the stables around a courtyard to give protection against robbers and wolves.

In many villages of Őrség, in the village of Őriszentpéter or in Szalafő, for example, there are houses still built in this traditional style and reformed churches with typical freestanding belltowers.

Őriszentpéter

Zalakaros

Velemér

In the southern part of Őrség, 17km/11 miles south of Őriszentpéter, on the Hungarian-Austrian border, the little village of Velemér with its beautiful 13th c. church is worth a visit.

The interior contains well preserved frescos by the Austrian painter Johann Aquila from 1378. The curved contours of the figures and the "soft" facial features are typical of the so-called International style, which was prevalent in European painting and sculpture around 1400.

Zalakaros

See Nagykanizsa, Surroundings

Zemplin Hills (Zempléni-hegység)

See Tokaj, Surroundings

Zirc

C 2

Region: Veszprém
Altitude: 282m/925ft
Population: 11,000

Situation and History

Zirc, 56km/35 miles south of Győr in the wide Cuha valley, which traverses the Bakony Forest, was first documented in 1139. The Cistercian abbey, which dominates the town and served important economic and cultural functions in the Middle Ages, was founded by King Béla III in 1182 and occupied by monks from Clairvaux (hence the Latin name Nova Claravallis). During the Turkish period it was completely devastated and not reinhabited until the beginning of the 18th c. by German settlers.

Sights

Cistercian church

The Baroque Cistercian church (Rákóczi tér 1) was built by Martin Athanasius Witwer and Matthias Kayr in 1739–53; the two 45m/148ft high towers of the façade were added later in 1854. The interior is finely decorated in Late Baroque style: paintings by Franz Anton Maulbertsch (high altar "Maria's Ascension", 1754, first side altar on the right Maria Magdalena); frescos by Josef Wagenmeister; richly decorated choir stalls and pulpit.

Monastery

The monastery is built on to the right of the church, the wings having been built in several stages between 1732 and 1854. The oldest, from 1732 making it older than the church, is the one next to the church; the last one to be completed was the Classical west front (by the main entrance).

The library of the Cistercian monks became the basis for the Antal Reguly library in the monastery, which is named after the pioneering Finno-Ugrian researcher of ethnology and linguistics Antal Reguly (1819–58). The five rooms beautifully furnished with inlaid floors and cabinets by the Zirc carpenter Michael Wild (1853–57) contain a protected collection with 60,000 volumes and many valuable incunabula (open: Tue.–Fri. 10am–noon, 2–4pm).

In the monastery there is also a museum of natural and local history (open: Tue.–Sun. 9am–5pm).

Behind the monastery complex (Damjanich utca) there is an attractive park which was a wildlife reserve even in the 15th c.; from 1737 it became the monastery's botanical garden.

Arboretum

Remains of an abbey church dating from around 1180 with a Baroque statue of St Imre (1749) are to be found by the wall which surrounds the arboretum.

Medieval column

Practical Information from A to Z

Accommodation

See Camping
See Hotels
See Holiday Accommodation
See Young People's Accommodation

Air Traffic

Several large international airlines as well as the national MALÉV serve Hungary through the Budapest Ferihegy Airport. There are flights to all important centres in Europe, North Africa and the Near East, as well as to the USA and Canada.

International airlines

Since Hungary is a rather small country and has a relatively extensive rail network, inland air traffic is not of great importance. When there is a demand flights are made to Győr, Miskolc, Debrecen, Szeged and Pécs, as well as to areas of touristic importance, and these services are increasing.

Inland flights

Airports

Ferihegy International Airport is situated 16km/10 miles south-east of the city centre. It has two terminals and is the only international airport in Hungary. It is also the base for the National MALÉV airline. From here there are regular connections with the important towns in central Europe.

Budapest Ferihegy International Airport

After the fall of the "iron curtain" air traffic with the provincial airports of Debrecen, Győr, Miskolc, Pécs and Szeged, as well as with a number of places of economic or touristic importance, has increased.
These airfields are served mainly from Budapest as and when required.

Provincial airfields

Airlines

The Hungarian airline MALÉV maintains connections to all important European towns and also to North Africa and the Near East. Comparatively recently direct flights were started to New York.

Magyar Légiközlekedese Vallalat

MALÉV

MALÉV-Generaldirektion, Roosevelt tér, H–1051 Budapest; tel. 1–266–90 33; Fax 1–266–26 85

MALÉV Offices in Hungary
Budapest

Ticket sales: Apáczai Csere J. u. 19 H–1051 Budapest; tel. 1–266–90 33
Dorottya u. 2, H–1051 Budapest; tel. 1–266–59 13

Seat reservations and telephone ticket sales: tel. 1–267–43 33

Airport: tel. 1–157–91 23

Kálvin tér 4/B Debrecen; tel. 52–16–545

Debrecen

◀ *Shops in the street in Szentendre*

Air Traffic

Győr	Aradi Vertánúl útja 2, H–2021 Győr; tel. 96–19–085
Miskolc	Széchenyi u. 105, H–3530 Miskolc; tel. 46–34–34 06
Pécs	Széchenyi tér 16, H–7621 pécs; tel. 72–24–378
Szeged	Oskola u. 5, H–6720 Szeged; tel. 62–24–200

Getting to and from Budapest airport

Taxi:
It is relatively expensive to go by taxi from the airport to the city and it is advisable to negotiate the fare beforehand.

Hotel buses, shuttle buses:
A number of the first-class hotels run their own bus service. This service is normally free for guests who have booked into the hotels concerned.

Airport bus:
Express bus connections every 30 minutes between Ferihegy terminals I and II and the city centre are provided at reasonable cost. The single journey takes 30–40 minutes.

Underground/municipal bus service:
The cheapest way into the city is by bus and underground. First take the red BKV bus no. 93 as far as the Kőbánya-Kispet terminus of Metro Line 3. It is then just a short trip by underground to the city centre.

Antique Dealers

Hungary is well-known as a good source of antiques. In Budapest especially, but also in the provinces, valuable old objects can be obtained; these range from engravings to well-preserved furniture from the "k.-u.-k" (imperial and royal) time. However, visitors should beware for quite often these goods are more or less well-made replicas or even fakes.

Anyone wishing to export articles of artistic merit or antiques of great value must first obtain clearance from the appropriate museums:

Hungarian antiques

Hungarian National Gallery (Magyar Nemzeti Galéria), Budapest I., Budavári Palota (Buda Castle Palace), Szent Győrgy tér 1; tel. 1–175–75 33

Folk art

Ethnographic Museum (Néprajzi Múzeum), Budapest V., Kossuth Lajos tér 12; tel. 1–132–63 40

Books and Music

Széchenyi National Library, Budapest I., Budavári Palota (Buda Castle Palace), Building F; tel. 1–175–75 33

East Asian works of art

Museum of Applied Art (Iparmuvészeti Múzeum), Budapest IX., Üllői út 33/37; tel. 1–117–52 22

Foreign antiques

Museum of Fine Arts (Szépmuvészeti Múzeum), Budapest XIV., Dózsa György út 41; tel. 1–142–97 59

Permit from the National Bank

If the value of the work of art intended for export exceeds 3000 Forint then a permit must be obtained from the Hungarian National Bank: Budapest V., Szabadság tér 8; tel. 1–111–34 46

Bathing, Swimming

Warning

It is not advisable to bathe in rivers such as the Danube (Duna) or the Tisza. Rivers in Hungary are in some stretches contaminated with pollution from industrial plants and from agriculture.

Lakes

The quality of water in Lake Balaton is strictly controlled and the level of pollution is very small. Along the shore one beach follows another. The southern shore is relatively shallow and therefore ideal for families with children. The north bank, on the other hand, slopes steeply.

Balaton

It is possible to bathe in the Velence Lake (Velncei-tó) between Budapest and Lake Balaton.

Velence Lake

For some time the Tisza Reservoir (Tisza-tó) near Tisafüred in eastern Hungary has been a popular rendezvous for water sports enthusiasts.

Tisza Reservoir

See Spas and Health Resorts

Héviz Thermal Lake

Bus Excursions, Sightseeing

General and special sightseeing tours are organised by most travel bureaux, both in Budapest and in the provinces. Qualified guides speaking foreign languages are available from tourist offices or can be hired individually.

Leading bus excursion offices

Alfa Tourist, Régiposta utca 11, H–1053 Budapest; tel. 1–118–57 20
Blaguss-Volánbusz, Erzsébet tér, H–1051 Budapest; tel. 1–117–77 77
Budapest Tourist, Roosevelt tér 5, H–1051 Budapest; tel. 1–118–60 00
Cityrama-Mecsek,Báthori utca 22, H–1054 Budapest; tel. 1–132–53 44
Cooptourist, Kossuth Lajos tér 13/15, H–1054 Budapest; tel. 1–111–88 03
Express, Szabadság tér 16, H–1054 Budapest; tel. 1–131–77 77
Falcon Pannonia, Alkotmány u. 20, H–1054 Budapest; tel. 1–111–14 75
Hungarocamion, Hungária kőrút 140, H–1146 Budapest; tel. 1–252–76 79
IBUSZ Travel Service, Bulcsú utca 19, H–1134 Budapest; tel. 1–140–93 60
IBUSZ-Zentrale, Felszabadulás tér 5, H–1053 Budapest; tel. 1–118 68 66
Idea Tours, Semmelweis utca 14, H–1052 Budapest; tel. 1–118–60 46
Omnibusz, Erzsébet tér, H–1051 Budapest; tel. 1–118–21 22
OTP-Penta, Bajcsy-Zsilinszky út 12, H–1051 Budapest; tel. 1–138–20 99
Pegazus Tours, Ferenciek tér 5, H–1053 Budapest; tel. 1–117–16 44
Volántourist, Üllőo út 21, H–1091 Budapest; tel. 1–138–25 55

Selection

Business Hours

Mon.–Fri. 7am–6pm, Sat. 8am–1pm. In Budapest and some larger centres more and more food shops are open throughout the day.

Food shops
Supermarkets

Mon.–Fri. 10am–6 pm. Larger shopping centres and stores are open also on Sunday at least for a few hours.

Stores

Kiosks, flower shops, tobacconists, confectioners, etc. are usually open every weekday.

Kiosks, etc.

Mon.–Fri. 9am–5pm, Sat. 9am–2pm

Financial institutions

Mon.–Fri. 8 am–6pm, Sat. 8 am–2pm.

Post offices

Cafés

Every visitor to Hungary ought to pay a visit to a coffee house. There are also many confectioners, expressos and cafés to be found, especially in Budapest.

Note

Coffee houses   Among the best in the capital are:

Gerbeaud, V, Vörösmarty tér
Hauer, VIII, Rádóczi út 49
New York (Hungária), VII, Erzsébet körút 9
Angelika, I, Batthyány tér
Korona, I, Disz tér
Ruszwurm, I, Szentháromság u. 7

Camping and Caravanning

Note   In Hungary there are more than 200 camp sites and new ones are opened
every year. Although prices are low the facilities (especially toilets) sometimes leave much to be desired. On most sites caravans and motor caravans can be accommodated; a number also have caravans or simple camp
huts for rental. Camp sites are crowded during the main holiday season
(May to October) and on fine weekends. Early booking of a pitch is advised.

Information   Magyar Camping es Caravaning Club (MCCC), Kalvin tér 9, Budapest; tel.
1–117–7248

"Wild" camping   Camping on open land is forbidden and sleeping in vehicles or caravans is
only allowed at specially indicated places. It should also be mentioned that
caravans and motor caravans sometimes have great difficulty in finding
places where sewage or rubbish can be disposed of.

Camp sites

Classification   Most Hungarian camp sites are divided into categories classified by stars;
these indicate whether the site has certain mininum facilities (*), simple
facilities (**), comfortable (***), or very good (****).

Best areas   The best run camp sites are situated in the area of Lake Balaton and near the
leading spas, as well as in the vicinity of Budapest (the Danube Knee).

Camp sites
literature   Brochures giving details of camp sites can be obtained from MCCC (see
above) and from the Hungarian Tourist Association (see Information).

Car Rental

Note   The easiest way of renting a car is to do so at Budapest Ferihegy Airport
(both terminals). Also in the capital there are a number of Rent-a-Car
stations. In the provinces car rental was unknown until recently; only in a
few towns and tourist centres can cars be rented. On the other hand it is
possible almost everywhere to obtain a car with a driver at reasonable
rates.

Car rental firms (selection)

Balatonföldvár   Europcar-Interrent, Balatonszentgyörgyi út 14; tel. 84–400–66

Balatonfüred   Avis-IBUSZ, Hotel Annabella, Deák Ferenc u.; tel. 86–42–222

Budapest city   Avis-IBUSZ, Martinelli tér 8; tel. 1–118–42 07
Budget, Hotel Buda Penta, Krisztina körút; tel. 1–155–04 82
Europcar-Interrent, Than Károly út 3–5; tel. 1–166–45 15
Hertz-Főtaxi, Aranykéz u. 4/8; tel. 1–177–788
Hertz-Főtaxi, Kertessz u. 24/28; tel. 1–111–6116

Avis-IBUSZ, Terminal 2; tel. 1–361–84 70	Budapest Airport
Budget, Terminal 2; tel. 1–157–84 81	
Europcar-Interrent, Terminal 1; tel. 1–157–66 88	
Hertz-Főtaxi, Terminal 1; tel. 1–578–629	
Hertz-Főtaxi, Terminal 2; tel. 1–578–606	
Hertz, Szabadság utca 27; tel. 52–708–88	Debrecen
Hertz, Bartok Béla utca 10; tel. 76–299–95	Győr
Europcar-Interrent-Mit-Car, Huszar utca 1; tel. 46–326–245	Miskolc
Hertz, Marx u. 4; tel. 46–70–754	
Hertz, Lanc u. 2; tel. 72–279–44	Pécs
Avis-IBUSZ, Petőfi sétány 38; tel. 84–111–05	Siófok
Hertz, Hotel Pelikan, Kossuth Lajos utca 18; tel. 56–47–747	Szolnok
Hertz, Savaria tér; tel. 94–147–65	Szombathély

Caves

Caves have been formed in the course of years in some of the karst mountain ranges of Hungary. Some of these have been opened up to tourists.

Castle Cave (Várbarlang – see A to Z Budapest, Buda)
Essentially an artificial cave system in the Castle Hill of Buda. Part has been set up as a panopticum. Entrance: Uri utca 9; Information: tel. 1–175–65 58

Budapest

Pálvölgyi barlang (see A to Z Budapest, Buda)
A cave preserved as a natural monument in the Buda hills. Entrance: Buda, Szépvölgyi út 162; Information: tel. 1–188–95 37

Szemlőhegyi barlang
Practically free of dust, germs and allergies. Interesting aragonite formations. Entrance: Buda, Pusztaszi út 35; Information: tel. 1–115–08 42.

Abaliget-barlang
Dripstone cave, about 500,000 years old; also used as a therapeutic tunnel for treating asthma. Information: tel. 72–78–054

Southern Hungary

Aggtelek-Baradia Cave (see A to Z, Aggtalek)
Fine series of dripstone caves; source of important archaeological finds; also used as a curative cave. Because of its excellent acoustic concerts are occasionally held here. Information: tel. 48–12–700

North-eastern Hungary

Lillafüred, Anna-barlang and István-barlang (see A to Z, Miskolc)
Dripstone caves with interesting lighting. Information: tel. 36–12–791

Tappolca Cave (see A to Z, Lake Balaton)
A cave through which once flowed a river, now dried up, with interesting dripstone formations. The cave is also used for therapeutic purposes. Information: tel. 87–12–579.

Lake Balaton Hinterland

Casinos

The first casino to be opened after the Second World War was set up in 1981 with Austrian help in the Hotel Budapest Hilton. Since then a number of similar establishments have been opened in various parts of the country which have had marked success.

Stakes   Stakes must be made in German Marks; all convertible currencies can be exchanged on the spot. Winnings are free of tax and can be taken out of Hungary without difficulty.

Location of Casinos

Budapest   Casino Hotel Budapest Hilton, H–1014 Budapest, Hess András tér 1/3; tel. 1–175–10 00

Casino Citadella, H–1118 Budapest, Gellérthegyi sétány; tel. 1–166–76 86

Casino Gresham, H–1051 Budapest, Roosevelt tér; tel. 1–117–24 07

Casino Imperial, H–1052 Budapest, Szabad sajtó út 5; tel. 1–118–24 04

Casinoship Schönbrunn (anchored in the warmer months at the head of the Pest Bridge), H–1051 Budapest, Roosevelt tér, Lower Quay; tel. 1–186–88 59

Casino Las Vegas, H–1051 Budapest, Roosevelt tér 2, Hotel Atrium Hyatt Budapest; tel. 1–117–60 22

Héviz   Casino Héviz, H–8360 Héviz, Hotel Termál Kossuth Lajos utca 9/11; tel. 82–18–961

Sopron   Casino Sopron, H–9400 Sopron, Liszt Ferenc tér 1; tel. 99–14–475

Pécs   Casino Imperial, H–7621 Pécs, Jókai tér 6; tel. 72–13–449

Chemists (Patika, Gyógyszertár)

Note   Although there are a great number of chemists in Hungary it may be difficult to find a particular product and it is advisable to take the required medicaments from home.
Prescriptions which have been issued abroad can be made up in Hungary provided the necessary medicines are available. A number of remedies can be obtained without prescription.

Day and Night Chemists   In the district of Budapest at least two chemists are open throughout the 24 hours, generally in rotation. Also in the large provincial towns there are chemists with a service at night. The addresses of chemists on duty can be obtained from information offices and hotel reception desks.

Currency

The Hungarian monetary unit is the forint (Ft). One forint=100 fillérs. In circulation are banknotes in denominations of 10, 20, 50, 100, 500, 1000 and 5000 forints, coins worth 1, 2, 5, 10 and 20 forints and 10, 20 and 50 fillérs.

Warning   The 10 forint note and 1000 forint note are very similar, care should be taken. The same applies to the newly issued 5000 forint note which can very easily be mistaken for the 50 forint note.

Currency regulations   For foreigners the import and export of a maximum of 500 forints per head is permitted. If a family of three, for instance, has 1500 forints the value of the highest bank note must not exceed 500 forints (i.e. the individual allowance). The Hungarian National Bank publishes daily the official exchange rates of more than 20 currencies

There is no compulsory exchange in Hungary. To avoid difficulties it is advisable to exchange foreign currency at the branches of banks, at post offices, at hotel reception desks or at the exchange offices at frontier crossings, airports, rail stations and camp sites.

Changing money

Exchange rates are subject to fluctuation. The current rates are obtainable from banks, etc.

Exchange rates

In the larger hotels and restaurants and in shops and stores frequented by tourists credit cards (American Express, Bank of America, Carte Blanche, Diners Club, Eurocard, Interbanc, Access and Visa) are accepted.

Credit cards

Eurocheques, together with a Eurocheque Card, will be cashed by banks, hotels and guest houses and travel bureaux (e.g. IBUSZ, Budapest Tourist, Blaguss-Volán) who display a Eurocheque sign.
In Hungary a Eurocheque must be made out in forints (maximum per cheque 15,000 forints).

Eurocheques

Customs Regulations

Personal effects and food for three days can be taken into Hungary without formality. In addition the following can be imported for personal use: 250 cigarettes or 50 cigars or 250 gr. of tobacco, two litres of wine and one litre of spirits.
Gifts to a value of 5000 forints can be imported by one individual in any one year.
Video equipment must be declared on entry. Radio equipment and mobile telephones can only be imported with special permission.
The import of sports and hunting equipment must first be cleared with a Hungarian embassy. A permit will only be granted if a letter of invitation from a Hungarian sports or hunting association is produced, or an order for such equipment from a hunting association. Other weapons may not be imported.
There is an absolute ban on the import of pornographic material, drugs, horror videos, films and pictures which are directed against Hungary.
Fresh meat and milk products are not allowed to be imported.

Entry

Articles brought into the country may be taken out without formality.
In addition the following may be exported: provisions for three days, and, for persons over 16 years of age, 200 cigarettes or 50 cigars or 200 gr. of tobacco, two litres of wine and one litre of another alcoholic drink. Gifts to a value of 3000 forints (no one article exceeding a value of 1000 forints). Such goods can only be exported if they have been obtained using freely convertible currency or bought with a credit card, and provided a receipt can be produced.

Exit

The export of works of art, precious metals and articles incorporating precious metals, as well as postage stamps, is only possible with special permission. Information can be obtained from the Hungarian National Bank and customs authorities.

Export of
valuable articles

Detailed current customs regulations for visitors may be obtained from the representatives of the Hungarian Tourist Authority or from IBUSZ trade and tourist offices.

Cycling

Hungary is one of the countries of Europe which have been seized by the cycling boom. Some years ago a start had already been made to mark cycling routes and tracks suitable for cyclists. Considerable progress has been made with these facilities in the conurbation of Budapest, on both sides of the Danube Bend, in the area of Mátra – Bükk – Eger – Aggtelek-Jósvafő, in the Zemplén Mountains, in the Nyírség, in the area of Debrecen – Hortobágy, around Lake Tisza near Tiszafüred, in the areas of Szeged and Pécs – Mohács and in the uplands of Sopron.

Popular Cycle Tours	Budapest–Danube Bend (Visegrad)–Tata Tata–Zirc–Vesprém–Lake Balaton–Keszthely Sopron–Szombathely–Zalaegeszeg–Sümeg–Lake Balaton–Keszthely–Eger Tour–Hortobágy–Tokaj
Cycles at the Station	The Hungarian Railways (MÁV) have also taken note of the popularity of cycling and at certain stations cycles can be rented.
Carriage of cycles by train	Passengers' cycles can be transported on certain trains of the Hungarian National Railways (MÁV), the Budapest Suburban Railway HÉV (Budapest–Szentendre) and the Budapest Rack Railway.
Information	Magyar Kerékpáros Túrazók Egyesülete (Association of Hungarian Cycle Tourists), Bajcsy-Zsilinszky út 31, H–1065 Budapest; tel. 1–111–24 67, 1–111–92 89.

Diplomatic Representation

Great Britain	Budapest V, Harmincad út 6; tel. 1–118–2888
United States	Budapest V, Szabadság tér 12; tel. 1–112–6450
Canada	Budapest II, Budakeszi út 32; tel. 1–176–7711

Electricity

Hungarian electricity supply is at 220 volts A.C. In the larger hotels electrical apparatus can be used with a continental adaptor.

Emergencies

Note	The Hungarian emergency services are currently being modernised throughout the country. Soon there will be common emergency telephone numbers everywhere. For the telephone districts of Budapest, Baja, Debrecen, Eger, Győr, Miskolc, Nyíregyháza, Pécs, Siófok and Szeged the following telephone numbers apply:
Ambulance Fire Service Police	Tel. 04 Tel. 05 Tel. 07
	In all other areas an additional "0" must be dialled
OMSZ	Hungarian Rescue Service OMSZ (air rescue); tel. 1–120–24 70

Events

Programme of events	Local tourist offices (see Information) publish comprehensive monthly programmes of events. In addition information about events can be found in the newspapers and obtained from the Hungarian Tourist Office.

Events

Important events (a selection)

Budapest: Peretten Gala (Peter Vigadó; Jan 1st.) — January

Budapest: Fashion Forum; Debrecen and Surroundings: Hajduságer Shrovetide Carnival; Kaposvár: Dorothy Ball (Dorottya-bal, 1st Saturday) — February

Mohács: Buscho Masked Procession (1st weekend); Budapest: Spring Festival; Culture Festivals in Debrecen, Gödöllő, Kaposvár, Kecskemét, Sopron. Szentendre, Szombathely; Utazàs Tourist Fair and Exhibition in Budapest (3 weeks); Hollókő: Folklore (Easter Monday) — March

Szekszárd: Wine Festival (1st Friday); Budapest: Technical Exhibitions; Pécs: Easter-egg painting. — April

Balatonfüred, Siófok: Opening of the season on Lake Balaton (last Sunday); Borbáspuszt: Riding Festival; Hajós: Hungarian-German Wine Festival on St Urban's Day (last weekend); Székesfehérvár: Alba Regia Cultural Festival; Budapest: International Spring Fair (BNV); operetta concerts in the Pest Vigadó (May to October), Folklore Market in the Castle district; in many places at various centres, especially in Szentendre, folk-art and handwork, revival of old customs (May to October). — May

Békéstarhos: Music Festival (June/July); Győr: Music in Summer (June/July); Kisvárda: Theatrical festival in the Castle (June–Aug.); Miskolc: Music in Summer (June–Aug.); Pécs: Summer Theatre (June–Aug.); Sopron: Festival weeks and music days (June–Aug.); Budapest: Open-air performances on Margaret Island (Margitsziget; June–Aug.); Chamber music evenings in the Béla Bartók Memorial House (June–Sept.); organ concerts in St Matthias Church and St Stephen's Basilica (June–Aug.); summer concerts in Pest Town Hall (June–Aug,); Tata: banquets in Renaissance style (June–Aug. at weekends); Szántódpuszta (south Balaton): equestrian and folklore programmes (June–Aug.); Balatonföldvár: folklore meetings (end of June); Őriszentpéter: Folklore Market (last weekend). — June

Sümeg: historic Castle Festival; Mátapuszta (Hortobágy National Park): International Equestrian Festival (1st weekend); Apajpusta (Kiskunság National Park): puszta folklore with equestrian competitions: carriage driving, shepherd shows (last weekend); Szombathely: International Bartók Festival; Badacsony (north bank of Lake Balaton): Folklore Market (at weekends in July/Aug.); Balatonfüred: Anne Ball with election of beauty queen (last weekend); Debrecen: International Jazz Festival; Fertőd: Haydn concerts in the Castle (July/Aug.); Keszthely: chamber concerts in the Castle (July/Aug.); Gyula: perfomances of plays by contemporary Hungarian authors in the Castle (July/Aug.); Martonvásár: Beethoven open-air concerts (July/Aug.); Budapest: Folk-dancing Festival in the Castle (July 20th–Aug. 20th); Szeged: festival on the cathedral square (end of July–end of Aug.); Nyírbátor: music in historic buildings. — July

Buzsák: Consecration Fair (Kirmes); Esztergom: International Guitar Festival (every two years); Budapest: Formula One Hungarian Grand Prix (on the Hungaroring, mid-Aug.); Debrecen: Carnival of Flowers (Aug. 20th, every two years); Mátapuszta (Hortobágy National Park): Folklore Market (Aug. 20th); Körmend: Water Carnival, fireworks (Aug. 20th); Budapest: St Stephen's Procession, fireworks (Aug. 20th); Ópusztaszer: festivities commemorating Árpád, conqueror of the country (Aug. 20th). — August

Wine Festivals in Badacsony, Balatonboglár, Balatonfüred, Sopron, Szekszárd, Eger (Sept./Oct.); Budapest: International Wine Festival (mid Sept.), Art festival (Sept./Oct.), International Autumn Fair (BNV); Szombathely: Savaria Festival (Sept./Oct.). — September

Pécsvárad: Maidens' Market (every two years). — October

339

| November | Budapest: Automobile Show; Sopron: Martini Balls (11th–13th); Budapest: Opening of the ball season (Elizabeth and Katharina Balls). |
| December | Christmas Markets in the towns (especially Sopron); New Year's Eve Ball (Dec. 31st). |

Fishing

| Fishing permits | On production of a passport a fishing permit can be obtained on request from the relevant municipal and local authorities (normally tourist bureaux or fishing authorities) at relatively low charges. |
| Information | Magyar Országos Horgász Szvövetség (MOHOSZ), H–1051 Budapest, October 6th and 20th; tel. 1–325–315. |

Folklore

Almost everybody who thinks of Hungary has visions of pastoral scenes around a well, of beautiful dark-eyed maidens in colourful green, white and red costumes, and of romantic gipsy violin music. Yet the popular culture here is not only seen and heard at festivals but is also marketed in the tourist sector and is highly commercialised.

Basic traditional Hungarian folklore can be experienced in the open-air museums and within the framework of organised programmes, which are presented, for example, in the Hortobágy (See A to Z) or in the János-Arany Theatre in Budapest.

Food and Drink

Food

Hungarian cuisine, like Austrian, stresses dishes which include meat, flour or cereal, and great attention is paid to spices and other added ingredients. Old recipes which have been handed down are particularly prized and these are characterised by a liberal use of fat and spices, especially paprika. Fresh-water fish (especially carp, catfish and pike-perch) caught in the lakes and numerous fishpools, are also a great favourite. Most people enjoy a glass of Hungarian wine with their meal; wines from Lake Balaton are particularly popular.

	Some specialities:
Bécsi szelet	Fried veal cutlet (Wiener schnitzel)
Borjúbecsinált rizzsel	Veal fricassée with rice
Fogas	Perch from Lake Balaton
Guba	Yeast buns with poppy seeds
Gulyásleves (goulash)	Well-spiced stew of beef, potato cubes, paprika, onions, tomatoes, garlic and caraway.
Halászlé	A soup delicately spiced with hot paprika and often consisting of several kinds of fish (carp, catfish, etc.) with the addition of vegetables, onions, croûtons and sour cream.
Halleves majgomboccál	Soup with liver dumplings
Harcsaszeletek roston	Baked catfish
Kalács	Plaited pastry

Goulash from the pot!

Layers of vegetables with sausage, bacon, minced meat, potatoes and slices of red pepper.	Koloszvári rakott káposzta
Soup with diced potatoes, croûtons, smoked bacon, tomatoes, slices of red pepper and herbs.	Lebbencs
Slices of red pepper in pork fat, steamed with tomatoes, aubergine, onions and salt.	Lecsó
White cabbage prepared with a roux and sour cream, and added bacon.	Lucskos káposzta
Noodles with poppy seed.	Mákos metélt
Pancakes	Palacsinta
Chicken with paprika in pastry	Paprikás csirke galuskával
Pastry cases filled with minced meat or finely chopped cabbage and baked.	Piroggen
Various kinds of pastry.	Pgácsa
"Thieves bite" (various pieces of meat, bacon, potato and onion baked on a spit).	Rablóhús nyárson
Fried chicken	Rántott csirke
Sweet strudel usually filled with apples, nuts, poppy seeds, curd cheese or cherries.	Rétes
Chocolate cakes with jam.	Rigó jancsi
Pieces of biscuit soaked in rum and served with cream.	Somlói galuska
Stewed beef with a thick well-seasoned sauce.	Tokány
Pasta dough with curd cheese and bacon	Túróscsusza
Larded pheasant.	Tüzdelt fácánsült
Boiling fowl in the Ujhaz manner (with vegetables, onions, garlic, mushrooms, parsley and vermicelli).	Ujház tyúkleves
Hare, "hunter style".	Vadas nyúl
Soup with green beans.	Zöldbableves
Mange-tout peas prepared with butter	Zöldborsó vajjal
Bread dumplings.	Zsemlegombóccal

Drinks

Hungarian fruit brandies are famous and popular, especially Barack (apricot brandy), Szilva (plum brandy) and cherry brandy.	Spirits
As well as local beers, German and Austrian beers are becoming more and more popular.	Beer (sor)
See entry	Wine

Getting to Hungary

By air	There are scheduled flights daily by British Airways and Malév from London to Budapest, either direct or via Rome or Frankfurt. From the USA and Canada visitors normally fly to Amsterdam, Copenhagen, Paris, Madrid or Vienna and continue on connecting flights to Budapest.
By rail	The best service from the UK leaves Victoria Station in the morning and arrives at Budapest the following afternoon, via Dover, Ostend and Vienna. It is possible to change in Paris and continue on the Orient Express. An alternative route is via the Hook of Holland and Vienna.
By road	Visitors taking their cars to Hungary are advised to travel on the German autobahns between Cologne and Munich to Salzburg and from there to Budapest. The AA in Great Britain and the AAA in the United States can provide further information.
By boat	During the summer (April–September) there is a hydrofoil service on the Danube between Vienna, Bratislava and Budapest, the journey taking between four and five hours. Information: tel. 1–118–1758.

Gliding

Gliding Club	Budapest Sport Gliding Club (Mezqgasági Repülökj Klubja) Towing: Technical University, Budapest.
Gliding Fields	Hármashatár-hegy gliding field, north-west of Budapest; for the location of other fields apply to information offices (See Information).

Golf

Information	Hungarian Golf Association, H–1143 Budapest, Dózsa György út 1–3; tel. 1–188–33 05.

Golf Courses

Bük	Birdland Golf and Country Club (18 holes) Information: Thermal & Sport Hotel, H–9740 Bükfürdo; tel. 94–58–500.
Kisoroszi	Kisoroszi Golf Course (18 holes) on an island in the Danube 38km/24 miles north of Budapest centre Information: Hotel Budapest Hilton, H–1014 Budapest, András tér 1–3; tel. 1–175–10 00.

Help for the Disabled

Information	Mozgáskorlátozottak Egyesöleteinek Országos Szövetsége (Nation Association for the Physical Handicapped), San Marco utca 76, H–1032 Budapest; tel. 1–188–8951; Fax 1–68–92–92.

Holiday Accommodation

Note	In all the important holiday and weekend leisure areas numerous holiday houses, flats and rooms are available, but furnishings vary considerably.

This accommodation is, in most cases, quite inexpensive. However, especially in the major tourist regions (Budapest, Danube Bend, Lake Balaton) some landlords are becoming inclined to raise prices to the level of those usually found in western Europe.

Local tourist offices (see Information) and the Hungarian Tourist Office IBUSZ keep a comprehensive catalogue of holiday houses, flats and rooms.

Information and catalogue

In the Budapest area especially a great many pensions and owners of rooms to let are represented by the Delfintour Agency (Szarvas G. u. 24, H–1175 Budapest; tel. 1–201 93 86, Fax 1–201–91 86.

Budapest area

Hotels

Hotels in Hungary are officially classified according to the standard of their furnishing and facilities. The categories range from five star (luxury class) to one star (lowest category). However within an individual category there may be considerable differences in quality as far as furnishing and service are concerned. The prospectus "Hotel – Camping" with a list of all hotels in Hungary can be obtained from any branch of IBUSZ.

General

A popular, even though relatively expensive, alternative to standard hotels are the castle hotels (Kástely hotel) which are usually beautifully situated and often still have their "socialist" furnishings. They are in the former residences and estates of the Hungarian nobility (Szirak Castle near Gyöngyós, Seregélyes Castle near Székesfehérvár, Nagycenk Castle near Sopron, etc.)

Castle hotels

In 1993 prices in Budapest hotels for a double room with bath (normally including breakfast) were:

Prices

```
***** £190–£290
**** £165–£210
*** £50–£105
** £25– £60
```

Quite often prices within a particular category show considerable variations. Generally prices are similar to those in hotels in central Europe.

In the main season (and in Budapest at any time of the year) hotel rooms should be booked in advance; for large hotels or hotel chains this is best done directly with the main booking office of the group:

Reservations

Danubius, Martinelli tér, H–1052 Budapest; tel. 117–36 52
Hungar-Hotels, Petőfi Sándor utca 16, H–1052 Budapest; tel. 118–30 18
Pannonia, Kigyó utca 4/6. H–1052 Budapest; tel. 118–36 58
Taverna, Váci utca 20, H–1052 Budapest; tel. 118–72 78

The cheapest overnight accommodation, usually below £8 per night, can be found in inns, most of which are situated in the mountainous parts of the country. However, the standard of comfort in these inns sometimes leaves a lot to be desired (dormitories, bunk beds, one shower on each floor, etc.) During the summer vacation student accommodation in university towns is often converted into youth hostels.

Inexpensive accommodation

Information can be obtained from the Association for Village Tourism, 1126 Budapest XII., Szoboszlai utca 2/4; tel. 155–53 33

Farm holidays

See Camping
See Holiday Accommodation
See Young People's Accommodation

Other accommodation

Hotels

Hotel Selection

<table>
<tr><td>

Budapest
*****Hotels

</td><td>

Atrium Hyatt Budapest, 1051 Budapest V., Roosevelt tér 2; tel. 138–30 00
Duna Inter-Continental 1052 Budapest V., Apáczai Csere János utca 4; tel. 117–51 22
Grand Hotel Corvinus Kempinski Budapest, 1051 Budapest V., Erzsébet tér 7/9; tel. 226–10 00
Budapest Hilton, 1041 Budapest I., Hess András tér 1/3; tel. 175 10 00
Thermal Hotel Margitziget (Margaret Island); tel. 111–10 10

</td></tr>
<tr><td>

****Hotels

</td><td>

Buda Penta, 1013 Budapest I., Krisztina körút 41/43; tel. 156 63 33
Dunapart Sállodahajó (ship hotel on Danube bank), 1011 Budapest I., Szilágyi Dezső tér, Alsó rakpart; tel. 155–9001
Flamenco Occidental, 1113 Budapest XI., Tax vezér utca 7; tel. 161–22 50
Forum, 1052 Budapest V., Apáczai Cs. J. u. 12; tel. 117–80 88
Gellért, 1111 Budapest XI., Szent Gellért tér 1; tel. 185–22 00
Grand Hotel Hungaria, 1074 Budapest VII., Rákóczi út 90; tel. 122–90 50
Korona, 1053 Budapest VII., Rákóczi út 90; tel. 117–41 11
Novotel Budapest, 1121 Budapest XII., Alkotás utca 63/67; tel. 186 95 88
Olympia, 1121 Budapest XII., Eötvös út 40; tel. 156–8011
Panoráma, 1121 Budapest XII., Rege utca 21; tel. 175–05 22
Ramada Grand, Margitsziget (Margaret Island); tel. 111–1000
Grand Hotel Royal, Budapest VII., Erzsébet körút 47/49; tel. 153–3133
Thermal Hotel Aquincum, 1036 Budapest III., Árpád fejedelem útja 94; tel. 188–63 60
Thermal Hotel Helia, 1133 Budapest XIII., Kárpát utca 62/64; tel. 129–86 50
Victoria, 1011 Budapest I., Bem Rakart 11; tel. 201–86 44

</td></tr>
<tr><td>

***Hotels

</td><td>

Aero Hotel, 1091 Budapest IX., Ferde utca 1/3; tel. 127–46 90
Alba, 1011 Budapest I., Apor Péter utca 3; tel. 175 92 44
Astoria, 1053 Budapest VI., Kossuth Lajor utca 19; tel. 177–34 11
Benczúr, 1068 Budapest VI., Benczúr utca 35; tel. 142–79 70
Budapest Hotel, 1026 Budapest II., Szilágyi Erzsébet fasor 47; tel. 202–00 44
Emke, 1072 Budapest VII., Akácfa utca 1/3; tel. 122–92 30
Erzsébet, 1053 Budapest V., Károlyi Mihály utca 11/15; tel. 138–2111
Expo Hotel, 1101 Budapest X., Albertsirsai út 10; tel. 184–21 30
Hunor, 1039 Budapest III., Pümkösdfürdő utca 40; tel. 180–09 49
Liget, 1068 Budapest VI., Dózsay Gyorgy út 106; tel. 111–3200
Normafa, 1121 Budapest XII., Eötvös út 53/54; tel. 165–34 44
Orion, 1013 Budapest I., Döbrentei utca 13; tel. 156–89 33
Rege, 1021 Budapest II., Pálos utca 2; tel. 176–73 11
Regina Hotel Budapest, 1223 Budapest XXII., Művelődés utca 21/27; tel. 226–63 44
Rubin Apartman Hotel, 1118 Budapest XI., Dayka Gábor utca 3; tel. 166–68 11
Stadion, 1148 Budapest XIV., Ifjúság útja 1/3; tel. 251–22 22
Taverna, 1052 Budapest V., Váci utca 20; tel. 138–49 99
Volga, 1134 Budapest XIII., Dózsa György út 65; tel. 129–02 00

</td></tr>
<tr><td>

**Hotels

</td><td>

Csalogány Hotel Buda Center, 1027 Budapest II., Csalogány utca 23; tel. 201 78 43
Danubius Sport, 1138 Budapest XIII., Váci út 185; tel. 129–76 63
Eravis, 1114 Budapest XI., Bartók Béla út 152; tel. 166 72 76
Gulliver, 1135 Budapest XIII., Békeút 26; tel. 131–95 70
Ifjúság, 1024 Budapest II., Zivatar utca 1/3; tel. 115–42 60
Minol, 1039 Budapest III., Batthyány utca 45; tel. 180–07 77
Platánus, 1087 Budapest VIII., Könyves Kálmán körút 44; tel. 113–50 14
Római, 1039 Budapest III., Szent János u. 16; tel. 188–6167
Sport Hotel, 1038 Budapest III., Márton utca 25; tel. 180–36 31
Studium, 1108 Budapest X., Harmat utca 129; tel. 147–41 47
Számalk, 1115 Budapest XI., Etele út 68; tel. 166–93 77
Tusculanum, 1031 Budapest III., Záhony utca 10; tel. 188–7673

</td></tr>
</table>

Ventura, 1119 Budapest XI., Fehérvári út 179; tel. 181–07 58
Wien, 1118 Budapest XI., Budaörsi út 88/90; tel. 166–54 00

Citadella, 1118 Budapest I., Citadella sétány; tel. 166–57 94   *Hotels
Csillaghegyi Strand, 1038 Budapest III., Pusztakúti út 3; tel. 168–40 12
Épitök Sport Club Hotel, 1101 Budapest X., Vajda Péter utca 38/42; tel.
113–90 35
Lidó, 1031 Budapest III., Nánáse út 67; tel. 188–6865
Touring Hotel, 1039 Budapest III., Pünkösdfürdő utca 38; tel. 180–31–84

Agárd Hotel*, 2484 Argárd, Akácfa utca ; tel. 22–55–016   Agárd

Cseppkö*, 3759 Aggtelek; telex: 63–13 31   Aggtelek

Duna*, 6500 Baja, Szentháromság tér 6; tel. 79–23–224   Baja
Sugovica***, 6500 Baja, Petőfi-sziget; tel. 79–21 755

Pirat Hotel***, 8220 Balatonalmádi, Neptun utca 15; tel. 80–39–150   Balatonalmádi

Neptun***, 8623 Balatonföldvár, Park; tel. 84–40–388   Balatonföldvár

Annabella***, 8230 Balatonfüred, Beloiannisz utca 25; tel. 86–42–222   Balatonfüred
Margaréta***, 8230 Balatonfüred, Széchenyi utca 29; tel. 86–43–824
Marina***, 8230 Balatonfüred, Széchenyi utca 26; tel. 86–43–644

Tó Motel*, 2653 Bánk, Petőfi út 73   Bánk

Boróka***, 7570 Barcs, Bajcsy-Zsilinszky út 39   Barcs

Touring Hotel**, 5309 Berekfürdő. Berek tér 13; tel. 59–11–666   Berekfürdő

Fiume***, 5600 Békéscsaba, István király tér 2; tel. 66–28–250   Békéscsaba

Thermal Hotel Bük****, 9740 Bükfürdő; tel. 94–58–500   Bükfürdő

Gabona**, 3557 Bükkszentkereszt; tel. 46–92–915   Bükkszentkereszt
Galyateto**, 3234 Galyatető, Kodály Zoltán sétány 10; tel. 37–76–011

Korona Motel***, 9300 Csorna, Felszabadulás utca 1   Csorna

Aranybika***, 4025 Debrecen, Piac utca 11/15; tel. 52–16–777   Debrecen
Civis***, 4025 Debrecen, Kálvin tér 4; tel. 52–18–522
Thermal Hotel, 4025 Debrecen, Nagyerdei körút 9/11; tel. 52–11–888

Arany Csillag***, 2400 Dunaújváros, Vasmü út 39; tel. 25–10–044   Dunaújváros

Eger****, 3300 Eger, Szálloda utca 1/3; tel. 36–13–233   Eger
Flóra***, 3300 Eger, Fürdőutca 5; tel. 36–20–211
Senator-Ház***, 3300 Eger, Dobó Tér 11; tel. 36–20–466

Esztergom Hotel***, 2500 Esztergom, Primás sziget; tel. 33–12–883   Esztergom
Fürdő Hotel**, 2500 Esztergom, Pázmány Péter út 14; tel. 33–11–688

Kastély*, 9421 Fertőrákos, Fő út 153; tel. 99–12–376   Fertorákos

Varsa**, 2483 Gárdony, Holdfény sétány 13; tel. 22–55–110   Gárdony

Mátra***, 3200 Gyöngyös, Mátyás király utca 2; tel. 37–12–057   Gyöngyös

Rába***, 9021 Győr, Árpád utca 34; tel. 96–15–533   Győr
Klastrom***, 9021 Győr, Zechmeister utca 1; tel. 96–15–611

Aranykereszt***, 5700 Gyula, Eszperantó tér 1; tel. 66–62–144   Gyula

Hotels

Hajdúszoboszió	Délibáb***, 4200 Hajdúszoboszió, József Attila utca 4; tel. 52–62–366
Harkány	Siesta Club Hotel***, 7815 Harkány, Kossuth Lajos utca 17; tel. 72–80–611 Dráva**, 7815 Harkány, Bartók utca 3; tel. 72–80–434
Héviz	Thermalhotel Aqua****, 8380 Héviz, Kossuth Lajos u. 13–15; tel. 82–18–947 Hotel Termál Héviz, 8380 Héviz; tel. 82–11–090
Hódmexővásar-hely	Fáma**, 6800 Hódmexovásarhely, Szeremlei utca 7; tel. 64–44–444
Jászberény	Touring Hotel**, 5100 Jászberény, Serház utca 3; tel. 57–12–051
Kalocsa	Béta Hotel***, 6300 Kalocsa, Szentháromság tér 4; tel. 64–61–244
Kecskemét	Aranyhomok***, 6000 Kecskemét, Széchenyi tér 3; tel. 76–20–011 Három Gúnár***, 6000 Kecskemét, Batthyány utca 11; tel. 76–27–077 Szauna***, 6000 Kecskemét, Sport utca 3; tel. 76–28–700
Keszthely	Helikon***, 8360 Keszthely, Balaton-part 5; tel. 82–81–944 Phönix**, 8360 Keszthely, Balaton-part 3; tel. 82–12–630
Kiskunhalas	Csipke**, 6400 Kiskunhalas, Semmelweis tér 16; tel. 77–21–455
Lillafüred	Palota*, 3517 Lillafüred, Erzsébet sétány 1; tel. 46–54–255
Mátrafüred	Avar***, 3232 Mátrafüred, Parádi utca 5; tel. 37–13–195
Mátraháza	Bérc Hotel Mátra***, 3233 Mátraháza; tel. 37–74–095
Miskolc	Pannonia***, 3525 Miskolc, Kossuth utca 2; tel. 46–16–434
Miskolctapolca	Juno***, 3519 Miskolctapolca, Csabai utca 2/4; tel. 46–64–133 Park Motel, 3519 Miskolctapolca, Bak Dénes utca 4; tel. 46–60–811
Moson-magyaróvár	Szent István Hotel, 9200 Mosonmagyaróvár; tel. 98–13–011
Noszvaj	De la Motte Kastély Hotel (castle hotel)*, 3325 Noszvaj, Dobó utca 10; tel. 36–12–419
Nyíregyháza	Szabolcs Jorona**, 4400 Nyíregyháza, Dózsa György út 1/3; tel. 42–12–333
Orosháza	Alföld***, 5900 Nyíregyháza, Szabadság tér 12; tel. 68–12–166
Pécs	Mediterrán***, 7627 Pécs, Dömörkapu; tel. 72–15–987 Palatinus***, 7621 Pécs, Király u. 5; tel. 72–33–022 Pannonia***, 7621 Pécs, Rákócai út 31; tel. 72–13–322
Pécsvárad	István király Hotel**, 7720 Pécsvárad, Vár utca 45; tel. 72–27–577
Ráckeve	Savoyai Kastély*, 2300 Ráckeve, Kossuth Lajor u. 95; tel. 25–85–253
Salgótarján	Karancs***, 3100 Salgótarján, Fő tér 21; tel. 32–10–088
Sárospatak	Bodrog**, 3950 Sárospatak, Rákóczi út 58; tel. 41–11–744
Sárvár	Thermal Hotel Sárvár****, 9600, Rákóczi út; tel. 94–23–999
Seregélyes	Taurus Kastély Hotel***, 8111 Seregélyes, Zichy-Hadfik Kastély; tel. 22–65–030
Siófok	Európa***, 8600 Siófok, Petőfi sétány 15; tel. 84–13–411 Hungária***, 8600 Siófok, Petőfi sétány 13; tel. 84–10–677

Taurus country-house hotel in Seregélyes

Ezüstpart Hotel**, 8600 Siófok, Liszt Ferenc sétány 3; tel. 84–13–622
Vénusz**, 8600 Siófok, Kinizsi utca 12; tel. 84–10–660

Lövér***, 9400 Sopron, Várisi utca 4; tel. 99–11–061   Sopron
Palatinus***, 9400 Sopron, Új utca 23; tel. 99–11–395
Solar Club Hotel***, 9400 Sopron, Panoráma út 16; tel. 99–11–675

Vár Hotel*, 8330 Sümeg, Vak Bottyán utca 2   Sümeg

Hungaria***, 6721 Szeged, Marcos utca 1; tel. 62–21–211   Szeged
Royal**, 6720 Szeged, Kölcsey utca 1/3; tel. 62–12–911

Alba Regia***, 8000 Székesfehérvár, Rákóczi utca 1; tel. 22–13–484   Székesfehérvár
Arév*, 8000 Székesfehérvár, József utca 42; tel. 22–27–051

Alisca**, 7100 Szekszárd, Kálvária utca 1; tel. 74–11–242   Szekszárd
Gemenc***, 7100 Szekszárd, Mészáros L. utca 2; tel. 74–11–722

Danubius Hotel Ister**, 2000 Szentendre, Ady Endre utca 28; tel.   Szentendre
26–12–511

Doimolos Kastély Hotel***, 7900 Szigetvár, Pf. 108; tel. 70–11–222   Szigetvár

Kastély Hotel***, 3044 Szirák, Petőfi utca 26   Szirák

Pelikán***, 5000 Szolnok, Jászkürt utca 1; tel. 56–43–855   Szolnok
Tisza***, 5000 Szolnok, Tiszapark 2; tel. 56–31–155

Claudius****, 9700 Szombathely, Bartók Béla körút 39; tel. 94–13–760 Szombathely

Gabriella*, 8300 Tapolca, Batsányi tér; tel. 87–12–642   Tapolca

Information

Tata	Kristály***, 2890 Tata, Ady Endre utca 22; tel. 34–80–577
Tatabánya	Árpád Hotel***, 2800 Tatabánya, Felszabadulás tér 20; tel. 34–10–357
Veszprém	Veszprém Hotel***, 8200 Veszprém, Budapest út 6; tel. 80–24–876
Visegrád	Silvanus***, 2025 Visegrád, Fekete-hegy; tel. 26–28–311
Zalaegerszeg	Aranybárány***, 8900 Zalaegerszeg, Széchenyi tér 1; tel. 92–14–100
Zalakaros	Liget Hotel**, 8749 Zalakaros, Gyógyfürdőtér 6; tel. 93–18–105
Zamárdi	Hotel Familia Zamárdi****, 8612 Zamárdi, Endrédi utca 1/2; tel. 84–31–350

Information

Great Britain	Danube Travel Limited, Central Agent IBUSZ Hungary, 6 Conduit Street, London W1R 9TG Tel: (071) 493 0263
United States	IBUSZ Hungarian Travel Limited, Suite 520, 630 Fifth Avenue, Rockefeller Center, New York, NY 10020 Tel: (212) 582 7412; toll free 800/367–7878

Information in Hungary

Budapest	Hungarian Tourist Office, Vigad u. 6, H–1051 Budapest, IV floor; tel. 1–118–07 50, Fax 1–118–52 41
	Tourinform, Sütő utca 2, H–1052 Budapest; tel. 1–117–98 00 (postal address: Box 185, H–1364 Budapest), Fax 1–117–95 78
	Dunatours, Bajcsy-Zsilinszky út 17, H–1065 Budapest; tel. 1–131–45 33, Fax 1–111–68 27
	Hungarotours Akácfa u. 20, H–1072 Budapest; tel. 1–141–38 89, Fax 1–122–74 53
Balaton	Balaton Administrative Commission of the Hungarian Tourist Office, Blaha Lujza u. 2, H–8230 Balatonfüred; tel. 86–42–801
Békéscsaba	Békéstourist, Andrássy u. 10, H–5600 Békéscsaba; tel./Fax 66–23–448
Debrecen	Hajdútourist, Kálvin tér 2a, H–4026 Debrecen; tel. 52–15–588, Fax 52–19–616
Eger	Heves Tourist, Szarvas tér, H–3300 Eger; tel. 36–11–225, Fax 36–10 639
Győr	Ciklámen Tourist, Jókai u. 12, H–9021 Győr; tel./Fax 96–16–050
Kecskemét	Puszta Tourist, Szabadság tér 2, H–6000 Kecskemét; tel. 76–29–499
Közép – Dunavidék	Administrative Commission of the Hungarian Tourist Office Közép – Dunavidék (Middle Danube), Múzeum u. 11, H–1088 Budapest; tel. 1–138–48 18
Közép – Tiszavidék	Administrative Commission of the Hungarian Tourist Office Közép – Tiszavidék (Middle Tisza), Kossuth tér 1, H–5350 Tiszafüred; tel. 58–11–753
Mátra – Bükk	Administrative Commission of the Hungarian Tourist Office Mátra – Bükk, Deák u. 11, H–3300 Eger; tel./Fax 36–12–564

Borsod Tourist, Széchenyi út 35, H–3525 Miskolc; tel. 46–350–645, Fax 46–350–617   Miskolc

Nyírtourist, Dózsa György ut 3, H–4400 Nyíregyháza; tel. 42–11–544, Fax 42–13–546   Nyíregyháza

Mecsek Tourist, Széchenyi tér 9, H–7621 Pécs; tel. 72–13–300, Fax 72–14–866   Pécs

Nógrád Tourist, Erzsébet tér 3, H–3100 Salgótarján; tel. 32–10–660   Salgótarján

Siótour, Batthyány u. 2b, H–8600 Siófok; tel. 84–13–111, Fax 84–10–803   Siófok

Administrative Commission of the Hungarian Tourist Office Sopron – Kőszeghegyalja, Uj u. 4, H–9400 Sopron; tel. 99–11–303   Sopron – Kőszeghegyalja

Szeged Tourist, Victor Hugo u. 1, H–6720 Szeged; tel./Fax 62–11–711   Szeged

Albatours, Szabadság tér 6, H–8001 Székesfehérvár; tel. 22–12–494, Fax 22–27–082   Székesfehérvár

Tolna Tourist, Széchenyi út 38, H–7100 Szekszárd; tel. 74–12–144, Fax 74–15–252   Szekszárd

Tiszatour, Verseghy Park 8, H–5000 Szolnok; tel. 56–37–502, Fax 56–41–441   Szolnok

Svarian Tourist, Hollán E. u. 1, H–9700 Szombathely; tel. 94–12–348   Szombathely

Komtourist, Ady Endre u. 24, H–2890, Tata; tel. 34–83–211, Fax 34–80–694   Tata

Administrative Commission of the Hungarian Tourist Office Velencei-tó, Tópart u. 17, H–2484 Agárd; tel. 22–55–051   Velence Lake

Balatontourist, Kossuth Lajos u. 21, H–8200 Veszprém; tel. 80–26–277, Fax 80–26–072   Veszprém

Zalatour, Kovács Károly tér 1, H–8900 Zalaegerszeg; tel. 92–11–443, Fax 92–11–469   Zalaegerszeg

Insurance

It is essential to take out short-term health and accident insurance when visiting Hungary. It is also advisable to have baggage insurance. Arrangements can be made through a travel agent or insurance company; many companies organising package holidays now include insurance as part of the deal.

See also Medical Assistance

Language

Visitors will have little difficulty in making themselves understood in Budapest, for a knowledge of foreign languages is a traditional part of general education, especially as Hungarian is a language which is understood by relatively few non-Hungarians and does not figure among the recognised international languages. German is widely understood in Hungary and many young people also speak quite good English.   Foreign languages

Hungarian belongs to the Finno-Ugrian family and therefore has a special place in Europe. The varying pronunciation of consonants and vowels will cause difficulty for the uninitiated.   Hungarian

Language

In Hungarian the first syllable is the one always stressed.

The alphabet and its pronunciation

Approximate equivalent in English
a = short open o (as in hot)
á = long a (as in calm)
c = ts (as in bits)
cs = ch (as in chat)
e = short e (as in bet)
é = long e (as the ai in fair)
gy = i (as adieu in French)
i = short i (as in bit)
í = long i (as the ee in breeze)
ly = sound of a voiced y (as in yes)
ny = gn (as in Cognac)
o = short o (as in hot)
ó = long o (as in mow)
ö = short o (as the e in the)
ő = long o (as the u in fur)
s = sh (as in show)
sz = sharp z (as the se in purse)
ty = ch (as in chance)
u = short u (as in butter)
ú = long u (as the oo in boot)
ü = short u (as in hue)
ű = long u (as in French tu)
v = v (as in very)
z = voiced z (as in buzz)
zs = voiced j (as in judge)

Numbers

0	null, zéró, semmi	20	húsz
1	egy	21	huszonegy
2	kettő, két	30	harminc
3	három	40	negyven
4	négy	50	ötven
5	öt	60	hatvan
6	hat	70	hetve
7	hét	80	nyolcvan
8	nyolc	90	ilencven
9	kilenc	100	száz
10	tiz	200	kétszáz
11	tizenegy	1000	ezer
12	tizenkettő		

Days of the week

English	Hungarian	English	Hungarian
Monday	hétfő	Friday	péntek
Tuesday	kedd	Saturday	szombat
Wednesday	szerda	Sunday	vasárnap
Thursday	csütörtök	Holiday	ünnep

Important words and phrases

English	Hungarian
accommodation	szállas
address	cim
airport	repülőgép
autumn	ősz
bed	ágy
bill	számla
blue	kék
boat	csónak
bread	kenyér
bridge	hid
café	kávéház

English	Hungarian
castle	kastély
closed	zárva
day	nap
departure	indulás
diversion	terelőút
doctor	orvos
door	ajtó
early closing day	szimnap
east	kelet
embassy (consulate)	követség
emergency exit	vészkijárat
entrance	bejárat
evening	este
exchange	pénzváltás
exit	kijárat
express train	gyorsvonat
filling station	benzinkút
first-aid	elsősegély
free	szabad
frontier	határ
German	németül
Goodbye	viszontlatasra
Good day	jó napot
Good evening	jó estét
Good morning	jó reggelt
help, assistance	segitség
hill	domb
hour, clock	óra
How much?	mennyi?
How much is that?	mennyibe kerül
Hungary	Magyarország
I (don't) understand	(nem) értem
information	Információ, felvilágositás
inn	vendéglő
island	sziget
lake, pond	tó
left	balra
letter	lévél
look out!	vigyázat!
luggage	poggyász
Madam (addressing a lady)	asszony
May I?	megengedi?
milk	tej
name	név
night	éjszaka
no parking	várakozni tilos!
north	észak
pardon	pardon!
pâtisserie	cukrászada
play street	játszótca
please	kérem
polics	rendőrség
post office	Posta
prohibited	tilos!
railway	vasút
red	piros
restaurant	etterem
right	jobbra
road, street	utca, út
road works	útjavitás
room	szoba

Language

English	Hungarian
shop, store	aruház
Sir (addressing a gentleman)	úr
south	dél
spring	tavasz
station	állomás, pályaudvár
storey	emelet
summer	nyár
telegram	távirat
Thank you	köszönöm
tip	borravaló
toilet (gentleman)	urak, Férfiak
toilet (ladies)	nők
town	város
tram	villamos
village	falu
water	viz
weather	időjárás
week	hét
west	nyugat
What is that?	mi ez?
When?	mikor?
Where?	hol?
white	fehér
wine bar	borozó
wine vault	borpince
winter	tél
year	év
yellow	sárga
yesterday	tegnap

Markets

Markets have had a long tradition in Hungary. In all the large towns there are one or more covered or open-air markets, where on weekdays from 6am to 5pm local horticultural and agricultural produce is on sale. In the warmer times of the year the stalls are loaded with vegetables, fruit, fish, meat, bread, cakes and pastries.

In addition skilled country women offer for sale colouful homemade table-cloths, blouses, gaily painted goose-eggs, carved cooking spoons and basketwork, together with herbal remedies, propolis (bee-glue) and "eau-de-vie".

Well-known Markets

Markets in Budapest

Central Market Hall (Központi Vásárcsarnok; IX District, by the Freedom Bridge, Vámház kórút 1–3), a unique and popular Budapest institution which has existed for almost 100 years.

Market place in the Közraktár utca (IX District)

Market on the Lehel tér (XII District), the largest and busiest Budapest market square (also open on Sundays).

Budapest Flea Market (Ecseri), XIX District, Nagykőrösi út 156, open: Mon.–Fri. 8am–4pm, Sat. 8am–3pm.

Other Budapest markets worth visiting:
Fény utca (II District); Fehérvári út (XI District); Klauzál tér (VII District); Rákóczi tér (VIII District); Batthyány tér (I District)

Folklore Markets

In the castle district of Buda (May); Szentendre; Őriszentpeter (last week-end in June); Badacsony (weekends in July and August); Hortobágy (market by the Nine-arched Bridge, Aug.)

Christmas Market

See Events

Medical Assistance

Budapest: tel. 04
Outside Budapest: tel. 004

First-aid and, in an emergency, an ambulance are in principle available without charge. Further treatment (including examination and hospital treatment) are chargeable.
In Budapest and in other large towns the services of a doctor are provided 24 hours a day. The relevant address can be obtained from information offices or from hotel reception desks.

Medical help

Before going to Hungary visitors are advised to contact their insurance company to ascertain what protection is available in Hungary. In general it is advisable to take out a personal medical and accident policy for the duration of the visit.

Insurance

Motoring

Hungary has some 30,000km/18,600 miles of well-engineered roads. All motorways and major traffic arteries radiate from Budapest.

Breakdowns

On the principal highways in Hungary, and particularly in the Budapest area, the Hungarian Automobile Club (Magyar Autóklub) has breakdown service points.

Up until now emergency telephones have only existed on the M 7 motorway. Members of the AA can obtain assistance from the emergency telephone centre of the the Hungarian Automobile Club (Magyar Autóklub MAK); tel. 1–135–3317 (English spoken). New independent breakdown services include: Hungaria tel. 1–189–1203; Budasegély tel. 1–188–6201; Start tel. 1–169–7495 and Toman tel. 1–147–5594. The Hungarian Automobile Club (Magyar Autóklub), Rómer Flóris utca 4/a, H–1277 Budapest; tel. 1–155 1220.

Emergency calls

The breakdown service can be contacted daily by telephone between 8am and 6pm (in summer until 8pm on busy roads). A 24–hour service operates from June 1st until September 15th.

Breakdown service

Budapest: tel. 1–252–80 00 (24–hour service)
Baja: tel. 79–129–17
Debrecen: tel. 52–145–67
Dunaújváros: tel. 25–182–39
Esztergom: tel. 33–119–06
Győr: tel. 96–179–00
Kaposvár: tel. 82–192–32
Kecskemét: tel. 76–201–59
Miskolc: tel. (46) 848–44
Mosonmagyaróvár: tel. 88–157–08
Nyíregyháza: tel. (42) 133–13
Pécs: tel. 72–127–38
Sopron: tel. 99–113–52
Szeged: tel. 62–261–66
Szekszárd: tel. 74–156–30
Tatabáya: tel. 334–117–09

Breakdown
telephone
numbers

Motoring

Emergency calls
(Segélykáro lap)

Assistance in the event of a breakdown can also be obtained with the use of so-called emergency cards, obtainable at the frontier or from a nearby filling-station. A driver suffering a breakdown can give a completed card to a passing motorist who will deliver it to the nearest emergency breakdown point.

Hitch-hiking

Hitch-hiking is permitted in Hungary, but not on motorways or their feeder roads. Hitch-hikers should, however, beware of assault, theft and similar risks.

Roads

Motorways

M 1 Budapest–Tatabánya
M 3 Budapest–Gyöngyös
M 5 Budapest–Örkény
M 7 Budapest–Balaton

Main Roads

N 1 Budapest–Tatabánya–Győr–Hegyeshalom
Nr 2 Budapest–Vác–Parassapuszta
Nr 3 Budapest–Gyöngyös–Miskolc–Tornyosnémeti
Nr 4 Budapest–Szolnok–Debrecen–Záhony
Nr 5 Budapest–Kecskemét–Szeged–Röszke
Nr 6 Budapest–Szekszárd–Pécs–Barcs
Nr 7 Budapest–Székesfehérvár–Siófok–Nagykanizsa–Letenye
Nr 8 Székesfehérvár–Veszprém–Körmend–Rábafüzes

Road signs

Road signs in Hungary correspond to those in most western European countries. Time-saving diversions around Budapest and other large towns are indicated by a sign with TIR in black on an orange ground.

Kilometer	Balatonfüred	Békéscsaba	Budapest	Bugac	Debrecen	Dunaújváros	Eger	Esztergom	Fertőd	Győr	Hajdúszoboszló	Harkány	Hegyeshalom	Hortobágy	Kecskemét	Keszthely	Kőszeg	Miskolc	Mohács	Parassapuszta	Pécs	Siófok	Sopron	Szeged	Székesfehérvár	Szekszárd	Szolnok	Szombathely	Tata	Veszprém
Balatonfüred	•	300	125	222	351	117	251	165	134	97	330	199	148	309	176	66	149	303	181	204	173	26	162	248	67	135	223	130	130	19
Békéscsaba	300	•	202	128	130	211	199	248	386	326	127	299	377	169	124	357	436	228	243	279	283	280	413	94	264	233	104	405	276	293
Budapest	125	202	•	131	226	69	126	46	184	124	205	223	175	184	85	182	234	178	189	79	197	105	211	172	62	143	98	228	74	116
Bugac	222	128	131	•	237	133	204	177	315	255	216	242	306	225	46	279	346	275	186	210	226	202	342	77	181	176	109	327	205	215
Debrecen	351	130	226	237	•	278	125	272	410	350	21	394	401	39	191	408	460	98	360	268	368	331	437	224	288	314	128	454	300	342
Dunaújváros	117	211	69	133	278	•	195	115	199	139	257	158	190	266	87	176	231	247	124	148	132	99	226	159	52	78	150	212	131	100
Eger	251	199	126	204	125	195	•	172	310	250	134	349	301	86	158	308	360	63	315	168	323	231	337	216	188	269	95	354	200	242
Esztergom	165	248	46	177	272	115	172	•	151	91	251	269	142	230	131	228	201	224	235	87	243	151	178	218	108	189	144	196	48	146
Fertőd	134	386	184	315	410	199	310	151	•	60	389	298	78	368	269	126	42	362	289	242	272	160	30	256	147	243	282	61	120	115
Győr	97	326	124	255	350	139	250	91	60	•	329	266	51	308	209	141	110	302	234	203	240	119	87	296	87	188	222	105	60	78
Hajdúszoboszló	330	127	205	216	21	257	134	251	389	329	•	373	380	60	170	387	439	119	326	277	347	309	416	228	267	293	107	433	279	321
Harkány	199	299	223	242	394	158	349	269	298	266	373	•	317	382	203	172	283	401	56	302	26	147	322	205	181	88	266	264	260	192
Hegyeshalom	148	377	175	306	401	190	301	142	78	51	380	317	•	359	260	186	117	353	285	254	291	170	105	347	138	239	273	123	111	129
Hortobágy	309	169	184	225	30	266	86	230	368	308	60	382	359	•	179	366	418	114	335	229	356	289	395	237	246	302	116	412	258	300
Kecskemét	176	124	85	46	191	87	158	131	269	209	170	203	260	179	•	233	300	200	156	164	177	156	296	87	116	123	63	281	159	169
Keszthely	66	357	182	279	408	176	308	228	126	141	387	172	186	366	233	•	120	360	186	261	146	77	135	305	133	177	280	101	196	85
Kőszeg	149	436	234	346	460	231	360	201	42	110	439	283	117	418	300	120	•	412	297	313	257	176	51	372	179	259	332	19	170	130
Miskolc	303	228	178	275	98	247	63	224	362	302	119	401	353	114	200	360	412	•	356	223	375	283	389	258	240	221	137	406	252	294
Mohács	181	243	189	186	360	124	315	235	289	234	326	56	285	335	156	186	297	356	•	268	40	137	316	149	147	46	219	278	228	174
Parassapuszta	204	279	79	210	268	148	168	87	242	203	277	302	254	229	164	261	313	223	268	•	276	184	290	251	141	222	175	307	153	195
Pécs	173	283	197	226	368	132	323	243	272	240	347	26	291	356	177	146	257	375	40	276	•	121	296	189	155	62	240	238	234	166
Siófok	26	280	105	202	331	99	231	151	160	119	309	147	170	289	147	77	176	283	137	184	121	•	187	228	47	91	203	157	128	45
Sopron	162	413	211	342	437	226	370	171	35	91	416	322	105	395	296	135	51	389	316	290	296	187	•	381	174	270	309	80	141	119
Szeged	248	94	172	77	224	159	216	218	256	296	228	205	347	237	87	305	372	258	149	251	189	228	381	•	207	139	121	253	246	241
Székesfehérvár	67	264	62	181	288	52	188	108	147	87	267	181	138	246	116	133	179	240	147	141	155	47	174	207	•	101	160	160	79	48
Szekszárd	135	233	143	176	314	78	269	189	243	188	293	88	239	302	123	177	259	221	46	222	62	91	270	139	101	•	186	240	182	128
Szolnok	223	104	98	109	128	150	95	144	282	222	107	266	273	116	63	280	332	137	219	175	240	203	309	121	160	186	•	326	172	214
Szombathely	130	405	228	327	454	212	354	196	61	105	433	264	123	412	281	101	19	406	278	307	238	157	80	353	160	240	326	•	165	111
Tata	130	276	74	205	300	131	200	48	120	60	279	260	111	258	159	196	170	252	228	153	234	128	141	246	79	182	172	165	•	111
Veszprém	19	293	116	215	342	190	242	146	115	78	321	192	129	300	169	85	130	294	174	195	166	45	142	241	48	128	214	111	111	•

See below

Budapest area: Fővinform; tel. 1–117–11 73, 1–117–82 86 (24–hour service); cross-country routes: Útinform; tel. 1–122–70 52, 1–122–76 43 (24–hour service).

Safety on the Road

Visitors taking their own vehicles to Hungary should have them properly serviced before leaving home.

However careful a driver may be, an accident can happen at any time. In such circumstances it pays to keep a cool head and take the following actions:

1 Switch on hazard lights; set a warning triangle at a reasonable distance behind the vehicle.

2 Attend to any injured person and if necessary send for an ambulance.

3 In Hungary every accident must be notified to the Police.

4 Note the names, addresses of all other persons involved; note the make and number as well as insurance details of any other vehicle involved. The time and place of the accident must also be noted.

5 Obtain, if possible, the names and addresses of any witnesses. Make sketches of the situation at the place of the accident, or, better still, take pictures of the scene from various angles.

6 Notify the insurance office given on your "green card" and obtain details of the insurance cover of third parties. On no account admit liability or sign any document written in a language which you do not understand.

7 Claim for repairs on your own insurance policy and notify the company if any claim is made against you. If the vehicle is completely wrecked the customs authorities must be informed.

Traffic Regulations

A national driving licence, the vehicle registration document and the "green insurance card" must be taken. (An international driving licence is not required.)

Foreign vehicles must be fitted with an oval nationality plate.

In Hungary drivers are forbidden to drink and drive.

Children under 12 years of age may not travel in the front seats of vehicles.

	Motor-ways	Main roads	Other roads	Built-up areas	Speed limits in km per hour
Cars	120	100	80	60	
Motorcycles	120	100	80	50	
Buses	80	70	70	50	
Cars towing	80	70	70	50	
Lorries	80	70	70	50	

A motorcyclist must wear a helmet at all times

Museums

Use of the horn	In populated districts the horn may only be used in an emergency.
Overtaking	Overtaking is forbidden on bends and at road or rail crossings.
Lights	In Hungary fog lamps and other additional lights must either be covered or disconnected. It is obligatory to drive with dipped headlights outside built-up areas in daylight hours

Petrol/Gasoline

Filling Stations	Near frontier posts, along the main traffic arteries and in towns and tourist centres there are plenty of filling stations.
Motor fuel	The following types of motor fuel are available: Super (92 octane), lead-free (95 octane), Extra-Super (98 octane) and Diesel. Note: Normal petrol in Hungary is only 86 octane.
Fuel in containers	It is forbidden to import or export fuel in containers.

Museums

The museums of Hungary are described in some detail in the A to Z section of this guide under the individual place names. Historical and specialised museums are naturally to be found in Budapest, but in other parts of the country there are many galleries, collections of paintings and museums documenting the history, culture and economy of the various regions.

Very popular are the open-air museums and museum-villages each of which presents a living picture of the rich culture of of a particular region of the country (architecture, way of life, economy, folk art, etc.).

Opening times	Most museums are open: Tue.–Sun. 10am–6pm. In the provinces smaller mueums sometimes have different opening hours; visitors should enquire locally.

Music

Hungarian music enjoys a world-wide reputation, to which, in addition to Franz Liszt, a considerable contribution has been made by Ferenc Erkel, Béla Bartók and Zoltán Kódály. In Budapest, but also in provincial towns (including Pécs, Debrecen, Szeged, Keszthely) the musical tradition of the country is highly cherished. A broad and varied programme of events, ranging from serious symphony concerts, through opera and operetta to imaginatively produced musicals, caters for every taste.

For those who like to indulge in traditional music there are in many places folkloric programmes, and stimulating gipsy music (*csárdás*) for dancing. Pop and rock fans will find ample opportunities to enjoy their music, especially in Budapest where numerous well-known groups can be seen and heard.

Concert venues	See Cafés, Casinos, Hotels, Restaurants

National Parks and Protected Areas

About 7% of the land area of Hungary is protected. As well as the National Parks and the planned biosphere reservation around the Fertő Lake (Fertő tó) there are a host of smaller protected areas and nature monuments.

Important Biosphere Reserves

Location: karst land in north-east Hungary. – Founded 1985. – Area 19,700ha/48,679 acres. Special features: dripstone caves, "sea eyes" (almost unspoiled forest); educational trail. For detailed description see Facts and Figures page 93.
Information: National Park Administration, H–3758 Jósvafő, Tengferszem oldal 1; tel. 48–12–700

Aggtelek National Park

Location: Bükk Uplands, north-east Hungary. – Founded 1976. – Area 38,800ha/95,880 acres. Special features: beech forest, about 400 different flowering plants, world-famous Lippizaner stud in Szilvásvárad; open-air museum of forest history; botanical trail. For detailed description see A to Z, Bükk Uplands.
Information: National Park Administration, H–3300 Eger, Sánc. u. 6 (Felnémet); tel. 36–12–791

Bükk National Park

Location: East Hungarian steppe region. – Founded 1972. – Total area of the various sections 52,000ha/1,228,492 acres.
Special features: flora and fauna of the Hungarian steppes; life and economic systems of the Puszta shepherds (csikos, csárdas); folkloric presentations in the holiday season. For detailed description see A to Z, Hortobágy.
Information: National Park Administration, H–4024 Debrecen, Sumen u. 2; tel./Fax 52–10–645

Hortobágy National Park

Location: Interfluvial area between Danube and Tisza. – Founded 1975. Total area of the various sections 30,600ha/75,613 acres.
Special features: bird sanctuary (especially great bustards); puszta (typical life and economic systems, especially in the Bugac puszta); typical Hungarian domestic animals such as grey cattle, Racka sheep, Mangaliza (woolly) pigs, dappled cockerel and crossbred horses. Riding schools, horses and carts, shepherds' museum. For detailed description see A to Z, Bugac and Kiskunfélegyháza
Information: National Park Administration, H–6001 Kecskemet, Liszt Ferenc u. 19; tel. 76–28–122, Fax 76–20–695.

Kiskunság National Park

As well as the above mentioned National Parks, there are over 150 smaller protected areas, some consisting of several sections or partially integrated biotopes. In the following list there are interesting protected areas, or specially protected places: Badacsony – Tapolca (volcanic cone), Fertő tó

Other Protected Areas

National Parks and Nature Reserves

Aggtelek National Park
Szatmár-Bereg (NR)
Ipolytarnóc (NR)
Hollókő (NR)
Bükk National Park
Pilis (NR)
Neusiedler See (NR)
Köszeg (NR)
Örség (NR)
Tihany (NR)
Szent-Györgyhegy (NR)
Badacsony (NR)
BUDAPEST
Ócsa (NR)
Kiskunsági National Park
Hortobágy National Park
Déványa (NR)
Mágorpuszta (NR)
Gemenc (NR)

NR = Nature Reserve (Protected Area)

© Baedeker

1 Buda (NR)
2 Eagle Hill (NR)
3 Szemiöhegy (NR)
4 Pálgövy Cave (NR)

(bird sanctuary), Gerrecsehégy Forest (near Tata), Hanság (marshy forest, north-west of Győr), Hollókő, Kőszeg, Löver Hills (near Sopron), Mecseg Hills, Örség (Hungarian Switzerland near Őriszentpéter), Pilis Hills, Sashegy (Eagle Mountain) near Budapest, branch of the Tisza at Martély (southern Hungary, near Szeged), Tihany (peninsula in Lake Balaton), Velancei tó (Velance Lake) bird sanctuary; and Visegrád (forest). Also of interest are the transdanubian arboretums of Agostyán (coniferous forests), Alcsút (ancient stands of trees), Jeli (rhododendrons), Szárvás (Altföld; over 1400 trees and bushes, many species of birds).

Information: Ministry of Conservation and Land Development, H–1011 Budapest, Fő u. 44–50; tel. 1–201–41 33, Fax 1–201–24 82.

Newspapers and Magazines

International Press

It is possible to buy some Western newspapers and magazines in shops and in the major hotels. The newspapers *The Times*, *The International Herald Tribune* (Paris edition) and the weekly *Time* and *Newsweek* magazines are available the day after their publication.

English-language publications

A bilingual English-German paper, *The Daily News – Neueste Nachrichten*, is published by the Hungarian news agency MTI and is widely available. There is also a free monthly magazine *Coming Events in Hungary* also with text in English and German and additionally in French. A new Hungarian quarterly in English deals with Hungarian life, culture and politics.

Nightlife

Note

Hungarian nightlife is concentrated in those cities and towns which profit from tourism and business interests. Since the fall of the "iron-curtain" Budapest has made every effort to live up to its title of "Paris of the East". In the capital discos, nightclubs, jazz-cellars, etc. have sprung up and revue theatres and casinos have proliferated.

Further note

See Casinos, Cafés, Hotels, Restaurants

Opening times

See Business Hours

Photography and Films

Films

For some time all popular films (Agfa, Fuji, Kodak, etc.) have been obtainable, but prices tend to be higher than in Great Britain. There are a number of processing laboratories, where films can be developed and printed speedily.

Cameras

Every reputable make of camera can be serviced in Budapest.

Restrictions

Military areas and sensitive military equipment may not be photographed. Normally notices to this effect are displayed.

Police (Predőrség)

The emergency number for the police is "07" throughout Hungary

Post (Posta)

Hungarian post offices are open on weekdays from 8am–4pm. In Budapest post offices at the West Station (Nyugati Pályaudvar) and at the East Station (Keleti Pályaudvar) are open 24 hours a day.

Post offices

The Budapest inner city post office (Belvárosi Postahivatal) in the Pest part of the city (Petőfi Sándor utca 17/19; open Mon.–Fri. 7am–9pm, Sat. 7am–8pm, Sun. 8am–1pm) has an international telephone, Telex and Fax service.

Postcards:		
within the Budapest city area	7 forints	Tariff
to the rest of Hungary and adjoining countries	10 forints	
to other countries	30 forints	

Letters:	
within the Budapest city area	9 forints
to the rest of Hungary and adjoining countries	15 forints
to other countries	40 forints

Registered mail costs an extra 20 forints, express post 26 forints. Airmail letters up to 20 gr. cost 22 forints to adjoining countries and up to 40 forints to other countries.

Stamps can be obtained from post offices and from most places where picture postcards are on sale.

Postage stamps

Letter boxes in Hungary are red and marked with a posthorn.

Letter boxes

Public Holidays

New Year	January 1st
Commemmoration day of Struggle for Freedom 1848	March 15th
Easter Monday	March/April
Labour Day	May 1st
Constitution Day or St Stephan's Day, Festival of New Bread	August 20th
Proclamation of the Republic	October 23rd
Christmas	December 25th–26th

Public Transport

In Budapest public transport comprises the Metro, trams, trolley-buses and buses which operate between 4am and 11pm, with some services throughout the 24 hours. In other towns local transport is generally carried out by bus services.

For cross-country travel the railway and buses play an important part. The Budapest–Danube Bend area is served by passenger ships and hydrofoils of the MAHART line.

Radio and Television (Magyar Rádió és Televizió, MRT)

There are brief bulletins in English broadcast on Budapest radio and television. There are two TV channels, and on Channel 2 imported programmes can sometimes be seen, either in the original language or with English sub-titles.

Railways

The first railway on Hungarian soil was opened in 1846 from Pest to Vác. At the end of 1850 the stretch from Pest to Vienna was completed and eighteen years later the Hungarian State Railways (Magyar Államvasutak – MÁV) came into being.

Now Hungary has a dense network of 7400km/4600 miles. Stretches which are important for international traffic have been electrified.

Railway Junctions | From the beginning of the railway age Budapest, with its three large stations, has been one of the most important junctions of the south-east European area. In recent years great attention has been paid to creating the right conditions for a connection between Hungary and the central and west-European Inter-City network. The line between Budapest and Vienna has been improved since the fall of the "iron-curtain" and is now used by many international trains.

Types of train | The Hungarian State Railways (Magyar Államvasutak – MÁV) run Euro-City and Inter-City trains as well as express trains (Gyorsvonat) and regional trains (Személyvonat).

Administration | Andrássy út 73/75, H–1061 Budapest; tel. 1–122–06 60, Fax 1–142–85 96.

Passenger services | Andrássy út 35, H–1061 Budapest; tel. 1–122–80 49.

Tickets | Single tickets are valid from two to four days, depending on distance. Return tickets are valid from three to thirty days.

Hungarian Railway Network

In comparison with present prices rail fares in Hungary are inexpensive. For certain stretches (e.g. Budapest to Lake Balaton) reduced rate return tickets are sold.
Children below five years of age travel free, children from five to eleven pay half-price. **Tariffs**

Young people below the age of 26 can take advantage of the Euro-Domino programme. On five days within one month as many journeys of unrestricted length can be made for a fixed price. **Euro-Domino**

Visitors from abroad have the opportunity of taking advantage of reduced rate period tickets, valid for 10, 20 or 30 days. These tickets are valid without restriction over the entire Hungarian railway network. **MÁV tourist tickets**

At more than two dozen stations in Hungary (see timetables) cycles can be rented at reasonable rates. **Bicycles at the station**

Old railways and railway museums

In Hungary there are more than fourteen old narrow-gauge (760mm/30 in.) railways running on 10 to 30km stretches, which all have a museum-like character.
This is true particularly of the line from Miskolc to Garadna (Bükk Hills) and the railway from Verőrce (Börzsony Hills) west of Vác.

A particular attraction is the narrow-gauge line from the resort of Balatonfenyves to the spa of Csiszta, on which in summer a curious steam locomotive is used. **Balatonfenyves –Csiszta**

From the west station in Budapest steam trains occasionally run to Esztergom. Prior enquiry is advisable. **Pest–Esztergom**

A curiosity is the private Győr–Sopron–Ebenfurth Railway (GYSEV) which crosses the Austrian frontier and runs along the southern side of Fertő tó **GYSEV**

Restaurants and Inns

Places for eating in Hungary are many and varied, ranging from simple self-service inns and comfortable wine bars to elegant restaurants. Even before the fall of the "iron-curtain" there were already a few pizzerias. Since that time all kinds of establishments of modern type (including bistros and fashionable bars) have sprung up. **Note**

Typically Hungarian are the Csárdás, those hospital inns which are often old converted coaching inns and in which the *csárdás* is danced. A rustic interior and gipsy music keep alive the memory of "the good old times". **Csárda**

In many areas Hungary's wine bars and wine cellars are highly esteemed. In these – as in the Viennese *heurige* – only bread and dripping or sausage snacks are served with the wine. Apart from Budapest particularly attractive wine bars can be found by Lake Balaton (especially Badacsony) and where Erlau (Bulls Blood) and Tokay predominate. **Bor pince (wine bars)**

See entry **Wine**

See entry **Cafés**

Selection

Alabárdos, I, Országház utca 2
Angelika Espresso, I, Batthyány tér 7 **Budapest**

Restaurants and Inns

Fehér Galamb, I, Szentháromság utca 9/11
Régi Országház, I, Országház utca 17
Tabáni Kakas, I, Attila utca 27
Kis-Buda, II, Frankel Leó utca 34
Margitkert, II, Margit utca 15
Trombitás, II, Retek utca 12
Vén Buda, II, Erőd utca 22
Postakocsi, III, Fő tér 2
*Sipos Halászkert (fish restaurant), III, Fő tér 6
Radeberger Beer Hall, III, Hidfő utca 16
Udvarház, III, Hármashatárhegy
Aranybárány, V, Harmincad utca 4
Kárpátia, V, Károlyi Mihály utca 4/8
*Légradi, V, Magyar utca 23
*Mátyás Pince, V, Március 15. tér 17
Ménes Csárda, V, Apácai Csere János utca 4
Ménes Mackó, V, Kigyó utca 4/6
Százéves, V, Pesti Barnabás utca 2
Nimród, V, Nádor utca 24
Otard Cogncbar, V, Kristóf tér 6
Vigadó Beer Hall, V, Vigadó utca 1
Vörös Sárkány, VI, Andrássay út 80
Prágai Svejk, VII, Király utca 59
Tuborg Beer Bar, VIII, Rákóczi út 29
Citadelly, XI, Gellérthegy
Kiskkakukk, XIII, Pozsonyi út 12
*Gundel, XIV, Állatkerti körút 2
Kanizsa, XIV, Gizella út 46
Thököly, XIV, Thököly út 80

Café New York (Hungáriá) in Budapest

Halszkert Fish Restaurant, Park utca 5 Kisfaludy House Restaurant	Badacsony
Hotel Sugovica Restaurant, Petőfi-sziget Neptun, Roosevelt tér	Baja
Bugac Csárda	Bugac
Hotel Termál Restaurant in Bük	Bükfürdő
*Hotel Aranybika Restaurant, Piac utca 11/15 Civis Beer Hallm Mester utca 1/3 Mandula Café	Debrecen
Dobos Café, Széchenyi utca 6 Fehérszarvas Vadástranya, Klapka utca 8	Eger
Pataki Café	Érd
Aranykereszt, Eszperantó tér 2 *Százéves cukrszda (traditional confectioners), Erkel tér 1	Gyula
Restaurant in the Thermal Hotel Aqua, Kossuth Lajos utca 13/15 Restaurant in the Thermal Hotel Hévíz, Kossuth Lajos utca 9/11	Hévíz
Kuckó, Arany János utca 38 Szürkebarát Pinceborozó, Arany János utca 20	Győr
Lehel Gyöngye	Jászberény
Három Búnár, Batthyány utca 7/9	Kecskemét
Hotel Helikon Restaurant, Balaton-part Béke, Kossuth Lajor utca 50	Keszthely
Aranypáva	Kiskunfélegyháza
Tanyacsárda	Lajormizse
Hotel Avar Restaurant, Parádi út	Mátrafüred
Alabárdos, Avas sor 5 Miskolc-Lillafüred, Restaurant in the Hotel Palota	Miskolc
Kakukk, Szabadság tér 1	Nyírbátor
Hotel Palatinus Restaurant, Király utca 5	Pécs
Kopár csárda	Piliscsaba
Valencsics Café, Fő út 132	Pilisvörösvár
Fehér Holló, Hősök utca 8	Polgár
Restaurant in the Sárvár Thermal Hotel, Rákóczi út 1	Sárvár
Restaurant in the Taurus Castle Hotel	Seregélyes
Csárdás, Fő utca 105 Hotel Európa, Petőfi sétány 15	Siófok
Szakál, Bácsai út 27	Soltvadkert

Riding

Sopron	Generális (food bar), Fő tér 7 Hotel Lövér Restaurant, Várisi utca 4 Hotel Palatinus Restaurant, Új utca 23 Pizzeria Corvinus, Fő tér 8 Hotel Sopron Restaurant, Fövényverem utca 7
Szántóppuszta	Ménescsárda
Szeged	Alabárdos, Oskola utca 13/15 Hotel Hungária Restaurant, Maros utca 1/3 *Virág Café, Klauzál tér 1
Szekesfehérvár	Velence, Március 15 utca Vörösmarty Café, Március 15 utca
Szentendre	Aranysárkány, Alkotmány utca 1/a
Szirák	Restaurant in the Castle Hotel Szirák
Szolnok	Marcipán Café, József Attila utca 111 Hotel Tisza Restaurant, Tisza Park 2
Szombathely	Claudia Café, Savaria tér Hotel Claudius Restaurant, Bartók Béla körút 39 Hotel Isis Restaurant, Rákóczi út 1 Kispityer Fischtscharda, Rumi utca 18 Savaria Café, Máritírok tér 4
Tatabánya	Hotel Árpád Restaurant
Tök	Patkó csárda
Visegrád	Hotel Silvanus Restaurant, Fekete-hegy

Riding

Riding enthusiasts can have a very good time in Hungary. Tens of thousands of Hungarian crossbred and thoroughbred animals are kept in extensive paddocks. Cross-country rides, riding trips lasting several days, trips in horse-drawn carriages and courses for beginners are available at many places throughout the country.

Studs, stables (selection)	Apajpuszta and Bugac, Kiskunság National Park Balatonfenyves, Nagyberek near Lake Balaton Hortbágy-Máta, Hortobágy National Park Mezőhegyes, south-eastern Hungary near the Romanian border Rádiháza Szilvásvárad, Bükk Hills Tata, Eszterházy Stable
Information	Pegazus Tours, H–1053 Budapest, Ferenciek tér 5; tel. 1–117–16 44, Fax 1–117 01 71 IBUSZ, H–1053 Budapest, Felszabadulás tér 5; tel. 1–117–77 23 MALEÉV Air Tours, H–1051, Budapest, Roosevelt tér 2; tel. 1–118–37 80

Sailing

Sailing on Lake Balaton is very popular either in one's own boat or in boats which can be hired on the lake (in Siófok, Balatonfüred, Keszthely and other places).

Large yachts on Lake Balaton need the sail indicator "A". | Sail indicator

Visitors who bring their own yachts to Hungary need a triptyque (carnet) which can be obtained from the national automobile clubs and sailing organisations. | Triptyque

Motorboats are banned on Lake Balaton, but sailing boats with auxiliary motors are allowed. | **Motorboats banned**

There are mooring places in almost every resort on Lake Balaton, and some hotels and bungalow complexes have their own moorings. Larger boats must tie up at Balatonföldvár Yacht Club; Balatonfüred near the hotels Marina and Annabella; in Tihany, sailing club; in Balatonalmádi at the sailing club and in Keszthely near the hotel Helikon. There are slipways for very large boats in Balatonfüred, Siófok, Tihany and Keszthely. | Mooring places

Yacht Club WG, Pegasus Tours, H–1053 Budapest, Károlyi Mihály utca 5; tel. 1–171–444 | Information

---

Shipping Services

Surprising as it sounds, Budapest, the capital of a country in the centre of Europe, is, after Vienna, the most important cruising destination on the Danube, the second longest river in Europe. The Lake Balaton too has developed since the 70s into a popular place for sailing.

Danube

International landing stage for Danube ships and hydrofoil, Belgrád rakpart (International customs point, issuing visas). | Landing stages

Landing stage for excursion ships and local services: Pest, Vigadó tér.

Hungarian Danube Shipping Company MAHART, General Direction H–1051 Budapest, Roosevelt tér 2; tel. 1–266–90 33; reservations; tel. 1–267–43 33 | MAHART

Lake Balaton

Between the peninsula of Tihany (north bank) and Szántód (south bank) there are frequent car and passenger ferries. | Ferries

Excursions operate from all the important holiday centres. Small craft link all the larger places with regular services. Sometimes evening excursions with dancing and entertainment are available. | Excursions

---

Shopping and Souvenirs

In all the major tourist centres souvenirs of various qualities are on sale. As well as the Rubik-cube there are handcrafted textiles (blouses, tablecloths and other household articles), often beautifully embroidered. | Souvenirs
Calocsa blouses, Matyó embroidery, jackets with textile decoration and rural woven articles are popular, as are porcelain from Herend, ceramics from Pécs, pottery and cutlery, and vessels carved from various woods in the style of the puszta shepherds. Various glasses, leather goods (especially ladies' handbags, shoes, ties, belts), and traditional remedies (pollens, propolis, honey and herbs) are readily bought by tourists because of

Hungarian handcrafted articles

their relatively low cost. Also to be recommended are records of the music of the famous Hungarian composers Bartók, Kodály, Goldmark and Liszt. Valuable old etchings and books can be found at very reasonable prices in the antique shops of Pest.

Popular with tourists are the Hungarian salami (brand names "Herz" and "Pick"), apricot brandy (called "barack") and the much prized "Szilva" (plum brandy), wines from specialised regions (especially Tokay) as well as paprika and garlic in various forms.

Shopping in Budapest

Although Budapest can not be compared with London, Milan, Munich or Paris as a shopping centre, nevertheless the Hungarian capital has the widest selection of goods in the whole of eastern Europe.

The principal shopping streets in Budapest are Vac utca, Kigyó utca, Kossuth Lajos utca, Rákóczi út, Múzeum körút, Várnház körút, Szabad sajtó út and the streets in the castle quarter.

Spas and Health Resorts

Among the most important raw materials of Hungary are the almost immeasurable supplies of thermal water. Because of the particular geological situation and, in many places, a surprisingly abnormal temperature, water with a high mineral content and trace elements can be extracted from just under the surface of the ground. 500,000 cu.m/654,000 cu.yds of thermal water issues every day from the Hungarian soil, one tenth of it within the area of Budapest (128 springs).

Tradition

The tradition of taking the waters in the Budapest area had already developed in Celtic times. The name of the Roman settlement of Aquincum is derived from the Celtic expression "ak ink" = "much water".

Spas in Hungary

Medicinal Baths in Budapest

Thermal Hotel on Margaret Island	Császár Baths	Király Baths
Gellert Hotel and Baths	Rudas Baths	Széchenyi Baths
ORFI (Hungarian Rheumatic and	Rác Baths	Hélia Spa Hotel
Physiotherapeutic Institute)	Lukács Baths	Aquincum Spa Hotel

In the 16th and 17th centuries the Turks were responsible for the development of the spas. In the area of Budapest alone they maintained three so-called Hamami, which survive today as Rácz, Rudas and Király spas. The Gellért spa is distinguished by bubbling and wave baths. The neo-Baroque Széchenyi bath in the City Woodland Park is both a spa and a swimming bath. In the Lukács baths various panels commemorate successful cures.

Spa Establishments (selection)

Rác fürdő, Hadnagy utca 8/10, H–1013 Budapest; tel. 1–758–373
Rudas fürdő, Dübrentei tér 9, H–1013 Budapest; tel. 1–754–449
Király fürdő, Fő utca 84, H–1027 Budapest; tel. 1–153–000
Gellért fürdő, Gellért tér 1, H–1111 Budapest; tel. 1–666–166
Széchenyi fürdő, Állatkerti körút 11, H–1146 Budapest; tel. 1–210–310
Lukács fürdő, Frankel Leó út 25/29, H–1027 Budapest; tel. 1–154–280
ORFI (Institute for Rheumatology and Physiotherapy), Frankel Leó út 17/19; tel. 1–154–680

Budapest

Spa Hotels:
Hotel Thermal Margitsziget, Margaret Island, H–1138 Budapest; tel. 1–111–1000
Grand Hotel Ramada, Margaret Island, H–1138 Budapest; tel. 1–132–1100
Thermal Hotel Helia, Kárpát utca 62, H–1133 Budapest; tel. 1–129–8650
Thermal Hotel Aquincum, Árpád fejedelem útja, H–1036 Budapest; tel. 1–250–3360

Thermal lake (slightly radio-active)

Hévíz

Spa Hotels:
Thermal Hotel Hévíz, Kossuth Lajos utca 9/11, H–8380 Hévíz; tel. 82–11–090
Thermal Hotel Aqua, Kossuth Lajos utca 26, H–8380 Hévíz; tel. 82–18–947
Beta Hotel Park, Petőfi Sándor utca 26, H–8380 Hévíz; tel. 82–13–243
Beta Hotel Napsugár, Tavirózsa utca 2/5, H–8380 Hévíz; tel. 82–13–307

Spas and Health Resorts

Széchenyi Baths . . .   *. . . and Géllert Baths in Budapest*

Sávár	Thermal Hotel Sávár, Rákóczi utca 1, H–9600 Sávár; tel. 94–16–088
Bükfürdő	Thermal Hotel Bük, Fürdőtelep, H–9740 Bükfürdő; tel. 94–13–366
Balf Balatonfüred	Balf thermal bath Baths for heart complaints (carbonic acid spring), north bank of Lake Balaton
	Spa Hotels: Hotel Annabella, Beloiannisz utca 25, H–8230 Balatonfüred; tel. 86–42–222 Hotel Margareta, Széchenyi utca 26, H–8230 Balatonfüred; tel. 86–43–824 Hotel Marina, Széchenyi utca 28, H–8230 Balatonfüred; tel. 86–43–644
Zalakaros	Iodine and bromine thermal spring south of Lake Balaton
	Kurhotel Napfény, Termál utca 10, H–8749 Zalakaros; tel. 93–18–202
Harkány	High-active carbon and sulphide thermal spring on the edge of the Mecsek mountains (south-western Hungary, near Siklós)
	Hotel Dráva, Bajcsy-Zsilinszky utca 3, H–7815 Harkány; tel. 72–80–434 Hotel Napsugár, Bajcsy-Zsilinszky utca 5/7, H–7815 Harkány; tel. 72–80–300
Hajdúszoboszió	Bitumen thermal spring near Debrecen (eastern Hungary) Hotel Délibab, József Attila utca 4, H–4200 Hajdúszoboszió; tel. 52–61–788
Debrecen	Silicic acid and borax thermal spring in eastern Hungary Hotel Aranybika, Piac körút 9/11, H–4025 Debrecen; tel. 52–16–777 Hotel Termál, Nagyerdei körút 9/11, H–4032 Debrecen; tel. 52–11–888
Gyula	Alkaline, iodine and bromine thermal spring on the south bank of the Great Hungarian Plain

Aranykereszet Hotel, Eszperantó tér 2, H–5700 Gyula; tel. 66–62–144
Hotel Hofőrrás, Rábai Miklós utca 2, H–5700 Gyula; tel. 66–61–544

Sport

Leisure activity is becoming more and more popular in Hungary and visitors will find plenty of opportunities for indulging in their favoured sport.

Covered bowling halls and skittle-alleys can be found in many hotels, some of which also have a fitness centre.

Bowling and Skittles

See entry
Fishing

See entry
Golf

See entry
Riding

Hungary has excellent facilities for shooting, whether for big or small game or for waterfowl. Information: Mavad, 1014 Budapest I., Uri utca 39; tel. 1– 155–67 15

Shooting

Covered tennis courts at the Hotel Flamenco Occidental, Budapest XI, Tas vezér utca 7; tel. 1–161–2250. Tennis courts can be found in many tourist centres.

Tennis

There are squash courts at the Marczibányi tér in Budapest (number 13 in the II district); tel. 1–115–9444.

Squash

On suitable lakes and rivers surfing, sailing, rowing, swimming and watertours can be enjoyed, provided there are no restrictions or ban in force. For environmental reason motorboats with petrol engines are forbidden in Hungary.

Watersports

Hungary has no high mountains, so winter sports are replaced by other attractions. However, should it snow, and, as in other similar European countries, the snowfall is not often very severe, then the ski-slopes are crowded. The chief venues are: Buda in the XII district, on the Normafa, in the Börsöny, Mátra and Bükk Hills (the highest point is the Kékes – 1014m/3328ft – in the Mátra).
The artificial ice-rink in the City Woodland Park (Városliget) in Budapest has been popular for years with both young and old. If Lake Balaton freezes then gliding along in a chair fitted with runners provides much amusement. Of the total population of 10.3 million Hungarians at least 500,000 go skiing, mostly in adjoining countries or in Italy.

Winter sports

Address of the Hungarian Ski Association: 1087 Budapest VIII, Dózsa György út 1/3; tel. 114–08 68.

Swimming

See Bathing/Swimming

Taxis

Hungarian taxi owners have formed an association. A taxi with an illuminated "Taxi" sign is free and will stop if given a hand signal.

Visitors should be on their guard to see that the taximeter is switched on. It shows a basic charge of 15 forints which increases by 10 forints for every completed kilometre.

Taximeters

Telephone

Special Airport charges	At the airport anyone hiring a taxi should agree a price to the chosen destination.
Limousine service	In Budapest and in other Hungarian cities with a reasonable amount of business travel, a limousine service on the American model is available at somewhat higher charges.
Car rental	See entry.

Telephone

Local calls	From coin-operated telephones: lift receiver; wait for continuous dialling tone; insert coins (at least 5 forints for three minutes) and dial the required number.
Inland calls with direct dialling	From coin-operated telephones: lift receiver; wait for dialling tone; insert coins (at least 10 forints); dial "06"; wait for another continuous dialling tone; dial local code and required number.
International calls with direct dialling	From coin-operated telephones: lift receiver; wait for dialling tone; insert coins (at least 20 forints); dial "00"; wait for another continuous dialling tone; dial the country code, prefix and required number.

International prefixes	Great Britain 44	Australia 61
	United States and Canada 1	Ireland 353
	Hungary 36	

Telephone service	Long-distance calls (abroad) tel. 09 Information (English-speaking) tel. 172–200 Telegrammes tel. 02

Theatres and Concerts

In Budapest and also in some provincial towns a varied cultural life has developed. The following should be specially mentioned: Pécs (world-famous ballet), Debrecen, Győr, Keszthely, Miskolc, Sopron, Szeged and Szombathely, where, especially in spring and summer, first-class performances are given.

Open-air stages	Budapest: open-air stage on Margaret Island; Buda: Hotel Hilton, Dominican Court Provinces: Esztergom, Castle Theatre; Gyula, Castle Theatre; Kisvárda, Castle Theatre; Kőszeg, Castle Theatre; Miskolc, Acropolis open-air theatre; Pécs, open-air theatre; Pápa, open-air theatre; Siófok, open-air theatre; Sopron, Fertőrákos cave theatre; Szeged, Cathedral Square; Szentendre, Teátrum; Tata, open-air theatre; Veszprém, castle; Visegrad, castle; Zsámbék, church ruins
Concerts	Budapest: Pest City Hall, Városház u. 7; Hotel Hilton, Dominican Court, Hess András tér 1; Matthias Church, Szentháromság tér; Pest Redoubt, Vigadáo tér 2; Museum of Musical History, Táncsics u. 7; Carmelite Court, Színház u. 1–3 Provinces: Eger, basilica; Felsőörs, church; Fertőd, Eszterházy Castle; Győr, cathedral; Keszthely, Festetics Castle; Majk, monastery; Miskolc, church; Szentendre, Peter and Paul Church; Tata, Knights' Hall; Veszprém, music court.

Details of current theatrical performances and concerts can be obtained from local information offices (see Information) and can be found in the daily newspapers and the publications of the Hungarian Tourist Office.

Programme
information

Time

Hungary observes Central European Time (Greenwich Mean Time + one hour); in summer Central European Summer Time (Daylight Saving) is two hours ahead of Greenwich Mean Time.

Tipping

Employees in the service sector generally consider themselves to be underpaid and expect a tip for personal attention notwithstanding the usual service charge included in a bill.

The normal tip is 10% of the bill. In superior establishments the head waiter and the wine waiter also expect a gratuity.

Restaurants

In many restaurants and inns gipsy musicians perform on their own account. After their performance they are often very insistant on a tip.

Gipsy musicians

A taxi driver usually receives 10% of the sum shown on the meter; for short trips he will often expect more.

Taxis

The usual tip is 10–20% of the bill.

Hairdressers

It is usual to give the attendant an additional five or more forints above the charge.

Cloakroom
attendants

The attendant expects up to 10 forints.

Filling station
attendants

Toilets

Public toilets can be found in bus terminals, railway stations and at a few other places.
Ladies' toilets (nök) and men's toilets (férfiak) do not always come up to expected standards.

Travel Documents

A passport is necessary to enter Hungary. No visa is required for a stay of less than three months for citizens of Great Britain, the United States and Canada. Citizens of other countries should enquire at a consulate about conditions for entry. Foreigners who wish to remain more than 30 days in Hungary must register with the local police.

Passport

Anyone losing a travel document or a permit must report this immediately to the nearest police station. New or replacement documents can be obtained (usually within three days) from the relevant embassy.

Loss of
documents

Vehicle documents, see Motoring

Walking

For some time Hungary has been engaged in creating a network of paths which will serve the interests of tourism as well as being environmentally acceptable. Excellent paths have been laid out in the Buda uplands and in other hilly areas near Budapest, as well as in the proximity of tourist areas (including the Balaton region, and the foothills of the eastern Alps near the Austro-Hungarian border). The large nature reserves are also provided with footpaths.

Blue Tour

The so-called Blue Tour covers the finest walking territory of Hungary. It leads from the 894m/2934ft-high summit of the Hagy-Milic in the extreme north-east of Hungary, passing through magnificent forests as far as Velem on the Austrian frontier.

Information

Tourist Department of the Hungarian Association of Friends of Nature, H–1065 Budapest VI, Bajcsy-Zsiliszky út 31; tel. 1–153–19 30

When to go

Note

The best time to visit Hungary is the period between March and October; spring and autumn can be particularly pleasant. In summer the climate can be very hot and dry, and at this time the water temperature of Lake Balaton can exceed 23°C/74°F.
In late autumn and winter it can be unpleasantly cold on account of the influence of continental climatic influence and there can be long periods when it is bitterly cold.
At Christmas time there are only a few tourists particularly in Budapest, which is seeking an all-year-round tourist trade, and in Sopron with its pretty Christmas Market.

Climate

See Facts and Figures, Climate

Wine (bor)

Vines were already growing wild in Hungary before the Ice Age. The actual viniculture of the country is about 2000 years old. When the Romans conquered the western half of present-day Hungary (Transdanubia) and made it into their province of Pannonia they found vines there. At the end of the 9th century the Magyars took over the growing of vines and brought it to perfection. Setbacks took place during the Turkish domination which lasted almost 150 years, and because of vine diseases which spread from America in the 19th century. In the 20th century the vineyards were steadily extended and wine-making techniques improved, so that the quality approached that of the level in western Europe. Marketing problems have recently led to a reduction of the area under cultivation. In the longer term there will still be about 100,000ha/247,000 acres where vines are grown.

Wine regions

Hungarian vineyards are spread over five large regions: northern Transdanubia (particularly in the north-west around Sopron and on the north bank of Lake Balaton); southern Transdanubia (especially in the south-west with the centres of Marienbad, Villány and the south bank of Lake Balaton); north-eastern Hungary (Eger, Kompolt, Matraberg, Tokaj-Hegyaja) and the Great Plain with the Danube Valley as its western border.

Wine Producing Areas

Tokaj

Eger
Gyöngyös

Sopron

Mór

Balatonfüred

Kecskemét

Badacsony

© *Baedeker*   Kiskörös

Szekszárd   Szeged

Pécs
Villány
Siklós

**Hungarian Vineyard
Regions and
their Centres**

In Hungary the majority of grapes grown are of the varieties known in western Europe. An important exception is the Furmint grape, the chief variety used to produce the world-famous Tokay (see A to Z, Tokaj), which apart from here is produced only in Burgenland, Austria.

Grape varieties

Grüner Veltliner (Zöld Veltelini)
Guteldel
Müller Thurgau (Rizlingszilváni)
Welschriesling (Olaszrizling)
Rheinriesling (Rajnai Rizling)
Silvaner (Zöldszilváni)
Muskat-Ottonel (Muskotály)
Sauvingnon
Chardonnay
Rulánder (Szürkebarát)
Zierfandler (Cirfandli)
Blaustengler (Kéknyelü)
Lindenblättriger (Hárslevelú)
Gewürztraminer (Tramini)
Königliche Mädchentraube (Királyleányka)

White Wines

Blaufränkisch, Lemberger (Nagyburgundi, Kékfrankos)
Cabernet Franc
Cabernet Sauvignon
Kadarka
Edelkadarka (Nemeskadarka)
Merlot
Spätburgunder, Poinot Noir (Burgundi)
Oporto

Red Wines

The red wine Bulls Blood (Egri Bikavér) which is well-known in the west, is a blend of various grapes (including Kadarka, Blaufränkish, Cabernet Sauvingnon). Traditionally it is a dry wine, but for export purposes it is also slightly sweetened.

The wine label   asztali bor = table wine
minőségi bor = good quality wine
különleges minőségu bor = high quality wine from fully-ripe and overripe grapes
Töppedt szölöböl készült bor = high quality sweet wine from over-ripe shrivelled grapes
fehér = white
vörös = red
száraz = dry (up to 4gr. per litre sugar)
félszáraz = semi-dry (4–15gr. per litre sugar)
félédes = semi-sweet (15–25gr. per litre sugar)
édes = sweet (from 25gr. per litre sugar)

Young People's Accommodation

Information   Magyarrországi Ifjúsági Szállások Szóvetzége (Hungarian Youth Hostel Organisation), H–1535 Budapest, Konkoly Thege Milkós út 21; tel. 1–156–28 57, Fax 1–175–93 27

Express Travel & Hotel Ltd., H–1359 Budapest, Szabadság tér 16; tel. 1–530–660, Fax 1–533–172
Individual booking: Reisebüro Express, Budapest, Semelweis u. 4; tel. 1–117–6634, Fax 1–176–634

Youth Hostels (b. = beds)

Baja   Ifjúsági Tábor (106 b.), Petőfi Sziget 5, H–6500 Baja; tel. 79–24–022, Fax 79–24–022

Balatonfenyves   Youth Camp, Bcs-Kiskun megyei Gyermek és Ifjúsági Alapitvány Tábora (100 b.), H–8646 Balatonfenyves, Kölksey u. 45; tel. 85–61–686

Balatonföldvár   Express International Youth Center, Hotel Juventus (200 b.), H–8623 Balatonföldvár, József Attila u. 9; tel. 84–403 79, Fax 84–403 79

Balatongyörök   Youth Holiday Center, Zalai Gyermek és Ifjúsági Alapitvány (240 b.), H–8313 Balatongyörök-Szépkilátó; tel. 92–11–010, Fax 92–11–358

Balinka   Balinka Tölgyes Tourist Center (200 b.), H–8055 Balinka

Budapest   Csillebérci Gyermek és Ifjúsági központ (200 b.), H–1535 Budapest, Konkoly Thege Miklós u. 21; tel. 1–156–57 72, Fax 1–175–93 27
Hotel Lido (260 b.), H–1031 Budapest, Nánási út 67; tel. 1–188–6865
Hostel Ananda (36 b.), H–1141 Budapest, Bonyhádi út 18/b
Hostel Bakfark (60 b.), H–1022 Budapest, Bakfark Bálint u. 1, Fax 1–135–83 21
Hostel Donáti (50 b.), H–1013 Budapest, Donáti u. 46
Hostel Felvinci (70 b.), H–1029 Budapest, Felvinci u. 8
Hostel Universitas, Kármán Tódor Kollégium (600 b.), H–1111 Budapest, Iriny József u. 9–11; tel. 1–181–11 22, Fax 1–166–68 08

Csopak   Ifjúsági Üdülő (290 b.), H–8229 Csopak, Sport u. 9; tel. 86–465–05
Dánfoki Ifjúsági Tábor és Kemping (220 b.), H–5630 Békés-Dánfok; tel. 66–41–830

Doboz   Békés Megyei Gyermek és Ifjúsági Alapitvány, Szanuzgi Tábora (220 b.), H–5624 Doboz-Szanazug; tel. 66–21–833, Fax 66–27–026

Hotel Aranypart (100 b.), H–9021 Győr , Aldozat u. 12; tel. 96–26–033, Fax   Győr
96–26–442

GAMF Ságvári Kollégium Hostel (230 b.), H–6001 Kecskemét, Izsáki út 10;   Kecskemét
tel. 76–21–916, Fax 76–22–865

Paradise Hostel, Esély Alapitvány (200 b.), H–4431 Nyiregyháza, Sóstói út   Nyiregyháza
76; tel. 42–14–822, Fax 42–14–822

Turisztikai és Szabadidő központ (230 b.), H–5001 Szolnok-Tiszaliget; tel.   Szolnok
56–44–705, Fax 56–39–323

Hotel Gubacs, Youth Camp Tábor (730 b.), H–2890 Tata, Fáklya u. 4; tel.   Tata
34–83–960

Hotel Avar (155 b.), H–9726 Velem, Petőfi út 16; tel./Fax 94–60–034   Velem

Express International Youth Center (200 b.), Verőcemaros; tel. 27–50–166   Verocemaros

Gyermeküdülő Centrum (140 b.), H–8250 Zánka, Balaton; tel. 87–48–440,   Zánka
Fax 87–40 084

Index

Notes